from
Bill

ONE CHILD

ONE CHILD

by

Torey L. Hayden

G. P. Putnam's Sons
New York

The author gratefully acknowledges permission to quote from *The Little Prince* by Antoine de Saint-Éxupéry, copyright 1943, 1971 by Harcourt Brace Jovanovich, Inc.

Library of Congress Cataloging in Publication Data

Hayden, Torey L
  One child.
  1. Child psychopathology — Case studies.   2. Child abuse — Case studies.   I.
Title.
RJ499.H398   1980   618.9′ 28′ 58   79-20265
ISBN 0-399-12467-5

Printed in the United States of America

To Sheila R., of course.

I am asked repeatedly about
the poem on my office wall.
It seems only right that
they should know the child
who wrote it. And I
only hope I have been
half as good a writer.

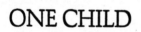

ONE CHILD

Prologue

For the better part of my adult life I have been working with emotionally disturbed children. The autumn of my freshman year in college I took a volunteer position in a day program for disturbed and disadvantaged preschoolers. From that season I have remained captivated by the perplexing aspects of mental illness in childhood. Since that time I have acquired three degrees; devoted several years as a teacher's aide, a teacher, a university instructor and a psychiatric researcher; lived in five states; and worked in private day-care centers, public schools, locked psychiatric wards and state institutions, all the while pursuing the elusive answers to these children, the magic keys that will finally open them to my understanding. Yet, within me, I have long known there are no keys, and that for some children, even love will never be enough. But belief in the human soul escapes all reason and flies beyond the frail fingers of our knowledge.

I am often asked about my work. Perhaps the commonest question is Isn't it frustrating? Isn't it frustrating, the college student asks, to live day to day with violence, poverty, drug and alcohol addiction, sexual and physical abuse, neglect and apathy? Isn't it frustrating, the regular classroom teacher asks, to work so hard for so little in return? Isn't it frustrating, they all ask, to know your greatest success will probably never have more than an approximation of normalcy; to know that these very little children have been sentenced to live a life which, by our standards, will never be productive, contributing, or normal? Isn't it frustrating?

No. No, it isn't really. They are simply children, frustrating at times as all children are. But they are also gratifyingly compassionate and hauntingly perceptive. Madness alone seems to allow the whole truth to be spoken.

But these children are more. They are courageous. While we turn on the evening news to hear of new excitements and conquests on some distant front, we miss the very real dramas that play themselves out among us. This is unfortunate, because there is bravery here unsurpassed by any outside event. Some of these children live with such haunted nightmares in their heads that every move is fraught with unknown terror. Some live with such violence and perversity that it cannot be captured in words. Some live without the dignity accorded animals. Some live without love. Some live without hope. Yet they endure. And for the most part they accept, not knowing any other way.

This book tells of only one child. It was not written to evoke pity. Nor was it intended to bring praise on one teacher. Nor to depress those who have found peace in not knowing. Instead, it is an answer to the question of frustration in working with the mentally ill. It is a song to the human soul, because this little girl is like all my children. Like all of us. She is a survivor.

10

CHAPTER 1

I should have known.

The article was a small one, just a few paragraphs stuck on page six under the comics. It told of a six-year-old girl who had abducted a neighborhood child. On that cold November evening, she had taken the three-year-old boy, tied him to a tree in a nearby woodlot and burned him. The boy was currently in a local hospital in critical condition. The girl had been taken into custody.

I read the article in the same casual manner that I read the rest of the newspaper and felt an offhand what-is-this-world-coming-to revulsion. Then later in the day it came back to me while I was washing the dishes. I wondered what the police had done with the girl. Could you put a six-year-old in jail? I had random Kafkaesque visions of the child knocking about in our old, drafty city jail. I thought about it only in a faceless, impersonal manner. But I should have known.

I should have known that no teacher would want a six-year-old with that background in his or her classroom. No parent would want a child like that attending school with his or her child. No one would want that kid loose. I should have known she would end up in my program.

I taught what was affectionately referred to in our school district as the "garbage class." It was the last year before the effort to mainstream special children would begin; it was the last year to pigeonhole all the odd children into special classes. There were classes for the retarded, classes for the emotionally disturbed, classes for the physically handicapped, classes for the behaviorally disordered, classes for the learning disabled, and then there was my class. I had the eight who were left over, the eight who defied classification. I was the last stop before the institution. It was the class for young human refuse.

The spring before I had been teaching as a resource person, supplying help to emotionally disturbed and learning disabled children who attended regular classrooms part of the day. I had been in the district for some time in a variety of capacities; so I had not been surprised when Ed Somers, the Director of Special Education, had approached me in May and had asked if I would be interested in teaching the garbage class the next fall. He knew I had had experience with severely disturbed children and that I liked small children. And that I liked a challenge. He chuckled self-consciously after saying that, aware of how contrived the flattery sounded, but he was desperate enough to try it anyway.

I had said yes, but not without reservations. However, I longed for my own classroom again with my own set of kids. I also wanted to be free of an unintentionally oppressive principal. He was a good-hearted man, but we did not see things in the same way. He objected to my casual dress, to my disorderly classroom, and to my children addressing me by my first name. These were minor issues, but like all small things, they became the major sore spots. I knew that by doing Ed the favor of taking this class, allowances would be made for my jeans and my sloppiness and my familiarity with the kids. So I accepted the job confident that I could overcome any of the obstacles it presented.

My confidence flagged considerably between the signing of the contract and the end of the first day of school. The first blow came when I learned I was to be placed back into the same school I had been in and under the same principal. Now not only did he have to worry about me but also about eight very peculiar children. Immediately we were all placed in a room in the annex which we shared with the gymnasium and nothing else. We were totally isolated from the rest of the school. My room would have been large enough if the children had been older and more self-contained. But for eight small children and two adults, plus ten desks, three tables, four bookcases, and countless chairs that seemed to mate and multiply in the night, the room was hopelessly crowded. So out went the teacher's desk, two bookshelves, a file cabinet, all but nine little chairs, and eventually all the student desks. Moreover, the room was long and narrow with only one window at the far end. It had originally been designed as a testing and counseling space, so it was wood-paneled and carpeted. I would have gladly traded all that grandeur for a room that did not need lights on all day or for a linoleum floor more impervious to spills and stains.

The state law required that I have a full-time aide because I was carrying the maximum load of severely disturbed children. I had been hoping for one of the two competent women I had worked with the year before, but no, I received a newly hired one. In our community, which had in close proximity a state hospital, a state prison and a huge migrant workers' camp, there was a staggering welfare list. Consequently, unskilled jobs were usually reserved for the unemployed listed with Social Services. Al-

13

though I did not consider my aide position an unskilled one, Welfare did, and the first day of school I was confronted with a tall, gangly Mexican-American who spoke more Spanish than English. Anton was twenty-nine and had never graduated from high school. Well, no, he admitted, he had never worked with children. Well, no, he never especially wanted to. But you see, he explained, you had to take the job they gave you or you lost benefits. He dropped his gargantuan frame onto one of the kindergarten-sized chairs, mentioning that if this job worked out, it would be the first time he had ever stayed north all winter instead of following the other migrant workers back to California. So then we were two. Later, after the school year started, I acquired a fourteen-year-old junior high school student who devoted her two hours of study hall to coming over and working with my class each day. Thus armed, I met the children.

I had no unusual expectations for these eight. I had been in the business long enough to have lost my naiveté. Besides, I had learned long before that even when I was shocked or surprised, my best defense was to never show it. It was safer that way.

The first to arrive that morning in August had been Peter. Eight years old and a husky black with a scraggly Afro, Peter had a robust body that belied the deteriorating neurological condition that caused severe seizures and increasingly violent behavior. Peter burst into the room in anger, cursing and shouting. He hated school, he hated me, he hated this class and he wasn't going to stay in this shitty room and I couldn't make him.

Next was Tyler, who startled me by being a girl. She slunk in behind her mother, her dark curly head down. Tyler was also eight and had already tried to kill herself twice. The last time the drain cleaner she had drunk had eaten away part of her esophagus. Now her throat bore an artificial tube and numerous red-rimmed surgical scars in ghoulish testimony to her skill.

Max and Freddie were both hauled in screaming. Max,

who was a big, strapping, blond six-year-old, carried the label of infantile autism. He cried and squawked and twirled around the room flapping his hands. His mother apologized because he always acted so unpredictably to change. She looked at me wearily and let the relief to be free of him for a few hours show too plainly in her eyes. Freddie was seven and weighed 94 pounds. The fat rolled over the edges of his clothing and squeezed out between the buttons on his shirt. Once allowed to flop on the floor, he ceased crying, ceased everything, in fact, to lie lifelessly in a heap. One report said that he, too, was autistic. One stated that he was profoundly retarded. One admitted not knowing.

I had known Sarah, age seven, for three years. I had worked with her when she was in preschool. A victim of physical and sexual abuse, Sarah was an angry, defiant child. She had been electively mute throughout the previous year when she had been in a special first grade class at another school. She had refused to talk to anyone except her mother and sister. We smiled upon seeing each other, both of us thankful for a familiar face.

A smartly dressed, middle-aged woman carried in a beautiful, doll-like child. The little girl looked like a picture from a children's fashion magazine, her soft blond hair carefully styled, her crisp dress spotless. Her name was Susannah Joy, she was six, and this was her first time in school. My heart winced. To be placed in my class upon entrance to school was not a hopeful sign. The doctors had told the parents that Susannah would never be normal; she was a childhood schizophrenic. She apparently hallucinated both visually and auditorily, and spent most of her days weeping and rocking her body back and forth. She rarely spoke and even when she did, seldom meaningfully. The mother's eyes implored me to perform the magic ritual necessary to turn her fairy child back to normal. My heart ached seeing those pleading eyes, because they signified nonacceptance. I knew the pain and agony that lay ahead

15

for those parents as they learned that none of us would ever have the type of magic they needed for Susannah Joy.

Last to come were William and Guillermo. Both were nine. William was a lanky, pasty-faced boy haunted by fears of water and darkness and cars and vacuum cleaners and the dust under his bed. To protect himself, William engaged in elaborate rituals, compulsively touching himself or chanting little spells under his breath. Guillermo was one of the countless Mexican-American migrants that came to work in the fields each year. He was an angry boy but not uncontrollable. Unfortunately, he was also blind. At first I was stymied that he had been placed in my class, but was informed that the classes for the blind and partially sighted did not feel equipped to deal with his aggressive behaviors. Well, I thought, that made us even. I did not feel equipped to deal with his blindness.

So, then we were ten, and with Whitney, the junior high student, we were in all eleven. When first I surveyed this motley bunch of children and my equally motley staff, I felt a wave of despair. How would we ever be a class? How could I ever get them doing math or all the other miracles that needed accomplishing in nine months? Three were not toilet trained, two more had accidents. Three could not talk, one wouldn't. Two would not shut up. One could not see. Certainly it was more of a challenge than I had bargained for.

But we managed. Anton learned to change diapers. Whitney learned to get urine out of the carpet. And I learned Braille. The principal, Mr. Collins, learned not to come over to the annex. Ed Somers learned to hide. And so we became a class.

By Christmas vacation we belonged to one another and I was beginning to look forward to each new day. Sarah had begun to talk regularly again; Max was learning his letters; Tyler was smiling occasionally; Peter didn't fly into rages quite so often; William could pass all the light switches in the hallway to the lunchroom and not say one charm to protect himself; Guillermo was begrudgingly learning Braille. And Susannah Joy and Freddie? Well, we were still trying with them.

I had read the newspaper article in late November and had forgotten it. But I shouldn't have. I should have known that sooner or later we would be twelve.

Ed Somers appeared in my room the day after school resumed following Christmas vacation. He came early, his kind face swathed in that apologetic expression that I was beginning to realize meant trouble for me. It was the expression attached to things like not getting a special tutor for Guillermo, or yet another hopeless report from the newest doctor Susannah's parents had found. Ed wanted things to be different; I believe he genuinely did, which made it impossible for me to be angry with him.

"There's going to be a new child in your class," he said, his face mirroring his hesitance to tell me.

I stared at him a long moment, not comprehending. I already had the state-allowed maximum and had never anticipated having another child. "I have eight now, Ed."

"I know, Torey. But this is a special case. We don't have any place to put her. Your class is the only option we have."

"But I've got eight kids already." I repeated dumbly. "That is all I can have."

Ed looked pained. He was a big bear of a man, tall and muscular like a football player but padded with the extra softness of middle age. His hair was nearly gone and what was left he had carefully combed across the shiny dome. But above all, Ed was gentle and I was amazed that he had ever made it to such a high position in education, a profession not known for its kind treatment of gentle people. But perhaps that was his secret, because I never failed to soften when he looked so hurt by what he was having to do to me.

"What's so special about this kid?" I asked tentatively.

17

"This is that girl who burned the little boy in November. They took her out of school and made arrangements to send her to the state hospital. But there hasn't been an opening in the children's unit yet. So the kid's been home a month and getting into all sorts of trouble. Now the social worker is beginning to ask why we aren't doing anything for her."

"Can't they put her on homebound?" I asked. A number of my children had been taught by homebound, a term referring to the practice of sending a teacher into the home to teach a child when for some reason he could not attend school. Often, severely disturbed children were handled in this manner until appropriate placement could be found.

Ed frowned at the floor. "No one is willing to work with her."

"The kid's six years old," I said in surprise. "They're scared of a six-year-old?"

He shrugged, his silence telling me more about this child than words could have.

"But I already have all the children I can handle."

"Choose a child to be transferred. We have to put this child in here, Torey. It will just be temporary. Until a place opens up at the state hospital. But we have to put her in here. This is the only place equipped to handle her. This is the only place she'll fit."

"You mean I'm the only one idiotic enough to take her."

"You can pick whom you want transferred."

"When is she coming?"

"The eighth."

By that point the children were beginning to arrive and I had to prepare for our first day back from vacation. Sensing my need to get to work, Ed nodded and left. He knew that, if given time, I would do it. Ed knew that, for all my bravado, I was a pushover.

After telling Anton the news, I looked over the children. As we went through the day I kept asking myself who

should go. Guillermo was the obvious choice, simply because I was least equipped to teach him. But what about
Freddie or Susannah Joy? Neither was making progress of
much note. Anyone could lug them around and change
their pants. Or maybe Tyler. She wasn't so suicidal now;
she hardly ever spoke of killing herself anymore; she no
longer drew those black-crayoned pictures. A resource
teacher could probably handle her. I looked at each one of
them, wondering where they would go and how they
would make it. And how our room would be without
them. I knew in my heart none of them would survive the
rigors of a less-sheltered class. None of them was ready.
Nor was I ready to give them up, nor give up on them.

"Ed?" I clutched the receiver tightly because it kept slipping in my sweating hand. "I don't want to transfer any of
my kids. We're doing so well together. I can't choose any
one of them."

"Torey, I told you we have to put that girl in there. I'm
really sorry. I hate to do it to you, but there isn't any other
place."

I stared morosely at the bulletin board beside the phone
with all its proclamations of events my children never
could attend. I was feeling used. "Can I have nine?"

"Will you take nine?"

"It's against the law. Do I get another aide?"

"We'll see."

"Does that mean yes?"

"I hope so," Ed replied. "But we'll just have to see. Will
you need another desk?"

"What I need is another teacher. Or another room."

"Will you settle for another desk?"

"No. I don't have any desks. There wasn't room for the
first eight. So we just sit on the carpet or at the tables. No, I
don't need another desk. Just send me the kid."

CHAPTER

2

She arrived January eighth. Between the time I had agreed to accept her and the morning she arrived, I had heard nothing, received no files, learned no background. All I knew was what I had read in a two-paragraph article under the comics on page six a month and a half earlier. But I suppose it did not matter. Nothing could have prepared me adequately for what I got.

Ed Somers brought her, holding tightly on to her wrist and dragging her behind him. Mr. Collins also came out to the annex with Ed. "This is going to be your new teacher," Ed explained. "And this will be your new room."

We looked at one another. Her name was Sheila. She was six and a half, almost; a tiny little mite of a thing with matted hair, hostile eyes and a very bad smell. I was surprised she was so small. I had expected something bigger. The three-year-old must have been nearly as tall as she was. Clad in worn denim overalls and a well-faded boy's striped T-shirt, she looked like one of those kids in the Save the Children ads.

"Hi, my name's Torey," I said in my friendliest teacher's voice while reaching for her hand. But she did not respond. I ended up taking the limp wrist from Ed. "This is Sarah. She's our welcome person. She'll show you around."

Sarah extended a hand but Sheila remained impassive, her eyes darting from face to face. "Come on, kid." Sarah grabbed her wrist.

"Her name is Sheila," I said. But Sheila bristled at these acts of familiarity and yanked her hand away, retreating backwards. She turned to run, but Mr. Collins was fortunately standing in the doorway and Sheila ran right into him. I captured one arm and dragged her back into the classroom.

"We'll leave you," Ed said, that apologetic look creeping across his face. "I left her cumulative folder in the office for you."

Anton slipped the bolt lock into place after closing the door behind Ed and Mr. Collins as they left. I dragged Sheila across the room to my chair where we always held morning discussion and set her on the floor in front of me. The other children cautiously gathered around us. Now we were twelve.

We always began each morning with "discussion." Ours was a school that enjoyed saying the pledge to the flag and singing patriotic songs before starting classes. I felt patriotism was not an appropriate topic for children who could not even communicate basic needs; however, the school board took a dim view of anyone who refused this display of nationalism. There were too many other issues I had to fight that were more important to me than the pledge of allegiance. So I compromised and created discussion. The children all came from such chaotic and disrupted homes that we needed something to reunite us each morning after being apart. And I had wanted something which would stimulate communication and develop verbal understanding. The first thing we did was the pledge, and I put it to good use by having one child lead it, which meant he had to learn it. Even this process was valuable because it presented words in an organized sense that implied meaning. Afterwards I started discussion with a "topic." Usually topic explored feelings, such as talking about things that made one happy; or topic was a roundtable for solving problems, such as what would one do if he saw someone else hurt himself. We went from there as a jumping-off point, making sure that everyone had a chance to participate. In the beginning I had brought all the topics in, but after the first month or two the children had their own suggestions and I had not started the discussion in ages.

After topic, I let each child have a few moments to tell what had happened to him since the release of school the previous day or Friday. These two aspects of morning discussion had gotten increasingly livelier, and even Susannah participated meaningfully on occasion. The kids all had a lot to say and I was hard put some days to terminate the activity. Afterwards, I outlined a schedule of the day and then we closed with a song. I had a repertoire of action songs that I could sing with more gusto than tune, usually pulling one of the kids through the actions puppetlike. The children loved that and we always ended laughing, even on those days when we had not come in merry.

So this morning I gathered the children around me. "Kids, this is Sheila, and she's going to join our class."

"How come?" Peter asked suspiciously. "You never told us we was getting a new girl."

"Yes, I did, Peter. Remember how we rehearsed last Friday things to show Sheila that we're glad she's with us? Remember what we did?"

"Well, I'm not glad she's with us," he replied. "I liked us just the way we was." He placed his hands over his ears to shut me out and began rocking.

"It'll take some getting used to, I imagine. But we will." I patted Sheila's shoulder and she pulled away. "Now, who's got a topic?"

Everyone sat around me on the floor. No one spoke.

"No one has a topic? Well then, I've got one: what do you suppose it feels like when you're new and don't know anyone, or maybe you want to be part of a group and no one wants you to? How's that feel inside?"

"Bad," Guillermo said. "That happened to me once and I felt bad."

"Can you tell us about it?" I asked.

Suddenly Peter leaped to his feet. "She stinks, teacher." He backed away from Sheila. "She stinks terrible and I don't want her sitting with us. She'll stink me up."

Sheila regarded him blackly but did not speak or move. She had folded herself up into a little lump, her arms wrapped tightly around her knees.

Sarah stood up and moved around to where Peter had reseated himself. "She does stink, Torey. She smells like pee."

Good manners were certainly not our forte. I was not surprised by the lack of tact, but as always I was dismayed. Silencing their clear-eyed perceptions of the world was an impossibility. For every step forward I made in teaching good manners, I took two back and six to the side. "How do you suppose that feels, Peter, to have someone say you stink?"

"Well, she does stink terrible," Peter retorted.

"That's not what I asked. I asked how you'd feel if someone said that to you?"

"I wouldn't want to stink everybody out of the class, that's for sure."

"That's not what I asked."

"It'd hurt my feelings," Tyler volunteered, bouncing up on her knees. Any displays of anger or disagreement frightened Tyler tremendously and sent her into rounds of appeasement, acting overly mature for her eight years and motherly toward those who disagreed.

"How about you, Sarah?" I asked. "How would you feel?"

Sarah stared at her fingers, reluctant to look at me. "I wouldn't like it too good."

"No, I don't think any of us would. What might be a better way of handling the problem?"

"You could learn her in private that she stinked," William offered. "Then she wouldn't get embarrassed."

"You could learn her not to," Guillermo added.

"We could all plug our noses," Peter said. He wasn't quite willing to admit yet that he had been inappropriate in his remarks.

"That wouldn't help any, Peter," William said. "Then you couldn't breathe."

"You could too. You could breathe through you mouth."

I laughed. "Everybody, try Peter's suggestion. Peter, you too." All the children except Sheila plugged their noses and breathed through their mouths. I urged her to try too, but she steadfastly refused to unfold. In a few moments we were all laughing, even Freddie and Max, at the funny faces we made. All of us, except Sheila. I was beginning to fear that she saw this as a joke at her expense and I hastened to explain it wasn't. She ignored me, not even looking at me. This was the way we solved our problems, I told her.

"How's this make you feel?" I asked her at last. There was a long silence, pregnant with our waiting. The other children became impatient.

"Don't she talk?" Guillermo asked.

"I used to not talk either, remember that?" Sarah offered. "Back when I was mad, I used to never talk to nobody." She looked over at Sheila. "I used to never talk, Sheila. So I know how it feels."

"Well, I think we've put Sheila in the hot seat enough for now. Let's give her some time to get used to us, okay?"

We went on with the rest of morning discussion and finished with a rousing chorus of "You Are My Sunshine." Freddie clapped gleefully; Guillermo directed with his hands; Peter sang at the top of his lungs; and I manipulated Tyler like a rag doll. But Sheila sat, her face stormy, her little body a solid lump in the way of the dancers.

After discussion we dispersed for math activities. Anton began orienting the others while I showed Sheila around the room. Actually, I did not show her. I had to pick her up and carry her around from place to place because she would not move. I was thankful I was not teaching adolescents. Then when I got her where I wanted her, she refused to look, covering her face with her hands. But I hauled her around anyway, determined she become part of us. I showed her her cubby and her coat hook. I introduced her to Charles, the iguana, and Benny, the snake, and Onions, the rabbit who bit if you bothered him too much. I pointed out the plants we had started before Christmas that I had had to come in on vacation to water; and the stories we read before lunch every day; and the dishes we cooked with on Wednesday afternoons. I showed her our aquarium and our toys. I lifted her up to view the scene from our lone window. All this was accomplished by lugging her from place to place and chattering as if she were very interested in what I had to say. But if she was, she did not let me know. She remained a dead weight in my arms, rigid and tense against my body. And she stank like an outhouse on a muggy July afternoon.

Finally I deposited Sheila on a chair at the table and got out a math paper. This evoked her first response. She grabbed the paper, wadded it up and threw it at me. I took another. She repeated the action. I took another. Again it was flung in my face. I knew I would run out of papers before she would run out of energy. So I took her on my lap, wrapping an arm around her wiry body so she could not get her hands free. I set another math paper down. It was simple addition; two plus one, one plus four, nothing fancy. I pulled a tray of blocks toward me with my free arm and spilled them on the table.

"Okay, now we do math," I stated. "First problem, two

25

plus one," I showed her two blocks and added a third. "How much is that? Let's count them." She averted her head, straining her stiff body against me. "Can you count, Sheila?" No response. "Come on, I'll help. One, two, three. Two plus one is three." I picked up a pencil. "Here, we'll write it down."

Everything was a battle. I had to pry a hand free from her body, then uncurl her fingers, then place the pencil in it. Suddenly those tightly clenched fingers lost their strength and the pencil slid effortlessly out of them and onto the floor. In the moment I bent to pick up the pencil she had grabbed two blocks with her free hand and flung them across the room. I clutched at the hand, shoved the pencil back into it and tried to recurl her fingers around it and grip it with my own hand before she could let the pencil drop again. But she had me at a disadvantage; I was left-handed and forced to use that arm to subdue her in my lap. Having to use my right to perform all these dexterous movements, I was just not fast enough. Perhaps I would not have been even with my left. She was skilled at this little bit of guerilla warfare and the pencil fell again. After another struggle I gave up.

"Evidently you don't want to do math just yet. Okay, you may sit. I will say to you that everyone in here does his work and tries his best. But we're not going to fight about it. You want to sit, you sit." I lugged her over to the corner where I isolated the children when they became too over-stimulated and needed to regain control, or when they acted miserably, trying to command attention. I pulled the chair out and sat Sheila in it. Then I returned to the other children.

In a few moments I looked up, "Sheila, if you're ready to join us, you may come over."

She sat, her face to the wall and did not move. I let her sit. In another few minutes, I reissued the conditions. And again a little later. It was obvious that she was not going to do anything I wanted. I went over and pulled the chair

26

away from the corner and into the room. Then I went back to the others. If she wanted to sit, she could. However, I was not going to let her isolate herself from us. If she sat, it would be right out in the middle of us.

Our morning routine went as usual. Sheila participated in nothing. Once ensconced upon that small wooden chair, she would not move, but instead drew in upon herself, folding knees up under her chin and wrapping her arms around them. She got off the chair one time to use the bathroom but returned to her seat to resume her contorted position. Even during recess she sat, only this time on the freezing cement. I had never seen such a motionless child. But her eyes followed me continuously everywhere I went. Brooding, angry, bitter eyes never left my face.

When lunch came, Anton helped the children prepare for their trek from the annex over to the cafeteria. Sheila had been lugged into line but I came and got her, taking her skinny wrist and pulling her out of the line. We waited until the others had gone. I looked down at her and she up at me. I thought that for a brief moment I saw an emotion other than hate flicker through those eyes, something other than anger. Fear?

"Come over here." I tugged her to the table and set her down in a chair opposite me. "You and I have something to get straight."

She glowered at me, her tiny shoulders humping up under the worn shirt.

"There aren't a lot of rules in this room. There are just two really, unless we need to make special rules for special times. But generally there are just two. One is that you can't hurt anybody in here. Not anybody else. And not yourself. The second is that you always try to do your best job. That's the rule I don't think you have straight yet."

She lowered her head slightly but kept her eyes on me. The legs came up and once again she began to fold in upon herself.

"You see, one of the things you have to do in here is talk.

27

I know that's hard when you're not used to doing it. But in here you talk, that's part of your best job. The first time is always the hardest, and sometimes it kind of makes you cry. Well, that's okay to do in here. But you have to talk. And sooner or later you will. It'll be a lot better if you do it sooner." I looked at her, trying to match her unflinching stare. "Is that clear to you?"

Her face blackened with anger. I was fearful of what might happen if all that hate got loose, but I tried to squash the fear, not letting it show in my eyes. She was a good reader of eyes.

I had always felt strongly about setting expectations for my kids. Some of my colleagues had been skeptical of my directness with the children, pleading the frailty of their egos. I disagreed. While certainly all of them had sad, well-trampled little selves, none of them was frail. Much to the contrary. The fact that they had survived long enough to be where they were after what most of them had been through was testimony to their strength. However, all of them lived chaotic lives and brought chaos on others by the nature of their disturbance. I did not feel it was my right to add to the chaos by leaving them to guess what I expected of them. I found establishing a structure a useful and productive method with all the children because it erased the fuzziness of our relationship. Obviously, they had already shown they could not handle their own limits without help, or they never would have arrived in my class to begin with. As soon as the time came that they could, I began the process of transferring the power to them. But in the beginning I wanted there to be no doubt about what I expected from them.

So Sheila and I sat in icy silence while she digested this bit of information. I did not have the endurance to stare her down, nor did I feel the need to do so. After a few moments I rose from my chair and went to collect the math papers from the correction basket.

"You can't make me talk," she said.

I continued shuffling through the papers trying to find the marking pen. Three-fourths of being a good teacher is timing.

"I said you can't make me talk. There don't be no way you can do that."

I looked over at her.

"You can't make me."

"No, I can't." I smiled. "But you will. That's part of your job in here."

"I don't like you."

"You don't have to."

"I hate you."

I did not respond. That was one of those statements that I find is often best left unanswered. So I continued my search for the pen, wondering who had walked off with it this time.

"You can't make me do nothing in here. You can't make me talk."

"Maybe not." I dropped the papers back into the basket and came over to her. "Shall we go to lunch?" I extended a hand to her. Some of the anger had dissipated to be replaced by a less readable emotion. Then without further urging she got off the chair and came with me, careful not to touch me.

CHAPTER

3

After escorting Sheila to the lunchroom I retired to the
office to have a look at her file. I wanted to know what
others had done with this perplexing child. From watching
her, it was apparent that she did not suffer from the crip-
pling, unexplainable disturbances such as Max and Susannah displayed. Instead, she was in surprisingly good control
of her behavior, more so than most of the children coming
into my class. Behind those hate-filled eyes I saw a perceptive and most likely intelligent little girl. She had to be in
order to manipulate her world with such conscious effort.
But I wanted to know what had been tried before.

The file was surprisingly thin for one that had worked
its way to me. Most of my children had thick, paper-bloat-
ed folders, glutted with verbose opinions of dozens of doctors and therapists and judges and social workers. It was
plain to me every time I read one of those files that the
people filling them never had to work with the child day
in and day out for hours at a time. The words on the papers

were erudite discourses, but they did not tell a desperate teacher or frightened parent how to help. I doubt anyone could write such words. In reality, each of the children was so different and grew in such unpredictable ways that one day's experience was the only framework for planning the next. There were no textbooks or university courses specializing in Max or William or Peter.

But Sheila's file was thin, only a few bits of paper: a family history, test results and a standard data form from Special Services. I paged through the social worker's report of the family. Like so many others in my room, it was filled with lurid details that, despite my experience, my middle-class mind could not fully comprehend. Sheila lived alone with her father in a one-room shack in the migrant camp. The house had no heat, no plumbing, and no electricity. Her mother had abandoned Sheila two years earlier but had taken a younger son. She now lived in California, the form stated, although no one actually knew her whereabouts. The mother had been only fourteen when Sheila was born, two months after a forced wedding, while her father was thirty. I shook my head in grim amazement. The mother would only be twenty years old now, barely more than a child herself.

The father had spent most of Sheila's early years in prison on assault-and-battery charges. Since his release two-and-a-half years before, he had also had stays at the state hospital for alcoholism and drug dependency. Sheila had been shifted around among relatives and friends of the family, mostly on the mother's side, before finally being abandoned on a roadside, where she was found clinging to a chain-link fence that separated the freeway lanes. Taken to the juvenile center, Sheila, then four, was discovered to have numerous abrasions and healed multiple fractures, all the results of abuse. She was released to her father's custody and a child-protection worker was assigned to the case.

A court statement appended to the file said that the

31

judge felt it was best to leave the child in her natural home. A county-appointed physician had scrawled across the bottom that her small size probably resulted from malnutrition, but otherwise she was a healthy Caucasian female with well-healed scars and fractures. Loose behind these two assessments was a memo from the county's consulting psychiatrist with the single statement: Chronic Maladjustment to Childhood. I smiled at it in spite of myself; what an astute conclusion this man had drawn. How helpful to us all. The only normal reaction to a childhood like Sheila's would be chronic maladjustment. If one did adjust to such pornography of life, it would surely be a testimony to one's insanity.

The test results were even more obscure. Beside each title on the battery, written in tight, frustrated printing: Refused. The bottom summary simply stated she was untestable and underlined the fact twice.

The Special Services questionnaire contained only demographics. The father had filled out the form and he had been in prison all those crucial years. She had been born with no apparent complications in a local hospital. Nothing was known of her early developmental history. She had attended three schools in her short educational history, not including the one she was in now. All the moves had resulted from her uncontrollable behavior. At home she was reported to eat and sleep within the normal limits. But she wet the bed every night and she sucked her thumb. She had no friends among the migrant workers' children at the camp; nor did she appear to have any solid relationships with adults. The father wrote that she was a loner, hostile and unfriendly even to him. She spoke erratically at home, usually only when she was angry. She never cried. I stopped and reread that statement. She never cried? I could not conceive of a six-year-old who did not cry. He must have meant she seldom cried. That must have been a mistake.

I continued reading. Her father saw her as a wayward child and disciplined her frequently, mostly by spanking or taking away privileges. I wondered what sort of privileges there were in her life to be taken away. In addition to the burning incident, she had been reprimanded for setting fires in the migrant camp and for smearing feces in the restroom of a bus station. By six-and-a-half, Sheila had encountered the police three times.

I stared at the file and its bits of random information. She was not going to be an easy child to love, because she worked at being unlovable. Nor was she going to be an easy child to teach. But she was not unreachable. Despite her exterior, Sheila was indeed probably more reachable than Susannah Joy or Freddie, because there was no indication that her functioning was garbled with retardation, or neurological impairments or other mysteries of the brain. From what I could glean, Sheila was a normally functioning child in that respect. Which made the battle ahead for me even harder because I knew it rested solely with us on the outside. We had no cute phrases, no curtains like autism or brain damage to hide behind when we failed with the Sheilas. We had only ourselves. Deep down behind those hostile eyes was a very little girl who had already learned that life really isn't much fun for anybody; and the best way to avoid further rejection was to make herself as objectionable as possible. Then it would never come as a surprise to find herself unloved. Only a simple fact.

Anton came in while I was paging through the file. He pulled up a chair beside me and took the forms as I finished them. Despite our clumsy beginning, Anton and I had become a fully functioning team. He was an adroit worker with these children. Having spent all his life prior to this year in the fields, and still living in the migrant camp in a small hut with his wife and two sons, Anton knew much more intimately than I the world my kids came from. I had the training and the experience and the knowledge, but

Anton had the instinct and the wisdom. Certain aspects of their lives I never would understand because in my existence warm houses and freedom from violence and hunger and cockroaches was my due. I had never had reason to expect otherwise. Now as an adult, I had learned that others lived differently and that this different way of life, to them, was also normal. I could accept the fact, but I could not understand it. I do not believe that anyone for whom it is not a living reality can; anyone claiming that extra measure of understanding either lies to himself or is a deluded braggart. But Anton compensated for my lack and together we had managed to build a supportive relationship. He had come to know without being told when and how and whom to help. An additional benefit was that Anton spoke Spanish, which I did not. Thus, he saved me innumerable times when Guillermo went beyond his limit of English. Now Anton sat beside me, quietly reading Sheila's folder.

"How did she do at lunch?"

He nodded without looking up from the papers. "Okay. She eats like she never sees food. But she probably doesn't. And, oh, so bad on the manners. But she sat with the children and did not fuss."

"Do you know her father out at the camp?"

"No. That's the other side of the camp, where the whites live. The junkies are all over there. We never go over."

Whitney came in and leaned over the counter. She was a pretty girl in a nondescript way: tall, slender, with hazel eyes and long, straight, dishwater-blond hair. Although Whitney was an honors student at her junior high and came from one of the community's most prominent families, she was a painfully shy girl. When she had come in the fall she had carried out all her tasks in great silence, never looking me in the eye, always smiling nervously, even when things were going wrong. The only time she did talk was to criticize her work, to put herself down or to apologize for doing everything wrong. Unfortunately, in

34

the beginning that seemed all too true. Whitney made every mistake in the book. She dropped half a gallon of freshly mixed green tempera paint on the gym floor. She forgot Freddie in the men's room at the fairgrounds. She left the door to our room ajar one afternoon after school and Benny, the class boa constrictor, escaped and went to visit Mrs. Anderson, the first grade teacher. For me, Whitney was like having another child. If I had not been so desperate in those early months for a third set of hands to help, I might not have had the patience for her. Those first weeks I was always reexplaining, always cleaning something up, always saying, "Don't worry about it," when I did not mean it. Whitney was always crying.

But like Anton, Whitney had been worth the trouble. Because she cared so much about the kids. Whitney was hopelessly devoted to us. I knew she skipped classes occasionally to stay longer with us, and she often came over on her lunch hour or after school to help me. From home she brought her own outgrown toys to give the children. She came with ideas for me that she had found in teaching magazines she read in her spare time. And always that hungry, pleading look to be appreciated. Whitney very seldom talked about the rest of her life outside my classroom. Yet, despite her affluence and the prominent name of her family, Whitney, I suspected, was no better off in some ways than the kids in the class. So I remained tolerant of her clumsiness and ineptitude and tried to make her feel a valued part of our team. Because she was.

"Did you get your new girl?" Whitney asked, stretching over the counter and causing her hair to tumble onto the papers I was reading.

"Yes, we did," I said and mentioned briefly what had transpired during the morning. That was when I heard the screaming.

I knew it was one of my children. None of the regular kids seemed to have that high vibrant note of desperation in their voices when they yelled. I looked at Anton, asking him wordlessly what was going on. Whitney went to look out the door of the office.

Tyler came careening in, wailing. She motioned out the door but her explanation was strangled in her sobs. Then she turned and ran.

All three of us sprinted after her toward the door that led to the annex. Normally over the lunch hour, lunch aides were in charge of the children. In the cold months, the kids all played inside in their rooms and the aides patrolled up and down the halls keeping order. I kept telling them that my children could not be left unattended at any time, but the aides hated supervising my room and avoided it by congregating outside the annex door and keeping an ear cocked for disaster. My children had the latest lunch hour, which meant the aides only had about twenty minutes of actual supervision. But they still protested and still refused to stay in the room with the kids. I usually ignored the aides, because I had worked hard to instill in my kids the independence to function without my physical presence. Lunch hour was a daily test of this skill. Moreover, both Anton and I desperately needed that half-hour break. Still things occasionally got out of hand.

Tyler was sobbing something out to us as we ran, something about eyes and the new girl. I came storming into a room in chaos.

Sheila stood defiantly on a chair by the aquarium. She had apparently caught the goldfish one by one and poked their eyes out with a pencil. Seven or eight of the fish lay flopping desperately on the floor around the chair, their eyes destroyed. Sheila clutched one tightly in her right fist and stood poised threateningly with the pencil in the other. A lunch aide was near her, dancing nervously about, but too frightened to attempt disarming Sheila. Sarah was wailing, Max was flying about the room flapping his arms wildly and screeching.

"Drop that!" I shouted in my most authoriative voice. Sheila glared at me and shook the pencil meaningfully. I had no doubt she would attack if at all provoked. Her eyes had the glazed wildness of a threatened animal. The fish flopped hopelessly about, leaving little bloody spots on the floor where their empty eye sockets hit. Max crunched through one on his flight around the room.

Suddenly a high-pierced shriek knifed the air. Behind us Susannah had entered the room. She had a psychotic fear of blood, of any red liquid, and would go into a frenzy of crazed screaming while darting senselessly about when she thought she saw blood or even hallucinated it. Now, seeing the fish, she bolted off across the room. Anton moved after her and I took that moment of surprise to disarm Sheila who was not so off-guard as I had suspected. She slammed the pencil into my arm with such vehemence that for a moment it stuck, waving uncertainly before falling to the ground. My mind was filled with too much confusion to feel any real pain. Freddie had joined Max in circling the room. Tyler was wailing; Guillermo hid under the table; William stood in one corner and cried. Whitney was off trying to capture Max and Freddie as they reeled around the perimeter of the room screaming. The decibel level was unbearable.

"Torey!" came William's cry. "Peter's having a seizure!" I turned to see Peter collapse to the floor. Passing Sheila to Whitney, I ran for Peter to remove the chairs among which he had fallen.

Sheila gave Whitney an audible crack in the shins and won her freedom. Within seconds she was out the door. I fell onto the floor beside Peter, still writhing in his seizure, and felt the pressure of what was happening lie upon me. It had all happened within minutes. Everyone had lost the tenuous control we fought so hard to keep. All the children except Peter were crying. Sarah, Tyler and William wailed on the sidelines, their bodies huddled together against catastrophe. Guillermo sobbed from his retreat under the table. He kept his hands protectively over his head and pleaded in Spanish for his mother. Susannah struggled frantically in Anton's arms. Max and Freddie still flew deliriously around the room, colliding with furniture and other children only to rise and resume their flight. Peter lay incoherent in my arms. I looked around. Whitney had disappeared after Sheila. The lunch aide had left long ago. We were in shambles. After months and months of careful effort, everything had fallen around our ears.

Mr. Collins and the school secretary appeared in the doorway. Normally I would have been horrified to have him see my classroom in such distress. But things had gotten completely out of control and I needed help. I had to admit that. After all the years he and I had worked together, I had managed my crazy children and we had never had a major slip. But now I had failed. Just like he always predicted. My crazies had gotten loose at last. I knew he must be thanking God he had put us in the annex where no one could see.

The secretary took Peter to the nurse's office to be sent home because he always needed to sleep after a major seizure. Mr. Collins helped me round up Freddie and Max and get them to sit in chairs. I dragged poor Guillermo out from under the table and hugged him. What this must have sounded like to him, who could not see . . . Anton was still trying to soothe Susannah Joy. Once we seemed to recapture some semblance of control, Tyler and Sarah were willing to sit down in the discussion corner and comfort each other. But William remained glued to the spot, quaking and sobbing. Mr. Collins made an effort to calm him, but he could not bring himself close enough to hug the child. We kept crunching and sliding on the dead goldfish, grinding gold scales into the carpet, the sound our shoes made stepping on them a muffled squeak. At last I had all the kids herded together and the crying had diminished.

Whitney and Sheila were still gone but I couldn't let myself think of that at that particular moment.

Mr. Collins had the decency not to ask what had happened. He had simply done as I asked, his face unreadable. When I got all the children settled down, I thanked him at the door for his help and asked if he could send me Mary, one of the regular school aides, who had been such a competent helper of mine the year before. I still had one on the loose, I explained, and the afternoon would be difficult. With one extra adult, I could get around to more of the children individually and try to set things straight.

When Mary arrived, the kids helped her choose a story they liked and I went in search of Sheila. Evidently when she had bolted, she was confused by the maze of doors and hallways connecting us to the main building. Whitney had been able to secure the outside doors before Sheila found them and she had been trapped into going into the gym, more by accident than design. Whitney stood in the doorway of the huge cavernous room and Sheila was on the far side.

Tears streamed over Whitney's cheeks as she held her post. My heart ached when I saw her. This was too much to expect of a fourteen-year-old. I should never have put her in this spot. Yet, my string of miracles had run out. Two adults alone could not manage that many disturbed children. I had been surviving on good luck, and now it had finally expired.

I entered the gym, gave Whitney a pat on the shoulder, and approached Sheila. She clearly had no intention of being caught. Her eyes were wild, her face flushed with terror. Each time I moved closer, she tore off in another direction. I spoke softly, my tone gentle and coaxing. But it quivered with my own frenzy. Slowly I edged closer. It did not matter. She could elude me forever in the huge gymnasium.

Pausing, I looked around, my mind racing for ideas. I had

to catch her. Her eyes mirrored her uncontrolled panic. She had gone beyond the limits she could comprehend in the situation and was reacting from animal instinct alone now. At this point she was far more dangerous to herself and to others than back in the classroom with the fish.

I could not think what to do. My head pulsed. My arm throbbed where the pencil had sunk in. Blood had soaked through my shirt sleeve. If a number of us approached her, that would undoubtedly terrify her even more. If I boxed her in, that too would heighten her irrationality. She had to relax and regain some control of herself. She was too dangerous this way. Despite her size and her age, I had the experience to know that in this condition she posed a very real threat, if not to me, then to herself.

I went back to Whitney and told her to return to the classroom and tell Anton to manage as best he could with Mary. Then I closed the door to the gym. I pulled closed the heavy divider that separated the room into two parts, because I remembered it having a door in it that locked. I could not afford to let Sheila escape again. Then, together in the far half of the gym, I came as close to her as I dared and sat down.

We regarded each other. Frantic terror gleamed in her eyes. I could see her trembling.

"I'm not going to hurt you, Sheila. I'm not going to hurt you. I'm just going to wait until you're not so scared anymore and then we'll go back to class. I'm not angry. And I'm not going to hurt you."

Minutes passed. I scooted forward on my seat. She stared at me. The tremors had taken over her entire body and I could see her scrawny shoulders shake. But she did not budge.

I had been angry with her. God Almighty, I had been angry. Seeing our beloved fish on the floor, their eyes gouged out, I had been livid. I had an intolerance of cruelty to animals. But now the anger had faded and as I watched

40

her, I was awash with pity. She was being so brave. Frightened and tired and uncomfortable, she refused to give in. Her world had been a very untrustworthy one and she was confronting it in the only way she knew how. We did not know each other; there was no way of determining that I would not hurt her. There was no reason why she should trust me and she was not going to. Such a courageous little being to face up to all of us who were so much bigger and stronger and more powerful, to face us unflinchingly, without words or tears.

I inched closer. We had been there waiting at least a half hour. I was within ten feet of her now and she was beginning to view my approach with suspicion. I stopped moving. All the while I spoke in gentle tones, reassuring her that I meant her no harm, that we would go back to the classroom together, that nothing would happen. I spoke of other things too; things the children liked to do in our room; things we enjoyed doing together; things she would do with us.

Endless minutes passed. I was getting sore from not moving. Her legs were shaking from standing so long without shifting position. This had become a test of endurance. An eternity was strung out over the ten feet separating us.

We waited. The frenzy was fading from her eyes. Tiredness was taking over. I wondered what the time was but was afraid to move my arm to see my watch. Still we waited.

The front of her overalls darkened and a puddle of urine formed around her feet. She looked down at it, taking her eyes from me for the first time. She caught her lower lip in her teeth. When she looked up, the horror of what had just happened showed plainly.

"Accidents happen. You haven't had a chance to go to the bathroom, so it really isn't your fault," I said. It amazed me that after the havoc she had wreaked in the classroom, this was the act that caused her regret.

41

"We can clean it up," I suggested. "I've got some rags back in the room for when this sort of thing happens."

She looked down again and then back at me. I remained silent. She took a cautious step backwards to better survey the situation. "You gonna whip me?" she asked hoarsely.

"No. I don't whip kids."

Her brow furrowed.

"I'll help you clean it up. We won't have to tell anybody. It can be our secret, because I know it was an accident."

"I didn't mean to."

"I know it."

"You gonna whip me?"

My shoulders dropped in exasperation. "No, Sheila, I don't whip kids. I said that to you once."

She looked at her overalls. "My Pa, he gonna whip me fierce when he sees I do this."

Throughout our exchange I had remained motionless in my spot fearful of breaking this tenuous relationship. "We'll take care of that, don't worry. We've still got a while before school is over. It'll dry by then."

She rubbed her nose and looked at the puddle and then at me. For the first time since she'd arrived, she seemed uncertain. Very slowly I rose to my feet. She took a step backwards. I extended an arm to her. "Come on, we'll go get something to clean it up. Don't worry about it."

For a long moment she regarded me. Then cautiously she came toward me. She refused my hand but walked back to the classroom at my side.

Things had quieted in the room. Anton and the children were singing songs. Whitney was holding Susannah and Mary was rocking Max. The dead fish were all gone. Heads turned toward us but I motioned to Anton to keep them busy. Sheila accepted the rags and bucket from me and we went back to the gym and cleaned the floor without speaking. Then she followed me back to the room.

42

Surprisingly the remainder of the afternoon went quietly. The children were all subdued, fearful of toppling their frail control again. Sheila retreated to the chair she had occupied all morning, folded herself up in it and sucked her thumb. She did not move for the rest of the afternoon. Yet she continued to watch us. Her eyes were unreadable. I went around to each of the children and cuddled them and talked with them trying to soothe their unworded feelings. Finally I came to Sheila.

Sitting down on the floor beside her chair, I looked up at her. She regarded me seriously, thumb still in her mouth. The toll of the afternoon showed on her. I made no attempt to touch her. Anton was conducting the closing exercises and no one was watching us. I did not want to spook her by being too intimate, but I did want her to know I cared.

"It's been kind of a hard afternoon, hasn't it?" I said. She did not respond other than staring at me. I got the full benefit of her odor from this position. "Tomorrow will be better, I think. First days are always hard." I tried to read her eyes, to glean some understanding of what was going on in her head. The open hostility was gone, momentarily at least. But I could see nothing beyond that. "Are your pants dry?"

She unfolded and stood up, inspecting them. They were passably dry, the damp outline barely distinguishable from the other filth. She nodded slightly.

"Is that going to be good enough so you don't get in trouble?"

Again an almost imperceptible nod.

"I hope so. Everybody has accidents. And this wasn't really your fault. You didn't have a chance to use the bathroom." I kept some spare clothes around because this sort of thing happened all too frequently in our room. I hadn't mentioned it, being afraid of frightening her with too much familiarity. But I wanted her to know that such problems were acceptable in here.

43

The thumb rotated in her mouth and she turned away from me to watch Anton. I remained near her until dismissal.

After the children were gone, Anton and I cleaned up the room in silence. Neither of us mentioned what had happened. Neither of us said much of anything. This certainly had not been one of our better days. When I got home after work, I washed out my pencil wound and put a Band-Aid on it. Then I lay down on my bed and wept.

CHAPTER

4

Life in my classroom was a constant battle whether I wanted to acknowledge it or not. Not only with the children but with myself. To cope with these youngsters from day to day I locked up my own emotions in many ways because I found that when I didn't I became too discouraged, too shocked, too disillusioned to function effectively. My days were a constant shooing of my own fears back into the little corners where they dwelled. The method worked for me but every once in a while a child came along who could really rock my bulwark. Out came tumbling all the uncertainties, the frustrations, and the misgivings I had so carefully tried to ignore and I became overwhelmed with defeat.

Basically, though, I was a dreamer. Beyond the children's incomprehensible behavior and my own vulnerability, beyond the discouragement, the self-doubts, soared a dream which admittedly was seldom realized, a dream that things could change. And being a dreamer, my dream died hard.

This time was no exception. The tears were short-lived and instead, I fell asleep. Later, I settled down with a tuna fish sandwich to watch "Star Trek." I had never watched much television and had never seen "Star Trek" when it had been a prime-time program. But now, years later, it was shown in syndication each evening at six. At the beginning of the school year when our classroom adjustment had been slow to come and my disillusionments had been many, I had started watching the program while I ate dinner and it had become a ritual. It divided my day into the work part and the rest part; that hour being the recuperative time when I put away all the problems and frustrations that had occurred at school. Marvelously emotionless Mr. Spock became my after-work martini.

So by the time Chad arrived at seven, I had recovered. Chad and I had been seeing each other regularly over the previous eighteen months. At first it had been the typical courting relationship: the endless rounds of dinner, movies, dances and mindless conversation. However, neither of us was suited for that sort of affair. So we drifted into a warm comfortable alliance. Chad was a junior partner in a law firm downtown and spent most of his time as a court-appointed attorney for the drifters and ne'er-do-wells that found themselves in jail. Consequently he did not have a good track record of winning cases. So we would spend our evenings together commiserating good-naturedly over my kids and his clients. We had talked once or twice about marriage, but that had been the extent of it. Both of us were sociable loners, satisfied with the status quo.

When Chad came over bringing a quart of Baskin-Robbins chocolate fudge ice cream, I told him about Sheila as we fixed sundaes. I had met my match, I stated firmly. The kid was a savage and I did not think I was the one to civilize her. The sooner the opening at the hospital came up, the better.

Chad laughed amiably and suggested I call her former

teacher. After our ice cream orgy when I was feeling comfortably full and a little more mellow about things, I looked in the telephone book for Mrs. Barthuly.

"Oh my gosh," Mrs. Barthuly said when I told her who I was and why I had called. "I thought they had put her away for good."

I explained that there had been no openings yet at the state hospital and asked her what she had done while Sheila was in her class. I could hear her making little clucking sounds, those indescribable little noises of defeat.

"I've never seen such a child. Destructive, oh my gosh, every time I took my eyes off her she destroyed something. Her work, the other children's work, bulletin boards, art displays, anything. One time she took all the other kids' coats and stuffed them down the toilets in the girls' lavatory. Flooded the entire basement." She sighed. "I tried everything to stop her. She always destroyed her work before you could get a look at it. I started laminating the worksheets so she couldn't tear them up. You know what she did? She shoved them into the cooling system and jammed the air conditioner. We went three days with no ventilation when it was ninety-four degrees."

Mrs. Barthuly went on to describe event after event. Her voice was rapid at first as if she had never had an adequate opportunity to tell about the chaos visited on her the first three months of the school year. But then it began to take on a weary note. Despite everything, she had liked Sheila, drawn by the same enigmatic force that had attracted me. The child seemed so vulnerable and still so brave. She had wanted to do right by Sheila. But nothing she did helped. Sheila refused to speak to her. She refused to be touched, to be helped, to be liked. In the beginning Mrs. Barthuly had tried to be kind. She attempted to show affection to this unlovable child, to include her in special activities, to give her extra attention. The school psychologist had set up behavior-management programs to reward Sheila's good behavior. But Sheila appeared to delight in never doing whatever it was they decided to reward. Mrs. Barthuly was convinced that Sheila purposely set out to ruin the programs, going so far as to stop doing some things she had previously been doing well when those things were included on the program.

Next, Mrs. Barthuly tried contolling her outlandish behavior negatively. She took away privileges, confined her to a time-out corner, and at last ended up sending Sheila to the principal for paddling. Still Sheila continued to terrorize the class, attacking other children, destroying things and refusing to work. At last, Mrs. Barthuly gave up. This child took too much time away from the other children. So Sheila was left on her own and the first semblance of peace settled in the room. Allowed to do as she pleased, Sheila spent most of the day wandering around the classroom or paging through magazines. If countered, Sheila would scream and tear about in revenge, destroying whatever was in her path. However, left entirely alone, she was tolerable and would ignore the others if they ignored her. She still never spoke, never did any work, nor participated in any classroom activities. Then the event in November occurred and she was removed immediately from school in response to fears expressed by other children's parents.

The voice on the other end of the phone was sad and pessimistic. Mrs. Barthuly regretted that so little had been done. No one knew if Sheila had even the most basic command of letters or numbers. Nothing about the child's learning or feelings was known at all. She was, Mrs. Barthuly admitted, the closest thing to an unteachable child she had ever encountered. Whatever could be done for Sheila was beyond her patience, ability and time. She wished me luck, amending it to say she hoped the state hospital placement came through soon. Then she hung up.

The news filled me with renewed depression because I did not know what I could do that had not been tried. With my group of children, I did not have much more of a chance to give her one-to-one attention than Mrs. Barthuly. I discussed the matter with Chad and decided there was nothing I could do other than wait and see.

The next morning before school, Anton and I sat down to plan our course of action. Clearly the occurrence which had happened the day before could not be repeated. The other children could not afford to go through that sort of experience. Some disruption was healthy in the classroom because it taught them how to respond in a supportive environment when things went wrong; but we could not afford chaos for days on end.

The social worker came in dragging Sheila about fifteen minutes before class started. She explained that the only bus they could get to connect with Sheila's home was the high school bus. Therefore, Sheila would be arriving each day a half hour early and would not be able to catch the bus home in the evening until two hours after class had finished. I was horrified. First of all, I did not feel Sheila was in any shape to be riding a bus with a bunch of high school kids; I doubted seriously that she could be trusted on any bus. Second, what was I supposed to do with her for two hours after school? The mere thought had frozen my stomach into a cold, iron-heavy lump.

The social worker smiled blankly. We would have to go along with the idea because the school district would not pay for special transportation when existing buses could be used. Arrangements would simply have to be made for her to stay at school. Other buses out to the country came almost as late and other children had to be waiting somewhere in the school. Sheila could wait with them. Transferring Sheila's limp wrist to me, she turned and left.

I looked down at Sheila and felt all my anxiety from the day before flood over me. She was regarding me, her eyes round and guarded, the hostility more hidden than the day before. I smiled weakly. "Good morning, Sheila. I'm glad you're with us again today."

In the few moments we had before the other children all arrived, I brought Sheila over to one of the tables and pulled a chair out for her. She had come with me from the door without protest and sat in the chair. "Listen," I said, sitting down next to her, "let's get an idea about what's going to happen in here today so we won't have another one like yesterday. That wasn't very much fun for me, and I don't suppose it was for you either."

Her brow wrinkled in a questioning expression as if she did not understand what I was doing.

"I don't know how it was for you at your other school, but I want you to know how it's going to be in here. Yesterday, I think we may have scared you a little bit, because you didn't know any of us and it might not have been clear what we expected. So, I'm going to tell you."

She began hunching herself up into the chair, drawing her knees up and folding in upon herself again. I noticed that she was still wearing the same worn denim overalls and T-shirt. Neither had been washed since yesterday and she smelled very strongly.

"I'm not going to hurt you. I don't hurt kids in here. Neither does Anton or Whitney or anyone else. You don't have to be frightened of us."

The thumb was in her mouth. She seemed scared of me and looked so little and vulnerable, making it difficult for me to remember her as she had been yesterday. The bravado was gone, at least temporarily. But her gaze remained unflinching as she watched me.

"Would you like to sit in my lap while I talk to you?"

She shook her head almost imperceptibly.

"Okay, well, here's the plan. I want you to join us when we do things. All you have to do it sit with us. Anton or Whitney or I will help you find out what is happening until you get used to it." I went ahead to explain the day's schedule. I told her she did not have to participate if she did not want to, just yet. But she did have to join us and there was no choice on that. Either she came on her own accord or one of us would help her.

"And," I concluded, "sometimes when things get out of control, the place I will have you go is over to the quiet corner." I indicated our chair in the corner. "You go and you sit there until both of us think you have things under control again. You just sit, that's all. Is that clear?"

If it was, she did not let me know. By that point the others were arriving. I rose and patted her on the back before going to greet the other children. She did not pull away from my touch but then she did not acknowledge it either.

When morning discussion came, Sheila was still sitting in the chair. I pointed to the floor beside me. "Sheila, over here, please, so we can start discussion."

She did not move. I repeated myself. Still she remained folded up in the chair. I could feel my stomach tighten in anticipation. She regarded me, her thumb in her mouth, her eyes wide. I looked to Anton, who was settling Freddie into place. "Anton, would you help Sheila join us?"

When Anton turned to approach her, Sheila came to life and bolted off the chair. She made a mad dash for the door, falling hard against it when the latch did not respond.

"Torey, make her stop," Peter said worriedly. The other children were watching Anton as he circled to catch her. She had that trapped-animal stare again and was dashing recklessly about trying to avoid capture. But the room was so small it was a futile flight. She attempted to deter him by knocking books off the counters but within a minute Anton had her cornered on the far side of one of the tables. Briefly, they danced back and forth, but Anton unexpectedly shoved the table toward her pinning her against the wall just long enough to reach and catch hold of her arm.

For the first time she made a sound. She let loose with a

51

scream that startled all of us. Susannah began to cry, but the others sat in fearful silence while Anton wrestled Sheila over to the group. I remained sitting and pointed to the spot I had indicated earlier. Taking her by the arm from Anton I pushed her into a sitting position. She continued to scream, a throaty, tearless yell, but she sat without struggling.

"Okay," I said with fake brightness. "Who has a topic?"

"I do," said William straining to be heard over Sheila's screams. "Is it always going to be like this in here?" His dark eyes fearful. "Is she always going to be like this?"

The other children were watching me anxiously, and I realized, not for the first time, what a con job my position was, because I was honestly as frightened as they were. We had been together four months and had learned each other's differences and problems. I knew Sheila would have been hard on us even if she had been quiet and cooperative, simply because she was new, testing our tenuous hold on order. But she was in no way easy to accept and she shook us all to our foundation.

So the topic that day was Sheila. I tried to explain as best I could that Sheila was adjusting and like all the rest of us was having a hard time. She simply needed our patience and understanding.

Sheila was not entirely ignoring us as we discussed her. Her screaming had diminished to sporadic squawks, inserted when there was too great a gap in our conversation or when one of us looked at her and she caught us at it. Otherwise, she was quiet. I let the children ask questions and express their fears and unhappiness. And I attempted to answer them honestly. All except Peter had the sensitivity not to be too critical in front of Sheila. Peter did not. Like the day before when he had complained of her smell, he angrily stated that he wanted this girl out of his room. She was ruining everything. I did not attempt to protect Sheila from his comments because I knew he would make them to her later anyway. That was all part of Peter's own problems and I preferred to be present when he talked.

So instead we discussed alternate ways of dealing with the inconveniences put upon us while Sheila adjusted. Tyler suggested sending her to the quiet corner to save our ears. Sarah opted to get freetime every time Sheila started a ruckus. And Guillermo, who seemed to be feeling particularly magnanimous, thought the children might take turns sitting with Sheila and keeping her company while she hollered so she wouldn't get lonely. I suspected he was reflecting more on his own feelings than on Sheila's.

In the end we decided that when Sheila yelled or in other ways demanded Anton's or my attention and disrupted the class, the other kids were to get busy at their own work and the more responsible ones were to keep an eye on Max and Freddie and Susannah. I told them that at the end of the week we would have a treat if everyone cooperated. After a short discussion we decided that we would make ice cream on Friday if everything worked out. The children were full of ideas.

"If you get busy with Sheila and Freddie starts crying, I can read him a story," Tyler suggested.

"We could sing a song by ourselves," Guillermo added.

"I'll hold Susannah Joy's hand so she won't run and hurt herself."

I smiled. "Everybody's got good ideas. This is going to work out real well, I can tell. So you just think what kind of ice cream topping you want on Friday." I looked down at Sheila, who was still making angry grunts. I continued hanging on to one overall strap, but she was sitting peacefully. "Do you like ice cream?"

She narrowed her eyes.

"I'll expect you'll want some, won't you? Do you like ice cream?"

Cautiously she nodded.

* * *

Sheila was more cooperative about moving to a chair while we had math. She climbed on one and folded herself up, watching me suspiciously as I went from child to child. The rest of the morning passed uneventfully.

I did not dare let lunch follow as it had the previous day, not only because I did not want a replay of the disastrous afternoon, but because the lunch aides had stated that they unequivocally refused to supervise her until she was more predictable. So I took my lunch and ate with the children.

I sat next to Sheila, who inched away from me on the cafeteria bench. Anton came and sat down on the other side of her and she inched back in my direction. She bolted her lunch down in minutes by cramming it into her mouth as fast as she could chew. Her manners were atrocious, but she could maneuver a fork, which was more than some of the others could manage.

After lunch I escorted her back to the room, sat down at one of the tables and graded papers while the children played. Sheila resumed her seat on the chair, put her thumb in her mouth and stared at me.

All afternoon she moved as requested, although when given a choice she always returned to the same chair at the table and hunched up on it. She appeared considerably subdued from the day before, almost depressed, but I made no attempt to question her. She seemed unduly frightened of me, which I did not understand, so I did not want to intensify her concerns by forcing myself upon her. The other children seemed disappointed that nothing happened and Peter came up to me after closing exercises to ask if we would still have ice cream if Sheila never misbehaved again. With a grin I assured him that if we went all the way to Friday with no problems, there would certainly be ice cream.

After the other children left, we were alone, Sheila, Anton, and I. Those two hours after school were normally my preparation time for the next day, but I thought that perhaps for the first few days at least, I might use them to get better acquainted with Sheila. She still sat in her chair, having not even gotten up when the other children put on their snowsuits and prepared to go home.

I came over to the table and sat down across from her. She regarded me, her eyes wary. "You did a nice job today, scout. I really liked that."

She averted her face.

I looked at her. Under the dirt and tangles was a handsome child. Her limbs were straight and well-formed. I longed to hold her, to take her in my lap and hug away some of that pain so obvious in her eyes. But we remained a table apart, which might as well have been a universe. With me so close, she would not even meet my eyes.

"Have I frightened you, Sheila?" I asked softly. "I didn't mean to, if I did. It must be very scary for you, having to come to a new school and be with all of us when you don't know us. I know that's scary. It scares me too."

She put her hand up to the side of her face to block me entirely from view.

"Would you like me to read you a story or something while we wait for your bus?"

She shook her head.

"All right. Well, I'm going to go over to the other table and make plans for tomorrow. If you change your mind, I'll be glad to read to you. Or you play with the toys or whatever you like." I rose from the table.

As soon as I had settled at my work she put her hand down and turned to me, studying me as I wrote. I looked up a few times but there was no response from that steady gaze.

CHAPTER

5

The next day I decided it was time for Sheila to participate. The bus which brought her dropped her off at the high school two blocks away, so Anton had gone to get her and walk her to our school. When they arrived, Sheila pulled off her jacket and went straight to her chair. I came over and sat down, explaining that today she was going to be asked to do some things. I went over the schedule of the day with her and told her I expected her to join us for everything just like the day before, and that I also expected her to work some math problems for me at math time. Also on Wednesday afternoons we always cooked, I said, so I wanted her to help us make chocolate bananas. Those two things she was expected to do.

She watched me as I spoke, her eyes clouded with the same distrust they had shown the day before. I asked if she understood what I wanted. She did not respond.

During morning discussion Sheila joined us when requested after I gave her the evil eye. She sat at my feet and did nothing. Math was a different story. I had planned to do some simple counting exercises using manipulatives. So I got out the blocks and called her to come over to me. She remained sitting in the spot that she had been for morning discussion.

"Sheila, come over here, please." I indicated a chair. It was the one she was so fond of. "Come on."

She did not move. Anton began to move cautiously to catch her if she bolted when I approached. Instantly she perceived our plan and panicked. This child was phobic about being chased. Shrieking wildly, she darted off, knocking children and their work over as she fled. But Anton was too close and snagged her almost immediately. I came and took her from him.

"Honey, we're not going to do anything to you when we come to get you. Don't you know that?" I sat down with her, holding her tightly as she struggled and listening to her breathing, raspy with fear. "Take it easy, kitten."

"Hey, everybody," Peter hollered delightedly, "everybody be good now." Little heads bent eagerly over their work and Tyler rose solicitously to check on Susannah and Max.

Sheila resumed screaming, her face reddening. But she did not cry. Holding her in my lap, I spilled out the counting blocks. I lined them up evenly while waiting for her to calm down. "Here, I want you to count some blocks for me."

She yelled louder.

"Here, count three out for me." She struggled to break my hold. "I'll help you." I manipulated a writhing hand toward the blocks. "One, two, three. There. Now you try."

Unexpectedly she grabbed a block and hurled it across the room. Within a split second she had another which hit Tyler squarely in the forehead. Tyler let out a wail.

I pinned Sheila's arm to her side and stood up, lugging her over to the quiet corner. "We don't do that in here.

Nobody is hurt in here. I want you to sit in the chair until you quiet down and can come back and work." I motioned Anton over. "Help her stay in the chair if she needs it."

I returned to the other children, rubbed Tyler's sore spot, and praised everybody for keeping busy. Putting a check on the board to indicate our approach toward Friday's ice cream, I then settled in next to Freddie to help him stack blocks. Over in the corner all hell had broken loose. Sheila shrieked wildly, kicking the wall with her tennis shoes and bouncing the chair. Anton was grimly silent, holding her firmly in place.

Throughout math period Sheila continued the ruckus. By the time free play had started half an hour later, she was tiring of kicking and fighting. I came over.

"Are you ready to come do your math with me?" I asked. She looked up at me and screamed wordlessly in anger. Anton was no longer holding on to her, just to the chair, and I motioned him away to keep an eye on the others. "When you are ready for math, you may come over. Until then I want you in the chair." Then I turned and left.

Leaving her entirely alone startled her momentarily and she stopped yelling. When she became fully aware that neither Anton nor I was standing over her to keep her in the chair, she stood up.

"Are you ready to do math?" I asked from across the room where I was helping Peter build a highway out of blocks.

Her face blackened with my question. "No! No! No! No!"

"Then sit back down."

She screeched in rage, her sudden change in volume causing everyone to pause. But she remained beside the chair.

"I said sit down, Sheila. You may not get up until you're ready to do math."

For an eternal moment she stormed with so much loudness I felt my head pulse. Then suddenly, startlingly, everything was quiet and she glowered at me. Such obvious hate withered what little self-confidence I had about what I was doing.

"Sit down in that chair, Sheila."

She sat. She turned the chair around so she could watch me, but she sat. Then she resumed screaming. I sighed a deep, private sigh of relief.

Peter looked at me. "You know, Torey, I think we ought to get two marks for good behavior on this one. She's pretty hard to ignore."

I grinned. "Yeah, Peter, I think you're right. This is worth two."

Sheila screamed and yelled all through playtime. The ruckus had been going over an hour and a half by then. She stomped her feet and bounced and rocked the chair. She pulled at her clothes and shook her fists. But she remained in the chair.

By snacktime she was hoarse and all that came from the corner was little strangled croaks. But her rage had not diminished and the croaks continued furiously. I stayed inside while Anton took the others out for recess. This increased Sheila's agitation for a few moments and she gasped out a few more shouts and rattled the chair around. But she was tiring. By the end of recess there were no sounds at all coming from the corner. My head was throbbing.

I did not restate the conditions for leaving the corner. I believed she was bright enough to know by that time and I did not want to give her added attention. The other children came in, frosty and red-cheeked from recess, full of tales about playing fox-and-geese in the snow with Anton, who got caught every time. Reading period started without event, all of us settling down to our tasks as if the little lump on the chair in the corner did not exist.

Toward the close of the period I felt a feather-light touch on my shoulder as I worked with Max. I turned to see Sheila standing behind me, her skin mottled with her anxiety, her face puckered with that cautious expression so frequently reflected in her eyes.

"You ready to do math?"

She pursed her lips a moment and then nodded slowly.

"Okay. Let me get Sarah to help Max. You go over and pick up the blocks you threw and get the others out of the cupboard by the sink." I spoke in a casual, offhanded manner as if it were normal to expect her to comply, my tight chest belying the degree of the con. She looked at me carefully but then went and did as I had asked.

Together we sat down on the floor and I spilled out the blocks. "Show me three blocks."

Cautiously she picked out three.

"Show me ten." Again, ten cubes were lined upon the rug before me. "Good girl. You know your numbers well, don't you?"

She looked up anxiously.

"I'm going to make it harder. Count me out twenty-seven." Within seconds twenty-seven blocks appeared.

"Can you add?"

She did not respond.

"Show me how many blocks are two plus two." Four blocks appeared without hesitation. I studied her a moment. "How about three plus five?" She laid out eight cubes.

I could not tell if she actually knew the answers or was solving them as she went along. Yet she clearly understood the mechanics behind adding. I was reluctant to get out pencil and paper, knowing her tendency to destroy paper. I did not want to ruin our fragile, newly won relationship. But I did want to know how she was working the problems. So I decided to switch to subtraction, which would tell me more. "Show me three take away one."

Sheila flipped two blocks out. I smiled. That problem she obviously knew without having to place three blocks out and remove one.

"Do six take away four."

Again two cubes.

"Hey, you're pretty smart. But I've got one for you. I'll get you this time. Show me twelve take away seven."

She looked up at me and the very smallest hint of a smile colored her eyes although it did not touch her lips. She stacked one, two, three, four, five blocks on top of one another. She did it without even looking down at the cubes. The little devil, I thought. Wherever she had been these past few years and whatever she had been doing, she was also learning. Her abilities were better than the average child her age. She gave no indication of even hesitating before laying the blocks out. My heart leaped at the possibility of having a bright child under all that protest and grime.

She did a few more problems for me before I said enough and she could put the blocks away. It was reading period now and I had told her in the morning that she did not have to participate in this activity. I rose to check on the other kids and Sheila rose with me. Still clutching the box of blocks she wandered after me.

"Honey," I said turning to her, "you can put those away, if you want. You don't have to carry them around."

Sheila had other ideas. The next time I looked up, she was in her favorite chair at the other end of the table with the blocks spilled before her. Busily she was manipulating them, doing something, but I could not tell what.

Lunch subdued her again and she retreated to hunching up in the chair. But when it came time to cook, I coaxed her off quite easily with a banana on a Popsicle stick.

Every Wednesday we made something to eat. I had done it for a variety of reasons. For the more controlled kids, it was a good exercise in math and reading. For everyone it

61

encouraged social activity, sharing, conversation and mutual work. Moreover, cooking was fun. Once a month we repeated a favorite recipe that the kids had chosen and this afternoon it was chocolate bananas, a messy affair involving a banana stuck on a stick that was dipped into chocolate and rolled in topping and then frozen. I had decided not to tackle a new recipe on Sheila's first day out to simplify things, and chocolate bananas were a popular standby. Almost all the kids could manage all the parts by themselves. Even Susannah could do most of it, leaving only Max and Freddie to supervise carefully. Naturally, there was chocolate everywhere and a good share of the toppings were eaten before they found a banana to adhere to, but we all had a marvelous time.

Sheila hesitated to join in, clutching her banana tightly and watching from the sidelines as the others babbled gaily. Yet, she was not resistant and Whitney lured her over to the chocolate sauce when everyone else had finished. Once Sheila started, she became fully absorbed and began trying to roll all four different toppings onto her sticky banana. I watched from the far side of the table. She never spoke but it became apparent she had some definite ideas about how to get the toppings to stick by redipping the banana in the chocolate after each roll in a topping. One by one the other children began pausing to watch her as she experimented with her idea. Voices became hushed as curiosity got the better of them. Rolling the huge, sticky mass in the last dish of topping, she lifted it up carefully. Her eyes rose to meet mine and slowly a smile spread across her face until it was broad and open, showing the gaps where her bottom teeth were missing.

At the end of each day we had closing exercises which, like morning topic were designed to unite us and prepare us for our time apart. One of the activities was the Kobold's Box. I loved to make up stories to tell the children and had once told them back at the beginning of the year that kobolds were like fairies, but that they lived in people's houses and watched over them to keep things safe while people slept. Peter had suggested that there might be a kobold in our room who took care of all our things and kept Benny, Charles and Onions, the bad-tempered rabbit, company during the night. This spawned a number of tales about our kobold. So one day I brought a large wooden box and told the kids that this was where the kobold was going to leave messages. I said he had watched all of us at work and had been extremely pleased with how kind and thoughtful everyone in the room was becoming. Therefore, every time he saw a kind deed done, he would leave a message in the box. So during closing exercises each day, I read the notes from the Kobold's Box. After a few days I told them the kobold was getting writer's cramp and needed a helping hand because so many people were being kind. I asked the children to be on the lookout for others doing kind things and to write a note and put it in the box, or if they could not write, to come to me and I would write it for them. Thus, one of our most popular and effective exercises occurred. Every night there were about thirty notes from the kids to each other over perceived kindnesses. This not only encouraged the children to observe positive behaviors in others, but they also knocked each other over being kind in hopes that their names would appear in the box at the end of the day. Some notes were traditional but others showed particular insight praising a child for small but significant steps, sometimes for things I myself had missed. For instance, Sarah was complimented for not using a particularly favorite vulgar phrase during an argument one day, and Freddie was praised for finding a Kleenex instead of blowing his nose on his shirt. I loved opening that box every night because I seldom contributed to it myself except to make sure everybody had at least one note. The thrill of seeing what the children had perceived was so

63

exciting to me. And admittedly, I also enjoyed finding a note for myself in there.

So closing exercises after cooking on Wednesday were particularly fun because for the first time Sheila's name appeared in handwriting other than my own. Sheila who still sat apart from us kept her head down when the kids clapped over her notes. But she accepted the notes readily when I gave them to her.

Anton walked the other children out to their buses after school ended. I settled down at the table to grade papers and to bring some behavioral charts I was keeping on a couple of the kids up to date. Sheila had gone into the bathroom to clean the final dregs of the chocolate banana from her face. She had been in there some time and I had become involved in my work. I heard the toilet flush and she came out. I did not look up because I was completing a graph with marking pen and did not want to make an error. Sheila came over to the table and watched me a moment. Then she came closer, putting her elbows on the table and leaning way over so that we were only inches apart. I raised my eyes to look at her. She examined my face thoughtfully.

"How come them other kids don't go to the bathroom in the toilet?"

"Huh?" I sat back in surprise.

"I say, how come them other kids, them big kids, go in their pants and not in the toilet?"

"Well, that's something they haven't learned yet."

"How come? They do be big kids. Bigger than me."

"Well, they just haven't learned it yet. But we're working on it. Everyone's trying."

She looked down at the graph I was drawing. "They oughta know that by now. My Pa, he'd whip me fierce bad if I do that."

"Everybody's different and nobody gets a whipping in here."

She was pensive a long moment. She traced a little circle on the table with her finger. "This here be a crazy class, don't it?"

"Not really, Sheila."

"My Pa, he say so. He say I be crazy and they put me in a class for crazy kids. He says this here be a crazy kidses class."

"Not really."

She frowned a moment. "I don't care much. This here do be as good as that other place I be before. It be as good as anyplace. I don't care if it be a crazy class."

I was at a loss for words, not knowing how to deny the obvious. I had not expected to be involved with one of my children in this sort of discussion. Most were either not coherent enough to be that perceptive or not brash enough to say it.

Sheila scratched her head and regarded me thoughtfully. "Do you be crazy?"

I laughed. "I hope not."

"How come you do this?"

"What? Work here? Because I like boys and girls a lot and I think that teaching is fun."

"How come you be with crazy kids?"

"I like it. Being crazy isn't bad. It's just different, that's all."

She shook her head without smiling and straightened up. "I think you do be a crazy person too."

CHAPTER

6

"Sheila, come over here, please," I motioned to a chair near where I was sitting. "I have something for you to do." Sheila sat across the room in her favorite chair. Thus far, the morning had gone smoothly. Like the previous two days, I had used the time before school to tell her what would happen that day. She had been cooperative, joining us for morning discussion without being reminded, and then for math. Although she still did not speak, she appeared considerably more relaxed in the classroom. Now she watched me from her chair.

"Come here, hon. I want you to do something with me." I beckoned to her. She unfolded from her post hesitantly. I had borrowed a test from the school psychologist called a Peabody Picture Vocabulary Test or more affectionately the PPVT. Although I never cared much for the test, it gave a general idea of a child's functioning verbal IQ quickly and without the child needing to talk. After the previous day's encounter with the math cubes, I was intensely interested to know the level at which the girl was functioning. With such a severe disturbance as Sheila displayed, it was typical for her to be academically behind. Most seriously disturbed children simply do not have the extra energy available to learn. So when she evidenced normal math skill, I became alive with curiosity. I was also excited to think she might have above-average intelligence. I was already beginning to mellow about her placement in my room and wondering about keeping her out of the state hospital. Of all the things she needed right now, I realized that was not one of them.

"You and I are going to do something together." I had had to get up and bring her over to my table. "Here, sit down. Now, I'm going to show you some pictures and say a word. Then I want you to point to the picture that best shows what that word means, okay? Do you understand that?"

She nodded. I showed the first set of four pictures and asked her to point to "whip." What a picture to have to start with, I thought ruefully. She studied the four line drawings, looked up at me, then cautiously pointed to one.

"Good girl," I smiled at her. "That's just exactly right. Point to 'net.'"

As I read each word, Sheila would point to a picture, hesitantly at first, studying each of the four choices carefully, then more freely. After six or seven plates a small smile slipped across her face and she raised her eyes. "This be easy," she whispered hoarsely so the others could not hear.

She missed one, "thermos," a word she had probably not encountered in her short, destitute life. But the next one she did correctly. A child had to miss six out of eight to stop the test, and she gave no indication of reaching that level. We continued. The words were beginning to get harder and she was taking more time to consider the pictures. Occasionally she would miss one, sometimes two. I could see the concern in her eyes; she knew when she missed them, even if I made no comments.

I had stopped making comments some time back. I had suspected she was above average in intelligence, maybe even bright, but she had long since passed my expectations. We were moving into a part of the test I had never given before because none of my kids had ever gone that high. We were working with words like "illumination" and "concentric." Sheila was missing words regularly, but never six out of eight. Tension mounted around us. She was obviously trying very hard not to make mistakes and I was touched by her concentration. But we were up into the adolescent end of the test; there were words no normal six-year-old would know. Biting her lips between her teeth, she kept trying. In her lap, I could see her wringing her hands.

"Sweetheart, you're doing a nice job," I said. I hadn't expected her to take the test so seriously and become so involved, to try so hard and to last so long. I really could not believe she knew these words.

She looked up at me. Her eyes were dilated, the soft skin at her throat mottled with nervousness. "I ain't getting them all right."

"Oh, that's okay, honey. You aren't supposed to get them all right. These are words for great big kids and you're not expected to know them all. This is just to see which ones you do know. But it doesn't matter if you get some wrong. I'm proud of you for trying so hard."

Her face puckered and she looked on the verge of tears. "These be fierce hard words now." She looked down at her hands. "First they be easy, but these do be terrible hard for me. I don't know them all."

Her tiny voice, her slipping hold on her composure, her small shoulders hunched up under the worn shirt all combined to rip at my heart. Such innocence, even in the worst of these kids. They were all simply little children.

I reached an arm out. "Come here, Sheila." She looked up at me and I leaned over and pulled her up into my lap. Under my hands her little body was tense, the omnipresent odor of old urine floating around us. "Kitten, I know you're trying your best. That's all that counts. I don't really care which ones you get right or wrong, that doesn't matter. Why, these are really hard words. I bet there isn't another boy or girl in here who could do better."

I held her, smoothing back the tangled hair from her face. Waiting for her to relax I looked over the test score sheet mentally subtracting out the errors. I suspected she was very close to reaching the ceiling of her ability on the test. She was missing three and four at a time. But even so, she had surpassed any other child I had ever tested.

"How do you know all these words?" I asked, my curiosity getting the better of me.

She shrugged. "I dunno."

"Some of these are big kids' words. I just wondered where you heard them."

"My other teacher, she let me have magazines. Sometimes I read the words in there."

I looked down at her. Her body was still rigid against mine and light as that of a little bird. "Can you read, Sheila?"

She nodded.

"Where'd you learn to do that?"

"I dunno. I always read."

I shook my head in amazement. What sort of changeling did we have here? At first I had been titillated by the thought of a bright child, because as dear as the others were, most were slow learners and it was always hard to know where the disturbance left off and the retardation began. Some, like Sarah and Peter, were average, but I had seldom had an above-average child. At first, the thought had excited me. But clearly Sheila was not simply above average. She was way beyond the comfortableness that came with easy learning and mastery. Instead, she had been catapulted into that little-known realm of true giftedness. I feared that fact would not ease my job at all.

There was no scale to measure Sheila's score on the PPVT. For her age group the scale stopped at 99, which translated into a 170 IQ. Sheila had a score of 102. I stared at the test sheet. We don't have a concept for that kind of brilliance. Statistics tell us that less than 1 in 10,000 has that high a level of functioning. But what does it mean? It is a deviant score, an abnormality in a society that worships sameness. It would set her apart as surely as her disturbance could.

I looked across the room to where Sheila sat. It was playtime now and Sheila had resumed her favorite chair. I looked at her as she sat, thumb in mouth, limbs wrapped around herself protectively. She was watching Tyler and Sarah, who were playing with dolls in the housekeeping corner. I wondered. Under that long matted hair, behind those wary eyes, what kind of child was there? I now felt more concerned than ever before, because if anything, the situation had become more complicated.

After lunch I showed Anton the test, He shook his head in disbelief. "That can't be right," he muttered. "Where would she learn those words? She just had to guess lucky, Torey. No kid in the migrant camp is going to know those kinds of words."

I could not believe it myself. So I put in a call to Allan, our school psychologist. He was out of the office but I left a message with his secretary saying I had a child that I wanted tested.

One thing from the testing situation puzzled me. As Sheila spoke to me more, it became increasingly apparent that she used a highly idiosyncratic dialect. I hadn't heard her enough to pick out the unusual features precisely, but the grammar was bizarre. Most of the migrant camp children came from Spanish-speaking homes and often their command of English vocabulary was below age-level but within normal limits grammatically. There was no other major speech variation in the locality. Sheila was not from a Spanish-speaking home; the IQ test substantiated that there was nothing wrong at all with her vocabulary. I could not fathom why she spoke so oddly. To me her dialect almost sounded like the inner-city blacks I had worked with in Cleveland. But Sheila was not black and our small Iowa farming community was far from inner-city Cleveland. Perhaps it was a family speech pattern. I decided I would have to investigate because the phenomenon left me so perplexed.

The remainder of the day went uneventfully. I still made minimal requirements of Sheila. I wanted to give her ample time to adjust to us without taxing the other kids too much. After the first tumultuous days, this was a welcome relief. She moved willingly with us, but participated infrequently and only when coaxed. She would not talk to the other children or to Whitney. In most instances she would not speak to Anton or me unless we were quite isolated. Yet, she was peaceful, sitting in her chair when given the opportunity and watching us with guarded interest.

The next major step that had to be taken with Sheila concerned her hygiene. Every day she arrived in the same denim overalls and boy's T-shirt. Apparently, the clothes had never been washed from the first day she wore them and she reeked of urine. I suspected she wet the bed and dressed each morning without washing. Consequently, she was extremely unpleasant to be near for any length of time. Both Anton and I were used to the strong odors of unchanged pants, since Max, Freddie, and Susannah were

71

all not reliably toilet trained. But Sheila was even stronger than we were accustomed to. Moreover, the plain everyday grime was crusted over her face and arms. When I had sent her in to wash off the chocolate from cooking the day before, there were lines on her forearms indicating how high she had washed. Those same lines were visible today. She had long hair that went halfway down her back in tangled strands. I had checked the first day for lice or mites. We had struggled twice with lice already and I was not game for another encounter. The second time I had ended up catching them myself and had been furious. Sheila did not appear to have any, although she did have impetigo around her mouth, which I hoped none of the other children would catch.

A school nurse came once a week for an afternoon. I had tried to send my children down. Most of them had had impetigo or rat bites or other evils of poverty. But I ended up getting the salve and Kwell shampoo from the nurse and taking care of the kids myself, simply because once a week on Thursday afternoons was not often enough to tend to all the problems.

I waited until all the children had left at the end of the day to tackle Sheila's hygienic needs. She had remained sitting in her chair while the others had gotten ready to go home. She was still sitting when I went to the cupboard and got out the combs and brushes I kept there. The night before I had stopped at the drugstore and bought a little package of hair clips.

"Sheila, come here," I said. "I got something for you."

She rose and came over. Her brow was furrowed with wary interest. I handed her the sack. For a moment she just held it, looking at me quizzically. But I urged her to open it and she did. Taking the clips out she looked at them and then at me. Her forehead was still wrinkled in puzzlement.

"They're for you, sweetheart. I thought we could comb

your hair out nice and put clips in it. Like I've got in mine." I showed her my hair.

She fingered the clips carefully through the plastic wrapping. With a frown she regarded me. "How come you do this?"

"Do what?"

"Be nice to me?"

I looked at her in disbelief. "Because I like you."

"Why? I be a crazy kid; I hurt your fishes. Why do you be nice to me?"

I smiled through my own perplexity. "I just wanted to, Sheila. That's all. I thought you might like something nice for your hair."

She continued to rub the clips through the wrapping, feeling the plastic shapes with her fingertips. "Ain't nobody give me nothing before. Ain't nobody be nice to me on purpose."

I stood watching her in bewilderment. There was nothing in my experience to relate to that. "Well, things are different in here, kiddo," was all I could reply.

I brushed the tangles out of her hair carefully. It took much longer than I had anticipated it would because I did not want to hurt her in any way. I was fearful of this fragile relationship we were forming, of accidentally harming it because we were from such different worlds. She sat very patiently clutching the clips in her hands but never taking them out of the wrapping. Over and over again she fingered them, but she would not open the package. Her hair was that fine, soft, impossibly straight hair that fortunately never tangles too badly. When brushed out, it hung down below her shoulder blades in a thick curtain. In front I combed her bangs. They were too long, falling into her eyes. She was a pretty girl with bold, well-formed features. With soap and water she would be even lovelier.

73

"There you are. Here, give me the clips and I'll put them in your hair."

She squashed the clips to her breast.

"Here, let's put them in your hair."

She shook her head.

"Don't you want them there?"

"Pa, he take them away from me."

"He wouldn't do that, would he? Just tell him that I gave them to you."

"He say I steal them. Nobody give me nothing before." She held on to the clips tightly, looking at the plastic bluebirds and ducks through the wrapping.

"Maybe for now, you can leave them at school until I get hold of your dad and tell him I gave them to you. How's that sound?"

"You fix my hair nice again?"

I nodded. "I'll fix it tomorrow morning when you come."

She looked at the clips a long moment and then hesitantly handed them to me. "Here. You keep them for me."

My heart thumped within my chest as I took the clips. It was so obvious how hard she was finding giving them back. At that moment Anton came into the room with an armload of dittos he had been running off. He reminded me that it was almost time for him to walk Sheila over to the high school to catch her bus. I was surprised that so much time had slipped by. We hadn't even gotten around to washing up and she did smell so terrible.

"Sheila," I asked, "do you get a chance to wash yourself at home?"

She shook her head. "We ain't got no bathtub."

"Can you use the sink?"

"Ain't got no sink either. My Pa, he brings us down water in a bucket from the gas station." She paused staring at the floor. "It just be to drink out of. He'd be fierce awful mad at me if I get it dirty."

"Do you have any other clothes?"

She shook her head.

"Well, I'll tell you what. We'll see what we can do about that tomorrow, okay?"

Nodding she went to the coat hook to find her thin cotton jacket. I sighed as I watched her. So much to do, I thought. So much to change. "Good-bye, Sheila. Have a nice evening. I'll see you tomorrow."

Anton took her hand and opened the door into the blowy January darkness. Just as he was shutting the door behind him, Sheila paused, peering under his arm and toward me. She smiled slightly. "Bye, teacher."

CHAPTER

7

The next morning I came ready for action. Armed with three bath towels, a bar of soap, shampoo, and a bottle of baby lotion, I arrived at school. First I went down to check the church box in the office. Although the school I was in was in one of the upper-income areas, enough children like those in my room were bussed in to warrant a box of spare clothes that could be given away. I kept my own box in my room, but primarily it contained underwear. What was in there was far too large for little Sheila. Having found a pair of corduroy pants and another T-shirt, I went back to my room.

Thus when Sheila arrived, I was running water into the sink in the back of the classroom. The sink was a large, roomy, kitchen-sized sink and I figured I would get a good share of her into it, since we lacked shower facilities. The moment she saw me, Sheila yanked off her jacket and came trotting over. That was the fastest I had seen her move toward me since she had come. Her eyes were wide with interest as she leaned over to see what I was doing. "You gonna put clips in my hair now?"

"You bet. But first we're going to give you the full beauty-shop routine. We're going to wash you top to bottom. How does that sound?"

"It gonna hurt?"

I laughed. "No, silly. I don't think so."

She had pulled the bottle of baby lotion out of the bucket I had it in and she removed the top. "What do this be for? Do you eat it?"

I looked at her in surprise. "No, it's lotion. You put it on your body."

A sudden look of pleasure rippled across her face. "It do smell good, teacher. Smell it. It smell good and you put it on to be pretty smelling." Her eyes were animated. "Now that kid, he ain't gonna say I stink no more, huh?"

I smiled at her. "No, I guess he won't. Look here, I found some clothes for you to wear. Then Whitney can take your overalls over to the Laundromat when she comes this afternoon."

Sheila surveyed the corduroy pants, picking them up gingerly. "My Pa, he ain't gonna let me keep them. We don't take no charity things."

"Yes, I understand that. You just wear them until the others get dry. Okay?"

I lifted Sheila up onto the counter beside the sink and took off her shoes and socks. She watched me carefully as I eased off her clothes but she made no attempt to help. I felt pressed for time because the other children would be arriving in less than a half hour, and although they were used to washing and seeing others washed in the sink, I was afraid Sheila might feel too vulnerable at this point to have an audience. I asked her about it and she said she did not mind, but I still felt it would be better to finish before the others came.

She was a scrawny little whip of a child with all her ribs

showing. I noticed the many scars on her body. "What happened here?" I asked as I washed one arm. A scar two inches long ran up the inside of it.

"That be where I brokeded my arm at, once."

"How'd you do that?"

"Falling down playing. The doctor putsa cast on it."

"You fell down playing?"

She nodded matter-of-factly, inspecting the scar. "I fall on the sidewalk. My Pa, he says I do be a godawful clumsy child. I hurt myself a lot."

In my mind was forming the question I had learned to ask of my kids; a question I dreaded. "Does your Pa ever do anything that leaves scars like these? Like spank you hard or something?" I asked.

She looked at me, her eyes clouding over. She regarded me so long in silence that I wished I had not asked. It was a personal question and perhaps I had not laid a firm enough foundation in our relationship to be so intimate. "My Pa, he wouldn't do that. He wouldn't hurt me bad. He loves me. He just hits me a little bit to make me good. You gotta do that to kids sometimes. But my Pa, he loves me. I just be a clumsy child to get so many scars." Her voice was tinged with defiance.

I nodded and lifted her out of the sink to dry her off. For several moments she did not speak to me. I had her on my lap and was drying her legs when she twisted around to look me in the eye. "You know what my Mama done though?"

"No."

"Here, I'll show you." She lifted the other leg up and pointed to a scar. "My Mama she take me out on the road and leave me there. She push me out of the car and I fall down so's a rock cutted up my leg right here. See." She fingered a white line. "My Pa, he loves me. He don't go leaving me on no roads. You ain't supposed to do that with little kids."

"No, you're not."

"My Mama, she don't love me so good."

In silence I began combing out her hair. I did not really want to hear any more because it hurt to listen to her; her voice was so calm and matter of fact that I felt that I shouldn't be listening to what she was saying. It was like reading someone's diary, the very calmness of the print making the words more pathetic.

"My Mama, she take Jimmie and go to California. That be where they live right now. Jimmie, he be my brother and he be four-years-old, 'cept that he only be two when my Mama, she leave. I ain't seen Jimmie in two whole years." She paused thoughtfully. "I miss Jimmie sort of. I wish I could see him again. He be a real nice boy." Again she turned around in my lap so she could see me. "You'd like Jimmie. He be a nice boy and don't yell or be bad or anything. He be a nice boy to have in this here crazy kidses class. 'Cept I don't think he be crazy like me. You like Jimmie. My Mama do. She like Jimmie better'n me, that's why she tooked him and leaved me behind. You ought to have Jimmie in this here class. He don't do bad things like I do."

I hugged her to me. "Kitten, you're the one I'd want. Not Jimmie. He'll have his own teacher some day. I don't care what kids do, I just like them. That's all."

She sat back and looked at me, a bemused look falling across her face. "You do be a funny lady for a teacher. I think you be as crazy as us kidses be."

That fifth day, Friday, she still did not talk to the other kids although when asked a direct question she would answer any of the adults. At the end of the day after everyone had had ice cream and we had finished closing exercises, we were standing in line waiting for the buses to arrive to take the other children home. We had finished up a bit early and everyone was standing around in their snowsuits getting hot, so I suggested a song. Max shouted out that he wanted "If You're Happy and You Know It, Clap Your Hands," one of the few songs he would sing with the rest of us. It was a simple action song that required the children to clap, then stomp, then nod their heads. I looked over to see Sheila standing on the edge of the group not singing but paying close attention. When we had finished all the actions, the buses still had not arrived so I asked for suggestions for new actions. Tyler said, "If you're happy and you know it, jump up and down." So we sang a verse using Tyler's action. Again I asked for new actions. From her corner Sheila shyly raised her hand. With all our other problems and with so few children I just never got around to requesting that they do that unless we were having a moment of mass confusion. To see this little kid—who thus far had never spoken to the other children, who came in with a history of uncooperativeness—standing there with her hand up was a heart stopper.

"Sheila, do you have an idea?"

"Turn around?" she said diffidently.

And so we sang our song turning around. The first week had ended in the heat of success.

Sheila came alive in our room during the next weeks. She began speaking, first with reserve, and then with none. Sheila had thoughts on everything and was most articulate when given the chance. I was delighted to have a verbal child in the room. The other children enjoyed her company and I was tickled that she could tell me about so many things.

Sheila never brought up the burning incident, not during the early stages of our relationship, not later, not ever. Most of the more coherent kids in my class were aware of some of the reasons why they had been placed in there. We talked about those reasons regularly, during the times we set weekly and long-term goals for change, occasionally during morning topic and at other less formal times: out on the playground while we all stood shivering in the lee of the building too engrossed in conversation to go in, over lunch or art or cooking, alone together on the pillows in the secluded animal-cage corner. There seemed to be a pressing need in most of the kids to talk about these things.

The conversations were low-keyed and often casual, much experience having gone into my ability to discuss such topics as committing suicide or burning cats alive with the same casualness I made out my laundry list or asked about baseball scores. The kids did not need to know the behaviors were wrong or that they frightened or repelled others — they already knew that. Otherwise they would not have been in my room in the first place. Instead they needed to explore the width and breadth and depth of those acts, how they felt when they did them, how they had expected they would feel and the seemingly meaningless myriad of details surrounding the episodes. Mostly I listened, asked a question or two if things were not clear, mmmm-hmmmed a lot to let them know I heard. And I kept us busy at dozens of mindless tasks like coloring or making papier mâché projects so that we could talk without having to look at one another, without having to acknowledge we were talking.

Sheila knew why she was there. From the second day on she continued to refer to us affectionately as a "crazy class." And she was a crazy kid who did bad things. Often she would join the conversations. Yet not once was the abuse incident brought up. Not with the kids. Not with me or the other adults. Never. I did not suggest the topic either. Although I seldom avoided issues, this one I felt instinctively I should leave alone, for no other reason than what my gut told me. So we never discussed it. I never found out what had been going through Sheila's mind that cold November evening.

* * *

I remained perplexed about her speech patterns. The more she talked, the more obvious the discrepancy was between the way Sheila spoke and the way the rest of us did. There were no reports of her father speaking any sort of dialect. He was a native of the area and should have spoken in the same manner as the rest of us. The major variations were word insertions, especially "do" and "be," and the absence of a past tense. The word "do" was used as an auxiliary verb, inserted at will throughout Sheila's conversations. "Be" took the place of "am," "is" and "are." For Sheila, the past tense simply did not exist with very few exceptions. Everything was spoken as if it were in the present or future. This mystified me because she had a good command of very difficult tenses such as conditionals like "should" and "would," and was capable of putting together complex sentences far beyond the grasp of most six-year-olds. Repeatedly, I taped samples of her speech and sent them off to experts to be analyzed. In the meantime, I let her speak as she chose.

Allan, the school psychologist, gave Sheila an IQ and reading test. The IQ test Sheila topped out, earning the highest possible score. Allan was astonished, coming out of his little room shaking his head. He had never had a child do that on the test he was using, and certainly had never expected it from a child they would place in a class like mine. Sheila read and comprehended on a fifth grade level, despite the fact that no one had ever taught her to read. Allan left that day, vowing to find a test that could measure her IQ.

Each morning before school Sheila and I worked on hygiene. I brought a plastic bucket at the discount store and put a comb, brush, washcloth, towel, soap, lotion and toothbrush in it. Most days Sheila was willing to wash and brush her teeth, if I would fix her hair. She delighted in the hair clips. I bought another package like the kind that I wore and Sheila guarded them all like a king's treasure. Each morning she went through them, counting them and deciding which ones she would wear. Each evening she took them out of her hair, laying them carefully in the folds of the towel. Again she counted them to make sure no one had taken any. Her clothes were a bit more of a problem. I kept clean underpants at school and insisted she change every morning. We never discussed the problem because I deduced that after the first day, it was a sensitive area. I did, however, make sure she changed, regardless of what subjects we mentioned. On Mondays Whitney trotted Sheila's overalls and shirt down to the Laundromat around the corner from the school. It was hardly a foolproof solution but at least Sheila did not stink so much anymore. All in all, she was a handsome child cleaned up. She had thick, long blond hair and much to the pleasure of all of us she had sparkly eyes and a ready smile that showed three gaps on the bottom awaiting new teeth.

To my relief one problem which I had anticipated but which never materialized was Sheila's bus ride to and from the migrant camp. With such a terrible history of uncontrollable behavior, Sheila, unsupervised on a bus, was something I could not imagine working out well. However, my fears proved to be unfounded. Perhaps putting her with forty high school students was enough to intimidate even Sheila.

Anton or I walked her to and from the bus, but once on it, she settled down in a seat toward the back. The only incident that ever occurred was in late January after she had been on the route for some time. We had walked her to the bus in the evening and put her on. However, by the time the bus had arrived at the migrant camp and the high school students had climbed off, Sheila was not there. The bus driver stood up from his seat and looked back, but the bus was empty. Alarmed because the bus only made two stops before the camp and he had not seen her disembark at either of them, the driver called me at home to make sure she had gotten on. I told him she had. There were more than a few panicky moments before the bus driver called back. Apparently, Sheila had gotten down on the floor by the rear tire where the heat came in and she fell asleep. After she discovered that warm, vibrating spot, she regularly curled up on the floor under the seat and slept during the hour ride both in and out. The driver always checked after that, to make sure she awakened and got off. The high school students, at first only tolerant of her presence, began to save that seat near the heater for her, began also to give her book bags or extra sweaters for a pillow and to see she was walked home on those nights she was too sleepy to be reliable.

A problem that was not solving itself was Sheila's father. I had tried relentlessly to get hold of him for a conference. He had no phone so I sent a note home with Sheila asking him to come to school. No response. I sent a second note. Again no response. I sent a third note saying I was coming to visit him at his home. When the evening came that Anton and I went out, the house was empty. I was getting the distinct impression he did not want to see me. Finally I contacted Sheila's social worker. Together we went out only to be greeted at the door by Sheila. Her father was gone.

I wanted to see him very badly. First I wanted to make some arrangements for Sheila to get proper clothing. I had mentioned this to the social worker. Although Sheila had only one outfit, my main concern was her outerwear. She owned only a boy's thin cotton jacket, something like a baseball Windbreaker. She had no gloves, no hat, no boots. And it was, after all, January. The temperature hovered around 20 degrees most days and had even been below zero on occasion. Sheila would arrive at school almost blue some mornings after her walk from the high school two blocks away. In desperation I had taken my car to get her on the worst days. I gave her more to wear at recess, but the one time I sent things home, they came back the next day in a paper bag. Sheila remarked with embarrassment that she had gotten a spanking for accepting "charity." The social worker explained that they had repeatedly gotten on the father for this and had even taken him downtown once to buy clothes for Sheila from his welfare check. But apparently he had returned the clothes later. You couldn't force the man, she said, shrugging. She did not want to endanger Sheila by forcing the issue because it was a known fact that he took his anger out on the child. Wasn't that child abuse? I had asked. Not technically. There were not any marks on her. I had slammed the door in frustration after the social worker left. Not any marks on her, huh? Then what the hell was she doing in my class? If that wasn't a mark, I didn't know what was.

During the hours that school was in session, I tried to provide her with all the experiences that her disturbance or circumstances had robbed her of. She came alive. Every moment of her day was filled with exploring and chattering. The first weeks she followed me around all day long. Everywhere I went, when I turned around there she would be, clutching a book to her chest or a box of math cubes. A silly smile would spill over her lips when she caught my eye, and she'd scuttle up ready to share. I had to divide my time equally with the other children, of course, but this did not deter her. She would stand patiently behind me waiting until I had finished. Sometimes I would feel a hand tentatively take hold of my belt as she got braver and longed for more physical contact. Anton would laugh and kid me in the teacher's lounge about looking like a subway, because as I walked around the room helping the other children, Sheila would go with me, one hand locked into my belt like a seasoned straphanger.

During those first weeks of intense devotion, I was both

thankful and dismayed for the two hours we had alone after school. My planning time was shot. Much to Chad's displeasure I was having to haul my work home and do it in the evenings. Anton groused about never getting to talk over matters anymore unless we both came in at seven thirty in the morning. But for Sheila it was ideal. She needed undivided attention.

For all of her six years she had been unwanted, ignored, rejected. Pushed out of cars, pushed out of people's lives. Now there was someone to hold her and talk to her and cuddle her. Sheila soaked up every little bit of intimacy I could spare. Despite the inconvenience of losing those two hours of planning time, I felt less anxious about dragging her around all day hanging on my belt and ignoring her while I worked with the other children, because after school she had me all to herself.

The other children were as delighted as Anton and I were to see Sheila blossom. Notes filled the Kobold's Box scribbled in childish hand. Most of the children were relieved that she did not smell so often or so badly and were quick to comment on that. But they also perceived her budding attempts at kindness.

Sheila had evidently not had much of an opportunity to learn how to be considerate of others or how to be kind. She had been busy surviving and altruism had little place in survival. Consequently, she was used to having to fight for what she wanted. When someone got the place in line she had chosen, she socked that person hard enough to win it back. If another child had a toy she wanted, she grabbed it, wrestled it out of the child's hands and scuttled off to safety with it to hiss angrily at anyone who tried to take it away. In many ways she was much cruder and more obnoxious in her directness than even Peter, but hers was an animal-like aggressiveness, without malice.

I knew that, after six years, it was not going to be a simple matter to convince her that there was another way to do things. My reprimands and cautions and forced marches to the quiet corner did not noticeably dent her behavior. But the Kobold's Box did.

Each night Sheila listened carefully as I read the notes and complimented the children who earned them. Greedily she would count hers after each session and, if given the opportunity, she would count other children's also to see if they got more or less than she did. I tried to discourage that activity. The other kids were not competitive and did not feel the need to measure their worth by the number of notes they received. I did not want them to start. But Sheila could not resist. Her meager portion of self-confidence would not let her rest. Over and over again she wanted to prove that she was the best child in the class, the smartest, the hardest-working, my favorite. When I steadfastly refused to confirm that, she set out to prove it to herself with notes in the Kobold's Box. But that eluded her. She could show me how well she read. That was simple; it only entailed getting out a book. She could show me how well she did math. That, too, was simple. But she could not figure out how to be kind or polite or considerate in order to earn herself more notes.

One afternoon after school she had stayed by the table where I was taking apart a science experiment. "How come Tyler gets so many notes?" she asked. "She gets more than anybody else does. Do you give them to her?"

"No, you know that. Everybody writes out notes."

"How come she gets more?" She cocked her head. "What she do? How come everybody likes her so good?"

"Well," I considered the matter a moment. "For one thing, she's polite. When she wants something she asks, and almost always says please. And thank you too. That makes a person feel more like helping her or being with her, because she makes you feel good for it."

Sheila frowned, looking down at her hands. After a long pause she looked accusingly at me. "How come you never tell me you want me to say please and thank you? I don't know you want that. How come you tell Tyler and you don't tell me?"

I looked at her in disbelief. "I didn't tell Tyler, Sheila. It's just something people do. Everybody likes other people to be polite."

"I don't know that. Nobody ever told me," she said reproachfully. "I never know you want me to do that."

In considering the matter, I knew she was right. I probably never had told her. It was one of those things I took for granted a child would know, especially a bright child like her. I had just assumed she knew. But the unfairness of the assumption was dawning on me. Sheila might never have heard those words in her environment. Or perhaps they had never been meaningful to her before.

"I'm sorry, Sheil. I thought you knew."

"I don't. I can say them if I know you want me to."

I nodded. "I do. They're good words to use, because they make other people feel good. That's important. People like you better for it."

"Will they tell me I'm a nice girl?"

"It'll help them see that you are."

And so, little by little she began to attend to what others were doing to be kind and considerate. When she did not understand, she asked. At other times when it occurred to me that she did not know, I would tell her during one of our quiet moments.

8

Unfortunately as in all Gardens of Eden, there were a few snakes. During that first month there were two problems that we did not seem able to lick.

The first problem was perhaps not as major as it felt. Despite all her progress, Sheila steadfastly refused to do paperwork. The instant a piece of paper was given to her, she destroyed it. Occasionally under dire threat from Anton or me, she would not tear it up immediately but actually appear to be working on it. However, it never reached the correction basket. Partway through she would rip it to shreds or scribble over it or crumple it into a tight little wad, stuffing it under the radiator or into the rabbit's cage to be eaten.

I tried any number of methods to stop her. I taped the work to the table so that she could not get it up. Then she simply scribbled over it until it tore. I put it into plastic folders. She would sit before it and refuse to pick up her crayon. On one occasion, she even ate the crayon. I tried using workbooks. But they were more expensive and I got angrier when they were ruined in one sitting. I tried Mrs. Barthuly's technique of laminating, since we had no air conditioner. It was a costly, time-consuming alternative and when presented with one, Sheila would just sit, refusing to do anything. I put the work on the chalkboard. She would erase it when I wasn't looking. There was not a method I could think of that she could not foil.

Sheila was not selective. If it required a written answer, she would not touch it. This included all the academics, coloring sheets and even art projects. She had no objection to oral work or even letting Anton or Whitney or me fill out a paper for her. But she would not do it herself.

Needless to say, this caused considerable friction between us. I tried all my tricks. I sent her to the quiet corner. But she would sit motionless and soundless for such a long time that I felt that was not solving the problem. I did not want her to miss too much of the program simply sitting in a chair. Unlike the first week when the quiet corner provided a means of getting control of her behavior, this did not. The quiet corner was not intended as punishment. So I was not concerned when the children sat there crying or struggling. They were out of control and trying to regain it. But when the child simply went there and sat, it became punishment. Occasionally a few minutes of punishment were warranted, but not long stretches at a time. So if I sent her to the corner and she went and was still not willing to do paperwork after twenty minutes of sitting, I let it drop. My winning the power struggle was not so important as keeping her active and participating in class. Moreover, I was concerned that something else lay behind her refusal to do paperwork. Unless she were angry, there was little else Sheila refused to do outrightly. We had long ago settled who was boss in the classroom and I did not feel she was testing. She went to ridiculous heights to please me in other ways, so it did not make sense to me that she was holding out on this one thing simply to irk me.

But admittedly the behavior did. And not just a little. I became obsessed with it after the third week, storming into the teachers' lounge and raging at the other teachers after school. At night Chad bore the brunt of my frustrations. Finally, one day, in desperation, I dittoed one worksheet off on a whole ream of paper. I maneuvered Sheila over to a table and sat her down at math. I decided that if we had to sit there until Valentine's Day and go through all 500 copies, we would.

"We're going to do this math worksheet today, Sheila. All I want is this one sheet and it's got easy problems on it."

She looked at me distrustfully. "I don't wanna do that."

"Well, it isn't your choice today." I tapped the paper on the table agitatedly with one finger. "Come on, let's get started."

She sat staring at me. I could tell she was leery of the situation. I had never forced her in such a direct confrontation and she did not seem to be able to tell what to expect from me. Inside myself my own irritation was clenching my organs. My stomach was tight and knotted, my heart beating rapidly. For a split second I wanted to retreat, but my anger over all these weeks of refusal overwhelmed me.

"Do it." I could hear my voice louder and sharper in my ears than I wanted it to be. I reached over and grabbed a pencil, shoving it into her hand. "I said do the paper. Now do it, Sheila."

She wadded up the first paper. I carefully straightened it out and taped it down to the table. Sheila gouged it out with the pencil. Grimly we struggled, my putting out new copies, Sheila ripping at them. Math period passed and the litter of destroyed dittos deepened around our chairs. The others rose for freetime. Sheila glanced around in concern.

Freetime was her favorite period and already she noticed Tyler was getting out the little toy people she liked to play with.

"Finish this paper and you can go," I stated, taping a new one down. I had swallowed my anger but a subdued sort of frenzy remained, causing my pulse to continue to run faster.

Sheila was losing patience with me. Angry little grunts were coming out with her heavy breaths. We went through another half-dozen copies of the worksheet. Moving my chair close to hers I pinned her in her chair against the table. Then I taped down a new sheet. Holding down her free hand, I took her other in mine. "I'll help you, Sheila, if you can't do it by yourself," I said doggedly. I could feel perspiration soaking my shirt.

Sheila began to scream, cutting loose with an earsplitting yell. Thankfully she was left-handed as I was, so I could move her hand. I asked her the answer to the first problem. At first she refused to say but then angrily shouted it out. I pushed her hand along the paper, writing a 3. Sheila struggled violently, trying to knock loose my hold of her chair, trying to bite me. Second problem now. Again I dragged the answer out of her and forced her to write it.

We struggled the rest of freetime and finished the paper with her screaming protests and my forcing her hand. The second I let go, she scrabbled the paper up from the tape and shredded it before I could catch her hands. Angrily she threw the paper in my face and broke away from my hold, knocking over the chair. Running to the other side of the classroom she turned to glower at me.

"I HATE YOU!" she screamed as loudly as possible. The other children were finishing their snacks and getting ready for recess, but they paused, watching us. "I hate you! I hate you! I hate you!" Then her frustration with me overpowered her and she stood shrieking wordlessly from her corner behind the animal cages.

Anton cleared the other kids out to recess, but I remained sitting at the table. Expecting her to go off into one of her destructive rages, I was poised to catch her. But she didn't. After a few moments she regained her composure and stopped screaming. However, she remained across the room, staring at me reproachfully. She seemed on the verge of tears, her mouth turned down, her chin quivering. I was beginning to feel like a first-class heel. Her disappointment in me for behaving so antagonistically was bright in her eyes. As I watched her, I knew I had done the wrong thing. I had been desperate; my teacher's instinct to get work accomplished on paper having overcome my better sense. But I shouldn't have let that happen. It had been wrong. I hated myself for allowing such an unimportant thing rule me.

I regarded her. Bad feelings rippled through me, recriminations, self-doubt. Had I destroyed our relationship? We had been doing so well in the three weeks since she had come. Had I screwed it all up in one morning? She watched me. For long, eternal moments we looked at each other in silence.

Slowly Sheila came toward me. Her eyes were still on me all the time, big, wary, accusing eyes. She came over to the far edge of the table. Tracing an invisible design on the smooth top, she studied it before looking back up at me. "You not be very nice to me." Her voice was heavy with feeling.

"No, I guess I wasn't, was I?" I felt the silence again. "I'm sorry, Sheila. I shouldn't have done that."

"You shouldn't oughta be mean to me. I be one of your kids."

"I'm sorry. I just got upset because you never do papers. I just wanted you to do papers like everyone else does. It makes me mad that you won't ever do them because it is important to me that you do. I got angry."

She studied me carefully. Her lower lip was shoved out

93

and her eyes were hurt-looking, but she sidled closer. "Do you still like me?"

"Of course I still like you."

"But you be mad at me and yell."

"Sometimes people get mad. Even at people they like a lot. It doesn't mean they stop liking them. They're just mad. And after a while the anger goes away and they still like each other. I like you as much as ever."

She pressed her lips together. "I don't really hate you."

"I know that. You were just angry like I was."

"You yell at me. I don't like you to yell at me like that. It hurts my ears."

"Look, kitten, I was wrong. I'm sorry. But I can't make it not happen because it already did. I'm sorry. For right now we won't worry about paperwork. We'll do it some other time when you feel like it."

"I ain't never going to feel like it."

My shoulders sagged with discouragement. "Well, then maybe we'll never do any."

She looked at me quizzically. "There gotta be paperwork."

I sighed tiredly. "Not really, I suppose. There are things more important. Besides, maybe someday you will feel like it. We'll do it then."

And so I gave up the paperwork war. Or at least the battle.

I can never understand what it is about being human that allows one to become fixed on small matters and think the world will collapse if things don't go just the way one wants them. Once I got that struggle out of my system, I could never understand why it had been so important to me. But for those first few weeks, it had.

The second problem Sheila presented was much more serious and much less easily resolved. She had a keenly developed sense of revenge that knew no limits. When crossed or taken advantage of, Sheila retaliated with devastating force. Her intelligence made it all the more frightening because she could perceive quickly what was valuable to a person and that was what she abused to get back for being wronged. When Sarah kicked snow on her at recess, Sheila systematically destroyed all of Sarah's artwork around the room. For art-loving Sarah this was crushing. Anton got angry with Sheila running in the halls to lunch one day and she returned afterwards and throttled all the baby gerbils Anton had brought to school that morning on loan from his son. Her cold, clear-eyed appraisal of everyone's sensitivities left me chilled.

But it went beyond destroying papers or even baby gerbils. It was calculated and long-abiding, and often over events which were not intentional. Sheila had to be watched every second. Even when we did think we were watching her carefully, she managed to get away from us.

Lunch hour was the most dangerous time of day. Neither Anton nor I wanted to give up our only break to police Sheila constantly. The lunch aides were clearly still frightened of her, although they did supervise her once more.

One day while Anton and I were in the teachers' lounge finishing up our sandwiches, one of the aides came shrieking in to us, Sheila's name spilling out incoherently. Having nightmares of a repeat of the first day, we dashed out after her as she left.

Sheila had gotten into one of the other teachers' rooms. In a short period of time, only ten or fifteen minutes, she destroyed the room completely. All the student desks were awry or knocked over, personal belongings strewn about. The window blinds were pulled down, books were out of the bookcase, the screen of one of the teaching machines was shattered. I could not have dreamed of further destruction in such a short time.

I yanked open the door. "Sheila!" She whirled around, her eyes dark and forbidding. A pointer was clutched in one hand. "Drop that!"

She stared at me for a long moment but let the pointer drop. She had been with us three weeks. By now she knew when I meant business. If I could get her to drop what she was doing and come over to me, I could take her out calmly. I knew better than to spook her so that she would flee. She would do more damage if she bolted and would become so frightened that she could not be reasoned with. She already had that wild-animal, frenzied look in her eye and I realized how tenuous her hold on control was.

However, as I looked around the room at the disaster, I could not imagine what we were going to do. I was flooded with discouragement at the fact that she would do this kind of thing, that I had let it happen. Sitting in the quiet corner hardly seemed adequate to cover hundreds of dollars' damage. This was also not my room. It was somebody else's. So I knew the matter was out of my hands.

By the time I had coaxed Sheila over to the door, Mr. Collins and the teacher, Mrs. Holmes, whose room this was, were behind me. When I finally got hold of Sheila's hand, Mr. Collins began to roar.

I suppose he roared with very good reason. But I knew what his solution to the problem was going to include. Mr. Collins was of the old school where most infractions were cured, or at least helped, by the paddle. He took hold of Sheila's arm. I already had her by the overall strap and did not let go.

We eyed each other, neither of us speaking. Sheila was stretched out between us.

I could not let him take her. Not after all this time of reassuring her that she could never be hurt here. There had been too many spankings in her past already. And too many people who had broken their promises. I could not let this happen.

Still the principal and I did not speak. However, that did not diminish the strength of the challenge. Under my fingers on her shoulder, I could feel the tenseness of Sheila's muscles.

When he finally did speak, Mr. Collins' voice came out in a hoarse whisper pushed between gritted teeth. He made it clear that not only was Sheila going down to the office for a paddling but I was coming along as witness.

Oh cripes, I was thinking. All I wanted to do was argue with him while Sheila was strung out between us, like two dogs fighting over a bone. But there wasn't much choice. I could not agree with him. Certainly I did not want Sheila to think I did.

We were hissing back and forth, one- or two-word responses mostly. He was losing patience with me.

"So help me God, Miss Hayden, you come with me right now or you're not going to have a job by the time this day is out. I don't care what I have to do. Is that clear?"

I stared at him. All sorts of things came into my head then. I had tenure. I belonged to the union. He had no power to fire me. Those things all came to me, but on a very academic level. What came at gut level was fear. What would happen to me if I got fired? Could I ever find another teaching job in town? Who would take care of my class? I had a history of rash and impulsive actions. Was this going to be one more? And what for? A kid bound for the state hospital? Here I was about to lose my job over a kid I'd barely known three weeks, who sooner or later would be elsewhere anyway, and who by all accounts wasn't very important to anybody anyhow. What would everyone think if I lost my job? Would Chad still want me? How would I explain it to my mom? What would people think? For the worst excuse of all, I let go of that overall strap.

Mr. Collins turned and took Sheila down the hall. I followed at a distance and felt like Benedict Arnold. Yet maybe they were right. I had lost control in a major way twice in three weeks with this kid. Maybe she did need a state hospital placement. I did not know. This had gotten to be more than I could manage.

I flopped into a chair in Mr. Collins' office. Sheila was calm. Far calmer than I. She came in beside Mr. Collins and stood complacently, not looking at me and not making any sound. Mr. Collins shut the door. From his desk drawer he took out a long paddle. Sheila did not flinch as he sized it up next to her.

I was bitter. Why did he have to have such neolithic methods of education? What kind of man was he? A lusty, full-bodied hate rose in me. How could he do this to me? How could I let him? After all my reassurances to her that I did not whip kids, what would she think of me now? What would I think of myself, now that I knew when the going got rough I would opt for my own skin?

Through the chaos in my own head, I was suddenly and deeply touched by Sheila's innocent courage. She glanced at me briefly and then looked back at Mr. Collins. She looked very much like any other six-year-old just then. Her lips were parted to reveal the gaps where teeth had fallen out. Her eyes were wide and round, the fear in them disguised enough so that if one had not known her, one would not have recongized it for what it was. I saw the little white and orange duck barrettes in her hair and thought how much she liked them. Those were her favorites, her lucky clips, she told me one day. *Well, your luck's run out this time, kid,* I thought. Like so many other times before. The duck clips seemed obscene in this place.

She stood so staunchly; no six-year-old should be able to do that. I wondered how often a board had been shown to her. Yet about her persisted such a little child's innocence; the duck barrettes, the long, impossibly straight hair not quite captured in pigtails, the worn overalls. I felt like crying. But the tears would be for myself for finding out I did not have the kind of strength that she had.

My viscera crinkled. This should not be happening.

But it was. Mr. Collins stated flatly that he had had it. Did she know what she had done? No response. She might even be suspended from school, he said. I knew the lecture was as much for my benefit as Sheila's. We were both being put in our places. He told her she was getting three whacks of the board. She had sucked her lips between her teeth. She watched him without blinking.

"Lean over and grab your ankles."

She stared without moving.

"Lean over and take hold of your ankles, Sheila."

She did not move.

"If I have to tell you one more time, I'll add another whack. Now bend over."

"Sheila, please," I said. "Please do as he says."

Still no response. Her eyes flickered toward mine a moment.

Mr. Collins yanked her down roughly and with a whoosh the board hit her. She fell on her knees on that first whack, but her face remained unchanged. Mr. Collins lifted her back to her feet. Again came the whack. Again she fell to her knees. The last two whacks she stood up and did not fall. But not a sound came out of her, not a tear came to her eyes. I could tell this had infuriated Mr. Collins.

I sat watching, numbed. After all my reassurance to her, it had come to this. I had worked so hard, so damned hard on this kid. I normally never let myself fully realize how much I invested in the children. Like the little fears and discouragements that I kept shooing out of consciousness during day-to-day living, I also spooked away into hiding how much the kids really meant to me. Because I knew that if I was aware, I would feel even more disheartened when my kids failed. Or when I did. That was what burned so many people out in this business: knowing they cared too much. So I tried not to see it. I was a dreamer. But my dream was a very expensive one. For all of us.

Mr. Collins had me sign a witness form that I had been present when he had paddled her. Then wearily I took Sheila's hand and we went down the hall.

I did not know what to do next. My head was spinning. When I got to the classroom door, I peered through the window. Anton had started afternoon activities and Whitney was there. Things seemed peaceful enough. I looked down at Sheila. "We need to talk, kiddo."

Knocking on the door, I waited for Anton to answer. When he arrived, I explained that I wanted to be alone with Sheila a little while, that too much had happened and I needed to get some things straightened out. I asked if he thought he and Whitney could manage while we were gone. He nodded with a smile. So I left them, one uneducated migrant worker and a fourteen-year-old kid, in charge of eight crazy children. The ludicrousness of the situation struck me and I almost laughed. But I could find no laughter in me just then.

I ended up taking Sheila into a book closet because I could not find anywhere else we could be alone undisturbed. I hauled in two teensy chairs, turned on the light and sat down, shutting the door behind me. For a long moment we stared at each other.

"Why on earth do you do those things?" I asked, my discouragement ringing clearly in my voice.

"You ain't gonna make me talk."

"Oh geez, Sheila, come off it. I can't play games with you. Now don't do that to me." I could not tell if she were angry or what. Inwardly, I wanted to apologize to her for having given in and letting Mr. Collins take her. But I did not do it. The need was more mine. I wanted to be forgiven.

We regarded each other without talking and the silence seemed to draw into eternity. Finally I shook my head and sighed wearily. "Look, that whole thing didn't turn out so well. I'm sorry."

Still silence. She would not talk to me. Her gaze was unwavering and I had to look away. Outside the door of the book closet I could hear classes getting ready for recess, noisy and rambunctious, such that they thudded against the door. Inside it was so quiet no one would ever know we were in there.

I looked at her. Looked away. Looked back. She stared. "Good God, Sheila, what *is* it you want out of me?"

The pupils in her eyes dilated. "Are you mad at me?"

"You could say that, yes. I'm just a little mad at everybody right now."

"You gonna whip me?"

My shoulders sagged. "No, I'm not. Like I told you a million times now, I don't whip kids."

"Why not?"

I looked at her in dismal disbelief. "Why should I? It doesn't help any, does it?"

"It helps me."

"Does it? Does it really, Sheila? Did what Mr. Collins just do to you help you?"

"My Pa," she said softly, "he says it be the only way to make me decent. He whips me and I must be betterer, 'cause he ain't never leaved me on no highway like my Mama done."

My heart melted. I certainly hadn't intended it to. I had been so angry at her for all this trouble she had caused. But my heart melted when she spoke. Jesus, I thought, what did this kid expect out of people. I reached an arm out to her. "Come here, Sheil, and let me hold you."

Willingly she came, climbing up into my lap clumsily like a toddler. She wrapped her arms around my ribs and clutched me tightly. I pressed her close. I was doing it as much for myself as I was for her because I didn't know what to do. God Almighty, I hurt inside.

What were we going to do? She had to stop this destructiveness, that went without saying. But how? What were a bunch of tipped-over desks and broken window shades against a little girl? Even if she had done a million dollars' worth of damage, what was that against a life? If they sent her out of the school, suspended her, she wouldn't come back. I had been in the business long enough to know that. Sooner or later, it would be off to the state hospital as planned. What then? What chance did a six-year-old have of coming out of a state hospital to live a normal life? I doubted it had ever happened. We'd lose her, without most of us even realizing she had been there at all. This bright, creative little girl who had never had a chance at life, would never get one. Were a bunch of lousy desks worth that much?

"What're we gonna do, Sheila?" I asked, rocking her in my arms. "You just can't keep doing these sorts of things and I don't know how to stop you."

"I won't do it again."

"I wish you wouldn't. But let's not make any promises we can't keep just now, okay? I just want you to tell me why you did it to begin with. I want to understand that."

"I dunno. I do be awful mad at her. She yell at me at lunch and it not be my fault. It be Susannah's fault but she yell at me. I be mad." Her voice quivered. "Do they gonna make me go away?"

"I don't know, honey."

"I don't want them to." Her voice rose suddenly to a little squeak, betraying her nearness to tears. "I won't never ever do that again. I wanna stay. I wanna stay in this here school. I won't never do it again, I promise." She pressed her face against me.

I stroked her hair, feeling the duck clips under my

102

fingers. "Sheila," I asked, "I never see you cry. Don't you ever feel like it?"

"I don't never cry."

"Why not?"

"Ain't nobody can hurt me that ways."

I looked down at her. The cold perception in her statement was fearsome. "What do you mean?"

"Ain't nobody can hurt me. They don't know I hurt if I don't cry. So they can't hurt me. Ain't nobody can make me cry neither. Not even my Pa when he whips me. Not even Mr. Collins. You seen that. I don't cry even when he hits me with the stick. You seen that, didn't you?"

"Yes, I saw it. But don't you want to cry? Didn't it hurt?"

For a very long moment she did not respond. She took hold of one of my hands in both of hers. "It sort of hurts." She looked up, her eyes unreadable. "Sometimes I do cry a little, at night sometimes. My Pa, he don't come home 'til it be real late sometimes and I have to be by myself and I get scared. Sometimes I cry a little bit; it get wet right here on my eyes. But I make it go away. Crying don't do no good, and it makes me think of Jimmie and my Mama if I cry. It makes me miss them."

"Sometimes it does help."

"It don't never help me. I ain't never gonna cry. Never."

She had turned around so that she straddled my legs and was facing me. I had my arms around her back. She fingered my shirt buttons while she talked.

"Do you ever cry?" she asked.

I nodded. "Sometimes. Mostly when I feel bad, I cry. I can't help it much, I just do. But it makes me feel better. Crying is a good thing in a way. It washes out the hurt, if you give it a chance."

She shrugged. "I don't do it."

"Sheil, what're we gonna do to fix up what you did in Mrs. Holmes' room?"

Again she shrugged. She feigned involvement in twisting one of my buttons.

"I want your ideas. I'm not going to whip you and I don't think suspending you is a good idea either. But we've got to do something. I want your ideas."

"You could make me sit in the quiet corner the rest of the day and you could take away the housekeeping corner for a week or something. You could take away the dolls from me."

"I don't want to punish you. Mr. Collins did that already. I want a way to make it better for Mrs. Holmes. I want to fix up what happened in there."

A pause ensued. "Maybe I could pick it up."

"I think that's a good idea. But what about being sorry? Could you apologize?"

She tugged at the button. "I don't know."

"Are you sorry?"

She nodded slowly. "I be sorry this here happened."

"Apologizing is a good thing to learn to do. It makes people feel better about you. Shall we practice together saying you're sorry and offering to pick up, so it'll be easier to do? I can be Mrs. Holmes and we'll practice."

Sheila fell against me heavily, pressing her face into my breasts. "I just want you to hold me for a little bit first. My butt do be fierce sore and I wanna wait 'til it feels better. I don't wanna think now."

With a smile I clutched her to me and we sat together in the dim light of the book closet, waiting—she for relief for her bottom and the courage for what lay ahead; I for the world to change.

CHAPTER

9

Resolving that situation did not turn out to be simple. Sheila and I did go to Mrs. Holmes' room and Sheila apologized and offered to pick up. As I had hoped, Sheila's childlike innocence, her small size, her natural beauty all brought out the motherliness in Mrs. Holmes. She was willing to accept Sheila's attempts to make amends.

On the other hand, it was not so easy with Mr. Collins. This had been the last straw for him, not only for Sheila, but for my class. Everything came to a head—including things not even related to Sheila's destructiveness. The two of us simply had different value systems, each of which seemed better in our own eyes. It all came out in a full-scale war after Sheila's incident and finally Ed Somers had to come and mediate. In no uncertain terms Mr. Collins wanted Sheila out of the school. The child was violent, uncontrolled, dangerous and destructive. She frightened the other children with her behavior, as well as the other teachers and the staff. She had caused $700 worth of damage in Mrs. Holmes' room alone. There was a point, he said, when society had the right to protect itself from harm. An identified threat such as this child should not be allowed to run loose in a public school. She belonged in the state hospital. Why wasn't she there?

I tried to explain Sheila's progress in my room. I explained how it had only taken three days to crack through this child and get her to work productively in the classroom. I spoke of her IQ, of her history of abuse and abandonment. I implored Ed to let me keep her. This was just one incident, I said. I'd watch her better after this. I'd give up my own lunch hour if I had to. But give me another chance, I asked. Let me try again. I wouldn't be so careless.

The mood was grim. Ed explained to me that they had the very real pressure from parents to consider. When word got out from the children in Mrs. Holmes' class, parents would call. And the court had arranged for her commitment before I had ever entered the picture. My room was the holding tank. I shouldn't get so involved, Ed said politely, but firmly. It was affecting my better judgment. He smiled sadly. It was nice she was making progress, but that was not why she had been placed with me. She was there to wait until a space came open at the hospital. That was all.

As I listened to him I could feel the lump in my throat and the stinging in my eyes. I did not want to cry in front of them. I did not want them to know they were getting to me that much. But I could feel the tears starting. My rational side kept urging calmness. They were not being intentionally cruel; indeed, they probably were not being cruel at all. But it felt that way to me. Goddamn them, what were they doing to me? I was a teacher. My job was to teach. I wasn't a jailer. Or was that all Ed had wanted when he had established my class? I was full of recriminations. What had they thought they had given me but a little girl—a scared, hurt, mistreated six-year-old. What was it that was so frightening about her? Now they told me that I didn't have to worry about her; she was only with me to wait. She could have sat in that chair of hers for however many months it took for the space in the state hospital to come through, and then she could leave. I had obviously misunderstood the matter. I had thought I was supposed to be her teacher.

Ed leaned forward resting his elbows on the table and blowing into his hands. He tried to reassure me, telling me not to get upset. He was embarrassed that the situation was making me cry and for a moment I was pleased he was. I wanted everyone as unhappy as I. But the moment passed and the gloom settled over all of us.

I left the room still tearful, went directly to my car and drove home. Feeling bitter and resentful, I feared I would need more than "Star Trek" to calm me that evening. My idealism had taken a mighty blow. I had learned some people were not even worth $700.

As always, Chad proved the calm center in my storm. Listening to me rage, he shook his head good-naturedly. Go to bed, he advised, it wasn't so bad as it seemed. Despite my feelings, it wasn't me against the world. It'd come out in the end, everything always does. Not in a mood to be placated, I shut myself in the bathroom and sobbed through a forty-five-minute shower. Chad was still sitting in the living room pulling a string for the cat when I emerged. Chad smiled. And then I smiled. I wasn't happy, but I was resigned.

It did not turn out so badly as I had anticipated. An education had to be provided for every child and I was at that moment Sheila's only source of education. In compromise, Ed told Mr. Collins that he could have an extra lunch aide solely to supervise my room and that Sheila was never under any circumstances to leave my room except under

107

my direct supervision. The matter was at least temporarily settled.

Despite the furor over Sheila's placement, things were going smoothly in class. We were becoming a group again, adjusting to Sheila's being with us. February had dawned cold and crisp with a groundhog's promise of six more weeks of winter. Sheila was fitting in and we were quite happily twelve. I appreciated those unexpected days of peace because they were rare in our class.

Academically, Sheila was plunging ahead. I could hardly find enough to keep her agile mind busy. I had dropped the paperwork altogether, conceding her the victory, although I had to admit still thinking about it. Whitney, Anton and I tested her orally and had discussions with her over what she was doing. She was an avid reader, consuming books faster than I could find them. I was thankful for this new interest because without the paperwork, which makes up a good share of each child's academic day, she finished her assignments rapidly.

Socially Sheila was making slower progress, but it was steady. She and Sarah had become friends and were beginning to share the typical pleasures of small girls' friendships. I also assigned Sheila to help Susannah Joy to learn her colors. This had a multiple effect: it gave me a much-needed helper; it occupied Sheila's extra time; it gave her responsibility; and it helped Sheila learn the finer points of an interpersonal relationship. An added benefit was the boost to Sheila's self-confidence. She was elated to be on the giving end for once and have someone need her. Some evenings after school she would busily make materials and carry on long earnest discussions with Anton or me about things she could do with Susannah to help Susie learn. Watching her, I always wanted to laugh, wondering if I looked like that to someone watching me. But she took the job with such innocent seriousness that I contained myself.

Sheila was beginning to grow away from needing to follow me around all day long. She still watched me often and would sit nearby if given a choice, but she did not need physical contact all the time. On bad days when things had gone wrong before she came to school, or when the other kids gave her a hard time, or even when I reprimanded her, it was not unusual to feel her hand go through my belt and for a while once more, she would move around the room with me while I worked. I did not discourage it; I felt she needed the security of knowing I was not going to leave her. The line was fine between dependence and over-dependence, but I had noticed that most of my kids went through a period of intense involvement and attachment in the beginning. It seemed to be a natural phase and if things progressed right, the child outgrew the behavior, becoming secure enough in his relationships that he no longer needed such tangible evidence of caring. So it was with Sheila.

One good thing came out of the incident with Mrs. Holmes' room. I tracked down Sheila's father. After school one evening in early February Anton and I piled into the car and drove out to the migrant camp. Sheila and her father lived in a small, tarpaper shack beside the railroad tracks.

He was a big man, over six feet tall, heavy-set with a huge belly that slopped over his belt, only one tooth on the bottom and very evil-smelling breath. When we arrived he was carrying a can of beer and was already quite drunk.

Anton forged ahead into the tiny house. It was only one room really, divided by a curtain. A lumpy brown couch was at one end and a bed was at the other. Otherwise there was no furniture. The place reeked of stale urine.

Sheila's father came into the house behind us and motioned us to sit on the couch. Sheila was crouched in a far corner by the bed, her eyes round and wild. She had failed to acknowledge either Anton or me, but sat folded in upon herself as she had in the first days of school. I mentioned that perhaps it would be best if Sheila were not present, as I needed to discuss some things with her father that might be painful for her to listen to.

He shook his head and flapped a hand in Sheila's direction. "She's gotta stay in that corner. You can't trust that kid out of your sight for five minutes. She tried to set fire to a place down the road the other night. If I don't keep her in, the police will be here again." He went on to give us the details.

"She ain't really my child," he explained, offering Anton a beer. "That bitch of a woman who's her mother, that's her bastard. She ain't my child and you can tell it. Just look at her. And the kid don't have a decent bone in her body. I haven't in all my born days seen a child like that one for causing trouble."

Anton and I listened speechlessly. I was mortified for her sake that Sheila was in the room. If he told her these things every day, no wonder she had such a low opinion of herself. At least, though, it was private. To tell it to us in front of her—I was horrified even to be there. It was like some scene out of a poorly written novel. Anton made an effort to refute the man's view but that only made him angry with us. So we let him talk, fearful of bringing repercussions on Sheila if we upset him.

"Now Jimmie, he was my boy. Better little boy you never seen than my Jimmie. And that bitch, she took him. Just upped and took him right out from under my nose, she did. And what did she do? She leaves this little bastard." He sighed. "I told her if one more school person came out here about her, I wouldn't forget it."

"I didn't come to say anything bad," I said quickly. "She's doing a nice job in our room."

He snorted. "She should. With a class full of crazies, she should know how to act. Jesus Christ, woman, I'm at my wit's end with that child."

110

The conversation never improved. My blood was icy with horror and I wished I could shrink up and fall through a crack in the floor to save Sheila from the humiliation of having people she cared about hear his words. But I couldn't, nor could I stop him. Her father went on and on. I tried to tell him that Sheila was a gifted child with marvelous intelligence. That was not in his world. What did she need with that, he asked, it'd only give her more of a chance to think up trouble. Finally the conversation turned back to his beloved, lost Jimmie. He began to cry, big tears rolling over his fat cheeks. Where, oh where, had Jimmie been taken, and why had he been left with this little bogie that he did not even believe was his child?

In a detached way I felt sorry for the man. I think he did love the boy and the loss must have been difficult. In his tangled, immature way he seemed to see Sheila as somehow to blame for losing Jimmie. If she hadn't been so impossible perhaps his woman would have stayed. He did not know what to do with Sheila or himself. So he lost himself in a couple six-packs of beer and wept to two complete strangers about a life thirty years out of control.

As wretched as Sheila's life looked, I knew we would have a difficult time getting her removed from her father's care. This was a community with a huge population of losers. The migrants, the penitentiary, the state hospital, all combined to make a town within a town, one that was so large that the parent community could not meet its needs. There were not enough social workers and foster homes and welfare checks to sort out the disasters and repair the damage. Only the most severely abused children were removed from their homes because there was no place to put the others. Yet I felt compelled to ask her father if he had considered voluntary foster placement since he was having such a hard time.

My question was a mistake. From tears, he exploded into a rage, leaping up and waving his hands at me. Who was I to suggest he give his child up? What kind of person was I? He had never accepted help from anyone before; he was man enough to solve his own problems without any help from me, thank you. With that he demanded that Anton and I leave his house immediately. Filled with frustration and angry sorrow, we left hoping we had not endangered Sheila. It was a grim visit and I wished I had never gone.

Afterwards, I rode across the migrant camp to Anton's. He too lived in little more than a hut. There were three rooms which he shared with his wife and two young sons. It seemed pitifully inadequate to someone with my middle-class upbringing, but it was clean and well-kept. The Spartan furniture was offset by handmade rugs and needlepoint pillows. A large crucifix adorned a wall in the main room. Anton's wife was cheerful and welcoming, even though she spoke no English and I spoke no Spanish. His boys were eager, chattery little fellows who climbed all over me asking about the classroom their daddy had told them of. They were so verbal and spirited despite their youth that they seemed to be geniuses in my eyes. I had grown so used to viewing my kids as normal. The five of us shared three Cokes and a bowl of corn chips while Anton diffidently asked about the possibilities of his going back to school and earning a teaching degree. He did not even have a high school diploma yet, although he eagerly told me that he was studying for his General Equivalency Diploma. I had not previously heard about these secret dreams he had been nursing. He had grown to love the children in our class, in spite of his initial reluctance, and someday he hoped he might teach in a class of his own. I was touched by his dreams, because that indeed was what I feared they were. I doubted he was aware of all the time and money involved in attaining that level of education. But watching his wife beam as her husband talked of such great plans and seeing the little boys dance at the thought that their daddy was going to be a real teacher and someday they might live in a

real house and have bicycles, I did not mention the draw-
backs. Besides, my emotions had not fully recovered and
my mind still wandered across to the other side of the
camp, wondering what was happening in the shack by the
railroad tracks.

CHAPTER

10

During the two hours that Sheila and I had alone together, after school, I had begun reading aloud to her. Although she was perfectly capable of reading most of the books herself, I wanted to provide her with some extra closeness as well as share some of my favorite books with her. We also needed to talk about some of the things in the books, I found out, because Sheila had had such a deprived childhood that she did not understand many things. This was not because she did not know what the words meant, but because she had no idea how they applied to real life.

For instance, in *Charlotte's Web* Sheila puzzled the longest time over why the little girl wanted to keep the runt pig, Wilbur, in the first place. He was a runt after all, the poorest of the litter. In Sheila's mind it was perfectly understandable that the father did not want to keep him. I explained that Fern loved him because he was tiny and could not help being a runt. But Sheila could not conceptualize that. She lived strictly by the law of survival of the fittest.

So I read to her, holding her on my lap as we sat in the reading corner surrounded by pillows. When she did not understand a word or a passage, we talked about it, often wandering off into long discussions about the way things were. I was fascinated by this girl who possessed a child's innocence in reasoning and a child's directness, but an adult's comprehension. Her clear-eyed perception of things was in many ways frightening because it was so often nakedly right. But the child's way she put some things together made me laugh.

One night I brought in a copy of *The Little Prince*. "Hey Sheil," I called to her. "I've got a book to share with you."

She came running across the room, leaping squarely onto my stomach and snatching the book from my hands. Carefully she inspected all the pictures before we settled down to read. Once started, she sat motionless, her fingers gripping the cloth of my jeans.

The Little Prince is a short book and within half an hour I was almost halfway through it. When we came to the part about the fox she became even more intent. I could feel her bony little hips in my lap as she wiggled to become more comfortable.

"Come and play with me," proposed the little prince. "I am so unhappy."

"I cannot play with you," the fox said. "I am not tamed."

"Ah! Please excuse me," said the little prince. But, after some thought, he added:

"What does that mean—'tame'?"

. . .

"It is an act too often neglected," said the fox. "It means to establish ties."

"'To establish ties'?"

115

"Just that," said the fox. "To me, you are still nothing more than a little boy who is just like a hundred thousand other little boys. And I have no need of you. And you, on your part, have no need of me. To you, I am nothing more than a fox like a hundred thousand other foxes. But if you tame me, then we shall need each other. To me, you will be unique in all the world. To you, I shall be unique in all the world . . ."

. . .

"My life is very monotonous," he said. "I hunt chickens; men hunt me. All the chickens are just alike, and all the men are just alike. And, in consequence, I am a little bored. But if you tame me, it will be as if the sun came to shine on my life. I shall know the sound of a step that will be different from all the others. Other steps send me hurrying back underneath the ground. Yours will call me, like music, out of my burrow. And then look: You see the grain-fields down yonder? I do not eat bread. Wheat is of no use to me. The wheat fields have nothing to say to me. And that is sad. But you have hair that is the color of gold. Think how wonderful that will be when you have tamed me! The grain, which is also golden, will bring me back the thought of you. And I shall love to listen to the wind in the wheat . . ."

The fox gazed at the little prince, for a long time.

"Please—tame me!" he said.

"I want to, very much," the little prince replied. "But I . have not much time. I have friends to discover, and a great many things to understand."

"One only understands the things that one tames," said the fox. "Men have no more time to understand anything. They buy things all ready made at the shops. But there is no shop anywhere where one can buy friendship, and so men have no friends any more. If you want a friend, tame me . . ."

"What must I do, to tame you?" asked the little prince.

"You must be very patient," replied the fox. "First you will sit down at a little distance from me—like that—in the grass. I shall look at you out of the corner of my eye, and you will say nothing. Words are the source of misunderstandings. But you will sit a little closer to me every day . . ."

Sheila put her hand on the page. "Read that again, okay?"

I reread the section. She twisted around in my lap to look at me and for a long time locked me in her gaze. "That be what you do, huh?"

"What do you mean?"

"That's what you done with me, huh? Tamed me."

I smiled.

"It be just like this book says, remember? I do be so scared and I run in the gym and then you come in and you sit on the floor. Remember that? And I peed my pants, remember? I be so scared. I think you gonna whip me fierce bad 'cause I done so much wrong that day. But you sit on the floor. And you come a little closer and a little closer. You was taming me, huh?"

I smiled in disbelief. "Yeah, I guess maybe I was."

"You tame me. Just like the little prince tames the fox. Just like you tamed me. And now I be special to you, huh? Just like the fox."

"Yeah, you're special all right, Sheil."

She turned back around, settling into my lap again. "Read the rest of it."

So the little prince tamed the fox. And when the hour of his departure drew near—

"Ah," said the fox, "I shall cry."

"It is your own fault," said the little prince. "I never wished you any sort of harm; but you wanted me to tame you . . ."

"Yes, that is so," said the fox.

"But now you are going to cry!" said the little prince.

"Yes, that is so," said the fox.

"Then it has done you no good at all!"

117

"It has done me good," said the fox, "because of the color of the wheat fields." And then he added:

"Go and look again at the roses. You will understand now that yours is unique in all the world. Then come back to say goodbye to me, and I will make you a present of a secret."

The little prince went away, to look again at the roses.

"You are not at all like my rose," he said. "As yet you are nothing. No one has tamed you, and you have tamed no one. You are like my fox when first I knew him. He was only a fox like a hundred thousand other foxes. But I have made him my friend, and now he is unique in all the world."

And the roses were very much embarrassed.

"You are beautiful, but you are empty," he went on. "One could not die for you. To be sure, an ordinary passer-by would think that my rose looked just like you—the rose that belongs to me. But in herself alone she is more important than all the hundreds of you other roses: because it is she that I have sheltered behind the screen; because it is for her that I have killed the caterpillars (except the two or three that we saved to become butterflies); because it is she that I have listened to, when she grumbled, or boasted, or even sometimes when she said nothing. Because she is *my* rose."

And he went back to meet the fox.

"Goodbye," he said.

"Goodbye," said the fox. "And now here is my secret, a very simple secret: It is only with the heart that one can see rightly; what is essential is invisible to the eye."

"What is essential is invisible to the eye," the little prince repeated, so that he would be sure to remember.

"It is the time you have wasted for your rose that makes your rose so important.

"It is the time I have wasted for my rose—" said the little prince, so that he would be sure to remember.

"Men have forgotten this truth," said the fox. "But you must not forget it. You become responsible, forever, for

what you have tamed. You are responsible for your
rose . . ."

Sheila slid off my lap and turned around, getting on her
knees so that she could look directly into my eyes. "You be
'sponsible for me. You tame me, so now you be 'sponsible
for me?"
For several moments I looked into her fathomless eyes. I
was not certain what she was asking me. She reached up
and put her arms around my neck, not releasing me from
her gaze.
"I tame you a little bit too, huh? You tame me and I tame
you. And now I do be 'sponsible for you too, huh?"
I nodded. She let go of me and sat down. For a moment
she lost herself, tracing a design on the rug with her finger.
"Why you do this?" she asked.
"Do what, Sheil?"
"Tame me."
I did not know what to say.
Her water blue eyes rose to me. "Why you care? I can't
never figure that out. Why you *want* to tame me?"
My mind raced. They had never told me in my education classes or my child-psych classes that there would be
children like this one. I was unprepared. This seemed like
one of those moments that if I could only say the right
thing . . .
"Well, kiddo, I don't have a good reason, I guess. It just
seemed like the thing to do."
"Do it be like the fox? Do I be special now 'cause you
tame me? Do I be a special girl?"
I smiled. "Yeah, you're my special girl. It's like the fox
says, now that I made you my friend, you're unique in all
the world. I guess I always wanted you for my special girl. I
guess that's why I tamed you to begin with."
"Do you love me?"
I nodded.

119

"I love you too. You be my special best person in the whole world."

Sheila scrunched herself down and around, lying on the carpet with her head resting on my thigh. She fiddled with a piece of lint she had found on the floor. I prepared to read again.

"Torey?"

"Yes?"

"You ain't never gonna leave me?"

I touched her bangs brushing them back. "Well, someday, I reckon. When the school year is over and you go on to another class and another teacher. But not before then and that's a long time away."

She shot up. "You be my teacher. I ain't never gonna have another teacher."

"I'm your teacher now. But someday we'll be finished."

She shook her head; her eyes had clouded. "This here be my room. And I do be gonna be in here forever."

"It won't be for a long time yet. When the time comes, you'll be ready."

"No sir. You tame me; you be 'sponsible for me. You can't never leave me cause you be 'sponsible for me forever. It says so right there, and that's what you done to me, so it's your fault that I got tame."

"Hey honey," I pulled her into my lap. "Don't worry about it."

"But you gonna leave me," she said accusingly, pulling out of my hold. "Just like my Mama done. And Jimmie. And everybody. My Pa, he would if they wouldn't put him in jail for it. He told me that. You do be just like everybody else. You leave me too. Even after you tame me and I not ask you to."

"It won't be that way, Sheila. I'm not leaving you. I'm staying right here. When the year is over things will change, but I won't leave you. Just like it says in the story,

120

the little prince tamed the fox and now he's gone, but really he's always going to be with the fox because every time the fox sees the wheat fields he thinks of the little prince. He remembers how much the little prince loved him. That's how it'll be with us. We'll always love each other. Going away is easier then, because every time you remember someone who loves you, you feel a little bit of their love."

"No you don't. You just miss them."

I reached an arm out to her, bringing her close once again. She wasn't going to be convinced. "Well, it's a little too hard to think about right now. You're not ready to leave and I won't leave you. Someday you will be ready and it'll be easier."

"No, I won't. I won't never be ready."

I was rocking her in my arms, holding her very tightly. This was too scary a thing for her right now. I did not know how to treat the issue because the time would come when she would have to leave, either when the state hospital had an opening or at the end of the school year in June. I already suspected my class would not exist the next year for a number of reasons. There was no use hoping that I would have her beyond the end of the year. So the time was coming and I did not know if in four short months she would feel much differently than she did right now.

Sheila let me rock her. She was studying my face. "Will you cry?"

"When?"

"When you leave?"

"Remember what the fox said? 'One runs the risk of weeping, if one lets himself be tamed.' He's right. One cries a little. Every time someone goes away, you cry a little. Love hurts sometimes. Sometimes it makes you cry."

"I cry about Jimmie and my Mama. But my Mama, she don't love me none."

"I don't know about that. That happened before I knew

121

you and I never met your Mama. But I can't imagine that she didn't love you some. It's very hard not to love your kids."

"But she left me on the highway. You don't do that to your kids if you love them. Pa, he tell me that."

"Like I said, Sheila, I don't know. I don't know who's right. But it isn't always that way. I'm never going to leave you in that way. When school is over and you go somewhere else, we'll still be together, even if we don't see each other. Because like the fox said, every time he saw a wheat field he thought of the little prince. So in a special way the little prince was with him. That's the way it'll be with us."

"I don't want no wheat fields. I want you."

"But that's special too, Sheil. At first we'll be a little sad, but it'll get better and then it'll be good. Every time we think of the other, we will feel nice inside. You see, there won't ever be enough miles to make us forget how happy we've been. Nothing can take away your memories."

She pushed her face into me. "I don't want to think about it."

"No, you're right. This isn't the time to worry about it. It's a long ways away. In the meantime, we'll think of other things."

CHAPTER

11

Although I had ceased to be obsessed with our paperwork war, it was never completely out of my mind. First, I had a hard time keeping Sheila busy without needing one of the adults with her constantly. I also worried that she would not be acceptable to a regular class teacher if she would never do any worksheets or workbooks. While in my class we could get away with it, a regular teacher with twenty-five other children and an academic schedule to keep would never be able to afford such frivolity. Finally, I worried that she was finding out that her current method kept a lot of adult attention focused on her. She was perfectly capable of answering almost any question we thought up for her, but she thrived on capturing Anton, Whitney or me and reciting her answers. This was not particularly acceptable behavior even in my room.

I still had no firm idea why she was no negative about paperwork. I suspect that it had something to do with failure. If she never committed anything to paper, it was impossible to prove that she ever made a mistake. And Sheila fell apart when she did make an error and was corrected, regardless of how gentle the correction was. I had an awful suspicion from random comments she made that once she had taken a paper home and had had a bad encounter with her father regarding it. But she had a large number of bad encounters with him, so I doubted that that alone accounted for her phobia. Perhaps she simply was bright enough to figure out that this method saved her a lot of work and got her the attention she craved. I did not usually think that, because there were a lot of easier ways for a bright child to achieve the same end. After a particularly hectic day, though, Anton expressed those sentiments.

However, there was one thing Sheila seemed to be finding more and more irresistible. I encouraged a great amount of creative writing in class. The children kept journals in which they recorded what they felt, things that happened to them and other important events in their lives. Often when I tangled with a child and one or both of us got angry, the child had learned that one place for expression was in the journal. Thus, kids were scribbling in their journals on and off all day. Each night I went through and left notes or comments to the children about what they had written. It was a personal communication and we each valued the opportunity to find out how the other felt. In a similar manner I had formal writing assignments almost daily in which the children wrote on an assigned topic. I had found that after the children learned to write easily and to associate words with the feelings they could evoke, all of them, even Susannah, could express themselves in some instances better on paper than face-to-face. So in our room a great amount of written correspondence took place.

Needless to say, Sheila, with her distaste for paper, did not write. This seemed to bother her a bit. She would crane her neck to see what the other kids were writing, or wander close to them during creative writing time, instead of going over to the reading corner or somewhere to play as she was supposed to. Finally, a day came in mid-February when her curiosity got the better of her.

She came over to me after I had handed out the sheets for writing. "I might write something, if you give me a piece of paper."

I looked down at her. It occurred to me that I might be able to swing the whole paperwork issue around to my side with a little reverse psychology. So I shook my head. "No, this is paperwork. You don't do paperwork, remember?"

"I might do this."

"No, I don't think so. I can't risk wasting any more paper on you. You wouldn't like it anyway. You go play. That's more fun."

She wandered away for a few moments. Then she came back. I was leaning over William helping him spell a word. Sheila tugged on my belt. "I wanna do it, Torey."

I shook my head. "No, you don't. Not really."

"Yes, I do."

Ignoring her, I went back to William.

"I won't waste no paper."

"Sheila, writing is for kids who do paperwork. Now you don't do it, so writing isn't for you."

"I could do some paperwork. A little bit, maybe, if I could have a piece of paper to write on."

I shook my head. "No, you don't like it. You've told me that yourself. You don't have to do it. Go play now, so I can help William."

She remained standing beside me. After a few moments of not getting results, she went and asked Anton. "Torey's got the paper," he said, pointing in my direction. "You'll have to ask her."

"She won't give me none."

He shrugged and rolled his big brown eyes. "Well, then I'm sorry for you. I don't have any paper you can use."

Sheila came back to me. She was getting angry with me

125

and trying not to show it. "I want you to give me a piece of paper, Torey. Now, gimme it."

I raised an eyebrow in warning.

She gave a frustrated stomp with one foot and shoved out her lower lip. I bent back over William.

She changed tactics. "Please? Please? I won't wreck it. I won't tear it up. Cross my heart and hope to die. Please?"

I regarded her. "I can't believe you. Maybe if you do some papers for me tomorrow and I see you don't tear them up, then I'll give you writing paper during creative writing tomorrow afternoon."

"I want it now, Torey."

"I know you do. But you show me I can trust you and you can have some tomorrow. We're almost out of time today anyhow."

She eyed me carefully, trying to determine a way to make me give in. "If you give me paper I'll write something you don't know about me. I'll write you something secret."

"You write me something secret tomorrow."

At that she gave a grunt of anger and stalked off across the room to the other table. She pulled out a chair very loudly and sat down with great emphasis. Little snorts punctuated the air. I smiled inwardly. She was cute when she was mad, now that she was learning to handle it more appropriately. Giving me absolutely black stares, she remained at the other table.

After a few moments I wandered over in her direction. "I suppose, if you write fast, I could give you a piece of paper today."

She looked up expectantly.

"Except you can't tear it up."

"I won't."

"What will we do if you do tear it up?"

"I won't. I said I won't. I promise."

"Are you going to do other papers for me, if I give you this one?"

126

She nodded emphatically.

"You'll do your math paper?"

She frowned in exasperation. "I ain't gonna have no time left if you keep talking to me all day."

I grinned and handed her a piece of paper. "This better be a good secret."

Clutching the paper in both hands she scurried over to the other table to grab a felt-tipped pen. She had been eyeing the pens for some time and now with both the pen and the hard-earned paper she darted off to the far side of the room. Scrambling under the rabbit's cage, she began to write.

She *was* fast. Somehow I had expected her to have difficulty since she had not written in so long. But as in so many other ways, Sheila surprised me. Within minutes she was back, the piece of paper folded into a tiny square. She sidled up next to me when I wasn't looking and pressed it into my hand.

"This here be a secret now. You don't go showing it to nobody. It do be just for you."

"Okay." I began unfolding it.

"No, don't read it now. Save it."

Nodding, I slipped the little square of paper into my pocket.

I forgot about it until that night when I was changing for bed. Then the folded square fell out onto the floor. Carefully I picked it up and straightened it out. Inside, written in blue felt-tip, I found what must have been for Sheila, with all her dignity, a very personal note.

A special thing I want you to know but not tell Nobody
You know sometimes the kids make Fun of me and call me names and befor I used not to put on clene Close. But sometimes I dont cos you know what I do but please dont tell I wet the bed. I dont mean to Pa he wips me for it if he knows but He dont mostly. I just dont know why Torey I try real hard to Stop. You wouldnt be mad at me would you. My pa he is but I dont mean to Honest. it bothers me alot but it

127

Make me ashamed of myself. Pa he says Im a baby but I be 7 soon when I do then there aint no clene underpanz and the kids make fun of me. Please dont tell no kids about this ok. Or dont tell Mr Colinz. or Anton or Whiteney or anybody ok. I just want you to know.

I read the note through, touched by her openness and amazed by her writing ability. By and large the note was well-written, punctuated and spelled correctly. It puzzled me that she used "I'm," since I did not ever remember hearing her say it. I smiled to myself and sat down and wrote her a note back.

So the first break in the paperwork war had been made. The next day with help she managed to do a math paper. It was carefully done and I suggested it go up on the bulletin board where I displayed all the children's good work. This was too much for Sheila and I later found the math paper shredded in the trash can. I was more careful after that. She became able to do two or three written assignments without supervision. Occasionally she would slip back and destroy the paper partway through the assignment or after completing it, especially those that were difficult for her. But if I gave her a second sheet, she would try again. I never marked anything wrong because Sheila had such a tenuous hold on herself in committing her work to paper. It was far too fragile at that point to take any criticism, however well-meaning the critic's intentions. Instead, Anton or I always checked on her while she did the papers and discussed some alternatives to questions she was answering incorrectly. Otherwise I kept a low profile on her increasing ability to do this task. It was not that important a matter, despite what my teacher's instinct told me, and I never wanted her to feel that I measured her worth by how many papers she did. Obviously someone had already communicated that to her and I wanted it clear that that was not true in our classroom. Regardless of how inconvenient

128

her distrust of paperwork had been, she needed to know that nobody would be valued less than a stack of school papers.

Interestingly enough, Sheila found great outlet in creative writing. In this area the old fears seemed to drop away, and she wrote spontaneously and copiously. Line after line of her loose, rather sloppy writing would hurry across the page telling about things that often seemed too personal to say face-to-face. I could usually count on five or six extra pages in the correction basket each night.

I never learned whatever it was that motivated Sheila toward her paper phobia. Later interactions with her over it and later comments that she made reaffirmed my belief that it was related to a fear of failure. But I never really knew. Nor did I feel a pressing need to know, only because so few human behaviors can be reduced to such simple cause–effect terms. There were more important things to worry about, things more important than ferreting out a mysterious and ultimately academic "why."

Allan, the school psychologist, returned shortly after Valentine's Day with a whole battery of tests for Sheila, including a Stanford–Binet IQ test. I balked a bit when I met him and his armload in the office that morning. I knew to my satisfaction that Sheila was a gifted child; she proved it daily. What difference did it make if her IQ were 170 or 175 or 180? It was all so far beyond normal that the numbers were meaningless. Even a variation of thirty points did not matter much. I would not know how to handle her any differently if she had an IQ of 150 or 180; she was too discrepant. But I suspect Allan was excited over finding such an interesting specimen and wanted to test her more for his own education than for any added benefit to Sheila. I relented because I knew the time was coming when we would have to face the authorities who had committed her to the state hospital. She certainly did not belong there; I could see that beyond a doubt now. I was hoping all the illustrious IQ scores would serve us in the end.

She topped out the Stanford-Binet as she had done on the other tests. An extrapolated score gave her an IQ of 182. As I looked at it, I was affected in a mystical way; 182 is beyond anyone's comprehension. That is as far in the direction of genius as an IQ of 18 is in the direction of retardation. And everyone knows how very different from the normal population a child with an 18 IQ is. What people generally fail to realize is that a child with a 182 is just as different.

What moved me most was considering how she ever came to possess that kind of knowledge. It almost seemed to me as if it were some sort of anomaly like brain damage in reverse. Her father—if he was, indeed, her father—was of normal intelligence and from what I could make out, so was her mother. Where in Sheila's abused, deprived six years had she learned what words like "chattel" meant? How had that happened? It seemed as nearly impossible to me as anything I had ever encountered. I was flooded with thoughts that she must be proof of reincarnation. I could see no other explanation for this extraordinary child.

Almost before I realized what I was thinking, a second emotion entered into the mystery. In the back of my head I heard the chant of a TV commerical I had seen once: "A mind is a terrible thing to waste." My gut tightened. There was so much to do with this child, and so little time. I did not know if it would be nearly enough.

CHAPTER 12

The last week in February I was speaking at a conference out of state. I had known about the engagement since before school had started in the fall and had reminded Ed Somers periodically that I was still planning to attend. Now as the time grew near, I once again called Ed to make arrangements for my replacement.

The children had been with a substitute earlier in the year in November when I had gone to a workshop. It was only one day and I had prepared the kids, so things had gone well. I felt it was very important that they have these little tests of independence. Regardless of how much progress they had made during their year with me, it would be futile if they only performed reliably in my presence. I had seen more good teachers fail because of this problem than any other and was haunted by the thought that I might fall prey to that difficulty. I suppose what worried me was that I tended to form a closer, more intense relationship with my kids than did a number of teachers in the same general area as I. When I saw them breeding dependency in their more detached manners, I feared I was in trouble. Thus far, I hadn't been, but I took every opportunity to let my children cope without me.

Sheila worried me though. She had not been with us very long yet and was still quite dependent. I saw this as a natural stage for her at the time, but I worried that my leaving, even for a short period of time, might frighten her.

On the Monday before my absence, which would be Thursday and Friday of that week, I mentioned casually to the children that I would be gone. Again on Tuesday, I mentioned it. On neither occasion did Sheila appear to attend to the comment. But on Wednesday after lunch I sat the kids down for a discussion. I explained I would be gone the next two days and not in the room. Anton would be there and so would Whitney and there would be a substitute teacher. Things would go just as always and there was no need to worry. I would be back on the next Monday when we were all going on a field trip to the fire station. We discussed ways of behaving properly around a substitute teacher; things that would make the job easier for her and things that should not be done. We role-played how to talk to her and how to deal with the minor crises that always seemed to crop up with subs. Everyone participated actively in the discussion. Everyone but Sheila. As the reality of what I was saying dawned on her, she regarded me anxiously. Her hand went up.

"Yes, Sheila?"

"You gonna be gone?"

"Yes, I am. That's what this is all about. I won't be here tomorrow or Friday, but I'll be back on Monday. That's what we're talking about."

"You gonna be gone?"

"Jeepers, Sheila," Peter said, "you deaf or something? What you think we been doing all this time?"

"You gonna be gone?"

I nodded. The other kids were looking at her strangely.

"You ain't gonna be here?"

"I'll be back on Monday. Just two days and then I'll be back."

Her face clouded over, her eyes filling with wary concern. She rose to her feet and retreated backwards toward the housekeeping corner, watching me the entire time.

I went on to answer other questions and finally broke up the group when it seemed everyone was satisfied. It was almost time for recess and then cooking.

Sheila remained in the housekeeping corner fiddling aimlessly with toy pots and pans. Anton called her to get her coat on for recess but she refused to come, popping her thumb into her mouth and looking defiantly at him. I motioned to Anton to go out with the others and went over to her. Turning a chair around backwards, I straddled it, resting my chin on the back.

"You're upset with me, aren't you?"

"You never tell me you go away."

"Yes, I did, Sheil. Both Monday and yesterday in morning discussion."

"But you didn't tell me."

"I told everybody."

She threw a tin pan down so that it clattered. "It ain't fair you go leave me. I don't want you to."

"I know you don't and I'm sorry for your sake that I have to. But I am coming back, Sheila. I'll only be gone for two days."

"I ain't never, never gonna like you again. I ain't never gonna do anything you ask. You do be so mean to me. You tame me so's I like you and then you leave. You ain't supposed to do that, don't you know? That be what my Mama done and that ain't a good thing to do to little kids. They put you in jail for leaving little kids. My Pa, he says so."

"Sheila, it's different from that."

"I ain't gonna listen to you. I ain't never gonna listen to

133

you again. I liked you and you be mean to me. You are gonna go away and leave me and you said you wouldn't. That be a fierce awful thing to do to a kid you tame. Don't you know that?"

"Sheila, listen to me . . ."

"I ain't never gonna listen to you. Don't you hear me say that?" Her voice was almost inaudible, but pregnant with feeling. "I hate you."

I looked at her. She kept her face averted. For the first time since she had come I saw her bring a finger up to one eye to stop an unfallen tear. In panic she pressed her fingers tight against her temples, willing the tears back. "Look what you make me do," she muttered accusingly. "You make me cry and I don't want to. You know I don't like to cry. I hate you more than anybody and I ain't never gonna be nice in here again. No matter what."

For a single moment the tears glistened in her eyes. They never fell. She darted past me, grabbed her jacket and ran out the door to the playground.

I got my own jacket and joined the children. Sheila sat by herself in the very furthest corner. Hunched up against the chilly February wind, she sat with her face hidden in her arms.

"Not taking it so well, eh?" Anton said.

"Nope, she's not taking it so well."

After recess when the other children readied for cooking, Sheila remained in the housekeeping corner idly clattering toys around. I let her be. She was upset and had reason to be. Despite her isolation from us, she was handling her distress quite well. No tantrums, no destruction, no bolting. I was surprised and pleased with the manner in which she was coping. Sheila had come a long way in two months.

The other kids tried to coax Sheila into joining them. Tyler, ever the class mother, fussed over Sheila until Whitney told her to get back to the cookies. Peter kept asking why she was standing there and not joining us. I explained that Sheila was feeling a little angry just then and was keeping herself in control by not being with us.

After the cookies were done and everyone sat around eating, I joined William and Guillermo. Tyler had taken some cookies over to Sheila, who was still in retreat midst the dolls and dishes of the housekeeping corner. Guillermo was showing me a new Braille watch his grandfather had given him and he and William were testing me to see if I could read it with my eyes closed.

"Torey," Sarah shouted from the other side of the room, "come here, Sheila's throwing up."

Peter bounced over in delighted glee. "Sheila just puked all over everything." Peter loved gruesome catastrophes.

Anton went for the janitor and I went back to see what had happened. The other kids gathered around like we had a three-ring circus.

I lifted Sheila out of the area and set her down beside me. Pushing back her bangs, I felt her forehead. She wasn't hot.

"Maybe she's got a virus," Peter said. "Last year I puked about a million times one night and all over my bed and stuff, and my mom said I had a virus."

"No," I replied. "I don't think Sheila's sick. I think she's just a little nervous about things today and it got to her tummy."

"That happened to me once. My uncle was coming and I got really excited," William said. "And I got sick because of it. He was going to take me fishing."

Peter snorted. "I bet it was Tyler's cookies."

"I think it would help if everybody would clear out of here and go sit down someplace," I said.

When Anton returned, I took Sheila into the bathroom to clean her up. She was compliant but refused to look at me or to speak. So in silence I washed off her face and clothes.

135

"Do you think you might throw up again?" I asked.

No response.

"Sheil, cut that out. Now answer me. I asked how you were feeling. Are you going to be sick again?"

"I didn't mean to."

"I know you didn't. But I wanted to know if you thought you were still feeling sick, so we could be prepared if we needed to be. It's almost time to go home."

"My bus don't come 'til five."

"I think it would be better if you went home when school's out. They sort of have a rule about throwing up at school. They wouldn't want you on the bus. And I just think it'd be better for you to go home. Anton can take you after school."

"But I didn't mean to. I won't do it again."

"Honey, that's not the point."

"You hate me. You hate me and won't even be nice to me when I be sick. You do be such a mean person."

I rolled my eyes in exasperation. "Sheila, I do not hate you. Honestly, what can I do to get through to you that I am coming back? I will only be gone tomorrow and Friday. Just two short days. Then I'll be back. Don't you understand that?"

I was frustrated. She was a bright child, she knew how long two days were. Yet she stood there uncomprehending. I doubted her vomiting was any more than a physical reaction to emotional distress, but I did not know what to do with her. She would not hear what I was saying.

Rising from where I had been washing her off, I shook my head. Then I shrugged. "Do you want me to rock you a little while until school gets out? Maybe that will help settle your tummy some."

She shook her head.

The janitor was just leaving and the children were starting to get ready to go home. Anton looked questioningly in my direction. I spread my hands in a gesture of bewilderment.

The other kids were getting their coats on, and Sheila stood in the bathroom doorway and watched. When I looked at her, she seemed a little pale. Perhaps I had been too hasty in judging, perhaps it was a virus. But I didn't think so. There had been too many nervous stomachs in my experience. She was, after all, struggling with a hard thing.

I sat down in the rocking chair and turned in her direction. She remained in the doorway. The distance seemed so far between us. How fragile the bond was that held us. Uppermost in my mind was the frustration of being unable to convince her that I, unlike all the others, was not abandoning her. However, underneath the frustration blossomed such admiration for this child. She was so strong and courageous. There was no reason why she should suspect I was being honest with her. Nothing in her past gave her grounds to think that I would return, and she was doing the only sensible thing. Yet as she stood in the doorway watching me, a pantomime of self-doubt and fear and sorrow played across her face. She was trying so hard to believe me, the war between her experience and her dreams vivid in her eyes. I was filled with respect for her, such heart-grinding, unspeakable respect, because she was trying so hard. This was one of those moments that made all the others worthwhile. We were touching each other's souls.

I reached a hand out. "Come here, kitten. Let me rock you."

She hesitated, then slowly approached. Without a word she climbed into my lap.

"This has been a hard day, hasn't it?"

She pressed her fingers to her temples.

"I know you don't understand what's happening, Sheila. You don't understand how I can do this to you and still like you." I rocked her, pushing back her bangs and feeling the silky softness of her hair. "You're just going to have to trust me."

Her body was rigid against mine, like it had been in the

137

beginning. She did not relax. "You tamed me. I didn't ask you to, but you did. Now you leave. It ain't fair. You be 'sponsible for me. You said so yourself."

I puzzled over her sudden change to the past tense. I had never heard it except in rare, random instances. "Kitten, please trust me. I'll be back. It won't be so bad as you think. Anton will still be here, and Whitney. And the substitute will be real nice, I just know it. You'll have fun if you just give yourself the chance."

She did not answer, but simply sat, her fingers white against her temples. There wasn't any more to say. She did not believe me or else she could not bring herself to admit she did. I was too used to her verbal ability. I sometimes forgot she was a six-year-old child. I forgot how many problems she had and how short a time she had been with us. I was expecting too much in wanting her to understand.

The conference was in a West Coast state which had a milder February climate. Chad went with me and we spent most of the time on the beach walking in the surf. It was a marvelous change. I seldom realized how tied up with the children I was until a moment like this occurred and I got away. My interactions were intense and all-consuming for me. When I was working, I could never perceive how tense the involvement left me. Now, on the sunny beach, I felt the weariness drain away.

It was a good conference and an even better vacation. I never thought of the children at all except in bed at night. Even then it was a hazy recollection. I knew they would take care of themselves in my absence. For Chad and me it was a spiritual rebirth. Since Sheila had come, proving such a challenge and forcing me to take my planning home at night, Chad had been slighted. He understood my fascination with the kids, but he still resented the fact that they absorbed every moment. Four days alone together left us happy and relaxed.

* * *

On Monday morning I returned anxious to get back to work. We had the field trip to the fire station planned in the afternoon and I had to make last minute calls on arrangements and check with all the parents who had promised to help.

Anton met me in the hallway as I was returning from the phone. He bulged his eyes. "We had quite a time in your absence," he said.

I could tell from his tone of voice that the "time" had not been a good one and I feared to ask. "What happened?"

"Sheila went absolutely berserk. She refused to talk. She pulled all the stuff off the walls, all the books out of the bookcases. She gave Peter a bloody nose on Friday. She wouldn't do any work at all. I couldn't even get her to sit in her chair. On Thursday she broke the record player. And on Friday afternoon she tried to break the glass out of the door with her shoe."

"You're kidding!"

"Uh-uh. Jesus, Torey, I wish I was. She was a holy terror."

"Cripes," I muttered, "I thought she was getting over doing that kind of junk."

"She was worse than I've seen her in ages. She spent the whole time in the quiet corner, having to be held in the chair every moment of it. She was worse than she ever was when she came."

My heart sank. A vast cesspool of emotions gurgled unhappily within me. I had honestly believed I could trust her to behave while I was gone. It hurt to realize I had misguessed so badly. I felt like I had been personally insulted. I had trusted her; I had depended on her good behavior and she had let me down.

I planned to discuss the matter with her but her bus was late. The other kids began to arrive, all bearing tales. "You ought to have seen what Sheila done," Sarah said excitedly. "She wrecked the whole room."

"Yeah!" Guillermo chirped. "That substitute, Mrs.

Markham, she spanked Sheila and made her sit in the quiet corner and Whitney had to hold her all afternoon, 'cause she wouldn't.''

Peter bounced around me, his dark eyes blazing with delight. "And she was real mean to Whitney and Whitney cried and then guess what? Even Mrs. Markham cried. And Sarah cried and Tyler cried. All the girls cried because Sheila was so naughty. But I didn't. I socked her. I hit her good for being so bad.''

"Her bad," Max confirmed, twirling around me.

My dismal discouragement turned to anger. How could she have done this to me? She had apparently behaved worse than she ever had when I was there. I thought she should have had good enough control to make it for two days without my lurking about every minute. I was deeply disappointed, my confidence about handling her had reached an all-time low. She was getting back at me; she had behaved that way on purpose and all the time and effort I had given her had been to no avail.

Sheila arrived after we had started morning discussion. She regarded me suspiciously as she sat down. The familiar musty odor of stale urine wafted up. She hadn't even bothered to wash since I had left.

My own displeasure did not lessen when I saw her. I was feeling very defensive, believing that her behavior had been a direct assault on my credibility as a teacher. As with all the others with whom she had come into contact, she had figured out what was most important to me and had used it as revenge. The more I thought about it, the worse I felt. This was far harder for me to accept than the incident of the first day or even Mrs. Holmes' room, because it had been so directly aimed at me.

After discussion I called her over. We sat in chairs away from the others. "I hear you didn't handle yourself very well.''

She stared at me, her feelings unreadable.

"I came back and all I heard was about the bad things you did. I want you to explain that to me."

She said nothing but met me with unwavering eyes.

"I'm mad at you, Sheila. I'm the maddest I've been in a long time. Now I want to hear why you did that."

Still no response.

Rage rose within me as I saw those cold, distant eyes. In sudden desperation I grabbed her shoulders and shook her roughly. "Speak to me, dammit! Speak to me!" But what emotion that was there closed, and she gritted her teeth. Horrified at losing control of myself, I let go of her shoulders. God, this job was getting to be too much for me.

She remained in stony silence, glaring at me. My aggressiveness had brought up her own anger and she was an equal match for me, if not better. This was her world, this realm of physical force. She was more a master of it than I and I could tell I had made a mistake in touching her that way. I imagined that she could outlast any sort of physical devastation I was capable of and still not speak. But I was so full of disappointment. My shoulders sagged.

"I trusted you," I said, my voice soft, the discouragement undisguised. "I trusted you for two lousy days, Sheila. I trusted you, can't you see that? And you want to know how it makes me feel to come back and hear you behaved like that?"

Sheila exploded with a fury I had been unprepared for. "I never told you to trust me! I never said that; you did! I never said you could trust me. You can't! Nobody can trust me! I never said you could!" She tore off, careening frantically around the perimeter of the room before scuttling under the table the animal cages were on. Her distress was so great that she sat under the table emitting little strangled noises that were not exactly sobs or screams or words. But their emotion was clear enough.

Her response had surprised me and I sat in the chair without moving. The other children had paused to look at

141

us, their concern mirrored in one another's eyes. I just sat and looked at her in her hiding place under the table. I did not know what to do.

"Well, then you're not going anywhere with us this afternoon, Sheila," I said at last. "I'm not taking anyone I can't trust. You can stay with Anton."

She crawled out from under the table. "I can too go."

"No, I'm afraid not. I can't trust you."

She looked horror stricken. I knew that the field trip meant a great deal to her. She loved going places with us. "I can too go."

I shook my head. "No, you can't."

Sheila screamed, letting loose high-pitched earsplitting shrieks. She still stood over by the animal cages and began leaping up and down, beating the air with her hands.

"Sheila, cut it out or over to the quiet corner. Right now."

She was clearly out of control. Flinging herself on the floor she banged her head violently on the ground. Anton made a flying leap toward her to intercept the self-destruction. Never before had she done such a thing; I had expected her to go off into one of her destructive rages and evidently so had the children who were covertly putting their valuables out of the way. But she had never attempted to hurt herself before. Some of the other kids, particularly Max and Susannah, would do that, but never Sheila.

Anton had her tight in his arms. She struggled savagely, all the while screaming. I couldn't hear myself think. Then as suddenly as it started, it stopped, the room falling into unearthly silence. I dashed over fearing that she had hurt herself to stop so abruptly. Anton released his grip on her and she melted through his arms like warm butter, slithering into a little lump on the carpet. Her arms were over her head, her face into the tweed of the rug.

"Are you all right, Sheila?" I asked.

She turned her head. "Please let me go," she whispered.

After that terrible show of emotion I was alarmed. "I don't think you'd better." If she were behaving like this I was fearful of controlling her outside the room.

"I do be sorry for what I done. Let me go. You can trust me. Please?" Her voice was very small. "Gimme a chance. I'll show you how good I can be. Please? I wanna go."

I looked down at her. My own feelings were returning and I was beginning to think all that violent behavior was a con because she had stopped it so fast. That renewed some of my anger. "I don't think so, Sheila. Maybe next time."

She began screaming again, covering her face with her hands but remaining on the floor. She looked like a rag doll in the contorted position she lay in. I turned and walked away to work with the other children.

All morning she lay in a lump on the floor. She screamed for a while longer and then fell into silence, not moving, not looking up from her huddle. At first I was tempted to move her to the quiet corner, but I changed my mind. I was feeling defeated; I did not want to tangle with her.

By lunch my spirits had flagged completely. I was beginning to realize that I had been angry with her for exposing what I perceived as a teaching deficit in myself. I was mad because I was not able to leave her successfully. I was angry because she had done to me what I had watched her do to so many others. Somehow, I had honestly believed she would never take revenge against me. She had not until then and I had enough of an inflated ego to believe she never would. Now that I had been put on an equal footing with everyone else, my feelings had been hurt. With great embarrassment, I realized I had done back to her the same thing by taking away the field trip. She had hurt me and I had wanted to show her that she'd be sorry. I had chosen the one thing within my power that I knew would hurt her back.

Realizing this made me feel worse than ever. What a crass, egotistical boor. I hated myself, hated the world. Feeling absolutely bleak, I could not decide how to recover the situation.

Over our sandwiches at lunch, I unloaded my guilt on Anton. Boy, I blew it this time, I mumbled into my peanut butter. Why had I ever become a teacher if I had such lousy control over my own feelings. Anton tried to reassure me. She had behaved very badly, he reminded me. She deserved to know that it was unacceptable.

But I felt like a zero. The poor kid. Here this day should have been a happy reunion for everyone. And I came back a shrew. What she had done was not so unpredictable. The kid was upset and was showing it the best way she knew how. Hell, that was why she was in this room to begin with. But what about me? Was that my reason for being there too? This day should have been a joyous affirmation that she could trust me; I returned like I had promised. Instead I yelled at her. And I took away a privilege she didn't even know was in jeopardy. God, how had I ever gotten into teaching?

I spent the entire lunch hour feeling like a monster and not knowing how to fix things. Even if I apologized, I could not undo becoming so mad at her in the morning. I choked unhappily through the last of my sandwich. She had been right. She had never said I could trust her.

Back in the classroom, I sat down next to her. The other kids were getting ready to go and parents milled around. Sheila sat alone over in the corner.

"Honey, I have to talk to you. I did something wrong this morning. I got mad at you when I was really mad at myself. I told you that you couldn't go on the field trip, but I've changed my mind. You can go. I'm sorry I was angry with you."

Without responding, without even looking at me, Sheila rose and got her coat.

After school, when the other children had gone home, the strained silence between us lingered. I had tried to break it all afternoon, outdoing myself to be funny and make everyone laugh. But Sheila remained apart, holding on to Whitney's hand. I gave up. As in all things, the best healer, I decided, would be time. I was recovering, knowing that I had acted inappropriately, but also knowing, as Anton had pointed out, that I was human.

I took the papers from the basket and sat down to grade them. I had offered to read but Sheila declined and busied herself playing cars on the floor across the room. The first hour passed and Sheila got up to stand by the window and watch the shadows lengthen across the snow. When next I looked up, she was still by the window but she was watching me.

"How come you come back?" she asked softly.

"I just went away to give a speech. I never intended to stay away. This is my job here with you kids."

"But how come you come back?"

"Because I said I would. I like it here."

Slowly she approached the table where I was sitting. The hurt was clear in her eyes now.

"You really didn't think I was coming back, did you?"

She shook her head.

Across a tremendous gulf of silence we looked at each other. I could hear the clock jumping the minutes. Onions, the rabbit, rustled in his cage. I was looking at her eyes, wide and fluid and the color of the water where I used to go diving off the coast. I wondered what she was thinking. And I realized sadly, that we never do understand what it is like to be someone else. Nor do we ever seem to be quite able to accept that truth, feeling glibly omniscient despite the limitations of flesh and bone. Especially with children. But we really never know.

She stood twisting an overall strap. "Would you read that book again?"

"Which book is that?"

"The one about the little boy who tamed the fox."

I smiled. "Yeah, I'll read it."

CHAPTER

13

March came in breezy and warm, a welcome relief for the winter-weary North. The snow finally melted, and cool, brown mud rose through the grass from all the water. We were all anxious for spring that year. It had been a hard winter with more snow and cold than we usually received.

March was also peaceful as far as school went; as peaceful as one got in a class like mine. There were no vacations, no disruptions to cause friction, no unexpected changes. The migrant population was coming up from the South, the camp swelling to meet their influx. Teachers in the lounge groused because migrant kids were finding their way into their classes, but I had nothing to worry about in that way. The return of the workers, however, had a strange sad-sweet effect on Anton. When the first few trucks filled with migrants began arriving, Anton did not mention it but he became quieter and more distracted. I finally asked him about it. I was wondering if he were nostalgic for that less encumbered life-style.

He had smiled when I asked. Smiled and looked at me in

the compassionate way one does when an issue is completely beyond the other's comprehension. Then he drew up one of the tiny chairs and dropped his huge frame in it. No, he explained to me, he did not miss the migrant life-style. There was nothing about living that way for a man to miss. He smiled again, more to himself than to me. What was affecting him, he said, was realizing how much he had changed since the trucks had rumbled out in the autumn. How different from them he had become. How he had never noticed the changing until now. Like Rip van Winkle must have felt upon awaking, he said, then gave a laugh of disbelief. He hadn't even known who Rip van Winkle was last year and now had more in common with Rip than with his own people.

I watched him as he talked. I studied the dark Latin features, the angular bones, the physical stigmata of a hard life too early. We both had changed, in ways I could not quite give words to, but which were no less immense for lack of expression. I was awed that we could have such vast effect on each other's lives and for the most part never realize it, certainly not while it was happening. For several minutes we sat looking at one another, openly, admiringly, the taboo on staring temporarily suspended. So many differences: our backgrounds, our sex, our education, so much. Yet somehow, in some way, we had managed to touch each other. That flicker of understanding silenced the two of us as we sat at the table. There was no need for words.

Like the daffodils, Sheila bloomed in spite of the harsh winter. Each day she was back showing more and more improvement. Within the limits of her situation she was now always quite clean. She would come bounding in each morning, wash her face and brush her teeth. She paid close attention to how she looked, inspecting her image carefully in the mirror. We experimented with new hairstyles. After school some days we played beauty shop. I let her work with my long hair and in turn I was allowed to play with hers, devising new ways to braid or style it. She had become a truly handsome child, evoking comment from the other teachers.

Sarah and Sheila had become fast friends and I caught them sending notes during class occasionally. Sheila had gone home with Sarah to play on several occasions after school before her bus came. And Sheila and Guillermo played together at the migrant camp. Tyler was a bit too much of a priss for Sheila's taste, and she would rebuff Tyler's motherly attentions. I was pleased to see that she generally attracted the favor of the children in the class.

Academically Sheila sailed. She willingly did almost anything I gave her to do. A paper was occasionally destroyed, but only very occasionally. If it happened twice a week, that was the exception. Even at that she had learned to come up and ask for another one. I had her working on third grade reading material and fourth grade math. Both were considerably below her ability level, but because of her deprived background and her fear of failure, I felt it was better to keep her in work which could cement her knowledge and confidence more solidly.

She was still overly sensitive about correction, going off into great sulks or heartrending sighs if she made a mistake. Some days seemed worse than others in that respect and she would spend the whole day with her head buried in her arms in dismal despair over missing one math problem. But as a rule there were not many disasters. With a bit of extra cuddling and reassurance she would usually try again.

Oddly enough in my mind, our falling out over my two days' absence did not appear to have adverse effects on Sheila's emotional stability. For a few days after my return she resorted to hanging on to me again, but soon after, abandoned that behavior. Never again did she do it. We talked a lot about that incident. She seemed to need to rehash the event over and over and over. I had left her. I had come back. She had gotten angry and destructive. I had gotten angry and lost my temper. I had told her I was wrong and I was sorry. Each little piece of the drama she wanted to discuss again and again, telling me how she'd felt, what had made her throw up that day, how she'd been scared. The saga was repeated over and over and over until I thought I would never hear the end of it. It held some secret significance that I did not fully understand and the ritualistic retelling seemed to reassure her. Certainly the fact that I had come back was important, but that was not the only facet she dwelled upon. That we had been angry with each other and weathered that appeared equally significant in her mind. Perhaps she felt assured to have seen me at my worst. She could trust me now, knowing what I was like even when I was upset with her. Whatever it was, she was learning to solve her problems verbally. No longer did she need physical contact; words were enough.

Oddly, the destructiveness all but disappeared after the event of my absence and return. When she became angry, which she still did with great regularity, she did not fly into a rage, throwing things to the floor and rampaging about. Revenge was becoming less important. When I thought about it, I wished I could have fully understood the importance of that incident because in many ways it greatly altered Sheila's behavior. But the full picture always remained a mystery. Sheila still had a lot of problems, but they were becoming more readily solved and much more manageable.

One of the things which still puzzled me was her language. Visiting her father had substantiated that her peculiar speech patterns with the lack of past tense and overuse of "be" did not come from home. Being as bright as she was, I could not fathom why she persisted in speaking so oddly, although as time passed she did appear to be using more normal speech. During March I decided to finally ask her about it, pointing out that some words were said differently if you were talking about something that happened yesterday. She was surprisingly antagonistic toward my comments, saying that I understood her, didn't I? When I said yes, I did, she asked me what did it matter how she talked if I understood her? That took me off-guard because it made me feel that the behavior was more premeditated than I had previously thought.

No one had any suggestions on the matter. All the speech experts to whom I sent tapes answered saying it was a dialect and often asking if she were black. When I replied that no, she wasn't, and no, it wasn't a family dialect, they had no other ideas. One night Chad and I were discussing it and he suggested that perhaps by not using the past tense, she was trying to keep everything anchored in the present where she could keep better control of things. The more I pondered that, the more possible it seemed. In the end, I concluded it was a psychologically based problem and let it go at that. We did understand what she was saying and perhaps someday she would feel comfortable enough to want to change. Right now, though, she did not.

The issue still uppermost in Sheila's mind was abandonment. She was preoccupied with her mother and her brother, where they were and what they were doing. Often her conversations were punctuated with comments to the effect that if she could have done this thing or that thing better, maybe her family would still be intact. In my mind this was all directly tied to her intense fear of failure.

One night after school Sheila had busied herself doing math problems. She loved math and excelled in it beyond all other areas. From the time she had arrived, she could do basic multiplication and division problems. Together we had worked out the more complicated techniques. She had discovered a dittoed exam from one of the fifth grade classes in a trash can at recess and brought it in to do after school.

When she had finished it, Sheila came over to show it to me. The problems were in division of fractions. This was not an area we had ever covered. Consequently all the problems were wrong because she had not inverted the divisor.

"Here's this. Is it done good?" she asked, handing it to me to look at.

Regarding the paper, I wondered whether or not I should point out the error. "Sheil, I want to show you something." On the back of the paper I drew a circle and divided it into four parts. "Now, if I wanted to know how many eighths were in it . . ." She immediately perceived that the way she was solving the problem would not give the correct answer.

"I done them wrong, didn't I?"

"You didn't know, kiddo. No one showed you."

She flopped down beside me and put her face in her hands. "I wanted to do them right and show you I could do them without help."

"Sheil, it's nothing to get upset about."

She sat for a few moments covering her face. Then slowly her hands slid away and she uncrumpled the paper which she had mashed. "I bet if I could have done math problems good, my Mama, she wouldn't leave me on no highway like she done. If I could have done fifth grade math problems, she'd be proud of me."

"I don't think math problems have anything to do with it, Sheila. We really don't know why your Mama left. She probably had all sorts of troubles of her own."

"She left because she don't love me no more. You don't go leaving kids you love on the highway. And I cut my leg. See?" For the hundredth time the scar was displayed to me. "If I'd been a gooder girl, she wouldn't have done that. She might still love me even now, if I could have been gooder."

"Sheil, we don't really know that. It was a bad thing, but it's over. I don't think your being good or bad had anything

151

to do with it. Your Mama had her own problems to straighten out. I think she loved you a lot; mamas generally do. I think she just couldn't cope with having a little girl right then."

"But she copeded with Jimmie. How come she tooked Jimmie and left me?"

"I don't know, love."

Sheila looked over at me. That haunted, hurt expression was in her eyes. God, I thought, would I never fill that emptiness? Absently she twisted one pigtail. "I miss Jimmie."

"I know you do."

"His birthday's gonna be next week. He be five years old then and I never seen him since he be two. That do be an awful long time." She turned away from me and went to the window, staring out at the winter-wet March afternoon. "I miss Jimmie almost more than anything. I can't forget him."

"I can tell that."

She turned to look at me. "Could we have a birthday party for him? On March twelfth, that be his birthday. Could we have a party like we have for Tyler when it be her birthday in February?"

"I don't think so, kitten."

Her face fell and she shuffled back over to me. "Why not?"

"Because Jimmie isn't here, Sheil. Jimmie lives clear out in California and not here with us."

"It could be just a little birthday party. Maybe just you and me and Anton. Just after school maybe."

I shook my head.

"But I want to."

"I know you do."

"Then why not? Just a little, little party? Please?" Her face had puckered, her voice pleaded. "I'll be your goodest girl. I won't mess up any other math papers."

"That's not the point, Sheila. I'm saying no because Jim-

152

mie isn't here anymore. Jimmie's gone. As much as it hurts to think about, Jimmie may not be coming back. I know you miss him a terribly lot, kitten, but I don't think it's a good idea to keep remembering him the way you are. All it does is hurt you."

She covered her face with her hands.

"Sheil, come here and let me hold you." Without removing her hands she came and I lifted her into my lap. "I know you feel awful about this. I can just feel you hurt from sitting here. It's a very hard thing you have to do."

"I miss him." Her voice broke with a dry sob and she clutched at my shirt, shoving her face into my breasts. "I just want him to be here."

"I know you do, love."

"Why did it happen, Torey? Why did she tooked him and leaved me behind? What made me such a bad girl?" The tears shimmered momentarily in her eyes. But as always they never escaped.

"Oh lovey, it wasn't you. Believe me on this. It wasn't your fault. She didn't leave you because you were bad. She just had too many of her own problems. It wasn't your fault."

"My Pa, he says so. He says if I be a gooder girl she'd a never done that."

My heart sank. There was so much to fight and so little to fight with. Why should she believe me and not her father? What could I do to show her he was wrong in that respect? I felt discouraged. "Your Pa made a mistake on this one, Sheil. He doesn't know what happened either and he doesn't know what it's like to be a little girl. He's wrong on this one. Believe me, please, because it's true."

We sat in silence several minutes. I held her close, feeling her warm unsteady breath against my skin. My heart hurt. I could feel it in my chest and it hurt. Her pain soaked through my shirt and my skin and my bones to be absorbed into my heart. God, it hurt.

At last she looked up. "Sometimes, I'm real lonely."

I nodded.

"Will it ever stop?"

Again I nodded, slowly. "Yes. Someday I think it will."

Sheila sighed and pulled away from me, standing up. "Someday never really ever comes, does it?"

Despite our sad moments, Sheila surprised me by being filled with joy. She had a tremendous capacity for joy. Working with these kids whose entire lives were chaotic tragedies affirmed my faith on a daily basis that humans are by nature joyous creatures. Sheila's moods fluctuated a great deal and she was never able entirely to escape the emotional devastation she had suffered. But by the same course, she was never far from happiness.

The smallest thing would ignite a merry sparkle in her eyes and not a day went by now that we did not hear her skitterish laughter. This was heightened by the fact that she had been deprived for so long that everything was new to her. She could not get her fill of the wonders that the world held. Perhaps her greatest discovery in March was the flowers.

Our part of the state comes alive in March with crocuses and daffodils waving from every patch of ground. Sheila was fascinated by the flowers. None had ever grown in the migrant camp and, as unbelievable as it seemed to me, she had never before seen a daffodil up close. One morning I brought a huge bouquet from my landlady's garden into class.

Sheila came squealing over, toothpaste still in her mouth. She was just in her T-shirt and underpants, her bare feet slapping the floor as she ran. "What them things be?" she gurgled through the toothpaste.

"They're daffodils, silly. You've seen them before, haven't you?"

Peering at them she shook her head. "Uh-uh. Just in books, that's all. Them be real flowers?"

"Sure they're real. Touch them."

Putting down her toothbrush, she cautiously reached out, touching the edge of one flower with her fingertip. "Oooooh!" she squealed with delight, spraying toothpaste all around. Jumping up and down, she clutched herself with pleasure. Then stopping suddenly, she hesitantly touched another. Again the little dance of joy.

"Go finish brushing your teeth and get your clothes on, then you can help me put them in a vase."

Dashing back, she spit out the rest of the toothpaste, but was unable to contain her glee long enough to put on the overalls. She came running back. "They do be so soft. Let me touch them."

"Smell them. Daffodils don't smell as good as some flowers, like roses, for instance. But they have a special odor all their own."

She sniffed deeply. "I wanna hug them."

I chuckled. "Flowers don't especially like being hugged."

"But they smell that good and they do be so pretty. They make me feel like hugging them."

"Yes, they do, don't they?" I had gotten out one of the vases a child had made for me years earlier. There were too many flowers to fit in it. Beside me Sheila bounced in delight, first on one foot and then on the other. Her whole body reflected her joy.

"Sheil, would you like a flower of your own?"

She looked up at me, her eyes widening to what seemed to be the very perimeters of her face. "I can have one?"

"Yes, there's too many to fit in my vase. We could put it in a milk carton over by where you always sit at the table."

"Could it really be mine?"

I nodded.

"For me?"

"Yes, silly, for you. Your own flower."

Her face fell suddenly. "My Pa, he wouldn't let me keep it."

I smiled. "Flowers are different than that. They don't last very long, hardly even a day. Your Pa wouldn't care about something like a flower."

Tenderly she reached out and caressed one of the daffodils. "Remember in that book about the fox and the little prince? Remember, the prince had a flower and he tamed it. Remember that?" Her eyes were full of wonder as she looked up at me. "Do you suppose I could tame one? It would be my very own special flower and I could be 'sponsible for it and everything. I could tame it for my very own."

"Well, you'll have to remember flowers don't last too long. But they tame easily. I think you could do it. Which one would you like?" I pointed to the ones left over from the vase.

Considering them all carefully she chose one that looked no different to me from all the others, but it must have said something special. Perhaps the taming had already begun, because like the little prince and his rose, this daffodil was Sheila's and to her it was like no other flower in the world.

Holding the flower gently and stroking its golden cup, she smiled. I had gone over and gotten her overalls and came back, leaning over her, urging her to put her legs in. The other children were arriving, noisy and curious about what was happening. But Sheila stood oblivious, letting me dress her and not looking at the other children. Her lips were pressed tight between her teeth to keep a smile in check.

"My heart do be so big," she whispered, "it be so big and I do reckon I be about the happiest kid for it."

I kissed her soft temple and smiled. Then I picked up the vase of yellow daffodils and took them to the table.

CHAPTER

14

We laughed a lot.

Things were not always very funny in our room. Often the things I did find myself laughing about were matters that, if I had stopped and really thought about them, were only tragic. Perhaps the greatest magic of the human spirit is the ability to laugh. At ourselves, at each other, at our sometimes hopeless situation. Laughter normalized our lives.

Whitney, more than anyone else, kept us in line with what was normal. I loved her wholeheartedly for that quality, for never letting me or Anton or the kids ever quite convince her that this room was different.

Despite her shyness, Whitney had a sense of humor that sometimes did not know limits. Her wit could be dry and shockingly adult on occasion, especially when she was alone with Anton and me. However, Whitney was at her best when practical joking. Perhaps I would have been better prepared for that side of her if it had seemed more in keeping with her meek, bumbling exterior. Or maybe if our room had seemed a likelier place for playing practical jokes. Whatever it was, Whitney consistently took me by surprise. I never failed to be genuinely startled by the spring snakes that jumped out of Susannah's crayon box or the fake vomit sitting on the table while Peter and William and Guillermo feigned sudden stomachaches.

When Sheila arrived, that side of Whitney hit its zenith. The other kids loved Whitney's jokes and readily participated in them. Sheila, however, was bright enough to catch on to what Whitney was planning ahead of time, to make creative suggestions of her own, to see the inherent humor in a given situation. And Sheila was naive enough to do some of the crazier things Whitney suggested.

Much of March had passed and nothing happened. That made me suspicious. Each morning I began checking my drawers and my ceramic mug and other things that regularly fell prey to jokes. Usually I could count on Sheila to tip me off, primarily because she could not keep secrets well. Even when she was trying, she was not too sophisticated about hiding the evidence. However, nothing was happening. I did catch the two of them giggling together frequently enough to continue to be on-guard, but as the days went by, nothing occurred. Perhaps this was because Whitney had caught a bad cold and was absent almost a week.

Toward the latter half of the month Mrs. Crum, Freddie's mother, came to visit me after school. A small woman, sparrow-brown and mouse-scared, she slipped inside the door and apologized for bothering me. I had been playing cars on the floor with Sheila and assured her I did not mind being interrupted. Could I help her? Head down, she wrung her hands. So sorry to bother me with her problems. I asked Sheila to trot down to the office and help Anton who was there cutting mimeo stencils. Once we were alone, I invited Mrs. Crum to sit down.

She had come to ask me if the children had been eating

anything at school lately. I thought. It was Wednesday, so we had just had cooking. We'd made egg foo young, I told her. Other than that, they hadn't eaten anything. Except lunch, of course. She wrinkled her brow. Freddie had come home three times in the last week and vomited. That would not have surprised her so much, she said, if she could have figured out what it was he was vomiting up. Little bright red, green, blue and yellow balls about a quarter inch in diameter. A couple dozen of them every time.

I was genuinely perplexed. Nothing I could think of fit that descsiption. Not only did we not have any candy because I did not keep candy in the room, but also I did not keep any small nonedibles like that simply because the kids like Freddie or Max or Susannah would put them into their mouths. No, he couldn't be getting them at school, I reassured her. But I promised I would keep an eye on him to be sure.

The next few days went as usual. Whitney was still gone and I got bogged down with end-of-term report cards, so I spent part of the after-school time working while Sheila played by herself. The weekend came and went, then Monday again.

In the afternoon when I came back from taking the other children to their buses, I found Sheila on her knees in front of the cupboard under the sink. She had a colorful assortment of phrases she saved to use when she was especially perturbed. No matter what I did, she persisted in stringing them out when things did not go her way. Now as I came back into the room, I heard her muttering them half-aloud.

"What's wrong, Sheil?"

She leaped to her feet and whirled around. "Nothing."

"What were you swearing about?"

"Nothing."

I came over to the sink. "Didn't sound like nothing to me. What's going on?"

"Someone takeded something that be mine."

159

"Like what?"

"Just some stuff." She frowned. "I be gonna make an art project out of. I be looking for it and someone stole it. It ain't in here where I put it."

"Why did you put it there in the first place? You ought to keep your things in your cubby. You know that. Nobody knows what they find under there is yours. What was it anyway?"

"Just some stuff."

"What kind of stuff?"

She shrugged. "Just stuff. That belong to me."

"Well, you go over to the art box. Maybe there are some scraps in there you can use."

About an hour later, there was Mrs. Crum at my door again. Oh so sorry, she began apologizing, but Freddie vomited again. More little colored balls. She had brought some with her this time, all wrapped up in a paper napkin. Despite her timidity, she insisted I look at them and convince her they did not come from my room.

Gritting my teeth I unwrapped the damp napkin. There were eight or ten little not-quite-round spheres in bright, Day-Glo colors. Taking a pencil, I poked at one. It mashed easily to reveal a dark, greenish-brown center. I could not imagine what they were.

Anton, who had been down in the teachers' workroom, came into the room. I beckoned him over.

"Have you seen anything like this around here?" I asked.

He leaned over my shoulder for a closer look. "What the hell?" Taking the pencil from me, he mashed a second one. It, too, crumbled easily.

"Apparently Freddie has been finding them somewhere, eating them and then throwing them up when he comes home from school. Mrs. Crum thinks they're from around here."

"What are they?" Anton asked, skepticism undisguised.

"I haven't the foggiest idea."

160

Sheila had gotten curious and came over. She tugged at my jeans. "Lemme see."

I pushed her off. "Just a sec."

She went off to drag a chair over and climbed on it to be closer to our height. "Lemme see."

"You know," Anton said, now holding the napkin with its mysterious contents, "this is going to sound dumb, but they look like rabbit turds to me."

"Anton, they're red and green and blue," I replied.

"I know it. But look at the middles. Don't they look like it to you?"

I started to laugh in spite of myself. The ridiculousness of the situation struck me.

Sheila was balancing precariously on a chair beside me, one hand on my arm, one on the collar of my shirt. "Lemme see, Torey."

Anton leaned over toward her and showed the napkin. When she saw the contents of the napkin, she jerked back suddenly, throwing herself off-balance. Both she and the chair fell over.

"You all right?" I asked as she picked herself up.

She nodded. Something about the way she looked at me made me suspicious. Or more precisely, the way she did not look at me.

"Do you know something about this, Sheil? What these little things are?"

Taking a step backwards, she gave a huge shrug.

Anton's eyebrows came down in his I-mean-business look.

"Sheila, did you give something to Freddie he shouldn't have?"

She looked up at us. Innocence written all over her. Big, wide eyes round as china plates. Hair escaped from her ponytail, wispy around her face. She held her lower lip between her teeth and continued to move backwards. For Sheila such innocent demeanor implied guilt.

"Sheila, I want you to tell me about this," I said.

Still no response.

"We know you know," Anton added.

We stared at one another.

"Sheila." My most serious voice. I was having a hard time sounding that way. She looked so damned innocent in the face of such obvious guilt. How she could look that way and betray herself so badly, I did not know.

Finally I approached her, slowly, because fear had creeped into her expression and she still spooked occasionally if someone rushed at her. Putting a hand behind her shoulder, I propelled her back to the table. I kept my fingers on her back and stood behind her so she could not get away again.

"Now suppose you tell us what this stuff is, kiddo. I want to know and I want to know right now."

She stared at the damp napkin full of the colorful little balls which Mrs. Crum had laid on the table. I could feel Sheila pressing back against my hand. I jostled her shoulder.

"I'm losing patience, Sheil. Don't make me angry. These things could hurt Freddie and we need to know what they are. Now tell me."

"Rabbit poop," she said softly.

"Then how come they're all those colors?"

"I painted them with temperas."

The situation got the better of Anton and he began to giggle. A hand over his mouth, he smothered the sound.

"For crying out loud, Sheila," I said, "why were you painting rabbit poop?"

"For Whitney."

As I wormed the story out of Sheila, we learned that she and Whitney had been planning to play a joke. For Easter, we were making a large mosaic in the back of the room, which was to be hung in the hallway of the main school building for Parent's Night. It was to be titled "Hopping Down the Bunny Trail." Apparently Whitney had thought it would be funny to substitute the mosaic chips with painted rabbit dung. Sheer adolescent humor. Sheila had been given the ignominious task of wrestling the dung away from Onions, who did not like anyone messing around in his cage for any reason. She was painting it and then drying it under the sink where no one looked much. Freddie must have discovered all this covert activity and assumed the painted dung was candy. Or something. He ate it. From the way Sheila related the whole deal, I gathered that the last week must have been a frustrating one for her. Onions had been uncooperative, Whitney had been absent and Sheila's cache of painted poop kept mysteriously disappearing. No wonder I caught her cursing into the cupboard after school.

Anton could barely contain himself through this recital. Lips tight between his teeth, he rolled his eyes heavenward repeatedly, and coughed into one hand. Mrs. Crum did not see the humor inherent in the whole mess. I might have felt differently too, if it were my son. None of us knew about the toxicity of the substance. I knew the temperas were nontoxic but had no idea about rabbit dung. Anton went to call the poison center. However, since Freddie had been eating them over the last week and had apparently suffered no ill effects, aside from his upset stomach, I was not too worried. Besides, he had been throwing them up unchewed and undigested anyway.

I pointed out the quiet corner to Sheila and suggested she go sit there the rest of the time. She went without protest, but deep, melodramatic sighs were issued so frequently that I was afraid she would hyperventilate. Anton returned with the report from the poison control center and assured Mrs. Crum that no harm would come to Freddie. I apologized to her for the kids' foolishness and escorted her to the door.

Anton and I discussed the situation and decided that we ought to have Whitney come in right then. She lived near the school and I felt it was better to get the matter taken care of when the other children were not around. Although it had been meant as a joke, the affair could have had serious consequences. I preferred to talk it over with Whitney and see how things were.

Anton left to call Whitney. I came over to the quiet chair. Sheila looked up.

"Listen, it's just about time for you to go to your bus. You get your jacket and get started. Anton and I are both too busy to walk you tonight, so you're going to have to take responsibility for yourself. I don't want to hear one single word from anybody that you messed around between here and the bus. Is that clear?"

Sheila nodded.

"Good-bye then. I'll see you tomorrow."

"I do be sorry."

"That's okay. We've talked about it and it's over now."

"You be mad at me?"

"I'll live through it. I know you guys did it as a joke and didn't mean to hurt anybody with it. I understand that. And you know now that it was a kind of dumb thing to do. So we'll just forget it, now that it's over."

She stood up but did not move away from the chair.

"Hurry up or you'll miss your bus."

"You be mad at me?"

"No, Sheil, I'm not mad at you. Now get moving."

"How come you don't smile at me, if you ain't mad?" The worry showed too plainly in her eyes.

Grinning, I came down on my knees to be her height and hugged her against me. I kissed her soundly on the cheek. "You're still a little short on faith, aren't you?" I pushed back her bangs. "Now don't you go home and worry about it, because I'm all done being mad. I wasn't very mad to begin with because what you did wasn't on purpose. Mostly I was just worried about Freddie and when I get really worried, it comes out like I'm mad. But it's all over. Okay? Does that settle it for you?"

164

She nodded.

"All right. Then scoot or you'll miss that bus."

Whitney was another matter entirely. She arrived with her mother about ten minutes after Sheila left. I had not meant it to become that big a deal. I simply wanted to talk to her. I was not angry. As I had told Sheila, I never really had been. Mostly, I had been worried and also a little embarrassed in front of Mrs. Crum. Yet there had been potential danger in the situation and I felt Whitney needed to be aware of that. However, Whitney's mother made a federal case of the deal.

Anton had had to talk to her on the phone and had explained a little bit of the problem. She came storming into the school, hauling Whitney by the arm as if she were a little girl. A tall woman with starched blond hair, Whitney's mother marched into my room and demanded I tell her what happened. I explained best as I I could. At that she turned to Whitney with an anger I could not have managed if Freddie had died from the stuff.

"Mrs. Blake? Mrs. Blake?" I kept trying to interrupt. "If I could just talk . . . Mrs. Blake?"

Anton was in the middle of the fray too, trying to distract her. "Would you like a cup of coffee, Mrs. Blake?"

All the time Whitney sat in one of the little chairs and sobbed.

I don't remember how we shut her mother up. We did finally, and Anton took her down to the lounge for coffee. I figured that was a just reward for her. By that time of day, the coffee would have been in the pot for over eight hours.

Whitney and I were alone. I was embarrassed to be there, to have heard her mother talk to her like that. She must have felt humiliated. I was embarrassed to the point that I did not know what to say. Bringing over a box of tissues, I set them on the table in front of her. I hesitated momentarily, wondering if I should apologize or something. I mumbled something about giving her a few min-

165

utes to collect herself while I sorted out the kids' papers and put them in their cubbies for the next morning.

When I came back, I sat down beside her and put an arm around her shoulder. Whitney turned and clutched me. The move had been unexpected and my chair wobbled with her weight against me but I closed my arms around her; she was so hungry for comforting.

"Listen, things aren't this bad, Whitney." I smoothed her hair back from her face. "Anton and I, we're not that mad at you. I'm not that mad at all."

She straightened up in her chair and took an umpteenth Kleenex. "I was just joking."

"I know you were. And I'm not mad. I didn't mean to get you in all this trouble. Believe me, I wouldn't have had you come over if I'd known it would be this bad for you."

"Oh, my mom gets mad at anything."

"Yeah, well, it wasn't that big a deal. I just wanted you to know that you have to be a little careful around here. These aren't normal kids, Whitney. You have to watch things so much more around them."

She nodded and wiped at more tears.

"Kids like Freddie don't know what's edible and what isn't. And Sheila's too little to know she shouldn't be doing that sort of thing."

"I didn't think anybody would get hurt. I didn't mean this to happen."

"Oh, sweetheart, I know that. And this time, nobody did get hurt. We just came awfully close. It was only a silly thing you did without thinking. I love your sense of humor, Whitney, and I love the way you show the kids how to laugh. But these are special kids. We need to take extra good care of them."

She braced her head in her hands and stared at the tabletop. "I never do anything right. I screw up everything I do."

"It just seems that way right now. But you know that isn't true."

"My mom's going to kill me."

"This isn't any of your mom's worry. It's just yours and mine. Anton will take care of your mom and if he doesn't, I'll talk to her."

"I am sorry, Torey."

"Yeah, I know you are."

"What's going to happen to me?"

"Nothing."

Whitney would not look at me; she continued to stare at the table. I had a hand on her shoulder still and could feel the warmth through her shirt. We sat a long, long time in silence.

"Can I tell you something, Torey?"

"Yeah."

Still no way she could look at me. "This is about the only place in the world I like to be. Everybody teases me about it. All the time. They say: Why do you want to hang around with a bunch of crazy people all the time? They think I'm crazy too. You know, not nice crazy, but really mental. Because otherwise why would I want to be here so much?"

"Well," I replied, "then they must think the same thing about Anton and me. We must be crazy too."

"Do people ever say that to you?" For the first time she looked at me.

"Not to me. But I suspect there are more than a few who think it."

"Why are you here?"

I smiled. "I guess because I like very honest relationships. So far the only people whom I've found to be that honest are either children or crazy. So this place seems to be a natural for me."

Whitney nodded. "Yes, I guess that's what I like too— the way everybody shows exactly what they feel. So at least if someone hates you, you know it." She smiled wanly. "The funny thing is, these kids don't seem as crazy to me sometimes as normal people do. I mean . . ." her voice trailed off.

I nodded. "Yes, I know what you mean."

Chad was waiting for me when I arrived home, none too patiently. He had brought over a couple of cartons of moo goo gai pan from Jeno's Chinese Take-Out.

"Where on earth have you been? It's practically seven o'clock." He had been trying to keep the food warm by setting cartons and all in a frying pan. The kitchen smelled of scorched paper.

"At school."

"This late? Jesus, I've been here practically an hour. What were you doing?"

"Well, one of my kids had been vomiting up these little colored balls at home and his mom was suspicious that it was something he got into at school. So she brought this soggy napkin full of what he'd been throwing up."

Chad began to giggle. He had turned away from me to jiggle the frying pan with the cartons in it. I could see his shoulders shake.

"So Anton and I began dissecting these little balls and they turned out to be rabbit turds."

Chad's giggles became full laughter. And contagious. I began to chuckle.

"Anyway, Sheila had been getting the turds out of Onions' cage and painting them with temperas. God only knows when she was doing it, but evidently Freddie found them and was eating them. I guess he thought they were candy or something."

Both of us were laughing. I could hardly get the last words out. The smell of scorching cartons wafted up between us but by that time the tears were rolling down our cheeks. My side hurt. And still we laughed.

"I'm sorry I asked," Chad finally gasped.

"I'm not," I replied.

15

The call that I had been dreading came the third week in March. Ed Somers' low, rumbling voice came over the telephone. When the secretary had called my room that evening after school to tell me I had a phone call, I had a premonition this was the one. When I heard Ed's voice I knew, even before he said it.

"Torey, the director called today. They have an opening at the state hospital."

My pulse began to race when I heard him say that. The beating was so hard in my ears that I could not hear easily. "Ed, she doesn't have to go, does she?"

"Tor, I told you this was only a temporary placement. The court ordered that she be placed in the state hospital when an opening came up. It really is out of our hands. Your placement was only temporary."

"But she's changed so much. She's not the same child. Ed, she won't make it in the hospital."

"Listen, it was all settled before either of us got into it.

You know that, we discussed it before. Besides, it'll be in her best interest. Look at that terrible home situation she has. She hasn't got a chance in hell to make it anyway, Tor. You know that. Christ, you work every day with these kids. You, of all people, should know when a kid's got too much stacked against her."

"But she hasn't, Ed," I cried. "This kid has so much. She could make it. She can't go into the hospital now."

Ed could be heard making clucking noises on his side of the phone. There was a long silence as he lit a cigarette. "Tor, you've done a hell of a good job with those kids. I honestly don't know how you do it sometimes. But you've gone too far with this one. You've gotten too involved. I could tell that back with that incident in January. This kid's case was decided long before she ever reached us."

"Then undecide it."

"It's out of my hands. After that burning incident, the state committed her. To placate the boy's parents, that was the only alternative."

"Ed, this is ludicrous. God Almighty, the child is six years old. This can't happen."

"I know how you're feeling, Torey, I really do. I'm awfully sorry this is having to happen this way because I know you've gotten involved with the girl. But she's a court case. We both knew how it would turn out. And I am sorry."

I went down to the teachers' lounge, unable to go back to my room where Sheila was playing. I sat and drank coffee, which I normally never touch, all the while trying to keep the tears back. Ed was right. I had gotten too involved; she mattered too much to me. I could not verbalize my frustration; I was not finding the right words. The chattering over lesson plans and art projects and the school carnival got to me. Finally I ended up going back to my room to get away from the lounge-dwellers who were so filled with after-school merriment.

When Anton saw me, he did not ask what had happened—he knew. He motioned Sheila over to the table where he was setting up a project for the next day and asked her to help him. I stood in the doorway looking around the room. Not a very remarkable place by the looks of it, I thought. Too long and narrow, too dark, too crowded with animal cages that smelled and pillows that lost all their stuffing on the carpet. Not even room for a teacher's desk. I could have used a teacher's desk right then; something to go and hide behind; something that shouted, "LEAVE ME ALONE," without my saying it. But there was none. Wearily, I went over to the pillows behind the animal cages and sank down onto them.

Within seconds Sheila was standing before me, her eyes scrutinizing my face. "You ain't happy," she stated quietly. She had her hands stuffed into the pockets of her overalls. How much she had grown, I thought. There must have been two inches between the overalls and her shoes. Or perhaps there always had been and I hadn't noticed.

"No, I'm not happy."

"How come?"

"Sheila, come over here," Anton called. Sheila remained motionless, her eyes piercing mine, probing my mind. I was wondering if I really had gotten too involved. She was such a beautiful child to me. To be sure, an ordinary passerby would have thought she looked like any of a hundred thousand other children. But she alone was more important to me than all the rest of them together. I loved her, although I certainly hadn't intended to. And loving her had made her so important to me. Now I was " 'sponsible." I could feel the tears in my eyes.

Sheila knelt beside me, the worry rippling across her face. "How come you cry?"

"I'm not very happy."

Anton came over and lifted Sheila to her feet. "Come on, tiger, you come help me put away papers."

171

"Uh-uh," Sheila twisted out of his grasp, moving out of reach.

I waved a hand at him. "That's okay, Anton. I'm all right." He nodded and left us.

For a long moment Sheila regarded me, her eyes flooded with concern. The tears remained unfallen in my own but I could not make them go away. Nor could I bring myself to look at her. I was embarrassed to show such shaky composure and I was worried about frightening her.

But she stood apart watching me. Then slowly she came over and sat beside me. Touching my hand tentatively, she spoke. "Maybe if I hold your hand, you'll feel better. Sometimes that helps me."

I smiled at her. "You know, kid, I love you. Don't ever forget that. If the time ever comes and you're alone or scared or anything else bad ever happens, don't forget I love you. Because I do. That's really all one person can do for another."

Her brow wrinkled. She did not understand what I was saying. I suppose I knew she wouldn't because she was so young. But I had to say it. I had to know, for my own peace of mind, that I had told her I had done my best.

I rolled over on the bed to look at Chad. We had been watching TV all evening and not talking. I was too preoccupied to concentrate on conversation. At first I had not even told him the particulars of what had happened; but as the evening wore on, my mind was coming out of the first haze of shock and beginning to tick again.

"Chad?"

He looked in my direction.

"Is there a legal way to contest what they plan to do with Sheila?"

"What do you mean?"

"Well, you know. Is there a legal way to fight the commitment? I mean could someone like me do it? Someone who isn't her guardian?"

172

"*You* fight it?"

"Someone has to. I think the school district would back me. Maybe."

"I suppose you could try."

I frowned. "My problem is that I can't figure out where to start. To whom do we appeal? The courts committed her and you can't take a court to court, can you? I don't have any idea how to go about this."

"I imagine you'd have to call a hearing with her father and the parents of the little boy she abused and the child protection workers and all that. You could go through due process. You know all that."

I did not know. I had about as much understanding of the judicial system as I did the theory of relativity. But I hated Chad to think so. "Would you take it on, Chad?"

His eyebrows shot up. "Me?"

I nodded.

"I don't know anything about that kind of thing. What you need is someone specializing in that sort of law. Cripes, Tor, my experience is confined to getting the drunks out of jail."

I smiled. "Your experience and my bank account are about equal. I'm supposing that if I advocate, I'll have to pay for it."

Chad rolled his eyes. "Another charity case, huh?" He grinned. "I guess no one ever promised me I'd get rich."

"Oh, someday you will. Just not this year."

When the superintendent of school discovered that I had engaged a lawyer to look into the case, there was a meeting scheduled immediately. For the first time I met Mrs. Barthuly, Sheila's former teacher, face-to-face. She was a petite woman in her early forties with a delicate smile. As all five-foot-nine-inches of me in my Levi's and tennis shoes towered over her, I could well imagine Sheila might have been a trial to her. She wore an Anne Klein scarf and platform shoes and looked like a model for a Chanel No. 5

advertisement on television. Smelly, earthy-minded Sheila must have been hard to contend with.

Ed Somers was also there, as well as Allan, the psychologist, Mr. Collins, Anton, the superintendent and the resource room teacher who had had Sheila in kindergarten the year before. In the beginning it was not a particularly comfortable meeting for me. Not knowing my relationship with Chad, the superintendent felt that I had overstepped my boundaries in consulting a lawyer on this case without going through him. Perhaps he was right. I explained that I had discussed the matter with Ed and he felt there was no way we could touch the case, so I had simply checked into the legal recourse available.

Despite our touchy start, once the meeting got underway, a transition took place. I had brought along examples of Sheila's schoolwork and some videotapes that Anton had made of her in class. Allan reported on the test results. Sheila's former teachers were impressed and said so. Even Mr. Collins, whom I feared would be angry about this next example in a long history of my impulsive acts, commented on the overall improvement in Sheila's behavior. Unexpectedly, I felt a rush of affection toward him as he spoke.

The superintendent was less enthusiastic, saying that this really wasn't our matter because of the abuse incident. Yet he was encouraged by Sheila's progress and by her unusual IQ. He cautiously agreed to stand behind me in stating that the state hospital was not the most appropriate placement for Sheila and that he thought she could be maintained in the public school system without endangering the other students. He asked that Chad come in and see him. Despite the superintendent's attempt to keep the mood of the meeting low-key, I left in jubilant spirits.

The other major person to involve was Sheila's father. Anton went on scouting duty. The next time he saw the man home, Anton called me, and Chad and I came out immediately.

As the time before, Sheila's father had been drinking. He had had a bit more this second time and was a little jollier.

"Sheila doesn't belong in the state hospital," I explained. "She's doing very nice work in school and I think she might even be able to go back to a regular class next fall."

He tipped his head slightly. "Why do you care what they want to do with her?"

The question echoed in my head, a repeat of what Sheila so often asked me. Why *did* I care? "You've got a special daughter," I replied. "Going to the state hospital would be the wrong move for her. I don't want to see that happen to her because I think she can lead a normal life."

"She's crazy as a loon, that girl is. They told you what she done, didn't they? She damn near burned that little kid to death."

"She doesn't need to be crazy. She's not. Even now, she's not crazy. But she will be if she goes down there. It'd get worse in the long run. You don't want your daughter down in the state hospital."

He heaved a great sigh. He did not understand me. All his life people had been after him. Things had always gone wrong. He'd been in trouble, Sheila had been in trouble. He had learned to trust nobody. And so had his daughter. In their world it was safer that way. Now I came and he could not understand.

We talked far into the night. Chad and Anton drank beer with him while I made notes. Sheila, who was keeping her usual vigil on us from the far corner, fell asleep on the floor while we talked. I did not know if she understood why I was there and what was going on. I had not told her anything specific because I did not want to frighten her needlessly, nor did I want to give her false hopes. But after that night I suspected she would know. It would be better in the end, I supposed.

Her father agreed with us eventually. At last we convinced him that it was not "charity" or "do-gooding" or a nasty trick. He began to perceive the real reasons, which I had trusted he would if we persisted long enough. I had trusted that he did have some paternal instinct under that crust. In his own way, he loved Sheila and needed as much compassion as she did.

That was a strange evening. All of us were a little tipsy. Chad with his experience of defending the skid-row residents seemed to get along with Sheila's father better than the rest of us. He and her father would slap each other's backs in boozy camaraderie when I tried to get the conversation back onto the track and then they'd ply Anton and me with another can of beer. In a way, I was glad the hospital situation came up. It forced us to recognize each other's places in Sheila's life; that was better for everybody.

The hearing was held on the very last day of March. It was a dark, cold, windy day, promising snow on the eve of April. Not a good day to boost spirits. I had to take the afternoon off from school as did Anton. Mr. Collins came with us too. Surprisingly, in my opinion, he was very supportive of me, coming into my room in the morning and talking in a warm, fatherly way. Of all the people I had encountered, I would have least expected this change in him, because I had nursed a childish one-dimensional picture of him since the incident in Mrs. Holmes' room. At first I was suspicious of him, wondering what prompted this change, if he were simply protecting his own interests. But as I aired out some of the closed portions of my own mind, I came to see that he cared in his own way as much for the children as I. Even for Sheila.

It was a closed hearing. Across the room from us were the parents of the little boy and their lawyer. Milling about were a multitude of state and county people. With us were Anton, Allan, Mrs. Barthuly, Ed, and the superintendent. Sheila's father arrived late, but he did come finally and he was sober. My heart ached seeing him. He had on a suit that must have been a reject from Goodwill. The seams were frayed, the jacket stained and worn, the pants mended. His huge belly pulled the jacket tight and made it gape, straining on the buttons. Obviously, though, he had tried to look nice. His face was freshly shaven and he reeked of dime-store after-shave.

Outside the courtroom on a hard oak bench sat Sheila. Chad felt it would be best if she could be there. He thought perhaps he might need her if things did not go smoothly.

Sheila had come dressed in her overalls and T-shirt. I had so wished we could have dressed her nicely, but time had run out. So over the lunch hour I had given her a very thorough bath in the sink and brushed her hair until it was neat and shiny. If nothing else, she was clean. She had to sit alone outside the courtroom so we had brought a number of books to entertain her. However, when the judge found out that the child in question was being left unattended, he sent a court clerk out to sit with her.

The hearing went much differently from what I had expected. I had never been in a court before and all my information came from television. But this was not like TV. The lawyers spoke quietly and each of us presented our material. I had brought along the videotapes to illustrate Sheila's growth in my classroom in the three months she had been with us. Allan reiterated his findings from the tests. Ed spoke of the possible programs for her in the public schools should she continue to need special services after my class.

Then the parents of the little boy were questioned about the incident in November. Sheila's father was asked about how carefully he watched his daughter and if, in his opinion, she had seemed to improve in the last months. It was a very quiet hearing. No one raised a voice. No one even appeared emotionally involved. It was so different from what I had expected.

Then we were all asked to leave the courtroom while the

lawyers and the judge finished up the case. I was so proud of Chad. Despite our long, enduring relationship, I had never seen him work professionally. Now in front of me I saw a different man from the one I knew lounging on the bed in front of the TV. He seemed so sure of himself, so at ease in the court surroundings. I was so proud of him for taking on the hassle of a case he knew would never earn him any money and for taking my bewildered queries and turning them into a real chance to keep Sheila with us.

Down the hallway the boy's parents sat. The strain showed on their faces. Mouths pulled tight and grim. Eyes staring without seeing. I wondered what they were thinking. I could not tell from their faces. Did they have the compassion to forgive Sheila for what she had done? Or were their hearts still too burdened with grief and with fear. Were they still nursing in deep, unspeakable recesses the hope that her life would be as crippled as they feared she had made their son's? I could not tell from looking at them.

The father turned his head and met my eyes briefly. Both of us looked away. They were not bad people. Not the kind I could work up a hate for. When they had testified, their voices had been soft without detectable anger. If anything, they spoke sadly. Unhappy to have the issue reopened. To be in court a second time. To have their lives once more disrupted by this child. In a way I wished I could have hated them, it would have made the decision either way easier for me to accept. But I could not. They had only done what they thought best. Their fault, if anything, was nothing more than ignorance of mental illness. And fear. Now a judge, a man who did not know either of us, nor either of the children, would be the one to decide — on an issue that had no black or white. I wondered how they felt. I wished I had the courage to get up and go to them and ask. I wished there were a way it could be different.

Sheila was sitting on my lap. She had been drawing a

178

picture when we had come out and was now trying to tell me about it. My self-absorption was annoying her. She put a hand up and physically moved my head to look at her. "Look at my picture, Tor. It be a picture of Susannah Joy. See, she gots on that dress she wears to school so much."

I looked down. Sheila had long been envious of Susannah Joy. Susie was the only child in our classroom to come from an affluent family. She was always immaculately dressed and had a splendid wardrobe of frilly little frocks. Sheila was inelegantly envious. She longed for a dress, just one dress like Susannah had. Day after day, she would page through catalogues and pick out dresses she would like to have. Time and again would come entries on the subject into her journal. Only the week before I had found in the correction basket Sheila's creative writing paper.

> I do my best writing for you Torey from now on I do be a gooder girl and do my best work I promise. I want to tell you what I do last night. I go down and wait for my father he be at the opptomrix who fistes eye glasses. So I got to walk around for a while and I look in them windows sometimes. Some times I wish I could by the things in them windows. Some times they be so prety. I seen a dress that be red and blue and be white too and it gots lace on it and be long and beutiful. I ain't never had a dress like that and it was prety torey. I sort of wish I could have it. It be my size to I think. I ask my pa if I could by it but he sad "no". That be too bad cos it be so nice and I aint never had a real dress. And I could a wored it to school like Susannah Joy do. She gots lots of dresses. But I couldnt so we went home and my pa he by me some M&Ms instead and toled me "to go to bed Sheila" so I did.

That little essay had hurt me in a funny, unidentifiable way. It seemed one of the saddest things she had ever written. But Sheila went on, knowing she could not have a dress, accepting it and continuing to dream.

Sheila prattled on about the picture she was holding, showing me intricacies in the drawing. Yet she noticed my

179

mind was wandering. She hadn't been called in, which I took as a good sign, but she was aware of the tension among us.

Then at last the doors to the judge's chambers opened. From the minute I saw Chad's face, I knew what the ruling had been. He stopped about eight feet from us, a crisp smile tight on his face. Then he grinned. "We won."

Noise erupted in the hallway and we danced about hugging one another. "We won! We won! We won!" Sheila shrieked, bouncing midst everyone's legs. We all laughed at her jubilance although I doubted she knew the impact of what she was saying.

"I think this calls for a celebration, don't you?" Chad asked. He was pulling on his trench coat. "What do you say we go down to Shakey's and order the biggest pizza they have?"

The others were beginning to leave. I glanced briefly down the hallway toward the boy's parents, who were putting on their coats. Once again I wished I had the courage to walk those twenty feet down the corridor and speak to them. Chad was talking to me about pizza, Sheila was jumping around my legs, scrabbling at my belt to be acknowledged, school people were yelling good-byes.

"Well, what do you say?" Chad asked again. "You want to go or are you going to stand there all evening?" He gave me a playful nudge.

I turned back to him and nodded.

"What about you?" Chad said to Sheila. "You want to come with Torey and me to get pizza?"

Her eyes widened and she nodded. I bent down and picked her up to bring her up to our level of the conversation.

Apart from us stood Sheila's father. Alone. His hands stuffed into the pockets of his ill-fitting suit. He stared at the floor. He seemed lonely to me, lonely and forgotten. This had not been his battle we had just won and it was not to him Sheila had gone. She had waited with us in the hallway and now she celebrated with us. It was our victory. He had not been a part of it. Courts had only been bad places for him in the past; they were frightening places. In his tattered suit and cheap after-shave lotion, he made a strange and striking contrast to the school district and government people. I realized with great sadness that even his daughter was not his own. She was one of us; he was not.

Chad must have perceived the same loneliness I did. "Do you want to join us?"

For a moment I thought I saw a flicker of pleasure on his face. But he shook his head. "No, I have to be going."

"It is all right if Sheila comes with us, isn't it?" Chad asked. "We'll bring her home later."

He nodded, a soft smile on his lips as he regarded his daughter. She was still in my arms, still wiggling with excitement, mindless of her father.

"You're sure you won't come with us?"

"No."

For a long moment we looked at each other, the universe between us never bridging. Then Chad reached into his pocket and took out his wallet. Pulling out a twenty-dollar bill, he handed it to Sheila's father. "Here. Here's your share of the fun."

He hesitated and I did not think he would accept it, knowing his disdain for charity. But uncertainly he extended his hand and took the bill. He mumbled a thank you, then he turned and walked away down the long corridor.

Sheila, Chad and I all piled into Chad's little foreign car and sped off to the pizza parlor. "Hey, Sheila, what kind of pizza do you like?" Chad asked over his shoulder to Sheila in the back seat.

"I don't know. I ain't never had no pizza."

"Never had pizza?" Chad exclaimed. "Well, we might have to do this more often, huh?"

181

If she never had pizza before, one would never have known it from Sheila's behavior. Her eyes were wide and shiny when the pizza arrived and she grabbed for it like a pro. Chad ordered the biggest, fullest-topped pizza he could find on the menu as well as a pitcher of soda pop. It was a magical moment. Sheila was alive and animated, talking constantly. She was intrigued by Chad and ended up sitting on his lap while we listened to the piano player entertain us. Chad commented that he had never seen a little kid eat so much food in one sitting in his life. Teasingly, Sheila told him she could eat at least a hundred pizzas if he had money to buy them and burped loudly to prove it.

Except for having seen her briefly the night we had gone to visit her father, Chad had never met Sheila. Early in the evening it was clear he thought she was one special person. Obviously the feeling was mutual. They laughed and kidded each other throughout the stay at the pizza place.

Night had fallen and the evening crowd was beginning to drift in. We had eaten the entire gigantic pizza, plus the pop, plus a round of soft ice cream. We had listened to the piano player so long that he coaxed Chad up to play "Heart and Soul" with him. But it was apparent that Chad and Sheila were not ready to part company.

Chad leaned way over the table to look at Sheila. "What's the thing you'd like best in the world, if you could have it?" he asked. My heart flinched because I knew Sheila would answer that she wanted her Mama and Jimmie back and that would dampen our mood.

Sheila pondered the question a long moment. "Real or pretend?"

"Real."

Again she sat pensively. "A dress, I think."

"What kind of dress?"

"Like Susannah Joy gots. One that gots lace on it."

"You mean all you'd want in the whole world is just a dress?" Chad's eyes wandered above Sheila's head to me.

182

Sheila nodded. "I ain't never had a dress before. Once a lady from a church bringed us out some clothes and there be this dress in it. But my Pa, he don't even let me try it on. He says we don't 'cept no charity from no one." She frowned. "I didn't think it would hurt just to try it on, but my Pa, he said I'd get a pounding if I did, so I didn't."

Chad looked at his watch. "It's almost seven o'clock. I don't think the stores in the Mall close until nine." He looked from me to Sheila. "What if I told you this is your lucky day?"

Sheila regarded him quizzically. She still did not know what was going on. "What do you mean?"

"What if I told you that in a few minutes we were going out to the car and go buy you a dress? Any dress you want."

Sheila's eyes got so big I thought they would break her face. Her mouth dropped and she looked at me. Then suddenly she was crestfallen. "My Pa, he wouldn't let me keep it."

"I think he would. We'll just tell him that's your share of the fun. I'll go in with you when we take you home. I'll tell him."

Sheila was beside herself. She leaped from her chair and danced in the aisle, colliding with unsuspecting patrons. She hugged me. She hugged Chad. Surely she would have exploded then and there if we hadn't left.

The next hour was a giddy one. We walked the aisles of the two big department stores in the Mall, Sheila holding on to our hands and swinging between us. Once we found the little girls' dresses, she turned unexpectedly shy and would not even look at them, instead shoving her face into my leg. Dreams close up can be quite hard to handle.

Finally I selected a few that were pretty and had lace and I dragged Sheila into a fitting room to try them on. Once we were alone she came back to life. Stripping off the overalls and shirt until she stood naked except for her underpants, Sheila lifted the dresses up to inspect them carefully.

She was such a scrawny little thing with a sway back and a little kid's fat stomach that only emphasized her skinniness. Now alone with the dresses she became too excited to try them on and danced around the small room in circles. I captured her around the waist and shoved her into one dress. What a magic moment. Sheila preened herself in front of the three-way mirror and then ran out to show Chad. We must have spent a half hour closeted in that little room while Sheila tried to decide among three dresses. She tried each of them on at least four times. At last she chose one, a red-and-white dress with lace at the neck and around the sleeves.

"I'm gonna wear it every day to school," she said enthusiastically.

"You look so pretty."

She was watching me in the mirror. "Can I wear it home?"

"If you want."

"I do!" Her sudden smile faded and she turned to me. She climbed onto my lap, touching my face softly with one hand. "You know what I wish."

"That you could have all three dresses?"

She shook her head. "I wish you was my Mama and Chad was my Daddy."

I smiled.

"It almost seems that way now don't it? Tonight, I mean. It almost seems like you are really my folks, huh?"

"We're something better than that, Sheil. We're friends. Friends are better than parents, because it means we love each other because we want to, not because we have to. We choose to be friends."

She looked at me for a long time, sitting on my knees and gazing into my eyes. Finally she sighed and slid off. "I wish we could be both. We could be family and friends both."

"Yes, that would be nice."

Her forehead wrinkled. "Could we just pretend?" she asked tentatively. "Just for tonight, could we pretend? Pretend that you and Chad was my folks and you was bringing your little girl out to buy her a dress? Even though she gots lots of dresses at home, you was bringing her out to buy another 'cause she wanted it and you loved her a lot?"

All my psychology class training urged me to say no. But as I saw her eyes, my heart wouldn't let me. "I suppose just for tonight we could pretend. But you have to remember it's just pretend and just for tonight."

She leaped up in a great bounce and tore out of the dressing room, still in her underwear. "I'm gonna tell Chad!"

Chad was amused to find out that while we were in the fitting room he had become a father. He played the part to the hilt. It was a mystical night filled with a lot of unspoken magic for all three of us. Sheila fell asleep in my arms on the way out to the migrant camp and after Chad parked the car, I woke her.

"Well, Cinderella," Chad said opening the door, "it's time to go home."

She smiled at him sleepily.

"Come on, I'll carry you in and tell your Daddy what we've been up to."

She hesitated a moment. "I don't wanna go," she said softly.

"It's been a nice night, hasn't it?" I replied.

She nodded. A silence fell between us. "Can I kiss you?"

"Yes, I think so." I enveloped her in a tight hug and kissed her. I felt her soft lips touch my cheek. And she kissed Chad as he lifted her out of my lap and carried her into her house.

We drove home in silence. Pulling up in front of my

place we sat in the car, not speaking. Finally Chad turned to me, his eyes shining in the wan glow of the streetlight. "She's a hell of a little kid."

I nodded.

"You know," he said, "it probably sounds dumb to say, but I pretended right along with her tonight. I wished we were a family too. It seemed so easy. And so right."

I smiled into the darkness, feeling a comfortable quiet drift down around us.

CHAPTER

16

April came in with a snowstorm. Although everyone bemoaned this parting shot of winter, it was one of those deep white fluffy snowfalls that are so lovely to look at. However, it stalled everything with its fierce depth, so school was suspended for two days.

When we returned, Sheila announced during the morning discussion that her Uncle Jerry had come to live with them. He had been in jail according to Sheila, although she couldn't remember what for, and now he was out looking for a job. She seemed quite excited about this new member of her family, telling us how Uncle Jerry had played with her all day during the snowstorm when she was bored.

We quickly returned to our routine. There was a trace of euphoria remaining from our victory in court. Although the children were not aware of what had happened, both Anton and I remained in high spirits. And if we were happy, Sheila in her new dress was positively radiant.

Every day she wore the red-and-white dress, parading in

front of the other kids in an obvious attempt to evoke the same kind of jealousy that Susannah had so successfully caused in her. She told them that how on her "trial day" she won and got to go to dinner with Chad and me and got her prized dress. Before long, everyone wanted a trial and I had to ask Sheila not to dwell on it. But while her speech with the other children lessened on the topic, with me after school it was the only topic. Like our incident in February over my absence, this had to be gone over repetitively, in minute detail: we had gone to Shakey's, we had had a tremendous pizza, Sheila had eaten lots and lots. Then we went to buy the dress and pretended we were a real family. Over and over and over she would recount the details, her face animated with memory. I let her go on about it because there seemed to be something therapeutic for her in it, just as in the February incident. Interestingly enough, Jimmie had been all but forgotten. I did not hear his name mentioned for days on end. That had been an evening of sheer, unspoiled happiness for Sheila and she didn't seem able to savor it completely enough. But then I suppose when those moments are far and few between, they are even rarer treasures. So I patiently listened, again and again and again.

One morning almost halfway into April Sheila arrived at school subdued. Anton had gone to meet her at the bus, but the bus had been late and she came in after morning discussion had started. She was wearing her old overalls and T-shirt again and was pale. Sitting down on the outer fringe of the group, she listened but did not participate.

Twice during the half-hour session she got up and went into the bathroom. I worried that she might be ill because she looked so pale and seemed so restrained. But the others were clamoring for attention and my mind was distracted.

When I was handing out math assignments I could not find Sheila, only to discover that she was in the bathroom again. "Don't you feel well today, hon?"

"I'm okay," she replied, taking the math papers from me and going over to her place at the table. I watched her as she went. She was speaking more now, using the proper verbs and I was pleased.

Late in the hour, just before freetime, I came over and sat down with Sheila to show her how to do a group of new math problems. I took her on my lap. Her body was surprisingly rigid as I held her. I felt her forehead to see if she were hot. But she wasn't. Yet she was certainly acting oddly. "Is something wrong, Sheil?"

She shook her head.

"You're all tense."

"I'm okay," she reasserted, and returned to the math problems.

As the lesson concluded, I lifted her off from my lap to the floor. On the leg of my jeans was a widening red spot. I stared at it not fully comprehending what it was. Blood? I looked at Sheila. "What on earth is going on?"

She shook her head, her face emotionless.

"Sheila, you're bleeding!" Down the inside of her right pants leg spread a red stain. Picking her up I rushed into the bathroom and shut the door behind us. Unbuckling the overall straps, I let them fall around her ankles. Blood had stained her underpants and ran down both legs. Wadded into her underwear were paper towels. Apparently that had accounted for the numerous trips to the bathroom earlier. She had been trying to staunch the blood flow so that it would not come through and show.

"Good God, Sheila, *what* is going on?" I cried, my voice sounding louder and more alarmed than I had meant it to. Fear rose in me as I pulled away the last of the towels from her clothing. Bright red blood trickled from her vagina.

But Sheila stood immutable. No emotion ran across her face. Her eyes were blank, looking at but not seeing me. She was paler than I had thought out in the dimmer classroom light; God, she was white. I wondered how much blood she had lost. In an attempt to wake her out of her stoicism, I grabbed her shoulders and shook her. "Sheila, what happened? You have to tell me. You can't play games now. What happened to you?"

She blinked like one coming out of a heavy sleep. She was paying a great price to cut off the pain and the emotion. "Unca Jerry," she began softly, "he tried to put his pecker in me this morning. But it wouldn't fit. So he tooked a knife. He said I was keeping him out, so he put the knife inside me to make me stop."

I went numb. "He put a knife in your vagina?"

She nodded. "One of the silverware knives. He said I'd be sorry for not letting him put his pecker in me. He said this'd hurt a whole lot more and I'd be sorry."

"Oh God, Sheila, why didn't you tell me? Why didn't you let me know?" Fearful that she had already lost too much blood, I wrapped a towel around her and picked her up.

"I's scared to. Unca Jerry told me not to tell. He said he'd do it again if I told on him. He said worser thing would happen if I told."

Rushing out of the bathroom carrying Sheila, I told Anton to watch the class. I grabbed my car keys and raced toward the office. Briefly I tried to explain to the secretary that I was taking Sheila to the hospital and to have someone find her father and get him there. Time had wound down to that eerie slow-motion pace it assumes in an emergency. Everyone around me seemed to react as if they were in a movie running at an improper speed. What was happening? The junior high aides peered out of the workroom. What was going on? All the time I could feel the warmth of Sheila's blood against my arm, soaking into my shirt as I held her.

Sheila was whiter now. Clad only in her T-shirt and shoes with the towel I had wrapped around her her only other protection, she was getting sluggish, closing her eyes and leaning heavily against me. I ran for my car. Still holding her in my lap, I turned the ignition and jammed the gears into reverse.

"Sheila? Sheila? Stay awake," I whispered, trying to maneuver the car and keep a hold on her at the same time. I should have taken someone with me, I thought absently, but there hadn't been time. No time to tell them what had happened.

"I do be awake," Sheila muttered. Her small fingers dug into my skin, pulling the tender area of my breast painfully tight as she gripped my shirt. "But it hurts."

"Oh, I'm sure it does, baby," I replied. "But keep talking to me, okay?" The distance to the hospital seemed interminable. The traffic impossible. Maybe I should have waited for an ambulance. I had no idea how much blood she had lost, nor how much was too much, nor what I could do about it. I cursed myself for never having followed through on my Red Cross training.

"My Unca Jerry, he said he was going to love me. He said he was going to show me how grown-up people loved each other." Her voice sounded small and childlike. "He said I better know how grown-up people loved. And when I screamed, he said nobody ain't gonna never love me if I can't learn how."

"Your Uncle Jerry doesn't know anything, lovey. He doesn't know what he's talking about."

She caught her lips in a tearless sob. "He said that be how you and Chad loved each other. He said if I want you and Chad to love me, I had to let him show me how, so I'd learn."

We neared the hospital. "Oh lovey, he's wrong. Chad and I love you already. He was just saying that so he could do something wrong to you. He had no right to touch you like he did. What he said and what he did were wrong."

Two young orderlies came running down the emergency ramp with a stretcher. Apparently Mr. Collins had alerted the hospital of our coming. As I placed Sheila on the stretcher for the first time she appeared to register pain and alarm. Moaning, she began to cry loudly but tearlessly. She refused to let go of my shirt and struggled fiercely as the men tried to pry her fingers loose.

"Don't leave me!" she wailed.

"I'm coming right along with you, Sheil. But lie down. Come on now, let go of me."

"Don't leave me! Don't let them take me away! I want you to hold me!" In a contorted mass the four of us and the stretcher moved toward the door. Sheila retained her terror-wrought grasp on my shirt, ripping the pocket. I did not know what brought her to life so fully. Perhaps she was frightened that I would leave her with these strangers; perhaps she could finally feel the extent of the pain. Whatever it was, she fought so valiantly that in the end it was easier for me to pick her up and hold her again than to pry her off and listen to her scream.

The emergency room doctor examined her briefly while I held her on my lap. Her father was still not there, so I signed a form stating that I would be responsible for emergency treatment until her father could be found.

A nurse came in with a needle and gave her a shot. Sheila had once again become docile and silent, not even flinching when the needle came. Within a short time after the shot, I could feel her fingers relaxing and I laid her on the examining table. Another nurse started an IV in one of her arms while a young Mexican-American intern was hanging a pint of blood above the table. The doctor gestured for me to come away. With a last look at Sheila, who lay with her eyes closed, pale and tiny on the table, I followed the doctor outside the swinging doors. He asked me what had happened and I told him to the best of my knowledge. At that point we saw Sheila's father stumbling down the corridor with the social worker. He was stone drunk.

The doctor explained that Sheila had lost a tremendous

amount of blood and they had to stabilize that first. Apparently, from what he could see in the examination, the knife had punctured the vagina wall into the rectum. It was a very serious injury because of the likelihood of infection and from the vast damage done. Once they had stabilized her blood level, the doctor believed there would have to be surgical intervention. Sheila's father weaved uncertainly beside us as the doctor spoke.

There was no more I could do. Undoubtedly my class back at school was in chaos. If Susannah had seen the blood, Anton would have more on his hands than he could handle alone or even with the other aides. And the children would be alarmed that I had left so suddenly. It was best that I get back to my job. I looked down at my clothes. Blood had stained the entire front of my shirt. The first spot on my Levi's had already dried into a dark blot. I stared at it. I was wearing part of somebody's life on me, little red tablespoons of a liquid more precious than gold. I was made uncomfortable by it, startled by how fragile life really is, reminded too fully of my own mortality.

I was back in school by eleven. When I looked up at the clock and saw how little real time had passed, I was shocked. Less than an hour had passed since I had lifted Sheila off my lap during math and seen the blood. The entire drama had taken place in barely fifty minutes. I had even gone home and changed my clothes before returning to class. I could not fathom that. To me it had felt as if a hundred years had been compressed into that fifty minutes. I had aged much more.

That night I did not go back to the hospital. I had called the doctor after school and he told me that they had just taken her into surgery and she was not yet out. Despite the blood administered, her condition had not stabilized but remained critical. He did not expect her out of the recovery room until quite late. She had been semicomatose most of

193

the day and he doubted that she was aware of who had been present. Sheila would go into intensive care after surgery to make sure the hemorrhaging stopped and she would stabilize before she was moved to the children's ward. I asked if I could come up, explaining I was as close to family as the child probably had aside from her father. He suggested I wait until the next day. She would not be conscious enough to know tonight and I would be in the way in the intensive care unit. They would make her as comfortable as they could, he assured me.

I asked if her father were still there, but the doctor replied no. They had sent him home shortly after I had gone. He was not sober enough to be coherent. The father's brother, Jerry, had been taken into custody.

In a way I was relieved not to have to go back. It had happened too fast and I could not conceive of the severity of the situation. She had talked to me. She walked all the way from the high school to our room and sat through an hour of class. And she had talked to me during the drive to the hospital. She could not be critically injured. I could not believe it.

The blood-stained shirt and jeans lay in a pile where I had hurriedly changed from them before returning to class in the morning. I put the Levi's to soak in the bathtub, but held the shirt, examining the pocket torn when Sheila had struggled with the emergency room attendants. Gently I folded the shirt and put it in the back of my closet. I could not bring myself to throw it away. Neither could I put it in the sink and wash it. I knew there was too much blood in it and if I did, the water would color. At that moment I was unable to wash the blood out, unable to see the water redden and go down the drain like so much filth. I would not be able to stand that.

After supper Chad came over and I related what had taken place. Chad was explosive. He paced the room at first saying nothing and shaking his head in disbelief. The anguish was not so much in the seriousness of the injury but in how it had happened. Chad raged with hatred, threatening to do physical harm to Jerry. He had no compassion for a man who would do such a thing to a little girl and I was frightened by the change in Chad, having never seen him so angry.

Although I was heartsick about the incident, a strange feeling twinged me. Five months earlier, Sheila had been the abuser and someone else had been the victim. Undoubtedly the boy's parents had felt very much the same way as Chad was now feeling toward Jerry. While it did not by any means excuse the gross inhumanity of the crime, it made me aware that the hurt and damage I had found in Sheila was probably in Jerry too. Neither was innocent, but neither was solely evil either. I was sadly plagued by knowing that Jerry was undoubtedly just as much a victim as Sheila. It made things so much more complicated.

The police called later in the evening and asked if I would come down and give them a statement. Together Chad and I went to the police department. In a gray-painted room at a gray-painted table, I told an officer what had happened in my classroom that morning. I repeated what Sheila had said to me and what I had done. It was a grim recounting of an even more grim occurrence.

During recess the next morning I called the hospital again to see how Sheila was coming along. The doctor's voice was more at ease this time. She had tolerated surgery well and had stabilized in intensive care during the night. By morning she was alert and coherent, so they had transferred her down to the children's ward. I could see her any time I wanted. I asked if her father had been in. The doctor said he had not. Please let her know I would be in right after school let out, I asked. The doctor agreed, his voice warm. She was a tough little kid, he said. Yes, I replied, there weren't any that were tougher.

Perhaps the most difficult task had been explaining what had happened to Sheila to the children in my class. We had already talked about abuse, both physical and sexual, in our room. My kids came from a high-risk population for abuse and I felt it was important for them to know what to do if they found themselves in such a situation or saw it happening to someone else. However, sexual abuse was hard to talk about. In a district where sex education had not made great popular strides in the schools, sexual abuse was taboo. I had worked up an informal unit for my children in which we simply discussed the appropriate and inappropriate ways of being "touched." An adult who held you and hugged you was okay. An adult who held your penis and hugged you was not. We discussed what one should do if that happened, because no one had the right to touch a boy or girl in some places. Neither should they ask to be touched there. We had done the unit in October and had gone over it a few times since. It provided a measure of relief for the kids to be able to talk about those things, expressing fears about not knowing what to do when someone touched them and it felt "funny."

But Sheila's case, I did not know how to handle. Sex and violence together are not good topics for primary-age disturbed children. Yet, I had to say something. They saw us leave so unexpectedly and they did see the blood. Then they saw me return without Sheila. I told them briefly that Sheila had been hurt at home and I had had to take her to the hospital because of it. Beyond that I said nothing.

The children made her get-well cards the next afternoon when I said I had called the hospital and Sheila was in the children's unit and feeling better. Poignant, brightly crayoned messages piled up in the correction basket. The event, however, affected the kids more than I had perceived. At closing time William burst into tears.

"What's wrong?" I asked as I sat down on the floor. The children were gathered around the Kobold's Box with me. William too was there but had suddenly dissolved into tears.

"I'm scared about Sheila. I'm scared she's going to die in the hospital. My grampa went to the hospital once and he died there."

Unexpectedly, Tyler also began to sob. "I miss her. I want her back."

"Hey, you guys," I said. "Sheila's doing really well. That's what I told you after lunch. She's getting better. She won't die or anything."

Tears coursed over Sarah's face although she made no noise. Max began to wail in harmony, although I doubt he had any concept of why everybody else was crying. Even Peter was teary-eyed, despite the fact that he and Sheila were sworn enemies most of the time.

"But you won't let us talk about it," Sarah said. "You never even said Sheila's name all day. It's scary."

"Yeah," Guillermo agreed. "I kept thinking about her all the time and you kept acting like she never was here. I miss her."

I looked at them. Everyone but Freddie and Susannah were in tears. I doubted they were all that loyal to Sheila, but what had happened had frightened everyone. Moreover, it had affected me. I had worried and in attempt to keep things calm I had said nothing. Moreover, in my classroom we had spent the better part of seven-and-a-half months learning openness and putting ourselves in other people's places. They had learned too well perhaps, because I could not disguise things from them.

So normal closing exercises went undone, the Kobold's Box was unopened, while I talked to them, telling them how I felt and why I had not been as honest as I usually was. We sat down on the floor, all of us together, and had a roundtable.

"Some things are kind of hard to talk about," I said. "What happened to Sheila is one of those things."

"How come?" Peter asked. "Don't you think we're old enough? That's what my mom always says when she don't want to tell me stuff."

I smiled. "Sort of. And sort of because some things are just hard to talk about. I don't even know why. I guess because they scare us. Even us big people. And when big people get scared about things, they don't like to talk about them. That's one of the problems with being big."

The kids were watching me. I looked at them. Each of them, individually. Tyler with her long, ghoulish throat scars. Beautiful black-skinned Peter. Guillermo, whose eyes never really looked anywhere, even when he was paying attention. Rocking, finger-twiddling Max. Sarah. William. Freddie. And my fairy child, Susannah.

"Remember I told you that Sheila got hurt at home. And remember back when we were talking about the ways people can touch you? I was telling you how sometimes people want to put their hands places on a little kid's body that they have no right to touch."

"Yeah, like down where it's private on you, huh?" said William.

I nodded. "Well, someone in Sheila's family touched her where he shouldn't have and when Sheila got unhappy about it, he hurt her."

Foreheads wrinkled. Their eyes were intent. Even Max stopped rocking.

"What did he do to her?" William asked.

"Cut her." As I listened to myself tell these kids, I wondered if I was doing the right thing. Instinctively I felt I was. Our relationship was grounded in the truth, however bad it might be. Moreover, I could not believe knowing could be worse than not knowing, nor worse than the many things these children had seen already. The fact that nothing in their lives was so bad that it could not be talked about had been a cornerstone in this room. Yet, deep inside of me nagged the knowledge that once again I was breaking the rules that I had been taught, overstepping the boundaries of proven educational and psychological practice. And as in all other times I had done that, the worry came that this occasion might be my downfall, that this time I might hurt more than I helped. The war between safety and honesty raged once more.

"Who done it to her?" asked Guillermo. "Was it her father?"

"No. Her uncle."

"Her Uncle Jerry?" Tyler asked.

I nodded.

For a minute there was silence. Then Sarah shrugged.

"Well, at least it wasn't her father."

"That don't make it any better, Sarah," Tyler replied.

"Yeah, it does," Sarah answered. "When I was little, before I came to school, my father sometimes he'd come in my room when my mother was at work and . . ." she paused, looked from Tyler to me, then down at the rug. "Well, he done that kind of stuff. It's worse when it's your father, I think."

"Let's not talk about this anymore, okay?" William said. Fear had creased his brow. He wrung his hands.

"No, I wanna," Sarah said. "I want to know how Sheila is."

"No," William said again. Tears returned to his eyes.

"You're scared, William," Guillermo stated. "What are you scared of?"

I reached a hand out. "Why don't you come over here and sit with me."

He rose and came over. I put an arm around him.

"This is a scary thing to talk about, isn't it?"

He nodded. "There's dust under my bed sometimes if my mom doesn't use the vacuum."

"William, that's off the subject," Peter said.

"That dust scares me. Sometimes I think maybe that used to be people. Maybe it's dead people under my bed."

"That's stupid."

"No, sir. It says right in the Bible, Peter, that you came from dust and you turn to dust after you die. It says so. My mom showed it to me. You ask Torey."

"I don't think that's what the Bible means, William," I said.

"And that might have been people under there, that dust. Might have been my grandpa after he went to the hospital. He might be under my bed now. Maybe it's Sheila."

"No, it's not Sheila. Sheila isn't dead, Will. She's in the hospital and she's going to get better," I replied.

"Torey?" Tyler asked.

"Yes?"

"How come Sheila's uncle did that to her? She just told us the other day that he was nice and played with her. How come he cut her?"

I regarded her. I did not have an answer. No matter how long I waited, an answer did not come to me. "I don't know, Ty."

"Did he have problems?" Sarah asked. "Like my father? They put him in the ward at the state hospital 'cause he had problems. That's what my mother told me. He never came back."

"Yes, I guess you could say he had problems. He didn't understand the right way to touch little girls. Or rather, I suspect he understood, but sometimes people do things without thinking first. They just do what sounds good to them at the moment."

"Is he going to go to the state hospital like my father?"

200

"I don't know. It's against the law to hurt people."

"When's Sheila coming back?" Peter asked.

"As soon as she's better."

"Will she be the same?"

"What do you mean?" I asked.

Peter frowned. "Well, if she got cut down there will she be the same?"

"I'm still not following you, Peter. Explain what you mean."

He hesitated, glanced nervously around the group, back at me. "Can I say some dirty words? I got to so you'll know what I'm talking about. I need to use dirty words."

I nodded. "This is different than yelling them at people. They aren't dirty when they mean something. Go a-head."

Again a hesitation. "Well, down there, that's a girl's cunt, isn't it?"

"Yeah."

"And down there, that's where a girl goes to the bath-room. Well, what if he cut her there? That's where babies come out. What if he cut her there?"

I still did not have the exact question Peter was asking. I decided to turn the question back on him to see if I could pull further information out of him. "What if he did cut her, Peter? What do you think would happen?"

His eyes widened with anxiety. "What if she grows up and has babies?"

"What if she does?"

There were tears in his eyes. "She might crap on them when they're being born." His mouth pulled down in a sob. "That's what my mom done to me. That's why I'm crazy."

"Oh, Peter, that's not true," I said.

He came crawling over on his hands and knees. I was sitting cross-legged on the floor with William against my right side. Peter laid his head in my lap. "Yes, it is."

"No, it isn't. I don't know where you got that idea, but it's wrong."

"Peter, you're not crazy," William said. "Nobody's really crazy. That's just a word. Isn't it, Torey? Just a word. And nobody's a word."

We talked a long time. The bell to go home rang, the buses came and went and we talked. About sexual abuse. About Sheila. About ourselves.

Afterward, I loaded all eight of them into the hatch of my car and drove them home. We never lost the seriousness of the discussion. Even in the car, the questions kept coming. No one ever kidded or made a joke or goofed off. The things we had to talk about were not funny to anyone. The need to talk about them surpassed all other needs that afternoon. And all our differences.

After I had dropped the other children off I collected the get-well notes and a few books I knew Sheila especially liked, and headed for the hospital. She had been placed in an observation room right off the nurses' station and the doorway I was to use was pointed out to me. I entered.

She was alone in the large room with glass windows on one whole wall, like a cage at the zoo. She was lying in a crib with high metal sides. An IV dangled above one post and next to it a unit of blood. The arm that the needles were in was tied to a rung of the crib with a restraint to immobilize it. She looked so young and small.

Tears filled my eyes before I could stop them and they spilled over my cheeks. The only thing I could think of was why had they put her in a crib? Sheila had a lot of dignity for a little kid. I knew that would humiliate her. I knew she would be embarrassed to have me see her in it. Why hadn't they given her a bed like a nearly seven-year-old child should have? Not a crib. Cribs were for babies.

Sheila turned her head toward me when I entered. In

silence she regarded me. "Don't cry, Torey," she said softly. "It don't hurt much. Really it don't."

Humble in the presence of such courage, I stared at her.
"Why did they put you in a crib?" I asked, my mind blank.
I let down the side nearest me and touched her free hand.
"You shouldn't be in a crib."

"I don't mind really," she said. I knew that was not true.
We had been friends long enough for me to know the extent of her carefully guarded sense of self. She smiled softly, as if I were the one to be comforted, and reached up to
touch my face. "Don't cry, Torey. I don't mind."

"It makes me feel better. You scared me so much and I
was so worried about you, Sheil. It makes me feel better to
cry a little bit and I can't help it."

"It don't really hurt bad." Her eyes had lost some of
their expression. Perhaps the medication was causing the
glassy effect. "But I do get sort of scared sometimes. Just a
little bit. Like last night, I didn't know where I was at.
That was kind of scary. But I didn't cry none or anything.
And pretty soon the nurse comed over and talked to me.
She be right nice to me. But I still be a little scared. I
wanted my Pa."

"I bet so. We'll see if we can't get someone to be with
you when you get scared."

"I want my Pa."

"I know, honey. And he'll be here when he can."

"No sir. He don't like hospitals none."

"Well, we'll see."

"I want you to stay with me."

I nodded. "I will as much as I can. And Anton will come
sometimes too. And I know Chad will want to. He's been
asking all day about how you are. We'll do the best we can.
I don't want you to get scared, love. I'll try my hardest to
help."

She turned her head away from me for a moment and
looked up at the IV. "My arm hurts some." Her eyes wan-

dered back to me and suddenly the hurt and the fear were alive in them. Her face contorted in a grimace. "I want you to hold me," she whimpered. "My arm hurts fierce bad and I do be so lonely. I want you to stay here and hold me and not go away."

"Kitten, I don't think they would like me to hold you. I think it'd mess up all the stuff they have hooked up to you. I can hold your hand, if you want."

"No," she whined. "I want you to hold me. I hurt."

I smoothed back her hair and leaned close to her. "Oh I know you do, sweetheart, and I want to. But we can't."

She looked at me a long moment and then that glaze of control filmed over her eyes. She took a deep, shuddery breath and that was all. Once again she was passive, locking up one more thing she could not bear to feel.

"I brought some books. Maybe you'd like me to read to you. It might take your mind off things."

Slowly she nodded. "Read me about the fox and the little prince and his rose."

CHAPTER

17

Sheila remained in the hospital through the rest of the month of April. During that time her uncle was arraigned and tried for sexual abuse. He returned to prison. Her father didn't go to see her the entire time she was hospitalized, pleading a phobia of hospitals. Instead he drowned his fears at Joe's Bar and Grill. I went every night after school to see her and usually stayed through dinner. Chad came up most evenings and played checkers with Sheila even after I had left. Anton visited regularly and Whitney was allowed on the unit for a couple brief stops even though she was underage. Oddly, even Mr. Collins came to see Sheila and I surprised him one Saturday afternoon playing a game with her. To the astonishment of the hospital staff Sheila turned out to be one of the most popular children on the unit with a whole entourage of well-wishers coming and going each day. I was thankful for the interest shown in her because much as I wanted to, I could not afford to spend more than a couple of hours up there every night.

Yet I knew that I probably would have stayed longer if no one else had shown up.

In a way the hospitalization was good for her. Being so physically attractive and having come through such a harrowing experience, she was the darling of the nursing staff. They showered her with attention. Sheila responded delightedly. She was cheerful and cooperative in most instances and, of course, never cried. Best of all, she was getting three balanced meals a day and was beginning to put on much-needed weight. It was not until the very end of her hospital stay that she began to get restless, not wanting to stay in bed, and getting cranky with those who insisted she did. Her emotional problems seemed totally eclipsed by this event. Certainly for as severely disturbed a child as she had been, there was almost no evidence of her acting up in the hospital. To the contrary the nurses were forever commenting on her outstanding behavior. This concerned me. While it made the stay more pleasant for everyone, I knew neither the hospitalization itself nor the reason she had gone in were anything other than vastly traumatic events. I feared that like her absurd ability to keep from crying, she had sublimated this misery, making it seem as if it had never happened. That was to me a greater indicator of the seriousness of her disturbance than anything else.

In the meantime the rest of the children had adjusted to life without Sheila. We enjoyed the April sunshine and the resurrecting earth around us. Things calmed down and, except for weekly letters to her, Sheila ceased to be a major topic of conversation.

During this time I learned for certain that my class would be disbanded permanently. A number of things had contributed to that situation and I had been aware of all of them. First, the district was doing some shuffling within itself and now felt that placement of many disturbed children such as Freddie and Susannah could be accomplished without maintaining another separate class as had been done this year. Second, the others had all made enough progress that, realistically, they could go into a less restrictive placement. Perhaps most important, rumblings were coming down of a new bill in Congress on mainstreaming handicapped children back into the normal classrooms. In response to this federal law, a number of special rooms were being eliminated altogether in an attempt to free some specially trained teachers for consultation to the regular classroom. As I had the most severe level, those in charge of placement were most interested in eliminating my level entirely. And last, and certainly most consequential, money was running tight. Maintaining children in classes like mine was very expensive. The low ratio of children to teachers, the greater training of the teachers who could thus command higher salaries, the special equipment all cost a great deal of money. The district could not afford to run as many special classes in the future as they had this year.

While I was saddened by the news, it was not unexpected. My sadness was only the same one I felt every year as it drew to a close and I wished we could start all over. In fact I had my own personal plans. The school district had offered me another position; however, I had applied to graduate school and had been accepted. I already possessed a master's degree in special education and my regular teaching certificate. But I did not have full certification for teaching special children. While the state was not yet requiring this full certificate in addition to the regular certification, I could see it on the horizon. Too many good teachers I had known had lost their jobs simply because they had not been able to keep up with the certification requirements. If the day came and I found myself in a job that I did not want to give up to go back to school, I would not want to be caught short of credits. This job was essentially over; I wouldn't be able to go back to the same kids and the same class in the fall anyway; so now seemed as good a time as any to return to school.

I was also toying with the idea of pursuing a doctorate. I had become increasingly involved in research during the previous years and had been appalled by the huge gaps in research in the areas of childhood withdrawal and depression.

While I loved teaching, the months just past had been filled with soul-searching about my future. In addition, Chad was renewing pressure to marry and settle down. That night after the trial with Sheila had affected him and he now openly acknowledged he wanted a family. Yet I was getting restless. When the acceptance from the university had come on April sixth, I had agreed to go, which meant when school let out in June, I would be moving half a continent away from Chad and Sheila and a place that had given me several of the best years of my life.

Sheila returned to school early in May. She came back with the same extroverted gusto she had displayed in the hospital, giving the distinct impression that she had been on an extended holiday. As I watched her resume her old place in the class I was more unsettled than ever by her attitude. One could not swallow that much pain and get away with it. I feared she might be even more disturbed than I had thought; that perhaps she was slipping off into some fantasy to protect herself from the horrors of the real world. But throughout the day and then the next couple of days she gave no indication of any problem. For all the world she seemed like some normal child who had stopped by to participate in our classroom activities.

By the end of the week the veneer was beginning to wear thin. The old hassles had begun to raise their heads again. I started demanding more out of her and she found herself making mistakes. This put her in a sulk for a few hours on Thursday. The other kids were readjusting to her return and were not giving her the attention to which she had grown so accustomed. This provoked a bit of angry fussing when things did not go her way. But most important she slowly began to talk to me again. That, I decided, was what had been missing. While she kept up a constant chatter in school and after, she never really did say anything. It was all just prattle over the immediate situation. Unlike before when she was open and voluntarily brought up her feelings, now she spoke only about safe things. Bit by bit, however, a statement would creep in that mirrored what was below the carefree surface.

She had returned to school wearing the old overalls and T-shirt. The blood stains were still visible and after having gained weight in the hospital, Sheila was too large to wear the overalls comfortably. They were too short and too tight. I wondered what had become of the red-and-white dress, so finally on Friday evening after school, I asked. Sheila was helping me cut out figures for the bulletin board; so we sat together at one table, the work spread between us.

She pondered my question a moment. "I ain't gonna wear it no more."

"How come?"

"That day . . ." she paused, concentrating on her cutting. "That day my Unca Jerry . . . Well, he says it be a right pretty dress. He could feel under it. He done it before but this time he wouldn't stop. He kept putting his hands under there. So I ain't wearing it no more. I ain't having nobody feel there."

"Oh."

"Besides, it got all blooded up. My Pa, he throwed it away when I was gone."

A long, heavy silence fell between us. I did not know what to say next so I just continued to work on what I was cutting out. Sheila looked up. "Torey?"

"Hmm?"

"Do you and Chad ever do that stuff together? Like Unca Jerry did to me?"

"What your uncle did to you, no one should do. That was wrong. Having intercourse is something grown-up people do with each other. It's not something kids do. And no one ever uses a knife. That was wrong."

"I know what it is. My Pa, he brings home ladies sometimes and does that. He thinks I be asleep but I ain't. It makes a lot of noise, so I wake up. I seen them. I know what it is."

Her eyes were cloudy. "Is it really love?"

I took a long breath. "You're not really old enough, Sheil, to understand altogether. Sometimes it's called love. But it isn't exactly. It's sex. Usually two people do it when they really love one another and then it's good and they like it. But sometimes people just do it but they don't love each other. It's still sex, but it's not love. Sometimes a person forces another to do it. And that's always wrong."

"I ain't never gonna love anybody if I have to do that."

"You're too little. Your body isn't ready to do those sorts of things yet, so it hurts you. But it isn't love, Sheil. Love is different. Love is a feeling. What happened was a really wrong thing. No one should do that to a little girl. It hurt you because it was not something that should have happened. You're too little."

"Then why did he do it to me, Torey?"

Putting down the figure I had been cutting, I pushed back my hair. "You're asking me awfully hard questions, sweetheart."

"But I can't understand that. I liked Unca Jerry. He played with me. Why did he want to hurt me?"

"I don't really know. Sometimes people just lose control. Like remember you and me back in Februrary when I went to the conference? I mean we sort of did that to each other. It's something that happens."

Sheila stopped her cutting, letting the paper and scissors

drop through her fingers to the tabletop. For a long, silent moment she sat motionless, staring at the paper and scissors and at her still spread hands. Her chin quivered. "Things never are the way you really want them to be, are they?" She did not look at me.

I did not respond, not knowing how to.

She lay her face down on the table in a gesture of defeat. "I don't wanna be me anymore. I just don't."

"Sometimes it's hard," I replied, still not knowing what to say but feeling the need to say something.

She turned her head so she could see me but let it remain on the table midst the shambles of her cutting. Her eyes were dull. "I wanna be somebody like Susannah Joy and have lots of nice dresses to wear. I don't wanna be here. I wanna be a regular kid and go to a regular kid's school. I just do not want to be me anymore. I'm sick of it. But I can't figure out how to do it."

I watched her. Somehow I always think I have finally lost my innocence. I always think, my God, I've seen the worst, the next time it isn't going to hurt me as bad. And I always find it does.

CHAPTER

18

I decided as a last major activity of the school year, our class would put on a Mother's Day program. One of the greatest tragedies to befall special education is that the special children almost never get to participate in the traditional fun activities of regular children. For the special kids, just getting through from day to day seems to be enough of an achievement. But I always hated that. Just "getting through from day to day" makes for a life hardly worth living. We all know it's the icing and not the cake that causes most people to eat cake. So I tried to make up for it by creating some of the more popular activities of the regular school program in our room.

We had had an assembly for the families in October that had gone off . . . not too badly. So I decided that was just what we needed to perk up May. To devise a program that children like Susannah and Freddie and Max could participate in was no easy task. But with the help of my parents' group we put together a few songs, a poem or two, and a skit full of the traditional spring flowers and mushrooms that always seem to bloom in small children's plays.

The kids were all excited about the event, except that Peter wanted to do a more ambitious skit. Most of them had just seen *The Wizard of Oz* on its umpteenth yearly run on television and were determined we should do that. I explained that with only five reliable actors that might be a bit difficult especially since no one except Sheila could read much. Peter in particular was adamant that he would not be any woodland flower and instead he wanted to be a Tin Man. Sarah agreed. Out on the playground they had been playing *Wizard of Oz* and she thought it went very nicely. I finally gave in, stating that if Peter and Sarah could develop a rough skit that would include parts for Freddie and the others, and Guillermo could play a good part despite his handicap, I would let them do it.

So we began practicing. Actually we had started working on the songs back in April, but Peter's change in script did not occur until Sheila was back with us in May. Obviously, our Mother's Day play was going to be a little late. I was eternally grateful for Sheila and her agile memory. She had a reasonable singing voice and could remember anything she was given. So I padded the program with her and with Max, whose disturbance had equipped him with the ability to repeat vast quantities of materials, although not necessarily on demand.

I had asked Sheila if she wanted her father to attend. Many of the other fathers were coming, since although the play was billed as a Mother's Day show, it was one of the only opportunities parents had of seeing their kids in a joyful and frivolous school activity. Besides, I wanted all the families to feel free to attend any of our school functions. So I asked Sheila about her father, knowing that if she wanted him, special arrangements would have to be made to get him there.

She screwed up her face a moment in consideration. "He wouldn't come."

"Anton could go out and get him, if he wanted to come. As long as we know ahead of time, it wouldn't be hard."

"I don't think he'd come anyways. He don't like school stuff too good."

"But he could see you in the play and singing your song. I bet your Dad would be proud to see you do all those things." I sat down on one of the little chairs so that I would be more at her level. "You know, Sheil, you've really come a long ways in here since January. You're like a different girl. You don't get into trouble nearly as much as then."

She nodded her head emphatically. "I used to wreck stuff all the time. But I don't anymore. And I used to not talk when I got mad. I used to be a bad girl."

"You've done a lot better, alright. And you know what? I bet your Pa would like to see how well you've done. I think he'd be proud of you because I don't think he realizes what an important girl you are in this class."

Sheila ruminated a moment while studying me through squinted eyes. "Maybe he would come."

I nodded. "Maybe he would."

The morning of the program Chad arrived in the classroom carrying a big box. Anton was setting up props and Sheila was brushing her teeth. "What are you doing here?" I asked, surprised to see him.

"I came to see Sheila."

Excitedly, Sheila leaped down from the chair she was standing on and ran over.

"Spit out your toothpaste first," Chad warned her. She scurried back to the sink to return in seconds, toothpaste still outlining her lips. "I understand you're going to have a play today."

"Yeah!" she cried, bouncing around him in excitement.

214

"I'm gonna be Dorothy and Torey's gonna braid my hair up in pigtails. An' I'm gonna sing a song and say a poem, and my Pa's gonna be here and *watch* me!" She was out of breath after the exclamation, having said it so rapidly. "Are you gonna come?"

"Nope. But I brought you a good-luck present for your debut."

Sheila's eyes widened. "Me?"

"Yes, you."

In glee she hugged his knees with such gusto that Chad wobbled unsteadily.

I knew what was inside the box—a long dress, red, white and blue with lace around the front placket. A beautiful and expensive dress that Chad had brought back with him from a recent trip to New York. I had told Chad about what had happened to the other dress and about Sheila's feeling that dresses made her too vulnerable. For that reason he had bought a long dress instead of a short one. The night he had come in to show me the dress, his eyes were all sparkly like a little boy's. I could just picture him in the New York stores, his tall football player's frame towering over miniature racks of little girls' dresses; his arms spread wide attempting to describe for the salesclerk the special little girl back in Iowa for whom he needed that very special dress. Chad had great confidence that he had found just what Sheila would dream for. That it would erase the horror of the last month and recapture at least a little of the magic we had found the night of the court hearing.

Sheila ripped open the paper and lifted the lid on the box. Momentarily she hesitated, gazing at the tissue paper still partly obscuring the contents. Very, very slowly she lifted the dress out of the box, her eyes huge and round. She looked at Chad who knelt on the floor next to her.

Then she let it drop back into the box and lowered her head. "I ain't wearing dresses no more," she whispered hoarsely.

Chad turned to me in bewilderment, his own disappointment clear in his face. I came over and knelt down with them. "Don't you think it might be okay this once?"

She shook her head.

I looked at Chad. "I think we need a minute alone, if you'll excuse us." I rose and took Sheila to the far side of the room behind the animal cages. I knew the confusion that must be filling Chad's head. I knew as well that Sheila must have been in torment. She loved pretty things so much and that was a stunning dress Chad had brought, far lovelier than the red-and-white one he had gotten her in March. Yet, what had happened to her was too fresh, the hurt too raw.

Her face contorted into a teary-eyed grimace by the time I had her behind the cages. She pressed her fingers to her temples in an effort to keep the tears back, but for the first time since she had come to my class she was unable to. Over her cheeks coursed rivulets and she dissolved into sobs.

The time had finally come. The time I had been waiting for through all these long months that I knew sooner or later had to occur. Now it was here.

For several minutes I sat with her behind the cages. She had surprised me so much by actually crying that for a moment I did nothing but look at her. Then I gathered her into my arms, hugging her tightly. She clutched onto my shirt so that I could feel the dull pain of her fingers digging in to my skin. When it became apparent that she had lost all control and was not going to regain it, I picked her up and came out of hiding. I needed to go somewhere where the other kids coming in and all the preparations for the program would not interrupt us.

"What did I do?" Chad asked worriedly, his gentle face distorted with concern. "I didn't mean . . ."

I shook my head. "Don't worry about it. Put the dress

216

over there. I'll get back to you after a bit, okay?" I turned to Anton. "Can you take care of things for a while?"

The only place I could think of where we would be entirely alone and undisturbed was the book closet. Attempting to manipulate a kiddie chair along with me while carrying Sheila, I unlocked the closet and went in, securing the door behind me. I put the chair against a stack of reading books and sat down, shifting Sheila to make her more comfortable.

She sobbed hard, but not in the hysterical manner in which she had started. But she cried and cried and cried. I simply held her and rocked the chair back and forth on its rear legs, feeling my arms and chest get damp from the tears and her hot breath and the smallness of the room. At first my mind was busy, wondering how Anton was managing alone with all the kids so high about the play, thinking about the program itself and how it would go, mulling over Sheila's situation. After a while my mind ran dry and I just sat and rocked, thinking of nothing in particular, except that my arms were getting tired.

Ultimately the tears stopped. Sheila had been reduced to a quivery, soggy lump. All her muscles had relaxed from exhaustion. The little room was humid and overly warm and both of us were awash with the saliva and tears and mucus that crying always brings. I smoothed her damp hair back from her face and wondered what had happened in her head to make Chad's gift the final snapping point.

"Do you feel a little better?" I asked gently.

She did not reply but lay against me. Her body convulsed with the hiccupy gasps and shudders that are the aftermath of hard crying. "I'm gonna throw up."

My teacher's reflexes came instantly into action and I let us out of the book closet and into the girls' restroom around the corner. When she came out of the toilet stall she looked battle-weary, her face red and swollen, her steps tottery. Faint lines of toothpaste were still visible on her chin. I picked her up.

"Sometimes that happens," I said as we returned to our haven in the closet. "Sometimes when you cry real hard, it makes you sick."

She nodded. "I know."

We had only the one chair between us but she willingly clung to my lap, leaning heavily against my soggy shirt. We sat for a while saying nothing.

"I can hear your heart beat," she said at last.

I touched her head gently. "Do you think we ought to go back to class? It must be the middle of math period by now."

"No."

Again silence drifted around us. A million things were running through my head, none of them finding words.

"Tor?"

"Yes?"

"Why did he buy me that dress?"

Across my mind trickled the thought that perhaps Sheila believed Chad had gotten her the dress for the same reason that her Uncle Jerry had told her he liked her red-and-white one. What a horrible thought that must have been for her; safe, kind, lovable Chad wanting her in a dress so he could have the same access to her that Uncle Jerry had had. It was no more than speculation on my part, but it made me certain not to reply that Chad had done it for "love."

"Because I told him your other one was ruined. He thought you might like something pretty to wear in the play." I ran my fingers through her silky hair. "I forgot to tell him you weren't wearing dresses anymore. That was my fault."

She did not respond.

"You know, don't you, that Chad would never do things to you like your Uncle Jerry did. He knows you shouldn't do those things to little girls. He didn't bring the dress to hurt you. He wouldn't ever hurt you."

"I know it. I didn't mean to cry."

"Oh sweetie, that's okay. Chad knows that things have been hard for you. No one minds that you cry. Sometimes that's the only way to make things better. We all know that. Nobody cares if you cry."

"I wanted the dress," she said softly, pausing. "I wanted it. I just got scared, that's all. And I couldn't stop."

"That's okay. It really is. Chad knows what little girls are like. We all do."

"I don't know why I cried. I don't know what happened."

"Don't worry about it."

The pressure of being gone so long when I knew the children would be excited about the play was getting the better of me. "Sheil, I have to go back to the room. The kids are all there and Anton's by himself. I have two ideas for you. You can come back with me or maybe if you don't feel up to it you could go down to the nurse's office and rest awhile."

"Do I gotta go home 'cause I throwed up?"

"No. You're not sick or anything."

She slid off my lap. "Can I rest a little? I'm tired."

I explained to the secretary that Sheila needed to lie down but didn't need to be sent home and I would be back in half an hour at recess to check on her. The secretary gave us a blanket and I settled Sheila down on one of the cots.

"Torey?" she asked as I tucked the blanket around her. "Do you suppose I could still have the dress? I wouldn't really mind wearing it."

I nodded and smiled. "Yeah. Chad left it for you."

I came back to the office at recess time and Sheila was

asleep. She slept the rest of the morning until I came down and woke her for lunch.

With good reason both L. Frank Baum and Judy Garland probably turned in their graves that May afternoon. Except for bearing the same title and characters as the famed story, the children's production had little in common with the book or the movie.

Sheila played Dorothy mostly by virtue of her ability to think fast and make up dialogue quickly. Both Tyler and Sarah had wanted the part, which resulted in some not-too-good-natured arguing for a while and a near-split of the Sarah–Peter production team. But Peter seemed to have authority in casting parts and he selected Sheila. Tyler was given the ignominious task of portraying all of the wicked witches. Sarah was transformed into the Scarecrow. William played the Cowardly Lion and Guillermo was the Wizard himself. Oddly, Peter selected Susannah to play the Good Witch Glenda, another fought-over part. The only reason for his choice I could think of was that Susie was so delicately pretty that she made a very realistic fairy even without a costume; but Peter had his own reasons that he would not disclose. Freddie was the sole Munchkin and Max a lone winged monkey. Peter, of course, was the Tin Man.

Only parents, teachers or folks with an uncanny love of unintentionally funny children would have properly appreciated *The Wizard of Oz* as produced by my class. Sheila had fully recovered from her troubles in the morning and had donned the dress Chad brought, refusing to wear the costume Whitney had made for her. Refreshed by a two-hour nap, she bounced all over as she spoke, knocking over scenery and props. Freddie on the other hand would not move. He simply sat in his place, a ridiculous Munchkin hat stuck on his head, and waved at his mother in the

audience. His fat legs tripped Sheila on one occasion causing her to fall into his lap. At last Anton had to drag him
off when his part was over. The Cowardly Lion was type-
casting for William and perhaps because he knew the feeling of fear so well, he gave the truest performance of all,
quivering and quaking about on the stage. Most surprising,
Susannah Joy did quite well as Glenda. She drifted onto the
stage and floated around as out of touch with reality as
always, muttering to herself in a high-pitched little squeak.
But in the setting of the play, it looked astonishingly natural.

The only major problem suffered during the course of
the play was when Sheila got long-winded in her dialogue
and often felt the need to narrate parts of the play in case
the audience hadn't figured out for themselves what was
happening. This left everyone else standing around dumbly while Sheila launched into lengthy monologues. Finally
Peter walked out onto the stage during one of her solilo-
quies and told her to get off.

The remainder of the program was delightful. No one
forgot their lines in the poems and the songs were sung
with rousing, albeit off-key, gusto. Afterwards we had
cookies and punch while the children showed their parents
things they had done in school.

Sheila's father did come. Dressed in the tattered suit that
buckled over his tremendous stomach and reeking, once
again, of cheap after-shave, he had eased his mammoth
bulk into one of the tiny chairs. All through the program I
kept praying it would not break as it creaked ominously
with his weight shifts. For the first time I saw him smile at
his daughter when she came bounding over to him after
the first performance. He had had the kindness to come
sober and appeared to enjoy being with us. He never commented about Sheila's new dress until I finally came over
and told him toward the end of the party that Chad had

221

bought it for her. He regarded his daughter carefully and then turned to me, pulling out a worn wallet from his coat pocket.

"I ain't got much here," he said quietly. I was terror-stricken, thinking that he was going to offer to pay for the dress and knowing it was obviously an expensive item. But he had other ideas. "If I give you money, would you take Sheila to buy some everyday clothes? I know she needs something and, well, you need a woman for that kind of thing . . ." his voice trailed off and he averted his eyes. "If I keep hold of the money . . . well, I got a little problem, you know. I was wondering . . ." He had ten dollars in his hand.

I nodded. "Yes, I will. I'll take her out after school next week."

He smiled at me, his lips pressed tight together in a faint, sad smile. Then before I knew it, he was gone. I stared at the bill. Not much clothing could be bought for that anymore. But he had tried. In his own way he had tried to make sure that the money went where it was supposed to before it went for a bottle. I liked the man in spite of myself, and I was flooded with pity. Sheila was not the lone victim; her father undoubtedly needed and deserved as much care as she did. Once there had been a little boy whose pain and suffering were never relieved. Now there was a man. If only there could be enough people to care, enough people to love without reservations, I thought sadly.

CHAPTER

19

Suddenly, only three weeks remained until school was through. My head was awhirl with all the things that had not been done. And there were plenty of them. I was also beginning to plan my move, which would occur shortly after school terminated. My evenings were filled with packing boxes and cleaning out all the garbage I had accumulated over the years.

I had not told the children yet that the class was to be disbanded. Some of them already knew that they would be returning to less restrictive placements the next year. William was going to a regular fifth grade class with resource help. For the last three months he had been going out of the room for both reading and math with a fourth grade class down the hall in the main building. Tyler was also going to a new program. She would still be in a self-contained room most of the time, but she would be closer to the life of a regular student.

We hadn't decided what to do with Sarah yet. Although

she coped nicely in our room, she still withdrew in a larger group. I suspected she would need at least another year in a special class, but she was almost ready. Peter would never leave a special setting, I feared. His behavior continued to deteriorate as a result of increasing neurological destruction. He was too violent and disruptive, his behaviors too impulsive for anything but a tightly structured classroom. Guillermo's family was planning to move. And Max, Freddie and Susannah would all go to special programs. Freddie was being placed in a room for the severly and profoundly retarded, and the teacher hoped he would not be too much of a problem. She had been over to observe him several times to see how his behavior was managed in our class. Max was doing beautifully. He was using much more normal speech and less echolalia. Both he and Susannah were going to a special program for autistic children.

And Sheila? Sheila. I had not spoken with her yet about the impending termination of class. I had put it off because I did not know what would happen when I did tell her. In short, I was scared. She had come a long way from that frightened little lump that was dragged into our room in January; far from the dependent belt-hanger of February. Jimmie had been forgotten and she almost never referred to being put on the highway anymore. But she was fragile. I did not think she would need a special classroom any longer. In fact, I feared she'd be ignored in one because she was so verbal and able to look out for herself. I was afraid that to place her in one now would force her to readopt some negative behavior just to get the share of attention she required. What she needed was simply someone who cared. I was tentatively thinking of suggesting to Ed that she be advanced to third grade, even though she was small, so she would be closer academically and socially to the other children. Despite her emotional problems, she was mature for her age. Besides, I had a good friend teaching third grade on the other side of town. The district would bus her there if requested because it was closer to the migrant camp than my school was and because maintaining her in a regular classroom was much less expensive than in a special one. And Sandy would take good care of Sheila for me. That assurance I needed for myself.

In an attempt to see Sheila into regular classroom life, I decided to mainstream her into a second grade class in our school for math. One of the second grade teachers, Nancy Ginsberg, was a pleasant, dedicated woman who had been among the first to invite my class and me to share activities with her group. So I approached her one afternoon in the lounge and asked if she would be willing to take Sheila for math. I explained that Sheila was considerably advanced beyond second grade math, but I wanted her out of the room for a period or so during the day in order that she could become readjusted to the strain of a regular classroom. Math was her most secure subject, so that seemed the best place to start. Nancy agreed.

"Guess what?" I said to Sheila as we were putting away toys from freetime.

"What?"

"You're going to do something neat from now on. You're going to go into a regular class for part of the day."

She looked up sharply. "Huh?"

"I talked to Mrs. Ginsberg and she said you could come have math in her room each day."

"Like William does?"

"That's right."

She bent back over the pieces of an Erector set she was putting away. "I don't wanna."

"You're just not used to the idea. You'll want to. Just think it'll be a regular class. Remember once, you told me that you wished you were in a regular class? Now you will be."

"I ain't going."

"Why not?"

"This here be my class. I ain't going in nobody else's class."

"It's just for math."

Her nose wrinkled. "But that's my favorite in here. It ain't fair you make me leave my favorite time in here."

"You can have math in here too, if you want. But you'll have math in Mrs. Ginsberg's room too, starting on Monday."

"No, I ain't."

Sheila was not keen on the idea at all. For every reason I had, she had a counter reason. The rest of the day she alternately sulked and stormed, not letting me ever change the subject. By afternoon I had had enough and flatly stated that I had heard all the protests out of her I wanted to hear. She was going, she had two days to get ready and I would do all I could to make the change easier, but she was going.

Sheila stomped her feet angrily and stalked off to rattle the bars on Onions' cage. After listening to the persistent clatter of the cage, which Onions fortunately was not in at the time, I went over and dragged her to the table, giving her the alternative of getting her act together better or sitting in the quiet corner. At that Sheila sprung to her feet and marched defiantly off to the quiet corner. Banging the chair around, she sat.

I let her sit. I went back to helping William with his art project and ignored her. She sat the remainder of the afternoon despite both Anton and my telling her she could leave if she calmed down, and even Sarah's offering to let her help with afternoon snacks.

Since she was obviously interested in making me feel bad, I left her with Anton after school and went down to the teachers' lounge to make lesson plans. If Sheila got into one of her moods, she was best left alone. When I returned just before five, she was lounging on a pillow reading a book.

"You done being mad?" I asked.

She nodded casually, not looking up from the book. "You're going to be sorry you made me go."

"And what is that supposed to mean?"

"I ain't going to be good if I have to go. I'm gonna be bad and she'll send me back here. Then you can't make me leave anymore."

"Sheila," I said in exasperation, "think about that one a while. That's not what you want to do."

"Yes, it is," she replied, still not looking up from her reading.

I glanced at the clock. It was dangerously close to the time when she had to leave. I hated it when she was like this. Coming over to where she was sitting, I dropped on my knees beside her. "What's up, kiddo? Why don't you want to go? I thought you'd like it, being in a regular class again."

She shrugged.

I lifted the book out of her hands so that she had to look at me. "Sheil, I want your thoughts. You know I can't send you in there if you're going to cause trouble. You got me on that one because I don't want Mrs. Ginsberg to have problems. But you can't want to do this."

"I do."

"Sheil . . ."

She finally looked directly at me, her blue eyes fluid. "How come you don't want me in here no more?"

"I never said that. I want you in here. Of course I want you in here. But I want you to learn what's happening in a real class too so you can go back to one."

"I already know what a real class is like. That's where I was before I came here. I wanna be in this crazy class."

The clock edged toward five. "Sheil, listen, we're out of

227

time. You're going to have to run to catch the bus as it is. I'll talk to you more about it tomorrow.''

Sheila would not discuss it further and she was true to her word. I sent her off on Monday morning for thirty-five minutes in Mrs. Ginsberg's class. Within fifteen minutes Anton had to go retrieve her. She had ripped up papers, thrown pencils and tripped some poor unsuspecting second grader twice her size. Anton came dragging her in kicking and screaming. The second the door shut behind them and they were safely in the classroom, Sheila stopped. A pleased smile touched her lips. I sank into a chair beside Max and covered my eyes while Anton escorted her to the quiet corner.

Because her behavior made mc extremely angry and I did not trust myself for a while, and also because I knew the time had come to discuss the whole matter of what was going to happen to her the next year, I did not confront her immediately about her behavior in Mrs. Ginsberg's room. After I had calmed down I told her she could leave the corner and rejoin us and then I went about our normal routine.

Directly defying me apparently frightened Sheila considerably. The remainder of the day she was oversolicitous toward me, trying to make sure I saw how good she was being. Also, the fact that I did not deal with the infraction except for the quiet-corner stay was novel, and this troubled Sheila even more. She asked me once when I was going to get mad at her. I smiled, not wanting her to think that my sudden indifference was another indicator of my desire to be rid of her. So I told her we'd discuss the matter later when we had more time. But she was nervous the rest of the day, shadowing me from a distance.

I walked out to the buses with the other children after school. When I returned to the room Sheila stood against the far wall by the animal cages, her eyes wide and fearful.

I jerked my head in the direction of one of the tables. "Come over here, kiddo. I think it's time we talked."

Hesitantly she approached, sitting in a chair across the table from me. Her face expressed her wariness, her eyes dilated. "You mad at me?"

"About this morning? I sure was this morning, but I'm not now. No, I just want to find out what is going on with you. I don't really understand why you don't want to go. Last week you refused to talk to me about it. So I just want to find out. You usually have good reasons for what you do; I trust you in that way."

She studied me.

"Well?"

"This here be my class," she replied, falling back on the word "be" which had become almost extinct.

"Yes, it is. I'm not trying to kick you out of it. That's just thirty-five minutes out of a whole day. Besides, I think it's time that you start thinking about a regular class for next year."

"I ain't going in no regular class. This here be my class."

I regarded her a long moment. "Sheil, it's May. The school year will be over in a few weeks. I think it's time to think about next year."

"I'm going to be in here next year."

My heart was sinking. "No," I replied softly.

Her eyes flashed. "I am too! I'll be the baddest kid in the whole world. I'll do terrible things and then they'll make you keep me. They won't let you make me go away."

"Oh Sheil," I wailed.

"I ain't going anywheres else. I'll be bad again."

"It isn't like that, kitten. I'm not kicking you out. God, Sheila, listen to me, would you?" She had her hands over her ears.

She raised her stormy eyes to me. They were angry and hurt-looking, the old flare of revenge glinting in them.

"This class isn't going to be here next year," I said so

229

softly that it came out almost inaudibly. Yet she heard it through her hands.

Like a wave the expression on her face changed and she lowered her hands. The anger drained away leaving her pale. "What d'you mean? Where's it going?"

"This class won't be here. The school district decided they didn't need it. Everybody can go to other classes."

"Didn't need it?" she shouted. "Of course they need it! I need it! I'm still crazy. I need a crazy kidses class. So does Peter. And Max. And Susie. We're all still crazy kids."

"No, Sheil, you're not. I'm not sure you ever were. But you're not now. It's time to stop thinking that."

"Then I will be. I'll do lots of bad stuff again. I ain't going nowhere."

"Sheil, I'm not going to be here either."

Her face froze.

"I'm moving in June. After school is over, I'm going away. It's really hard for me to say that to you, because I know we've gotten to be such good friends. But the time has come. I don't love you any less and I'm not leaving because of anything you did or didn't do. It's a separate decision I made. A grown-up decision."

She continued to look at me. With elbows on the table, her hands were clasped together and she rested her cheek against her fist. Her underwater-colored eyes studied my face without seeing.

"All things end, Sheil. I'm a teacher, so my ending comes in June. We've had terrific times together and I wouldn't have changed it for anything in the world. You've changed so much. And so have I, really. We've grown together and now it's time to see how good the growing was. I think we're ready. You too. I think you're ready to try it on your own. You're strong enough."

Tears suddenly filled her eyes and spilled over, making fast paths over her round cheeks and down to her chin. Yet she remained motionless and unblinking, her face still propped in her hands. I was running out of words to say. I often forgot she was only six. She would not even be seven until July. I forgot because her eyes were so old.

Slowly she lay her hands on the table and lowered her head. She sat a moment, still not wiping away the tears that continued to fall noiselessly. Then she rose and turned away from me, went over to the far side of the room and sat down amidst the pillows on the floor. Once there she covered her face with her hands. Still no sound came from her.

I sat in silence feeling acutely the pain she radiated, which I suppose was my own pain too. Had I gotten too involved, I wondered? Despite her apparent progress, had I let her grow too dependent on me? Would it have been better to have left her as I found her in January and simply taught her, rather than have accustomed her to the everyday trials of loving someone? I had always been a maverick among my colleagues. I belonged to the better-to-have-loved-and-lost school, which was not a popular notion in education. The courses, the professionals, all preached against getting involved. Well, I could not do that. I could not teach effectively without getting involved, and in my heart, because I did belong to the love-and-lost school, when the end came I could leave. It always hurt, and the more I loved a child, the more it hurt. But when the time came that we had to part or I had to honestly give up on the child because I could do no more, I could go. I could do it because I took with me, every time, the priceless memories of what we had had, believing that there is no more one can give another than good memories. Nothing I could do, even if I worked with Sheila the rest of her school career, could ensure happiness for her. Only she could do that. All I could give her would be my love and my time. When the end came, the parting would be just as painful. In the end my efforts would be reduced once more to memories.

Yet in watching her, I worried that there had not been

sufficient time to heal her hurts enough, that she might not be strong enough to tolerate my painful way of teaching. While it was right for me, perhaps I was unfair to her in giving her no choice about it. But what should I have done? My heart ripped with worry that at last I had been given the wrong child, the one I hurt instead of helped. Being a maverick is admissible when one is an academician. When one is a practitioner, it is usually safer to be a conformist.

Slowly I rose and came over to where she sat still noiseless, except for snuffling. "Go away," she stated quietly but firmly through her hands.

"Why? Because you're crying?"

The hands came down and she looked at me briefly. "No." She paused. "Because I don't know what to do."

I sat across from her, arranging a pillow and leaning back on it. For the first time I did not feel like putting my arms around her to soothe away the hurt. Dignity sat as tangible as a cloak about her. We were equals then, not one the older, one the younger. I no longer was the wiser one, the smarter one, the stronger one. We were equal in our humanity.

"How come you ain't staying to make me good?" she asked at last.

"Because it isn't me that makes you good. It's you. I'm only here to let you know that someone cares if you are good or not. That someone cares what happens to you. And it won't matter where I am, I still will always care."

"You're just like my Mama," she said. Her voice was soft and unaccusing, as if she had already resolved how things were and why.

"No, I'm not, Sheil." I regarded her. "Or maybe I am. Maybe leaving you was just as hard for your Mama as it will be for me. Maybe it hurt her that much too."

"She never loved me really. She loved my brother better. She left me on the highway like some dog. Like I didn't even belong to her."

232

"I don't know about that. I don't know anything about your Mother or why she did what she did to you. And really, Sheila, you don't either. All you know is how it felt to you. But your Mama and I are different. I'm not your Mother. No matter how much you want it to be that way, I'm not."

The tears renewed in intensity. She played with the waistband of her pants. "I know that."

"I knew you did. But I know you dreamed. In the same way, I guess I did too at times. But it never was any more than a dream. I'm your teacher and when the school year ends, I'll just be your friend. But I will be your friend. For as long as you want me, I'll always be that."

She looked up. "What I can't figure out is why the good things always end."

"Everything ends."

"Not some things. Not the bad things. They never go away."

"Yes, they do. If you let them, they go away. Not as fast as we'd like sometimes, but they end too. What doesn't end is the way we feel about each other. Even when you're all grown up and somewhere else, you can remember what a good time we had together. Even when you're in the middle of bad things and they never seem to be changing, you can remember me. And I'll remember you."

Unexpectedly she smiled, just a little smile, and rather sadly. "That's 'cause we tamed each other. Remember that book? Remember how the little boy was mad because he'd gone to all that trouble to tame the fox and now the fox was crying 'cause he had to leave?" She smiled in memory, looking within herself, almost unaware of me. The tears had dried upon her cheeks. "And that fox said it had been good anyways because he would always remember the wheat fields. Remember that?"

I nodded.

"We tamed each other, didn't we?"

"We sure did."

"It makes you cry to tame someone, doesn't it? They kept crying in that book and I never 'xactly knew why. I always thought you only cried when someone hit you."

Again I nodded. "You take a chance at crying when you let someone tame you. That seems to be part of being tamed, I guess."

Sheila pressed her lips together and wiped the last traces of tears from her face. "It still hurts a lot though, don't it?"

"Yeah, it sure still does hurt."

CHAPTER

20

Sheila went back to Mrs. Ginsberg's room the next morning and made it through the thirty-five minutes without too much trouble. Our problems were by no means resolved. Despite Sheila's recognition that the school year was ending and that we would no longer be together, she could not accept it gracefully. I doubted that she would in the two weeks left to us. Her behavior became a little less polished as she vacillated between anger at me for leaving and fear that I was going to. She could not separate out clearly that what was happening to us was different from what had happened between her and her mother. Time and time again we had to discuss the issue in far more detail than her previous conversational obsessions had required. She clung to *The Little Prince* as literary proof that people did part and it did hurt and they did cry, but they all still loved each other. The book was never far from her hands at any time and she could quote parts of it from memory. Because it was in print, it seemed to have more validity to her than my words.

She certainly had learned to cry. Most of the next days found her in tears or on the verge of them. Her eyes were almost like leaky faucets after a while; tears streamed over her cheeks even when she was smiling or playing. When questioned about them she often did not know why she was crying. I let the tears run and did not worry about them. So long had passed since she had cried that I believed she had to accustom herself to it, finding the width and breadth of the emotion, and if it helped her to prepare for what lay ahead, so much the better. Slowly the tears began to disappear.

Underneath it all her marvelous core of joy and courage gleamed. This was her hardest task. All else that had happened in her life had not been voluntary and she had had no choice but to let it happen and try to survive in the aftermath. But she knew this was coming and she struggled valiantly to take control of herself. As I watched her coping with her tears, hugging the mauled copy of *The Little Prince* to her chest and relentlessly plaguing me with questions about what was happening and why, I knew she would make it. She was strong; probably stronger than I. My work with the emotionally disturbed had deeply impressed upon me their resilience. Despite many popular notions, they were far from fragile. To have survived at all was testimony of this. Given the tools that so many of us take for granted, given love and support and trust and self-value that we often do not notice when we have it, they go beyond survival to prevail. In Sheila this was self-evident. She would not give up trying.

In the midst of all the flurry over the ending of the school year, my birthday came. We made a big thing about birthdays in our room, partly because most of the children did not get a celebration anywhere else and partly because I like parties. It seemed only reasonable that the kids should get to celebrate Anton's and Whitney's and my birthdays as well. After all, we had all been born too, and I did not have the modesty to pretend it did not matter. So when my birthday came I brought in a big yellow elephant-shaped cake and chocolate ice cream.

The day did not go well. Nothing especially terrible happened, just the little annoying things that kids seem to be best at doing. Peter had gotten in a fight on the bus and arrived with a bloody nose and a grudge. During recess Sarah got mad at Sheila, who in turn got mad at Tyler, who cried. Then Sheila kicked sand on Sarah and she cried. The quiet corner did a boomimg business all day long. However, it wasn't until afternoon that I lost my patience. When Whitney went down to the teachers' lounge for the ice cream, she found out one of the fifth grade classes had mistakenly thought it was theirs. I set the cake out anyway. Peter and William were horsing around with each other while we were getting ready. They had a couple of blocks which they were pretending to juggle. I had asked them to stop but they hadn't. One of the other kids was pulling on my arm and I was momentarily distracted. Then *crash*. William had thrown a block to Peter who, while backing up to catch it, bumped into Sheila sitting on the floor. He fell on her and they both came up swinging. Before I knew it Sheila had one of the blocks poised to throw at Peter. He picked up a chair and flung it angrily in her direction. The chair hit the table, then Max, then the cake. My yellow elephant splattered.

"Okay, you guys, that *is* it!" I shouted. "Every single one of you in your chairs with your heads down."

"But it wan't my fault," Guillermo protested. "I didn't do anything."

"*Everybody.*"

All the kids, even Max and Freddie, found chairs and sat down. Everyone except Sheila.

"It don't be my fault dumb old Peter tripped on me." She was sitting on the floor where Peter had knocked her.

"Get in a chair and put your head down like everybody else. I've had it with the whole lot of you. All you've done all day is bicker. Well, this is where it gets you. Sitting in a chair with your head down."

Sheila remained on the floor.

"Sheila, get up."

With a great sigh she rose and took a chair. Pulling it over next to Tyler, she sat and put her head down.

I looked at them. What a ragtag lot. Whitney and Anton were picking cake out of the carpet. Anton rolled his eyes when I came over. I smiled wearily. What I really felt like doing was crying. For no particular reason except that I had wanted a special day and had gotten an ordinary one. And for my yellow elephant cake that had taken so much time to make and ended up being ground into the rug.

When I turned around to look at the kids, Peter had one eye peering over the side of his arm. I pointed a finger at him and gave him the evil eye. He covered his face again. I looked at the clock and watched the second hand revolve.

"Okay, you guys, if you can act like human beings you can get up. There's about ten minutes left. Help pick up the rest of the cake and then find something quiet to do. I better not hear one single word of fighting."

Sheila remained at the table with her head down.

"Sheil, you can get up."

She remained unmoving, her head in her arms. I came over to her and sat down in a chair beside her. "I'm not so mad anymore. You can get up and play."

"Uh-uh," she said. "This here's my birthday present for you. I ain't gonna be no trouble for the rest of the day."

After school Whitney took Sheila out and Anton and I went down to the teachers' lounge. I was sitting in the one comfortable chair, my head back, my feet up on the table, my arm over my eyes.

"What a hell of a day," I said. When Anton did not

respond I sat up and opened my eyes. He was gone. I had not even heard him leave. Oh, well, I leaned back again. I almost fell asleep.

"Tor?"

I looked up. Anton was back, standing over my chair.

"Happy Birthday." He handed me a fat envelope.

"Hey, you shouldn't have done anything. That's the deal around here."

He grinned. "Open it."

Inside was a crazy cartoon card with a green snake on it. Out fell a piece of folder paper.

"What's this?" I asked.

"My present to you."

I opened the paper. It was the photostated copy of a letter.

Dear Mr. Antonio Ramirez:

With great pleasure Cherokee County Community College announces that you have been chosen as one of the recipients of the Dalton E. Fellows Scholarship.

Congratulations. We look forward to seeing you in our program this fall.

I looked up at him. Even though he was trying, he could not keep the smile on his lips in check. It spread from ear to ear. I wanted to congratulate him. To tell him how much this piece of paper pleased me. I said nothing. We just stared at each other. And smiled.

I had called Ed about Sheila's future placement and we held a team meeting. I continued to hold out for placing Sheila with my friend, Sandy McGuire, at Jefferson Elementary School. Sandy was a young, sensitive teacher whom I could trust not to lose Sheila in the crowd. She had talked to me about Sheila a number of times when I had first had the notion that Sheila might be ready to go back to a normal setting.

239

At first Ed did not favor the plan. He disliked advancing children ahead of their chronological peer group. Moreover, Sheila was a small child for her age. Most of the eight- and nine-year-olds would be half a head above her. We did a lot of soul-searching. She was at least two grades ahead of the second graders academically and she was smaller than they were as well. In her case there were no perfect solutions. I was more in favor of placing her with a teacher I could trust to continue supporting her emotional growth than worrying about her size or IQ. Clearly, she would never be normal academically, so there was no point in providing a source of new trouble. I feared that Sheila's unchained mind would go so unchallenged in second grade, that she would get into trouble just keeping herself occupied. In the end the team agreed to try Sheila in Sandy's room. She would also get two hours a day in a resource room to help meet her emotional needs and her advanced academic status.

The second to the last week of school I told Sheila she would be at Jefferson the following year. I said I knew her teacher very well and that we had been friends a long time. I asked Sheila if she would like to go visit Sandy in her classroom some day after school. The first time I suggested it was coupled with telling her where she was going the next year. Sheila could not accept that all at once and vehemently announced that she would not now nor would she ever want to meet Sandy. But later in the day, after the other kids had heard of Sheila's placement and had been all excited because she was skipping a grade, Sheila decided that she might not mind meeting Sandy so much after all.

Wednesday afternoon Sheila and I climbed into my little car right after the bell rang and started off for Jefferson Elementary on the other side of town. Because we had almost a half hour before Sandy's class was finished at three thirty, I stopped at Baskin-Robbins for ice cream cones. Sheila selected a double scoop of licorice. The mistake I made was in not taking any napkins with us when we got back into the car.

By the time we arrived at Jefferson, Sheila looked as if she had changed races. She had black ice cream all over her cheeks and chin, on her hair and down the front of her shirt. I looked at her in surprise because only fifteen minutes earlier she had been clean. I did not even have a Kleenex with me, so I wiped what I could off with my hand. With Sheila clutching at me tightly we went to see the school.

Sandy laughed when she saw Sheila. I couldn't blame her. Sheila looked like a four-year-old with all that ice cream on her and her fear gave her a waif-like solemnity. She pressed close to my leg.

"Boy, you look like you had something good," Sandy said, smiling. "What was it?"

Sheila stared at her wide-eyed. "Ice cream," she whispered. I wondered what Sandy must have been thinking just then. I had enticed her into accepting Sheila mostly by elaborating on Sheila's incredible giftedness and verbal ability. Right then Sheila sounded anything but the epitome of intelligence.

I should have trusted Sandy more. Bringing over chairs, she sat down with us and proceeded to get all the details of Sheila's ice cream passions. Then she took us on a tour of the room. It was a typical-looking classroom. Jefferson was an ancient, bulky, brick building with huge rooms. The room easily accommodated twenty-seven desks and a variety of "learning centers" around the perimeter. As usual for Sandy's room, it was messy. Stacks of workbooks defied gravity on the corner of a table, bits of construction paper were strewn through the aisles. I had never been known for my neatness, but Sandy's clutter surpassed even mine. The children must have had half-a-dozen projects going in all states of completion. In the back of the room was a well-stocked bookcase and a gerbil cage.

241

Slowly Sheila began to thaw out and come to life. The books interested her and finally got the better of her timidity. Soon she was wandering around on her own, inspecting the premises. Sandy flashed me a toothy, knowing smile as we watched Sheila in silence. She'd make it.

Standing on tiptoe to see the covers of the workbooks, Sheila took one from the top of the stack and paged through it. Still holding it, she came over to me. "This here's different than them you got, Torey," she said.

"That's probably the kind you'd use in here."

She continued to look through it. Then she turned to Sandy. "I don't like doing workbooks so well."

Sandy pursed her lips and nodded slowly. "I've heard other kids say that too. They aren't a lot of fun, are they?"

Sheila eyed her a moment. "I do 'em though. Torey makes me. I didn't used to, but I do now. This here one don't look too bad. I'd probably do this one." She examined a page carefully. "This here kid made a mistake. Look, it gots a red mark by it." She showed it to me.

"Sometimes people make mistakes," Sandy said. I made a mental note to tell her of Sheila's allergy to correction. That would be one of next year's tasks: reducing Sheila's anxiety about her errors.

"What d'you do to them?" Sheila asked.

"When they make a mistake?" Sandy said. "Oh, I just ask them to do it over again. If they don't understand, I help them. Everybody goofs up once in a while. It's no big deal."

"Do you whip kids?"

With a grin Sandy shook her head. "Nope. I sure don't."

Sheila nodded toward me. "Torey, she don't either."

We stayed with Sandy for almost forty-five minutes, Sheila becoming bolder and bolder with her questions. Finally I suggested we leave so we would get back in time for Sheila's bus. As we went out the door, Sandy mentioned that perhaps Sheila would like to come over for part of a day before school let out and see how it was in the third grade when the children were there. I thanked her for her time and we trotted out to the car.

Sheila was quiet through most of the ride back to our school. Just as I turned the car into the parking lot, Sheila turned to me. "She ain't so bad, I guess."

"Good, I'm glad you liked her."

We climbed out of the car. Sheila took my hand as we walked toward the building. "Tor, do you suppose I could go over to Miss McGuire's class sometime?"

"You want to?"

"I wouldn't really mind."

I nodded. Stretching up to pick a dogwood flower off the tree that leaned over the school doorway, I fastened it into her hair. "Yeah, Sheil, I reckon we could arrange that for you."

Monday of the final week Anton drove Sheila over to Sandy's class. She had elected to remain the entire day, although I had suggested she go just for the morning. But she wanted to eat in the cafeteria, paying for her own lunch and getting to select what she wanted to eat like the other children. At our school my class was the last to eat and their trays were all fixed for them and laid out on the table. Sheila wanted to see how it felt to be a regular kid. My heart lurched a little watching her leave with Anton, her small hand in his. She had come wearing the red, white and blue dress Chad had bought her rather than her everyday jeans and shirt that we had gotten with the money her father had given me. She asked me to put her hair in a ponytail and had found a piece of yarn from the scrap box to tie around it. She looked so tiny next to Anton as they left, and so vulnerable.

Sheila returned that afternoon a satisfied veteran. The day had gone smoothly and she smiled with pride as she related how she had carried her own lunch tray clear across the cafeteria without spilling anything, and how a girl named Maria, who had the longest, shiniest, prettiest black hair she'd ever seen, had saved a place for Sheila to eat with her. There had been hitches. She had lost her way coming back from the girls' restroom. In the tone of voice she used telling the incident, I gathered she must have been very frightened to find herself in such a spot. But she finally made it back. And, she smiled proudly, she never let on to anybody that she'd been lost. At recess she discovered the long dress, despite its being so pretty, was an impediment to play. She tripped while running and skinned her knees. Sheila pulled the dress up to show me. The scratches weren't very visible, but they hurt, she informed me. She hadn't cried about it. Sandy had seen it happen and had given Sheila comfort. Beaming, Sheila told me Sandy smelled good when she held you real close and she would blow on your knees 'til they felt better. All in all, it had been a successful day. Sheila affirmed that it would be an okay class to be in although she hoped Maria flunked, so she'd still be in it next year and they could be friends. I hastened to mention Maria and she might still be friends without wishing poor Maria such bad luck. For the first time Sheila did not get that stricken look about leaving my class; she didn't even mention it. Instead, her conversation was punctuated with "Next year, Miss McGuire says I can . . ." or "Miss McGuire's going to let me . . . when I'm in her room next year." It was a sweet-sad moment for me because I knew I had been outgrown.

On the last day of school we had a picnic. I contacted everybody's parents and a number met us over in the park a few blocks from school. We brought packed lunches from the cafeteria and the makings for ice cream sundaes, while the parents brought cookies and other goodies. The park was a huge one old and sprawling with a small zoo and a large duck pond. It had gardens of flowers all gleaming in the June sunshine. Children scattered in every direction with a parent in tow.

Sheila's father did not come; we had not really expected him. But when Sheila showed up in the morning she was dressed in a bright orange-and-white sunsuit. She seemed embarrassed about having so much of herself exposed and walked around clutching her body for the first half hour with us. But Anton raved about the beautiful color and teased her about stealing it if he got the chance. This loosened her up in a fit of giggles at the thought of Anton wearing her sunsuit and she danced for us across the floor of the classroom while we waited for the other children. Her father had bought the sunsuit for her the night before at the discount store and it was the first new thing she could ever remember him getting her. Her mirth bubbled up in her so brightly that she could not stay still. All the way to the park she pirouetted down the sidewalk, her blond hair swirling in the air as she turned.

Once at the park she continued her joyous movements and Anton and Whitney and I sat in the sun by the duck pond after lunch and watched her. She was apart from us, thirty or forty feet down the walk that circled the pond. She was listening to some inner music and gliding in harmony around on the sidewalk. Others on the walk had to step around her, their faces amused. A skip, now a twirl, then a few rhythmic bends. It was almost eerie watching her dance alone in the sunlight, her hair glistening in a wide yellow wheel. Completely oblivious to the strollers on the walk, to the other children, to Anton and Whitney and me, she satisfied some inner dream to dance. The others must have felt the same eldritch fascination that I did. Anton watched without speaking. Whitney cocked her head as if trying to catch the music none of us was hearing.

Anton turned to me. "She looks like a spirit, doesn't she? Like if you blinked too hard, she'd be gone."

I nodded.

"She's free," Whitney said softly. And that indeed was what she was.

The end of the day came all too quickly. We packed up our things and returned to the classroom to pass out the last of the papers and say our final good-byes. The narrow, wood-paneled room was almost empty now. Pictures and stories were down from the walls. The animals had all gone to my apartment. The names were removed from the cubbies.

The finality of what was happening dawned on Sheila and she lost her merry spirit. By the time we had given out all the papers and awaited the ringing of the bell to go home, Sheila had retreated to the corner, empty now of its pillows and animal cages. Lacking those, she squatted on the floor. The other children were all chattering, excited about summer vacation and their changes for next year. So while Anton led them in songs, I broke away to Sheila.

The tears coursed silently over her now-tanned cheeks. Without a Kleenex, she used her hair to wipe away the wetness. Her eyes were filled with hurt and sorrow. "I don't wanna go," she wailed. "I don't want this to be over. I wanna come back, Torey."

"Of course you do, honey." I took her in my arms. "But that's just how it feels now. In just a little while you'll have a whole summer ahead of you and then you'll be in third grade, a regular kid. It's just a little hard right now, that's all."

"I don't wanna go, Torey. And I don't want you to go."

I smoothed away her bangs. "Remember, I told you I'd write you letters. We'll still know what's happening to each other. It won't be like we're really apart. You'll see."

"No, I won't. I want to stay." She was struggling to regain control and her wiry little body shuddered in my arms. "I'm gonna be bad. I'm not gonna be nice at all in Miss McGuire's class and then you'll have to come back."

"Hey, I don't want to hear that. That's the old Sheila talking."

"I won't be good. I won't. And you can't make me."

"No, Sheil, I can't. That's your decision. But you know it won't change things any. It won't make this year come back or this class. Or me. I'll be going to school myself, like I told you. What you do with yourself only you can decide. But it won't bring this year back."

She was staring at the floor, her bottom lip pushed out.

I smiled. "Remember, you tamed me. You're responsible for me. That means we'll never forget we love each other. That means we'll probably cry a little right now. But pretty soon we'll only remember how happy we were with each other."

She shook her head. "I won't ever be happy."

Just then the bell rang and the room was alive with shouts. I rose and went to the other children. Hesitantly Sheila trailed over too. The good-byes came. Tyler and William were teary-eyed. Peter whooped with joy. We all exchanged hugs and kisses and they were gone, running out into the June warmth.

Sheila was catching the high school bus back to the migrant camp. On this last day, it left only a short time after the bus for the grade school children. I figured that, after saying good-bye to Anton and Whitney and collecting her things, Sheila would have just enough time to walk the two blocks to the high school and meet her bus.

Parting from Anton was hard for her. At first she covered her face and refused to even look at him. He kept coaxing her to smile, saying little things in Spanish, which I did not understand but Sheila did. After all, he reminded her, they'd still see each other at the migrant camp. He promised to bring her over to play with his two little boys. Finally I delivered an ultimatum. I'd walk her to her bus, but she had to leave right away. With this she turned to Anton and hugged him, her tiny arms locking him in a

247

wrestler's hold. Then she waved to Whitney and took my hand. At the doorway she paused, broke away and ran to hug Anton again. She kissed his cheek and trotted back to me. Tears sparkled as she picked up her things, a few papers and the worn copy of *The Little Prince*, a tangible memory of what had been. We descended the steps and went down the walk to the high school.

She did not speak the entire way. Neither did I. We had gone beyond needing words. Talking would have spoiled what we had. The bus was waiting in the semicircle drive of the high school, but the students had not yet loaded. The bus driver waved to us and Sheila ran over to put her things on a seat. Then she came out of the bus again, walking back to where I stood.

She looked up at me, shading her eyes from the light. I looked at her. It seemed a small eternity in the bright sunlight. "Bye," she said very softly.

I sank to my knees and embraced her. My heart was roaring in my ears, my throat too tight to speak. Then I rose and she ran to the bus. All the way to the steps of the bus she ran, but as she started up them she stopped. The older kids were there now and she had to wait to get in. She looked over at me. Then suddenly she came running back.

"I didn't mean it," she said breathlessly. "I didn't mean it when I said I would be bad. I'll be a good girl." She looked up solemnly. "For you."

I shook my head. "No, not for me. You be good for you."

She smiled slightly, oddly. Then in a second she was gone, back to the bus already, scurrying up the stairs and disappearing. In moments I saw her face at the rear window, pressed tight against the glass. The driver shut the door and the bus began to rumble. "Bye," she was mouthing, her nose squashed flat against the window. I could not tell if she was crying. The bus pulled around and down the drive. A small hand waved, frantically at first then more

248

gently. I raised my hand and smiled as the bus turned on to the street and disappeared from sight.

"Bye-bye," I said, the words squeezing themselves almost inaudibly from my stricken throat. Then I turned to go back.

Epilogue

In the mail a year ago came a crumpled, water-stained piece of notebook paper inscribed in blue felt-tip marker. No letter accompanied it.

To Torey with much
"Love"

All the rest came
They tried to make me laugh
They played their games with me
Some games for fun and some for keeps
And then they went away
Leaving me in the ruins of games
Not knowing which were for keeps and
Which were for fun and
Leaving me alone with the echoes of
Laughter that was not mine.

* * *

Then you came
With your funny way of being
Not quite human
And you made me cry
And you didn't seem to care if I did
You just said the games are over
And waited
Until all my tears turned into
Joy.

Life After Darkness

A doctor's journey through severe depression

Cathy Wield

Forewords by

Keith Matthews
and
Chris Thompson

Radcliffe Publishing
Oxford • Seattle

Radcliffe Publishing Ltd
18 Marcham Road
Abingdon
Oxon OX14 1AA
United Kingdom

www.radcliffe-oxford.com
Electronic catalogue and worldwide online ordering facility.

British Library Cataloguing in Publication Data

A catalogue record for this book is available from the British Library.

ISBN 10 1 85775 729 7
ISBN 13 978 1 85775 729 3

Typeset by Acorn Bookwork, Salisbury, Wiltshire
Printed and bound by TJ International Ltd, Padstow, Cornwall

Contents

Foreword

On first meeting Cathy, I was struck by three things. First, she looked so very frail. An empty husk. Although bearing a superficial resemblance to the woman she once had been, life and vitality had long since drained away. Second, she was defeated, despondent and desperate. In clinical terms, she was profoundly depressed and suicidal. Her speech, her thought processes and her movements were all slowed; it was as if she were submerged in an invisible mud. The suffocating effects of depression had helped to prevent her from finding the strength to inflict fatal self-harm. Beside her, however, sat her husband, clearly a life-sustaining source of care and support. Phil's concern and unwavering dedication was the third most memorable thing about what I now recognise as a 'godforsaken' impersonation of Cathy.

With the passage of time, I have enjoyed the relatively rare privilege of watching a remarkable transformation. I have witnessed the emergence of a humorous, sociable, highly intelligent and courageous woman from the depths of a chronic and severe episode of depression. In observing this metamorphosis, I have learned a great deal. For example, although *theoretically* sufficiently aware to mention it in medical student teaching, I had never *truly* recognised how different a personal history can be when it is provided at a time of good health. On reading Cathy's written account of her life before the years of 'darkness', I realised that my grasp of who she was had been grossly diminished, distorted and drained of all colour. Despite my best efforts, I did not really know who Cathy was, or who she had been. Psychiatrists rarely have an opportunity to hear a detailed account of someone's early life without it being filtered through the distorting lens of ill-health and adversity. The pressures of clinical practice do not usually permit psychiatrists to remain in contact with someone who recovers robust good health. Unfortunately, this means that, even as mental health professionals, we never fully appreciate how severely depression disfigures personal memories.

Perhaps most significantly, however, Cathy has educated me about stigma. One of Cathy's driving motivations for bringing her story to a wider public has been a fierce desire to combat the appalling stigma associated with depression, with self-harm and, more controversially, with neurosurgical treatment for mental disorder (previously known as psychosurgery). Stigma pervades every aspect of Cathy's story. Stigma drove many of the callous and unhelpful health service staff responses to the terrible self-harm she inflicted upon herself. Stigma elicited the sometimes misguided and

damaging comments from friends and acquaintances. Stigma shaped the fear-inducing misrepresentations of neurosurgery provided by MIND. Stigma has been defined by Webster's Dictionary as a '*mark of infamy or disgrace; a sign of moral blemish; stain or reproach caused by dishonorable conduct; reproachful characterization*'. The implications are clear. If we acknowledge that the experience of mental illness (and depression in particular) is almost universally tainted by stigma, we also acknowledge that there are widespread assumptions that such afflicted individuals are guilty of unprincipled and deceitful behaviour, or that they lack moral fibre and that they fail to behave as a 'decent' person would. Sadly, despite improved efforts at destigmatising mental illness, it seems that society is most comfortable with a moral explanation for the challenging behaviours driven by disorders such as Cathy's severe depression.

As if it is not enough that the condition itself be viewed with suspicion, misunderstanding and a lack of empathy, we also find that effective treatments themselves are widely misrepresented, ridiculed and reviled. I have always thought it fascinatingly perverse that certain psychiatric treatments – antidepressant drugs, electroconvulsive therapy (ECT) and neurosurgery in particular being good examples – are routinely portrayed and discussed in the media and beyond (by so-called 'experts' and lay public alike) as if they were belief systems rather than extensively evaluated therapeutic interventions. It seems that, as a society, we accept that it is reasonable for someone to appear on radio, television or in the press and to express the view that they '*are opposed to*' or '*do not believe*' in psychiatric treatments. Tom Cruise recently did just that when a television interview strayed on to the topic of actress Brooke Shields who had been prescribed antidepressant drugs to help combat postnatal depression. For reasons best understood by television and tabloid news editors, these comments were deemed sufficiently newsworthy to be given extensive airing. Such public exposure of 'beliefs' is widespread. Much more so for mental health than 'physical health'. Not that such beliefs have been formed following careful evaluation of the breadth of scientific evidence for and against. No, that seems entirely unnecessary. These people simply '*do not believe*' – rather as if the topic under discussion was the existence of God or extra-terrestrial life. Indeed, only this week, a high-profile clinical academic appeared on national radio expressing his firmly held beliefs about the 'barbarism' of neurosurgery for mental disorder. The fact that this individual has never met, nor professionally evaluated, *any* such patients before and after treatment failed to impede his enthusiastic denouncement of all neurosurgical treatment approaches. I wondered if the interviewer might have challenged these views had the topic not been such an easy, crowd-pleasing target?

Such media coverage of psychiatric treatment, although comforting and productive in terms of audience approval, is, ultimately, deeply damaging. Many people who suffer from the most severe forms of depression often

cannot quite believe that 'depression' offers an adequate explanation for how ill they feel and how dysfunctional their minds and bodies are. Failure to respond to recognised and proven therapeutic endeavours – a trial of antidepressant medication, a course of cognitive therapy – simply increases these doubts and discourages adherence with further treatment recommendations. Faith in psychiatry and in the scientific approach to health and therapeutics is quite easily jettisoned. Psychiatric explanations for mental disorder and carefully studied treatment outcomes are dismissed as the worst kind of cultural relativism. Rather like football, everyone has an equally valid and insightful opinion and there are no 'experts'. The explanation for 'treatment failure' then becomes all too clear. Psychiatry has 'failed' because the philosophy and the method has no real substance. The individual dimension has been missed. There is 'something wrong' with the individual themselves. Something that is not 'depression'. For the sufferer, this may be an unrecognised and much sought-after 'physical illness'. Alternatively, it may represent a punishment instituted by a higher being in response to some perceived previous misdemeanour. For friends and relatives, there is often a desperate search for 'the reason'. If only someone can 'get to the bottom' of the problem (usually with some form of counselling or psychotherapy), then all will be well. This is why some sufferers endure very lengthy exposures to analytic psychotherapy in the absence of any evidence that it is likely to improve their health. Thereafter, many sufferers are supported and directed towards all manner of alternative and complementary treatments. Better to place faith in crystals and the wisdom of the ancients than in evidence-based modern medicine.

Regrettably, the response of the health professional is often no more rational. Sufferers become 're-labelled', usually being described as having a 'personality disorder'. This helps the hard-pressed health professional to cope. At least then the treatment failures are down to the sufferer and not attributable to professional and therapeutic inadequacies.

Unfortunately, the explanations for failure to respond to treatment, although complex, are usually devoid of any such cause for blame. Depression is a poorly understood aggregation of physical and psychological changes that can, for poorly understood reasons, progress from a temporary impairment of optimal functioning to a prolonged, debilitating and dreadful illness. Yes, an illness. In every sense of the word. Existing explanations for depression, be they biomedical or psychological, are grossly inadequate and only marginally helpful to clinicians and sufferers. Depression is almost certainly not a single, discrete, clinical 'thing' any more than is 'breathlessness'. Failure to respond to antidepressant medication (and to ECT) is common. The reasons why one individual should respond and another not, remain essentially unknown. Psychotherapy (for example – cognitive therapy), as with drug treatment, is only helpful for a proportion of sufferers. Again, the reasons for this are complex and largely

not understood. In a particularly cruel manner, failure to respond to one treatment predicts further failure to respond to subsequent treatment interventions. When one reaches the position of having tried and failed numerous trials of medication and psychotherapy, what next?

For some such sufferers, neurosurgical treatment interventions appear to offer reasonable prospects for improvement. Neurosurgery for mental disorder has an uncomfortable and, in part, disreputable history. There is no question that, throughout that latter half of the last century, crude and damaging neurosurgical procedures (leucotomy and lobotomy) were used without sufficient discrimination and regard for adverse effects. Nevertheless, the history of 'psychosurgery' is not nearly so black and white as we often like to believe. If in doubt, the interested reader may wish to consult Jack El Hai's excellent recent biography of the US neurologist Walter Freeman – 'the father of lobotomy'.[1] Modern neurosurgical procedures bear little resemblance to those of the past. Undoubtedly, we have only a rudimentary understanding of how and why such interventions might alleviate depression. Further, we must remain vigilant to the possibility that there may be unrecognised and significant long-term adverse effects. However, I would invite the readers to place themselves, even for a moment, in Cathy's shoes throughout the year 2000. What would you have done?

Like Cathy, you may be most familiar with neurosurgery for mental disorder as depicted in Milos Forman's award winning 1975 movie *One Flew Over the Cuckoo's Nest*. To summarise the plot, a rebellious new patient (McMurphy – memorably played by Jack Nicholson) is admitted to a small US mental institution where his antics endear him to fellow patients (*and the audience*) whilst incurring the wrath of the stern, authoritarian and repressive nurse Ratched who runs the ward.

In this movie, the unspoken, feared, 'true' motives of psychiatry are laid bare – social control, forced compliance with damaging and debilitating medication, electroconvulsive therapy and psychosurgery to eradicate individuality and freedom of thought. McMurphy, who clearly suffers from no mental illness, is shown to have a superior understanding of his fellow patients than that of the strikingly non-empathic staff. Ultimately, he is punished for his audacity by forced lobotomy, rendering him compliant and devoid of spirit or soul. This post-psychosurgery state is considered so hideous and unworthy that his companion suffocates him in an act of mercy before escaping from the hospital himself. Such stigmatising stereotypes are difficult to change or evade. Ironically, society seems pleased to watch the latest high-tech neurosurgical 'miracle' treatments for Parkinson's disease or chronic pain. However, it remains reluctant to accommodate depression within this framework. Yet, if the substrates for the debilitating condition we call chronic, severe depression are not located in the brain, where are they?

As with any treatment intervention, when considering neurosurgical

treatments, all patients must weigh up the potential benefits, the risks of adverse events and the likely consequences of not proceeding with treatment. Much of the hostility to neurosurgery for mental disorder stems, I suspect, from a lack of awareness of how unbearable life can become for someone in the depths of a severe depression where all other 'reasonable' treatments have failed. If you read on, Cathy will describe this for you.

An important lesson for me has been recognising my own unwitting collusion with maintaining the stigma that surrounds depression and its treatment. When the possibility of writing a book was first mentioned by Cathy, I cautioned against the risks. I expressed concern over the degree to which deeply personal events could become public knowledge and the potential for this to impede her recovery and rehabilitation. At each stage, Cathy simply replied '... but why not?', or '... but why shouldn't I?' I never had a good answer to those questions. Having read Cathy's story, I appreciate that I was wrong. There are so many important messages in Cathy's story, I now believe that it should become required reading for *every* medical student, *every* doctor, *every* nurse (particularly those working in Accident and Emergency Departments and Psychiatric Units), *every* health service manager and *every* politician. There are elements of this story that make deeply uncomfortable reading. Much of the time we pretend that our health service is just about managing to respond adequately to the challenges of providing high quality healthcare for those with mental ill-health. The truth is very different.

Our mental health services are, in large part, grossly inadequate and unresponsive to the needs of the population they are supposed to serve. We tolerate appalling physical environments, particularly for in-patient care, that would never be deemed acceptable for other patient populations. Last week, I visited a patient in a psychiatric in-patient unit in a Scottish district general hospital to conduct an initial assessment for potential neurosurgical intervention. The path leading to the front entrance had to be negotiated with considerable care due to the liberal sprinkling of litter and a heavy overgrowth of 12 inch high weeds. The entrance was most notable for its unpainted, weathered woodwork, its dirty windows and lack of legible signs. Inside the vestibule, there was a reception area. The chairs and carpet conformed fully to Cathy's descriptions of the physical environment of the much-dreaded 'DOP'. There was a reception window. However, although clearly designed to accommodate a receptionist, there was no one there. There is, in fact, never anyone there. The unit has no receptionist. Any visitor must simply attempt to navigate by the scarce and unhelpful signs, or hope to meet a member of staff. It is difficult to imagine that we might tolerate such poor physical conditions for a cancer treatment unit. Why is this acceptable for mental health service users and carers? Can we attribute this to stigma, to apathy, or to our misguided complacency that mental illness will never affect us?

Of course, once in the wards themselves, the environment is usually no better. Cathy's heartbreaking descriptions can, sadly, be applied to many psychiatric units that I have visited. Perhaps worse, however, is the accuracy and generalisability of her description of the barren regime inside an acute psychiatric in-patient unit. Why do we provide barely sufficient numbers of trained staff to operate according to a custodial ethos rather than a therapeutic one? Psychiatric nursing is a challenging job. Very challenging. Why then, do we try to make it impossible for them? Our insistence on running units with the bare minimum numbers of staff, with the bare minimum of training and expertise, is counter therapeutic, wasteful and, sometimes, unsafe. Cathy also highlights for us the difficulties of effective multidisciplinary working. Faced with the challenges posed by seemingly intractable illness, we must find ways to work together more productively.

I hope that the reader will find Cathy's story compelling and thought provoking. Cathy raises many important issues that merit thoughtful responses. This story should engage and concern healthcare staff, health service managers and politicians. It will surely also engage and outrage every reader.

Listen to Cathy and keep an open mind. Also, remember that cuckoos don't actually build nests.

Professor Keith Matthews
Professor of Psychiatry
University of Dundee
Ninewells Hospital and Medical School
August 2005

Reference

1 El-Hai J (2005) *The Lobotomist: A maverick medical genius and his tragic quest to rid the world of mental illness.* John Wiley & Sons Inc, Chichester.

Foreword

The two words 'depression' and 'courage' are not often used in the same sentence. In the popular mind depression is associated with what unkind doctors sometimes call 'acopia', in other words a diffuse inability to cope with the stresses and strains of life in general. I hope that Cathy's book will demonstrate that people with depression can indeed deal with their illness courageously and emerge with dignity. Cathy's story, very ably and touchingly, describes many of the features of a chronic depression that are so damaging, not only to the sufferer, but also to their family and social networks. However, what is really outstanding about this story is the way Cathy uses her experience of being a doctor to try to understand what it was like for those of us who were trying to help her get better while taking responsibility for her safety during her periods of extreme self-harm. In so doing she illuminates a whole range of the effects of the illness that are seldom considered.

As a psychiatrist, whether you are biologically oriented or psycho-therapeutically oriented (and Cathy rightly valued both approaches during her illness) it is impossible to be useful to patients without feeling empathy and sympathy for their predicament. Although one is also taught to keep an emotional distance, that balance between empathy and professionalism presents its own predicament to the practitioner. Like Lewis Thomas, the great New York physician, I would go further than the need for empathy and use the simple human word 'affection' for the feelings of a doctor to a patient. One cannot help but be 'affected' by the pain and suffering of a severely depressed patient, even though one understands it to be an illness, and even though physical pain may be self-inflicted due to the compulsive thoughts of self-harm that are a part of the condition. I don't know if it was the fact that Cathy was herself a physician that made it harder to bear her pain for those of us looking after her. I don't know if it was the fact that she had a husband whose support was an inspiration. I don't know if it was the fact that she had four beautiful and successful children – children of roughly the same age as my own – and was desperate not to miss their growing up. It might have been all of these things put together with the extreme, unremitting and constantly life-threatening nature of her depression that had such a profound impact on me as well as on her other consultants and professional carers.

I have no doubt that some readers of this story will be critical of some aspects of her care from one standpoint or another. It is inevitable because psychiatry remains in many ways controversial despite the explosion of

scientific evidence in the last few decades. I am sure that those who detest biological interventions because they themselves have had side-effects, or because they think it places too much power in the hands of the psychiatrist, would be critical of the many attempts to find the right anti-depressant, the right anti-psychotic, or of the use of ECT. Even more so would they be critical of the eventual referral for neuro-surgery that led to her recovery. Against this view is the fact that a cognitive therapist found her too ill to concentrate on therapy. And while she found the additional time and empathy of the psychoanalytic form of therapy helpful, in retrospect she did not feel that a search for meaning in early childhood events was anything more than the scratching of psychological carbuncles raised by the illness.

So, indeed, there will also be those on the biological side of psychiatry who will criticise the long and frustrating hours of psychotherapy. To those I would simply say 'read Cathy's judgement on the importance of a listening ear'. Some may also criticise the long periods of time that we made Cathy stay in hospital under a section of the Mental Health Act. All I would say to that is that we simply had a duty to protect her life until she recovered.

So there came a point at which the team agreed that even we were losing hope that we could heal Cathy's depression and were becoming resigned to the probability that she would die by her own hand. That cannot be right if there is any other possible avenue for treatment. I remember that Cathy was at first very shocked when I mentioned to her the possibility of neuro-surgery. It is not a treatment that any psychiatrist prescribes often and without extremely careful thought. But despite the extremity of her distress, Cathy was able to make her own decision to go for the assessment and eventually to have the operation, and what a good decision that turned out to be.

So Cathy has many messages in this story.

To patients she is saying, 'don't give up hope, have courage, keep trying', and curiously, to mental health professionals her message is exactly the same.

To commentators on mental illness, particularly on controversial treatments like brain surgery, she is simply saying, 'keep an open mind'. Some treatments may be distasteful but life saving, as is the case in many other areas of medicine.

I think she is also saying do not denigrate what you don't understand. You can't understand me (Cathy) unless you enter my world as a caring professional and you can't understand the value of any treatment unless you ask me (the patient) before the treatment whether I want it, and ask me after the treatment whether it helped.

Finally, I think anyone who reads this would want to congratulate Cathy on her courage in adversity, her recovery, and her service to mental

health through being brave enough to revisit those terrible years and to set it down on paper for the benefit of everyone suffering from or caring for someone suffering from this grossly misunderstood illness.

Professor Chris Thompson
Director of Healthcare Priory Group
Surrey
August 2005

Acknowledgements

I cannot name every individual who has contributed to this book, but many have done so either by their encouragement or by talking to me of their memories of the years of my illness. Thank you to the many people who have allowed me to write about their involvement, I am grateful to all of you.

I would like to thank Gillian Nineham of Radcliffe Publishing who believed I could do this even before I had put pen to paper.

My thanks also go to Dr David Baldwin for writing his contribution 'A doctor's view' and his help and advice during my writing. This included answering my inevitable questions which arose when I had access to my medical record and checking my appendices for accuracy.

I am grateful to Ninewells Hospital for their kind permission to use the Neurosurgery Information Sheet in Appendix B. In particular I wish to thank Professor Keith Matthews for his ongoing support and encouragement. Thank you to both my foreword writers, Professor Keith Matthews and Professor Chris Thompson, for so willingly agreeing to do this for me.

I will always be grateful to the many health professionals who contributed to my care and without whose help I would not have lived to write my story. Thank you so much to the many doctors and nurses who work in psychiatry. You rarely receive the praise that you are due, in large part because the people you care for are the least able to tell you just how much your care and concern means to them. You are my unsung heroes.

Lastly it is hard to express the gratitude that I owe to our many friends and family for their support. Especially to Phil, Rebecca, Simon, Stephanie and Jonathan who have not only given their permission for me to write about them, but have also had to undergo the process of reliving some extremely painful memories.

Introduction

Since returning to normal life and living, I have often been struck by the similarities between my experience and those who have been held captive and then released. Melodramatic perhaps, but I was also taken prisoner against my will, held not just by my illness, but also as a result of it, forced to reside in the rather archaic institutions that are our present day mental hospitals. However, the enemy, Depression, may not fill you with terror at its name, unless of course you have met it yourself, either personally or at close quarters. The 'black dog', as Winston Churchill used to call it, encompasses a wide range of experience. It is obviously not one condition, but the common factor of 'low mood' prevails in each form it takes. My life journey took me through a single, but continuous, seven-year episode. It was a terrible nightmare of torture and imprisonment. I am one of the fortunate ones to have survived and recovered. I hope through my story, I will be able to bring to you some insights into this kind of suffering and I hope that the stigma which is attached to mental illness will lessen as a result.

Through my life, I had never experienced serious illness. However, once qualified as a doctor, I had been a patient on several occasions. I appreciated that this was indeed an uncomfortable position to be in and knew something of the vulnerability the role engenders.

This time, it was different. I was working as a junior doctor in the Accident & Emergency Department of my home town, Southampton. I enjoyed my job and had decided that this was the speciality I wished to make a career in. I was also the mother of four young children and had role-swapped with my husband three years previously; my long hours made it necessary for him to be a full-time parent. I was very happy with this arrangement. I knew that our children had a great father who cared for them just as well as I had done when I was at home. However, when the news came that I had secured funding to pursue my career working part-time, I was thrilled.

That was what seemed so strange. The onset of my illness could easily have been put down to the stress of my working life, but in fact my working hours were just about to dramatically improve. Out of all the specialities that I had worked in, I found Accident and Emergency the most enjoyable; I liked my work!

I remember well the morning that the penny finally dropped that I was seriously depressed. This was some time in early December 1994.

I had all the typical symptoms of depression. I was feeling low all the time, tearful (although I kept this well hidden), sleeping badly, poor

appetite, but more importantly I had a pervading sense of hopelessness and suicidal thoughts had begun to emerge.

Fortunately I had great faith in the medical system. Once I realised that I was ill and needed treatment, I lost no time in seeking help. At the end of my shift, I sought out the consultant, Rodger Sleet, who was head of our department at that time. It was not quite as simple as I thought it was going to be. Initially he did not believe me – well, not until I let the tears flow. He kindly referred me to the Counselling Service for Sick Doctors. At this stage, I was convinced that the cause of my illness was cumulative stress and so I had no reluctance to try one of the 'talking' therapies. It was not so easy once I found out where my appointment was to be held.

In Southampton, the mental health services had a certain notoriety. I had visited the Department of Psychiatry when I worked as a medical house officer. It is known by staff and patients alike as the DOP. The idea of going there as a patient sent shivers down my spine.

The DOP is situated at the Royal South Hants Hospital. It is housed within a building which had been constructed as a maternity wing, but was never used for that purpose. Not only is it in the middle of the city, but it is also in one of the poorer areas of town; the territory of drug abusers and also the local red light district. Not exactly the ideal set-up for the mentally ill.

My previous experience led me to believe that patients in the DOP were the 'difficult' ones, scary even, known by many medics as 'sad, mad or bad'. Known by outsiders as 'nutters', 'loonies', 'crazy'. Surely I could not be one of them?

I realised that I also needed to enlist the help of my GP. Once again this step required courage. The stigma attached to a psychiatric diagnosis was high. I had a few internal battles, but made up my mind that I required medical help and I felt that I should be signed off work; just for a week or so until I had recovered. How glad I am that I had no inkling of what the future would be.

It's interesting looking back at how much insight I had. Surprisingly, I was not afraid of the effect this illness would have on my future career, I guess because I was still certain that it was not going to be for long and that I would be able to start my part-time working.

Now, having done some voluntary work for an organisation which supports troubled doctors, I have often heard major concerns expressed by those suffering with a mental illness, about the effect it will have on their work and careers. Many shy away from seeking help, afraid of the consequences of stigma. Fortunately for me, the two consultants for whom I worked were very supportive and I was never made to feel that my return to work would be an issue. Instead I received a letter telling me not to worry about the staffing problems caused by my absence, but to concentrate on getting well. I wish everyone could have such understanding

employers. So my sick role started. Thankfully I had no idea of what turn life would take.

Writing my story in the context of my patchy memory loss has not been easy. I have used as many sources as possible. I have used my right to access my medical record, interviewed medical and nursing staff involved, as well as drawing on the recollections of my family and friends. I wrote things down on occasions during the illness, but these are often not dated. It was not until January 2001 that I started to write a regular diary. I have also used our family diary and photos to piece together the sequence of events.

It has been very strange reading about myself in the medical notes, sometimes disturbing, often incomprehensible. I would much rather they were referring to someone else. At times I have felt completely disassociated from the entries. At other times, I have felt so involved that I wish I could put the author right: 'it wasn't like that', 'that's not what I was thinking', misunderstandings or misinterpretations which inevitably occur on either side between the patient and the staff. Even the little errors of fact, for instance wrong dates or misspelt names, are irritating, and then I have to remember my own professional life. These were contemporaneous notes, written by busy people in demanding jobs. For the most part, I am very grateful that the letters and notes were so lengthy and descriptive and I now realise just how much time and effort was spent in providing my care. The notes have been an incredibly helpful resource. I am indebted to the dedication of the staff whose care has brought me through this terrible illness.

It has not been easy to revisit these years, either for me or for my family. I am truly grateful for all the support I have received during this process. I would especially like to thank my husband Phil and my children, Rebecca, Simon, Stephanie and Jonathan. They are part of my story and have allowed me to share a little of what they suffered too.

A promising future

Seven years lost. Seven years of being a prisoner, not just of my mind but of a rundown healthcare system, to a large degree still in existence. How can I best describe that place to you so that you may know a little of what many people still suffer along with their families, in this first world, educated society?

I admit my life was far from typical. There were many unusual features to it, but none that could predict the onset of this nightmare. Despite the 'vulnerability factors' which the psychotherapists and psychiatrists identified, nothing could account for this. Many people have far more traumatic or difficult upbringings than I had. In fact some would say my childhood was nothing other than advantaged.

I was born in New Delhi, in India, the daughter of a diplomat. My father's postings took us overseas for much of my early childhood. I had an older brother and two younger sisters and enjoyed being part of a large and interesting family. We lived in Nairobi, Kenya for four years and then after a short time in England we went by ship to Bangkok in Thailand. My education was privileged as a result of my father's job and just before my tenth birthday I started at Badminton School in Bristol, the first of two boarding schools.

I remember how on the first night I realised that this was not in fact going to be quite like *Jo of the Chalet School* (a series of books I had read by Elinor Brent-Dyer). Sadly this brought an abrupt end to the excitement and anticipation which I had felt at the prospect of going away to school. Instead, I experienced homesickness and a certain bewilderment, made worse by the matron's intolerance towards any girl seen weeping. However, there was a camaraderie and I settled in to some extent. But I spent most of my school life counting the days until the end of the term and then most of the holidays dreading the day I would go back. I loved going home for the holidays, but the parting from my parents was always extremely painful. I cried in anticipation and cried for most of the long flight back to England, but once I arrived back at school, life carried on. I never thought of myself as clever. I didn't work particularly hard and I hadn't really understood that there was any need to do so. That was until I was about 13.

There was a girl in my class who worked obsessionally hard, to the

extent that the staff started to worry about her and finally she had to go home, clearly unwell. I had observed this closely since she sat next to me in our classroom for prep (homework). I decided that working hard might give me an early holiday too, so I started to do my homework diligently and work beyond the prep time. Not surprisingly, since I was not ill, it did not achieve the same result. I suddenly found that my marks went up and I was moved to all the top sets in my year. I was called in to the headmistress, as Jenny had been. Only I was to be congratulated on my success, although she did warn me not to work too hard!

In the meantime, my parents had registered my distress and hoped that moving me to another school would help. They found a school near our English home, so that whenever they were on leave, it would be a convenient three-mile drive away and I would easily be able to see them. I had sisters who would be joining me at school in the future so it was a sound decision.

I started at St George's School in Ascot just before my fourteenth birthday. However, this was to be a different experience altogether. At that time, unlike Badminton School, it was not a particularly academic institution. I was unusual; my fees were paid by the Foreign Office and I lived abroad. I teamed up with another girl in similar circumstances, but most of my contemporaries' interests lay in their social lives and the talk revolved around their 'coming out' as debutantes. This certainly boosted my confidence academically as I was seen as being particularly clever, but I felt isolated. I was really very miserable at first, but I had learnt to hide my feelings well.

Back in Thailand, we had by then moved up to the North where my father had become the British Consul in Chiang Mai. We lived in the beautiful Consulate residence on the banks of the river Mae Ping. It had a huge garden, tended by several gardeners. The weather was much more temperate than Bangkok; the town was small, traffic-free and fascinating. I spent lovely times with my mother searching through the quaint little shops which sold all sorts of wares, ranging from new local crafts to antiques. My mother had developed an eye for Ming china and we used to browse these shops looking for the genuine amidst the many reproductions. I loved those holidays. We went swimming every day, often travelling to the local pool on the back of my brother's motorbike without even a helmet – it was here that I learnt to do back dives from a high diving board. The adventurous side of my personality was beginning to develop. There were not many tourists in those days; the foreigners who lived in the North were largely missionaries. I had started expressing a desire to do medicine and was introduced to a surgeon who worked in a leprosy hospital. He allowed me to come and watch operations. It seemed wonderful to me and the seeds of my future career were sown.

I was not in a competitive environment at school and somehow it never

occurred to me that entry into medical school would be in any way diffi-cult. In fact the school did not even offer the necessary subjects. Indeed, they had never had a pupil go to medical school and only eight in our year stayed on in the sixth form to study for A levels.

The move to Ascot played a very significant part in my life. For the first time I had contact with my uncle Douglas McBain and his family for exeats, since I was now within reach of Streatham in south-west London, where they lived. On the first weekend that I went to their house, I was rather dismayed that on Sunday morning I had to go to church with them. He was a Baptist minister, which actually meant very little to me. My family were not churchgoers and my only experience of the Christian religion was the occasional necessary Church of England service I had attended at school. Christianity seemed boring and irrelevant. It was certainly not one of my interests. However, I was intrigued by the differ-ence attending this service. More so that my uncle's preaching was fasci-nating, entertaining and relevant to me and my circumstances. Even as a young child, I had a sense that I was 'sinful', particularly since an incident where I had lied, which almost led to serious trouble. I was eight years old at the time and it had bugged me. But even though eventually I had confessed to my parents, I still felt it keenly. Uncle Douglas preached the Christian message, that Jesus' death had taken place in order that we could be forgiven. At the end of the service, I prayed the simple prayer silently as invited and surrendered my life to God. It seemed the most natural thing to do and I felt different immediately, as though a weight had been lifted from my shoulders.

I had no notion of being 'saved' or 'born again', but eventually my cousin teased out of me the reason for my enormous grin as we walked home from church. I was baptised a few weeks later. At school, my new found faith isolated me further. I could not understand why what had seemed like a wonderful experience to me was received with such hostility. I learnt to keep quiet about my faith.

When my parents arrived back in England for a home posting, the trips to my uncle's stopped and I lost touch with the church and related activ-ities. However, I never lost touch with the reality of what had happened or of my faith in God.

The sixth form was academically challenging. I taught myself O level physics and chemistry and I had to cycle to the nearby St Mary's Convent to do my chemistry A level in order to satisfy the entrance requirements for medical school. I was delighted to be offered a place at St George's Medical School which was about to move to Tooting, in south-west London. I was a little perturbed by the name being the same as my school, but when I started there, still aged 17, I was overwhelmed with delight. My experience was the complete opposite of starting at St George's School! I immediately felt at home with students from all sorts of backgrounds and threw myself

into student life. I saw my first 'X'-rated film just a few days before my eighteenth birthday at the medical school, *One Flew Over the Cuckoo's Nest.* With the benefit of hindsight I have to laugh that my first 'adult' movie was this; an introduction to mental hospital horror!

I decided to visit the Christian Union and, to my great surprise, there was a reception committee to meet me. I had not bothered to look at the geography of the area. My uncle had obviously heard I was starting there and his church was within easy distance. Students attending Streatham Baptist church were looking out for me. I had not made any efforts to reawaken the spiritual experiences of my earlier teenage years, but I decided to attend the church. However, I lost interest in the Christian Union when some of the students showed their disapproval – I had moved out of halls to share a flat with two of my male friends! I in turn thought they were rather unexciting and rigid in their beliefs. I always was a bit of a rebel, never one to follow the crowd and always ready for a challenge. However, I made good friends at medical school and enjoyed a variety of activities. I loved parties and practical jokes. I even wrote a comedy skit for our annual medical school review. I was not a particularly gifted clarinet-tist, but I managed to start the first St George's Medical School orchestra.

I did very well as a student and obtained a grant from the Medical Research Council to do an intercalated BSc. As a result of this I decided to postpone my summer vacation visit to see my parents, who by that time had moved to Brunei. Instead I took a summer job as a mortuary technician!

I continued to attend Streatham Baptist Church on Sundays. On this particular occasion I sat with a group of clinical students who did not go home for the summer. There was a friend of theirs named Phil and we got chatting. We all went out to the proms on that evening. Soon Phil became my first serious boyfriend. I had no intention of getting married young; after all, becoming a surgeon required dedication. But we fell madly in love with each other! Just three weeks after we started going out, we decided to get engaged and planned our wedding for the following summer, August 1980, when my parents would be back in England on leave and I would have completed my BSc degree.

Phil and I travelled out to Brunei at Christmas so that they would meet him before we told them of our good news. We did not anticipate their concerns! Their daughter, happily dedicated to her future profession and only 20 years old, was just about to embark on marriage to this man whom she had known for less than six months! I cannot blame them for their natural parental anxieties. However, Phil was equally committed to my future and though they had no way of knowing it at that time, he was to be dedicated to me in a way that few people could ever be.

I started my clinical studies in September 1980 as a married woman and celebrated my 21st birthday party a month later. However, my parents'

Our wedding day, 2 August 1980, with friends from St George's Medical School.

fears that my career aspirations would be jeopardised were well founded, but it was my choice to marry. It's a funny thing to have choice; it gives the illusion of control over one's destiny. When I fell pregnant in my penultimate year as a medical student, I had the strength to continue my training, despite being plagued by persistent nausea.

Medicine was still very much a male-dominated profession and there were certainly no concessions for me in my pregnant state. The doctors I studied under either ignored it or made derogatory remarks about my lack of commitment to the profession. It seemed that sex was an acceptable hobby for male students to pursue; I, on the other hand had just been careless! Maternity leave was not even spoken of and I continued my studies. The baby was due in October of my final year. The day I went into labour I was finishing a surgical attachment and the first contractions started while I was assisting at an operation – a vasectomy if my memory serves me correctly! I remember timing the labour pains on the operating theatre clock. Of course I did not say a word to those around me. I left there to go and inform my midwife and by early the following morning, 25 September 1982, we had a baby daughter, Rebecca.

The minute I held her, my maternal instinct took over. I was delighted with my new baby and incredibly happy even though I was exhausted from an all-night labour. I felt enormously fulfilled and loved being a

mother. I lost my ambition to become a surgeon very soon after Rebecca's birth, although I wanted to finish my medical training. I had no regrets.

The final year was very hard. The only break in my studies was for a short time during my elective; the Dean of the medical school was a paediatrician and she allowed me to stay at home with my newborn baby, although this was in order to study for exams! Rebecca developed severe eczema, so I was advised to breast feed exclusively until she was six months old. I was having to get up in the middle of the night, not only to feed her (she did not sleep through the night), but also to express enough milk to leave with our kind friend who looked after her during the day. I managed to get through the year and pass my finals in July. How, I do not know!

The next step was pre-registration house jobs. These consist of two six-month hospital posts in the specialities of medicine and surgery. I would be unable to practise as a doctor until these had been completed. There were no opportunities to work part-time. An easy rota was a one in three, which meant being resident in the hospital and on call every third night and weekend. The decision to postpone these jobs and stay at home with Rebecca was not difficult to make.

We had some amazing spiritual experiences in those days. We wanted to buy a flat but had no money for a deposit. Then we found a mortgage broker who was able to offer a 100% mortgage. We saw a run-down maisonette opposite Streatham Common station. It really was in a dreadful state, but we put in an offer for £20 000. It wasn't until near to the completion date that we started to worry and then pray about the fact that we had no money to pay either the solicitor or the surveyor. At the weekend we visited Phil's grandparents without warning them first. When we arrived on their doorstep, they were in a very excited state. 'We have been trying to get hold of you all day and here you are. We have some important news to tell you,' they said. They had decided to give us £1000. It was totally unexpected. We felt that God was indeed looking after us.

I became a full-time mother and housewife. Phil had trained as a computer programmer and worked first for the NHS and later on for an insurance company. I supplemented our income by doing some child-minding and we also had a lodger. This gave us enough money to pay for the mortgage and we had just about made the maisonette habitable before we moved in!

I had always wanted a large family and it wasn't long before I fell pregnant once again. I had been very impressed by Caroline Flint, who had lectured during my medical school training on natural childbirth. She had delivered Rebecca and agreed to be my midwife for this planned home delivery. She almost missed the birth as she left the room to 'spend a penny'. Simon's speedy arrival was just 21 months after Rebecca (June

1984). Our free time was spent in doing up the maisonette and I loved being at home with our growing family.

Since the property market was booming, we sold the maisonette at a reasonable profit and were able to buy a three-bedroomed terraced house. It also needed quite a lot of renovation but we did not find this daunting. Once again I fell pregnant and planned for a home delivery. I continued to enjoy being at home with my young children and was delighted at the birth of Stephanie in April 1986, also delivered by Caroline Flint. She was a bigger baby at birth than Rebecca and Simon, but by the age of seven months the health visitor was worrying about her small size. We were sent for an urgent outpatient appointment to a paediatrician. Fortunately he confirmed my own opinion, which was that she was a healthy, but tiny little girl. She remained small for her age until she grew as a teenager.

In the meantime both Phil and I had a desire to go and work in the Far East. Phil successfully applied to become country director of a charity known as Christian Outreach, working with the Cambodian refugees on the Thai–Kampuchean border. We left for our base in Bangkok in 1987 with our three children Rebecca, Simon and Stephanie.

It was wonderful to be back in Thailand. I was amazed at how readily I picked up Thai again. Phil took up this new role with remarkable ease. He had never done anything like it before, but the agency made a good choice and he loved the work running the team of engineers, nurses, teachers and an occupational therapist who like us had volunteered themselves for the project. We stayed there for two years. During this time, Rebecca started at the local English school and was very happy initially. Then suddenly her behaviour changed; she became reluctant to go to school and we found out that she was being badly bullied. The head teacher was not in the least bit sympathetic and so we took the decision to remove her from this environment. I had no option but to teach her at home, but the Worldwide Education Service provided good resources and encouragement enabling me to do this successfully.

It was good for all of us. Rebecca soon returned to her normal, happy self. We were friends with other families whose children were also home-schooled and there were also children who lived in the same apartment block, which had a communal swimming pool. So I had no need to be concerned about social interaction with other children. Rebecca and Simon had learnt to swim and they both could dive. Even Stephanie was swimming unaided before her second birthday (mostly underwater!)

We had sold our house in London, but had not realised to what extent property prices would continue to rise. This meant that we would not be able to buy again in the same area. Fortunately we had met a few people connected with a church in Southampton and Phil's sister who lived there agreed to help us find tenants. That was if we could find somewhere to buy. The property market was moving so fast that we made the decision

that I should return to the UK. A couple of days before I left, we remembered that the children were on my passport so that I could not leave without them. I flew back with the three children. I was feeling slightly nauseous. I managed to find a small house in Southampton, buy it, move in and unpack our furniture from storage, all within the space of three weeks! I found out that it was possible to exchange contracts and complete all on the same day. I also phoned Phil with the news that we were expecting our fourth baby – Jonathan was born later that year in October 1988 in a Thai hospital.

Phil, myself, Rebecca, Simon, Stephanie and our new addition to the family, baby Jonathan.

CHAPTER 2

Working mother

In some ways it was a relief to be back in England's temperate climate when we returned in March 1989. We had lived without air-conditioning in the Bangkok apartment. Southampton seemed so quiet and peaceful in comparison. Rebecca and Simon started at school and we settled into our new home. It did not need renovating, but it was very small. We joined Southampton Community Church and made new friends. This church did not belong to any denominational group but arose out of what is termed the 'house church' movement. It was large, had a membership in the hundreds, was active and enthusiastic about faith in Christ. This was good for both of us. Neither of us are particularly 'religious' and we enjoyed the freedom of expression and openness. We would find it difficult to align ourselves with groups who express intolerance or religious bigotry – here the Christians seemed to be showing love and concern towards anyone whatever their circumstances might be.

We did miss Thailand though, and in particular the biggest shock for us was that Phil was unable to find similar (charity) work in the UK. So he returned to his original occupation, computer programming. Just over a year later, we were able to move to a larger house. We had moved nine times in under 10 years of our marriage, but this was a lovely, big house able to accommodate us all. As usual we needed to do some work on it and once again we had the financial need of a lodger. We had fun, we socialised, we enjoyed having friends round for meals. We learnt to play mahjong and stayed up into the early hours having had far too much to drink and regretted it the following morning when bright-eyed children were pestering us for breakfast.

We had been back in England for 18 months when we started thinking about the possibility of my return to medicine. It was now seven years since I had qualified. Fortuitously, there was another Southampton student who was also looking to do her house jobs part-time, so we applied as a jobshare for the following August (1991). Meantime we were trying to sort out the logistics of looking after four young children, which was likely to be challenging. Even though I was only going to be working half-time, full-time was 84 hours a week! We decided to role swap since Phil's new job proved to be rather tedious after the challenge of Thailand. Phil became the househusband in February 1991 when I decided to get the surgical six

months out of the way, so I did this on a full-time basis – my first post as a qualified doctor.

I wrote a book of notes for Phil on how to run the house, which he soon abandoned in favour of his own regime. Our children did not seem to notice the change or if they did it was not a big issue for them. For me it was a bit more of a shock.

My first day as a surgical house officer was also my first day on call. I was used to being woken at night as my babies were not of the well-trained variety and it was not unusual for me to attend to them two or three times a night. However, I do not recall having to think during these episodes! Being woken by the bleep and being asked to run to A&E to assist with a patient who had been stabbed, left me sitting on the bed wondering what on earth I was doing.

I soon settled down and started to enjoy the work. The role swap became more comfortable and at least I had no concerns for the children's well-being knowing they were safe and happy with their dad.

After the requisite six months had passed, I went on to do my planned jobshare medical house officer post. This worked really well. Teresa and I worked on alternate weeks and we shared a morning handover on a Wednesday. However, the intention had been that Phil would be able to find computer work based at home, as half a house officer income was really insufficient for our needs. Unfortunately this proved to be extremely difficult as the IT industry was hitting its own recession. I ended up having to do extra work as a locum and we could no longer afford the fees for our children who were by this time happily settled in our church's independent primary school. This year was a big strain for us and so by the end of it we decided that I would once again work full-time.

I had lost my aspirations to do surgery and so assumed that I would become a GP. I planned my next jobs, which were at senior house officer grade (SHO) to fit in with the requirements for GP training. My first SHO post was in Accident and Emergency (A&E). Despite the arduous shifts, I really took to this work and enjoyed it more than anything I had done so far. However, I still felt that I ought to pursue general practice as a career. It would at least give good opportunity for part-time work once I was fully trained. At that time, I think I had a love–hate relationship with work. I loved the challenge of being a doctor and caring for patients and I was learning all the time. But unlike the present system, there was very little in the way of training or senior support. This meant that when I started a new post, I would often be asked to deal with situations which I may not have come across before, often on my own. It was not good for patients and not good for doctors.

A particularly frightening experience happened to me on one of the first days of my paediatric post in 1993. I was called to the labour ward urgently because a mother was having some difficulty delivering her baby.

The baby was born shortly after I entered the delivery room. He was pale, floppy and not breathing. Suddenly I was in the position of having to resuscitate this baby without proper training. I called for the consultant, but unbeknown to me, the switchboard put out test calls at the same time. The consultant ignored the call thinking that it was the usual test bleep. I continued to struggle with this infant, whose heart rate was getting slower – a sign that he was about to die. I literally shouted at the midwife to go and get help from anywhere and a consultant anaesthetist came to the rescue. I had given the baby a dose of adrenalin down the endotracheal tube but it was more than was necessary. By the time the consultant paediatrician arrived the baby had started breathing and had a good strong pulse. He reckoned my large dose of adrenalin had saved the baby's life. I was not so sure. I found the whole event devastating. This poor little patient of mine had somehow survived in the hands of an inexperienced junior doctor. I found it hard to see the positive side of the care I had given. I could not see that I had kept him well oxygenated and given him heart massage. I could not see that I had saved his life. Instead I kept thinking of my panic and how I had failed by giving the incorrect dose of adrenalin, despite being reassured that this had not been harmful; on the contrary, it had restored the baby's heart rate. I continued to ruminate over this. 'What if it happened again? What if I gave the wrong dose of another drug?' In addition, I was very tired. I was on call every fourth night and weekend. When I was at home I wanted to spend time with the children, taking part in their activities. I had little time for myself.

I fell ill with strange symptoms in the autumn of 1993; I had emergency surgery for a haematoma (a large blood clot) and 24 hours later, I developed severe sciatica and other physical symptoms including diarrhoea and weight loss. I was readmitted to hospital on regular morphine for the pain and underwent some very disagreeable investigations. There were no answers and the gastroenterologist decided this was all psychosomatic. The strain of the long hours was obviously beginning to show. I am sure he was right, this was induced by stress, but unfortunately his attitude was very unpleasant. He was rude, unsympathetic and disparaging. He told me I had wasted his time. His offensive manner was very upsetting to me and certainly did nothing to relieve the pressure I was under. I slowly recovered and returned to work shaken by this experience but determined to carry on despite it. I felt low, but this did not seem surprising considering what I had been through.

Our whole family had a wonderful holiday that Christmas 1993. My sister Mary was doing very well in her new line of work and decided to treat us all by paying for my parents, my brother, his two children, our family and my younger sister Sarah to come out to Hong Kong where she now lived. We then went on to one of the Philippine Islands to enjoy the tropical weather and warm seas. It was highly successful and we all

enjoyed ourselves. I was fully recovered when I came back from the holiday.

On our return, we had the serious business of Rebecca's future to sort out. Ever since she was a little girl, I had sent her to dance classes. It was something I had loved as a child. She had taken to this in a remarkable way and had even continued attending ballet classes in Bangkok. I had always regarded it as a fun activity and was reluctant to allow her to enter the examinations which the dance school at Southampton wanted their pupils to take. Shortly after we had arrived back in England, Rebecca, now aged six, had shown me one of her books which described White Lodge, the junior part of the Royal Ballet School for children aged 11–16. She told me quite determinedly that she was going to go there when she was 11. I found this amusing and related it to her ballet teacher. Sheila put me straight; Rebecca was extremely talented and Sheila advised me that this could be more than a childish dream. Shortly after this, Rebecca auditioned for the Junior Associates of the Royal Ballet School, which involved going up to a class in London once a month. She was successful. Simon kept saying 'I wish there was a Royal Football School!' Stephanie also loved her dancing and equally seemed to have a similar talent.

In the spring of 1994, Rebecca auditioned for White Lodge. I found this particularly testing. She was very determined to go, but I had been resolute

The children, just before the onset of my illness – Rebecca (11), Simon (9), Stephanie (7) and Jonathan (5).

that none of my children would go away to boarding school after my own unhappy experience. However, I recognised that Rebecca needed to do this and, by the time the audition came, I was as nervous as she was of the outcome. We were all very excited when she was awarded her place. She was a beautiful dancer and we were all very proud of her. Her new life was due to start in September. All of the children seemed content with their busy lives. In the meantime Stephanie had auditioned for Junior Associates and been successful in obtaining a place.

In August 1994, I decided to return to A&E to do the fourth and final hospital post which was required to complete my GP training. I had already spent six months in general practice, by this time. However, I found being back in A&E both challenging and enjoyable. When I was made aware that I could train in this speciality part-time, and was granted funding from the Deanery to do so, I was very pleased to have this opportunity to change my career direction. There was a new consultant in Southampton General A&E, Lynn Williams. I found her enthusiasm inspiring and both the consultants I worked for wholeheartedly supported my career aspirations. They also provided structured training and any confidence that I had lost in my skills through the traumatic 'baby incident' soon returned.

Once again I was faced with a child who was extremely close to death. This time, I really was on my own as I was working in the small casualty department at Lymington Hospital. This little boy had been found beside a bouncy castle at his birthday party. On this occasion I was able to resuscitate him in a calm and logical way. Sadly I was not able to save him. Later I found out that he had died of a previously undiagnosed heart defect and there was nothing that I could have done which would have helped him. I was distressed by his death and was self-reflective over the event. But I was not filled with self-reproach and I knew that I had done my best for this little boy, even though the outcome on this occasion was tragic.

I continued to enjoy looking after the many different patients who visit A&E departments with complaints ranging from minor cuts and bruises to life-threatening emergencies. I seemed to work well with the nursing staff and because I had worked in this speciality before I already had some experience, which helped to lessen the stresses of the job. My life was once again on an upward turn and I was full of hope for the future. I had less than six months to go until the part-time training was due to start and I was looking forward to the extra freedom it would bring so that I could spend more time at home with the family. Rebecca settled into White Lodge and came home every weekend. She showed no signs of homesickness and for that I was very relieved. I had no reason to become depressed.

CHAPTER 3

Falling into the pit

I cannot give an accurate picture of how the depression started. I do not know. It must have made its appearance sometime in late 1994; it may have been earlier than that. I believe after the 'psychosomatic' illness I had considered the possibility that I might in fact be depressed. I had even taken antidepressants for a short time, but I know that I was positive, hopeful and well when I started the A&E post in August 1994.

Sometime between August and the beginning of December, a relatively short period, not only had I self-diagnosed depression, but I had started treatment. I was prescribed medication by my GP and I was about to be assessed for psychotherapy courtesy of the sick doctors' counselling service. I took myself off work in mid December, still thinking that this was a treatable illness and I would soon be over it.

The Department of Psychiatry.

The referral to the sick doctors' counselling service had resulted in an assessment by a consultant psychotherapist at the dreaded DOP. This is an extract from the letter she wrote to my GP on 12 December 1994.

History

A 35-year-old married woman who has become the family bread-winner as the result of the recession. (Not true, it was my choice!) She presents with symptoms of depression and panic.

Her mood is depressed and she is close to tears most of the time. There is diurnal variation, being at her lowest in the morning with an improvement in the evening.

She has little interest in things, driving herself not to let her children and husband know the worst of her feelings. Given the opportunity she would stay in bed all day and did so yesterday.

Her concentration remains reasonable, though not at its usual high level. She uses computer games to occupy her mind and prevent herself from feeling terrible.

She has considered suicide and has made the decision that she must ensure her death if she moves down this path. She will take the amitryptiline she has, drive to a distant place and take the tablets (she may well have access to equally lethal tablets and knows how to kill herself). She has decided that although her husband would be better off without her, her children would suffer and she has chosen not to kill herself. It is important to her that she has been able to make this choice.

Her sleep has been disturbed for some time, with initial and early morning wakening. She is not troubled by dreams, but when she wakes, she does not feel rested. Her appetite is much reduced and she forces herself to eat. She has lost weight since August.

She is unable to cope with her job, becoming increasingly cautious and indecisive. She cannot withstand angry patients and ruminates later over what has happened. She is in a panic over decisions at work and about not being able to get herself back to work, if she should take time off.

Mental state examination

A thin, sad looking woman, dressed in an oversized jersey that accentuated her smallness and gave her a waif-like air.

She was sad and easily moved to tears by the horrors she has suffered and the difficulties she is facing in her present life. Her mood seemed to change when she talked about other matters, but this was more like putting a lid on things rather than her mood lifting. She is quick to smile but there is little pleasure in the smile, rather it is to distance patient and therapist. She expresses herself

well and honestly. She needed to be encouraged to elaborate matters, for example, her suicidal ideation, and to be shown that she has been heard and proper weight given to what she has been said. There was no evidence of thought disorder or psychomotor retardation. There was no evidence of hallucinations or delusions.

Diagnosis
Depression and panic in the context of present problems that have reactivated earlier conflicts.

I do not remember the interview and when I read this letter, I found it startling. Was this really me? I do remember wearing big jumpers but it certainly wasn't to give an impression of waif-likeness. However, on balance, I think it is fair description of what was happening at that time. After all, I can understand that although the future had been looking rosy, I was still a junior doctor working long hours in a stressful job. Despite finding the job very satisfying, I would have been the first to admit that A&E can be a particularly nerve-racking speciality. I had also recently seen Rebecca go off to boarding school and, not surprisingly, memories of my own departure from home must have been reawakened.

From then on I was to see the psychotherapist's colleague, Ian, but I now know that he was a registrar in psychiatry, training as a psychotherapist; the consultant was his supervisor. I was actually quite relieved when I met Ian. He was very pleasant and soon put me at ease. I do not remember much of the actual sessions except that he drew the boundaries early on. He was not seeing me as a 'doctor', but as a counsellor, so he was in no position to advise me over medical treatment.

It seems so weird that my sessions with Ian would have been subject to scrutiny and discussion by another party. I was under the impression that nothing would leave the four walls of the therapy room! (I am sure – or at least I hope – that I was told at some stage, but I certainly didn't retain that information.)

Oh that room, I remember it so well. It was someone's office that was conveniently vacant at the time that the sessions were run. The NHS chairs were covered with tasteless bright orange material. The outlook from the first floor window was on to another dreary building, the sky just visible. I remember dull weather and cloud. There were no signs of natural life, no trees, no grass, no garden to observe. There was not even a token pot plant in the room. I remember Ian, I liked seeing him; he seemed kind and understanding. The only problem was that despite pouring out my life history in great detail, delving into every nook and cranny where the root of the problem could lie buried, I did not feel any better.

Looking back at our family diary, I see that I had requested annual leave and then there are no further entries with shift times. The GP's notes

confirm that by this stage I was 'off sick'. My life had changed. The memories I do have are of long days spent in our bedroom doing very little, which concur with the document above. Phil was still the househusband, so I had no domestic responsibilities. Of course there is more to being depressed than feelings. It is more than just a state of mind. I felt very unwell and, when severe, the physical effects can become particularly apparent; they did so for me. I was continuously tired, exhausted and lacking in energy. I wanted to sleep, but often sleep would not come. When I did sleep, I would awake without feeling refreshed and with no desire to get up. Every task, however small, was a great effort. Eating was also a trial as I had little appetite and I was constipated. There seemed to be no activity which produced any comfort or respite apart from sleep, but even then dreams and nightmares could disturb that haven. As the illness progressed, I required treatment for low oestrogen, osteoporosis and an underactive thyroid. I was to learn that this disease seated somewhere in my brain was able to switch off hormonal systems. Historically the body had become divided in a completely artificial way as far as the medical world was concerned. The mind, body and spirit are considered separate entities; an attitude that has been highly influential, spilling over into modern society. Consequences are grave for the sufferer. I was entering the world of the 'mentally ill'; no flowers, chocolates and sympathy now. In fact I was experiencing increasing suicidal thoughts. I felt worthless, useless, a hopeless failure. This was real to me and I was also totally convinced that this was my fault in some way. I thought I was a weak person to have succumbed to such an illness and I must bear the blame of allowing this to happen. I loved the children dearly and in fact they gave me the only real protection from acting on my suicidal thoughts. I loved Phil, too, but my deluded mind and low self-esteem convinced me that he would have been much better off with someone else. How little I realised that his incredible love for me was to sustain all of us as a family, for what was to come through these long years.

The children – Rebecca 12, Simon 10, Stephanie 8 and Jonathan 6 – were blissfully unaware of what was happening to their mother and how it would affect their lives.

Rebecca had completed her first term at White Lodge, living out her dream of becoming a ballet dancer that had been present since early childhood. Simon was in his last year at the local primary school, a popular boy who loved his sport. Stephanie had become a junior associate of the Royal Ballet School, happily pursuing her own independent love of dancing. Jonathan was in the infant school, very sociable and particularly keen on football. Phil would pick Rebecca up every weekend, so we would be together, but the holidays became very precious times for us all and my annual leave had been booked over Christmas.

My new post was due to start on 1 February 1995. I was to be part-time

and supernumerary, which meant that I would have flexibility about when I worked, but still at Southampton General Hospital A&E. This was my dream job, training in my chosen career yet being able to spend more time with the children, but I never made it back – at least not for another seven years.

Christmas 1994 holds no memories for me. I have some photos, tacit reminders that it did actually take place. But even now the unforgettable is deep, somewhere irretrievable and I have no way of gaining access. I do not know to what extent this is a blessing; although many a time I have been told that it is. But how can anyone know how many rich, poignant moments are lost for me, or was every second of my life shrouded in darkness? This loss of memory continued throughout the years of my illness. It is not complete, but nonetheless disturbing. It is not right to have so many blank patches during this precious time when our children were growing up. It is something I bitterly regret.

As the New Year passed I remained off sick; the depression had not lifted at all despite the fact that I had been treated for several weeks now. Instead it was gaining momentum.

February 1995

On 16 February my desperation reached new heights. I had been on anti-depressants since December but there was no relief. In fact life was unbearable.

Depression is not easy to describe. The experience undoubtedly varies from person to person. However, I am sure everyone can relate to sadness. Yet this is different, principally because there appears to be no reason for it. In some instances it is possible for a sad event, a bereavement perhaps, to trigger an episode of depression. But this was not the case for me.

My experience was like a mist coming down. A dark mist, that clung to every part of my body and mind. I lived it and breathed it. It prevented me from moving because my arms and legs were so heavy and it shrouded my mind with a deep anguish that gnawed within. It hurt so much. I felt lonely, forlorn, lost, helpless. I felt very unwell. Alongside this ran thoughts of suicide. These were not logical thoughts, although they seemed so at the time. They were not just thoughts of escape, although who would blame me if they were. Somehow they seemed to run a parallel but separate path to the depressive feelings, related to some degree to the depths of my torment. However, my survival instinct was still alive and struggling against the ongoing battle over my life and being. It was as though I was stuck in a swamp up to my neck. I was reaching out to anyone who would take my hand and pull me free. I was being sucked under this dark, thick, disgusting quagmire. I believed someone would help me, so I held my arm up. I didn't want to die. Why should I? I had a loving, caring family. I had

a good job with strong career prospects. I was an extrovert personality, outgoing, and enjoyed my social life. I had great friends and I had a good sense of humour. I had a deep religious faith. All of this was in direct competition with thoughts of death and the suicidal thoughts were winning. They had taken over my mind. But why should depression kill me?

One of my friends was training in psychiatry and I felt desperate enough to call her. She took the call seriously and rang my GP. Phil took me to an urgent appointment the following day. From there we were sent directly for an emergency psychiatric assessment. Once again I had to attend the DOP but this time to see a consultant psychiatrist who decided that I needed to be admitted to hospital. Since I was a doctor, the policy was to be treated outside the geographical area of my work.

Phil recalls being told that he was to take me straight to the Old Manor Hospital in Salisbury, only stopping off at home in order to pack a few items. He was pretty shocked by this experience. He remembers arriving at this hospital and having to wait while I was being seen. I was given a private room on a ground floor, the window looking out on to the car park. Phil says that when he requested information, he was told that no one could say anything to him without my permission. Did this mean that the hospital doctors thought he was to blame in some way? That is what he wondered, anxious to know something more about my condition. The consultant interviewed me and then spent some time with Phil in order to explain what was happening. However, he still drove back to Southampton extremely concerned for me and worried for himself. That afternoon, he had to return home to caring for four children, his wife 30 miles away in a mental hospital. Neither of us had any experience of this. It was completely outside our territory.

I watched from the window as Phil drove away, tears rolling down my cheeks. This I do remember. What on earth had I done? This wasn't what I had anticipated when I asked for help – I felt so guilty. Every thought condemned me. Praying gave me no comfort. I wondered where God was.

Unfortunately having a mental illness leaves the sufferer open to many people's opinions, not just from the medical profession. Friends, family, anyone who knows you, are likely to have ideas about why this has happened.

In the weeks preceding this admission, inexplicably a few well-meaning people at church thought they had the answers. I pondered on their counsel. Clearly I wasn't being a good Christian. I had been advised to pray more, read the bible more, confess my sin, call on God … all well-intended but completely inappropriate. Of course I didn't pray enough. Who does? I certainly couldn't read the bible. I couldn't concentrate. My depression was telling me I was guilty, so confession of sin was easy. I was the worst person in the world, I could tell anyone that, no one had to tell me. As for

calling on God – oh yes, I knew about that. They were probably the only words I could muster. I did so now. Oh God … oh God … not in anger, but in desperation of spirit and of mind.

Back at home, of course, the majority of our good friends suffered with us. Without their love, prayers and support, I do not know how our family would have managed. However, on that day neither Phil nor I could find any reassurance from anywhere.

I had developed what was termed psychomotor retardation, although I was not aware of this at the time. This phrase describes the situation where the processes in the brain are slowed, so that not only is thinking slow, but it affects every sort of process including movement. The physical slowing can best be described as 'wading through treacle'. Everything is hard work including small tasks like eating or brushing teeth. One of the psychiatrists described how when he asked me a question, he would have to wait for a reply. It was almost as if he could see my mind trying to register the information and often the delay was so long that he would think that maybe I hadn't heard; just as he was about to repeat the question, my reply would come. This was the sort of slowness I was demonstrating. In this situation it is not unusual for a patient to be given electro-convulsive therapy, ECT, to rapidly alleviate these serious symptoms.

CHAPTER 4

Time is no great healer

I remember the first time the subject of ECT was mentioned during the admission. All in all it seemed a reasonable option to me. I had never seen it done, even as a medical student, and I was vaguely aware that it was still considered a controversial treatment. There is no doubt; I was scared at the prospect of having a jolt of electricity applied to my head in order to induce a seizure! However, I was reassured that I would not feel anything. I would be fully anaesthetised and I liked the idea of going 'off to sleep'. But the truth was that I was also incredibly desperate, so I wasn't really interested in the mechanisms of why or how ECT works, just whether it would.

The doctors convinced me that this treatment would be worth it – this would not be a cure, but it would make me feel a lot better. Unfortunately complications arose during the first ECT session. I woke to find myself surrounded by a number of people – nurses and doctors. It had taken me a long time to come round from the anaesthetic. It turned out that I have a genetic defect which means that I am unable to metabolise an anaesthetic drug called suxamethonium. It is given in these circumstances to briefly paralyse the body, which prevents painful convulsions. The drug remained in my system so I remained paralysed requiring artificial ventilation to support my breathing. This is most unusual and could have occurred with any anaesthetic. It was nothing to do with the actual ECT. In fact ECT, which has often been given a bad press, was given to me as a *life-saving treatment* on a number of occasions through the years, with obvious success.

Once the problem had been identified, different drugs were used and I went on to receive the whole course of treatment, which consists of a number of ECT sessions until an improvement is seen. The side effects could include memory loss for the time around the course of treatment and also a headache immediately after the ECT, which I did experience occasionally. We suspect the ECT is responsible for some of the persisting gaps in my memory for events during my illness and possibly even for the profound memory loss I have for the time preceding the treatment. However, I have learnt that severe depression in itself affects the ability of the brain to lay down memory, due to the patient's lowered concentration or inattention to general life and living. This probably explains much of what happened to

me and also the fact that what I do remember is often highly emotionally charged, i.e. situations which had gained my attention.

The good news was that the ECT lifted my mood. I was discharged from hospital, not completely well, but I had improved enough to go home.

March 1995

The admission had lasted for six weeks, which seemed an awfully long time to be in hospital. Apart from what I have described, I remember very little of that time; I do not even remember the layout of the ward. Visiting was difficult for Phil and the children as the journey to Salisbury took about 45 minutes. My parents, who had retired by that time, lived in Teffont, a Wiltshire village, so at least it was convenient for them to visit me.

In addition to the ECT, my antidepressant medication had been changed. However, when I was seen in outpatients two weeks after being discharged, the consultant was disappointed to see a marked deterioration. I was started on a different class of drug with a warning to the GP to prescribe only a week's supply at a time since they are dangerous in overdose. Nothing much had changed, I was still suicidal.

Extract from my writing on 20 March 1995
I feel terrible. I don't know where to turn. I want to talk to someone but I don't know who. I've told Phil and he's very patient, but I feel I need to unburden elsewhere as well. I don't feel like doing anything – the idea of watching TV, playing patience, housework ... any of the usual distractions is terrible. I wish I could sleep on and on and on. Oh yes, I've thought about it (suicide), it makes it less likely. I wondered whether if I talk about it, I won't be believed for that reason. Maybe I should keep quiet ... however when I think suicidal plans, it really does relieve some of the horribleness and I haven't found another way out. God help.

April 1995

One month later, an outpatient letter from the consultant sent to my GP:

I saw Cathryn and her husband as planned. As you know her mood has continued to deteriorate over recent weeks despite increasing the dose of dothiepin. As well as presenting in a depressed state, she was very miserable at the prospect of having to be readmitted ... In view of the fact that her husband is able to

work at home and ensure that she is never alone and the fact that he is able to supervise the medication, has led me to cautiously decide to attempt the option of adding in lithium ... I plan to keep a very close eye on the situation by at least weekly visits to the outpatient clinic, but please feel free to contact me and possibly arrange admission if you feel the situation is becoming unsafe to continue at home.

Summer 1995

One week later, on 3 May, I was readmitted for another course of ECT. I was discharged again in June on four different drugs – two antidepressants, one sedative and one to counteract the side effects. It is noted in the clinic letter two weeks later, that my 'mood is beginning to dip again'.

After this admission, a request was made to the Community Psychiatric Service for me to be allocated a CPN (Community Psychiatric Nurse), although it took three months before it actually became a reality. No doubt there had been a waiting list.

Since December, I had been on sick pay which was equivalent to my full salary for six months. This was coming to an end and I was due to have the final six months as half pay. Clearly this in itself was a major stress for both Phil and me. Meantime Phil had been applying for jobs. Finally he was offered a position back in his field of expertise – as a computer programmer – in Guildford. It was quite a journey to get there, but it was work and therefore a salary. Of course, this also brought with it the problem of childcare, which we had not had to face so far. At least now I was out of hospital, I would be able to look after the children. After a fashion.

I look back at the family diary; it's packed with the children's activities – dancing lessons, swimming, football, friends coming and friends to go to. Alongside these are doctors' appointments and the continuing psychotherapy every week with Ian. But there were also social events for us as a family and church events. In fact, I was quite adept at a presentation of normality on such occasions. (Although I record in my writing what a mask this was, how much effort it took to preserve this and suppress my true feelings.) I was obviously difficult to live with, which is entirely reasonable. I was irritable, unenthusiastic, disinterested and pessimistic; no wonder Phil and I had frequent disagreements from which arguments and rows would erupt.

So life continued through the long summer holiday behind a façade of coping. The children took it in turns to stay with their two sets of grandparents and we even had a two-week trip to a Eurocamp on the Costa Brava. I remember the long, hot drive to reach our destination but little else.

The children enjoying the holiday at Eurocamp.

September 1995

September brought little change and the outpatient letter confirmed this: 'Cathryn continues to be stuck in a moderately severe depressive illness and so far there has been no convincing improvement despite the change of medication ... I feel we must persevere with a biological approach to this disorder because I am not convinced that there are any psychological issues that can be dealt with in a productive way.' A further increase in one of the drug doses was the outcome of that visit. I had been allocated a CPN by this stage and he was paying me regular visits at home to monitor my progress and provide nursing support. One month later, the news from the clinic was good. There was some improvement and we even talked about the possibility of a return to part-time work the following year.

November 1995 – April 1996

November sadly proved that the improvement had been short-lived and I was given another increase in the dose of my medication. Throughout the years of depression, I was extremely conscientious in taking the drugs I was prescribed. I was highly motivated to get better and still firmly held the belief that medicine alongside the psychotherapy would provide a cure. I

was also terrified of becoming worse. I was prepared to put up with side effects and would rather take an additional drug to counteract them if possible, than risk decreasing the dose. The side effects varied with each different preparation. I remember in particular experiencing tremor, dry mouth and nausea. I also remember being in a semi-stuporous haze, but I am not sure whether this was the depression or the effects of the treatments.

My CPN wrote to the psychiatrist from the Old Manor Hospital at Salisbury and to my GP in December expressing increasing concern. He had developed a supportive relationship with me over the three months since he had started to visit. He was worried because this support had to be terminated since he was due to move. He also pointed out that I had had no input from female staff and was therefore requesting that his successor be a woman. This was not to be, but Andrew Eva, my new CPN, was also very understanding and I was more able to talk to him than to the medical staff. Twelve months had passed and I was obviously no better off than a year ago.

Despite this, my guilt at being off sick was immense. I continued to take active steps to get another job. Even though I knew that I wanted to do Accident & Emergency Medicine as a career, I was also near to the completion of my GP training. I was actually offered a job to do the final stage part-time. Once again this was not to be. I realised that I was not well enough and the psychiatrist strongly advised me to turn it down – I did so.

Another Christmas went by, another school holiday to endure. The children being home on holiday was definitely a mixed blessing! My desire to be a good mother gave me just enough strength to carry on, but it meant that I had to expend considerable energy in daily activities. I was quite determined that the children would not see my distress, but putting on a front took considerable effort. My CPN became increasingly worried and, in February, I had another urgent outpatient review. I had been treated in Salisbury for over a year now and the travel to outpatients had been manageable. However, the psychiatrist there realised that my illness was proving resistant to treatment. Admission to hospital so far away from home was a strain for our family, particularly now Phil was working 50 miles from home in another direction. It was for this reason that I was asked to see another psychiatrist back at the DOP. I needed admitting and fortunately there were no beds. This justified the referral to the local private hospital, Marchwood Priory.

There was no comparison in terms of comfort and facilities at this hospital. The grounds were beautiful, with a lovely view from the window of my room. All the rooms were private with en suite bathrooms. It was quiet and peaceful. There were facilities for exercise and communal rooms to relax in – it was more like a friendly hotel than a hospital. However, I was still very withdrawn and even though the staff encouraged me to take

my meals with the other patients in the communal dining room, I managed this on only a few occasions. My parents still visited and my mother sought permission for me to have a bird feeder erected on one of the trees visible from my window as I did little other than sit staring out of it.

Phil and the children continued at home, but of course this time it was different. Phil was working. He remembers well the strain of trying to organise for the children to be cared for. He became a single parent, but with the added responsibility of having to visit his very sick wife and beginning to wonder whether there really was going to be a medical breakthrough. Meanwhile the psychiatric teams had convinced themselves that my psychotherapy was going to get to the root of the problem.

Reading the account of my family history as written by the assessing psychiatrist at the DOP, I now have no doubt that the depression was exaggerating many aspects of my life, so that minor sad events were blown out of all proportion. In particular, I had become obsessed with the drug error which I had made in the paediatric post. I did not mention the fact that the baby had actually benefited as a result and had certainly come to no harm. I did not mention the fact that the resuscitation drug doses, normally up on a notice on the wall, had been removed to be edited on that day. I did not mention the fact that I had competently managed the situation on my own, despite lack of training. My negative and deluded thinking had changed the story to such an extent that the psychiatrist came to think that I had been responsible for causing serious harm or even the death of the baby. I relived the fear, the panic and my mistake. I chastised myself endlessly.

Similarly the circumstances of my childhood underwent comparable processes, magnification of small events – a molehill soon became a mountain. I had no ability to see the good or positive aspects of the past. There was no bright side to my life. My clouds had no silver linings.

During the psychotherapy sessions, I was talking about the past, recalling in great detail situations which had been difficult for me in some way. Negative emotions were surfacing with great regularity. In retrospect, I am not certain how helpful this was. However, we were all searching for a cause of my problems including my wider family and friends. The medical team also wanted to know why my depression was proving so resistant to treatment; I think this led to a preoccupation by everyone involved that the origin of the illness must lie somewhere in my past.

The positive side to this, I believe, lay in the support that I received from some wonderful friends, part of the pastoral team at our church. David and Marie Damp allowed me to talk over the memories of the past, but guided me through the spiritual process of letting go, forgiving those whom I needed to forgive, thus preventing bitterness from entering the situation. Unfortunately my emotion did not respond to this process either. The desperate, gnawing sadness continued to torture my soul. My suicidal thoughts

were changing. I was no longer thinking about 'medical' ways to end my life. Violent methods also plagued my thoughts. I required one-to-one nursing at this time.

The medical team did their best to exclude any other causes for the depression since I was displaying 'severe psychomotor retardation'. Eventually, after 17 ECT treatments, my mood improved sufficiently for me to be discharged. I had been in the Priory Hospital for two and a half months.

CHAPTER 5

Freely consenting?

April 1996

Now discharged from Marchwood Priory, I was back at home, still feeling very low, but at least I was home.

Unfortunately, just before I was discharged, Phil had an accident. He was playing a game of tennis with a work colleague and suddenly felt a very severe pain in the back of his ankle, causing him to fall to the ground. He had ruptured his Achilles tendon. His left leg was put in a full-length plaster cast. That made two of us out of action. He was still in considerable pain, not helped by the fact that he had also injured his shoulder. This meant that using crutches was impossible, so he had become effectively bed-bound. I was not really well enough to look after him myself, but we had no choice. We struggled on, calling upon our long-suffering friends and Phil's mother to help with practicalities like driving the children to their activities and taking Rebecca back to White Lodge

My medical care had once again reverted back to the DOP. The psychiatrist I saw had never actually met Phil, but was convinced that his demands on me were adding to my problems. When we learnt of this, we reeled with the shock. Phil did not choose to sustain this painful injury or to be immobile. However as a result of this, social services were brought in to help me with household activities, which did provide us with some relief. It was not long before he was up and about. Fortunately this psychiatrist decided that he needed to refer me to the care of the specialist in mood disorders, Prof Chris Thompson.

June 1996

Phil still had his leg in plaster, but had managed to sell the mini and buy a second-hand car – an automatic. This at least enabled him to drive and get back to work. My carer from social services came in every day for an hour and life had resumed some sort of routine. However, I was far from well. I was very low and my thoughts were often preoccupied with violent ways of ending my life. This was kept in check by the presence of the children, as usual reminding me that I had a duty to continue living. I had not yet

received an appointment to see Prof Thompson and my current psychiatrist was encouraging me to accept yet another hospital admission. My drug therapy had once again been altered and I was started on six-weekly depot injections. I was very lethargic.

I had started deliberately exposing myself to risky situations. I had always suffered with summer asthma and hayfever, being allergic to grass pollen. Now I was deliberately inhaling from a sack of hay, knowing it would make me wheezy, hoping that I could provoke an attack severe enough to kill me. Then at least I would have died from natural causes; at least that is what my sick mind was telling me. In fact, the breathlessness was so unbearable, I could not resist using the inhaler and after an hour or so, the attack would settle down, the children would return from school and I would be fine. However it was very unpleasant and my secret desperation was not abating. I started taking risks in all sorts of ways. I was lucky not to get knocked down on the road and maybe luckier still not to have been the cause of any accidents. Truly there must have been an angel watching over me.

Phil has described to me the day that he returned home to find me covered in blood. My memory of the actual event is hazy. I was alone in the house and vaguely remember being in our conservatory. I smashed up a plastic disposable razor with a hammer to remove the blade. It was the first time that I cut myself deliberately and something which I have regretted ever since. I have a total of 24 scars over both my arms, which I made on that one occasion. I believe that it was a sort of pain experiment: this is what people do, so I will try it. I reported to Phil later that it had relieved tension, but I cannot say this for sure. I did not seek help to get the wounds attended to afterwards and I only cut my arms on this one occasion, but it was on the area of the body where scarring has everlasting consequences. In fact for that sort of self-harm, the severe pain is relatively short-lived, but if a doctor were to ask your permission to use a scalpel to cut your skin, then it would be extraordinary to allow it without local anaesthetic. It hurts. For some reason, my brain had prevented the primitive pain avoidance mechanism we all possess from working. It had been over-ruled and more than that I had actively sought physical pain.

As I have said, it was regrettable and yet more than that, it was a disaster. Now I carry the hallmarks of my previously disturbed psyche. It is difficult to bear while stigma still pervades all through our society. Usually the people who see the scars do not understand why it may have happened. Rather there are looks of bewilderment, embarrassment, even revulsion. I have heard the snide remarks and the backchat when patients have arrived in A&E having done similar things to themselves or when like me they have scars revealing that they have done so in the past. (Unfortunately there are still many hospital and ambulance staff who see this only as a behavioural problem, failing to see the possible reasons behind it.) It is

hard for me to explain why I did it. It is hard for me to understand why I did it, more so now I am well. No wonder it is hard for someone close to me to comprehend, let alone a stranger. It is one of the battles with stigma that I am still facing and have not yet won. When I see or hear of anyone who might possibly do this to themselves, my plea is 'don't do it'. However tempting it might seem at the time, remember the effect, it takes a minute, but lasts a lifetime. It's just not worth it.

The frustration of the psychiatric team is evident in their letters written during that period. They wanted me to be readmitted to hospital, but I was not 'sectionable', meaning that they could not force me into hospital against my will. I had suicidal thoughts but I told them adamantly that I would not carry out my plans. I was receiving psychotherapy every week, on maximal medication, seeing my CPN once or twice a week and going nowhere, fast.

Letter to GP from the consultant's registrar
Problem: Recurrent depressive disorder, current episode severe.

At the request of the CPN Andrew Eva and in the absence of the consultant, I visited CW at home on 24/6/96. Andrew was concerned at her degree of retardation and the severity of her depressed mood as well as her intermittent suicidal ideation.

I note that her mood has been severely depressed for the past month and there have been associated suicidal ideas, including poisoning herself with carbon monoxide or of self poisoning with her prescribed medication. However she has not made progress to realising such thoughts and cites the incentive of responsibility to her family which is more borne out of duty than affection. On the Hamilton scale (a score for depression) she scores 25 but she has some atypical features so that it is important to emphasise *that she is suffering from a severe symptom pattern*. She is managing to cope with a minimal domestic routine and receives daily help from Social Services which appears adequate. She is compliant with prescribed medication. Apart from input from our CPN, she sees Dr R for psychotherapy and consultant psychiatrist in Outpatients.

How can we best help her when she is averse to hospital admission? The responsibility to her family makes her averse to hospital treatment and we will try and co-operate with her wishes up to a point. While she is significantly depressed we are continuing to monitor her closely in the community and aiming to optimise her drug treatment as well as keeping further ECT in mind. I note that she is due to see Prof Thompson on 3 July and I will inform my consultant of her progress on his return next week.

July 1996

The first visit to Prof Thompson took place as planned. Fortunately he was a good deal more understanding towards Phil and recognised well how much the community and psychiatric services were relying on him to provide care for the whole family as well as for me. He was also very concerned for me and was of the opinion that I should be back in hospital. But my guilt at leaving the children continued to make me unwilling to comply. However, he made more changes to the medication and Andrew Eva my CPN was by now visiting daily. Two weeks later, the team decided that it was urgent that I return to hospital, since there was no improvement and so pressure was put upon me once again to agree to admission. Since as a doctor I was still supposed to be treated out of the area that I practised in, I was once again admitted to the comfortable and pleasant environment of Marchwood Priory, but how little I appreciated this. What I did not know was that this was not in fact the reason for my admission to the Priory. It was because there were no beds at the DOP. The Trust fiercely rejected any idea that I should be given any privileged treatment just because I was a doctor practising in their city!

While I was there, I fell in the bathroom. It turned out that this was due to postural hypotension (low blood pressure on standing up) caused by a combination of the medication and dehydration. I had to be taken to my old workplace, Southampton General A&E, for stitches. It was very embarrassing for me to be brought there as a mental patient. I hoped that no one would know me, but not surprisingly that was not to be. However, I survived the embarrassment and humiliation that I felt.

We had a family holiday planned in Dorset, staying at a hotel with Phil's parents and sister. This, combined with the fact that the children were now on their summer holidays, enabled me to pick up sufficiently to be discharged after yet another course of ECT and further changes to my medication.

September 1996

The time away had not been easy. There were quite a lot of family tensions, no doubt exacerbated by our difficulties. I was relieved to get home. In fact, I felt quite good initially. I continued to faithfully take the prescribed medication and I had a new carer from social services to help me with domestic duties. Annette was a lovely lady who quite coincidentally went to our church. She was pleasant, helpful and understanding without being intrusive. However, I was holding out. The holidays were almost over and I was highly motivated to keep going only while I had the children around me most of the day.

Once they were back at school, I drove to a car park by the sea; my

intention was to kill myself with the exhaust fumes. Fortunately I started to think it over logically and I came up with a number of problems. Having worked in A&E, I was only too aware of the consequences of a failed attempt. I was worried about being found alive, but being left with brain damage, I was also worried that I would be forced into hospital. But probably my greatest concern was still for my children. I realised that they would have to live with the disgrace that their mother had committed suicide. I was desperately wondering how I could cover up my death, make it look accidental.

I abandoned this plan and drove back home. But I had decided to start overdosing slowly on lithium, knowing that it would eventually poison me and kill me. I thought this would go unnoticed. However, somehow it came to the attention of the psychiatric team, though I cannot remember how. It earned me a Section. I was admitted to the DOP against my will.

Being sectioned under the provisions of the Mental Health Act is not for the faint-hearted. Usually the process starts when a doctor decides that your condition warrants urgent hospitalisation either for assessment or for treatment when you do not agree. The law requires that two doctors independently examine you and that the Section is recommended by an approved social worker. All have to be in agreement, so at least three interviews with the patient have to take place. When faced with this situation as a patient you may not actually know what is going on. No doubt hospital admission will have been suggested, but in my case I was adamant that I did not want another admission. I had reached the point where I no longer believed that treatment would help me. I felt so down that death really did seem the only way out.

For all of us, every instinct that we are born with cries out to survive, but suddenly for me this was not the case. Living had become a kind of hell. Furthermore, the very people who were supposed to be helping me had suddenly assumed awesome power. They were able to dictate my whereabouts, to force me to the place that I had dreaded ever since I knew of its existence. That's how it felt. The children were taken to our friend's house, while I was removed from the house to the waiting ambulance. Not a pretty sight. The ambulance crew had seen it all before. It did not faze them at all. From their point of view, I was just another woman, probably a 'time waster'. There were far more urgent patients who needed their help.

This memory still lives on. I can see it now. Half-heartedly they attempt to persuade me to come voluntarily. Adrenalin is pumping through my veins, suddenly I possess energy. I want to run, but they drag me back. I cannot hold out against two strong men. Sobbing, I am dragged out of my house and into the back of the ambulance. This time it was not to March-wood.

Once at the DOP and on the ward, the doors were locked and now I had become a prisoner for my own good, for my own safety. The nursing staff

seemed oblivious to the enormity of what had happened. For them it was a common enough event. This was not the Priory, where you are shown to your en suite bedroom. This was a dreary, run-down, understaffed institution. The furniture was old, the carpet stained and even for people in the best of health, the general demeanour was in itself depressing.

I was clerked in by a rather disinterested junior doctor. I did not want to talk, I wanted to scream and shout. I had become the lowest of the low, humiliated. I did not know how to resist, but I did. I was very angry and my co-operation was limited. I refused to eat and drink. I refused to consent to ECT. But my autonomy had been taken away from me. I was even given ECT against my will.

Everyone was assigned a primary nurse. He or she was responsible for your nursing care whilst on the ward, but inevitably because of their shifts contact was erratic. The nurses' duties varied, as did their responsibilities. Personalities were different too and so sometimes it seemed like a lottery whether you would be looked after by a nurse you could relate to.

My bed was in a six-bedded dormitory and we were not allowed to stay in there for long periods during the day. As a non-smoker, there was only one alternative for me and that was to sit in the dayroom. This was a large room for men and women. Everyone was thrown together, regardless of diagnosis. I was extremely depressed, but was compelled to sit in a room where all sorts of 'carrying on' took place.

Most of the chairs were placed around the edges of the room. High-backed, not terribly comfortable chairs. The light blue, synthetic velvet was stained. There was that indescribable hospital smell pervading every area of the ward. The dayroom was the main thoroughfare for the men's dormitories and the smoking room, so there was plenty of coming and going. In one corner was a television, on continuously, usually a channel with daytime chat shows. It was only on rare occasions that there was something I would consider worth watching. I soon learnt to leave well alone. If another patient attempted to change channel, disputes would arise. I stayed away. There were drug abusers, alcohol abusers, those with psychotic illnesses, all thrown in together. I have memories of particular patients probably high on drugs swearing continuously, using filthy abusive language sometimes directed at staff, sometimes at a fellow patient and sometimes at no one in particular. Not infrequently, violence would break out and furniture would be overturned and at this point, every nurse on the unit would appear, to come and take control. The perpetrator would be escorted off, to be calmed down, but it left the rest of us far from calm. One of the entries in the medical notes describes how a chair thrown narrowly missed my head. It was very frightening.

I think it was during this admission that I felt as if I had lost every thread of my dignity. My previous occupation meant nothing now. Me, a doctor? It was laughable. How would I ever be able to work again after this, even if

I were to recover? Here I was in the worst place imaginable. There was no more privilege, no private room, no private bathroom. There was no place to go, no gardens to walk in, no retreat. I was forced to socialise. However much I wanted to be left alone, my fellow patients were having none of it. I was constantly badgered until I revealed my name and my reason for being in the DOP on a Section. The nightmare was never-ending. I took my anger out on myself in the only way possible within the situation. I started to self-harm. I was head banging, biting myself, behaving just like the stereotypical madman.

Unfortunately the nightmare was not confined to my experience of the ward. During one of the ECT treatments, the anaesthetist made the mistake of giving me the paralysing drug, before putting me to sleep. It seems that the needle in the back of my hand had ceased to work and so I was left paralysed, being unable to move or communicate, knowing what was about to happen, scared witless, praying like crazy. In my mind I was shouting at them, 'I'm awake, I'm awake, don't do it, please don't do it.' I do not remember the shock being delivered, thankfully. Apparently you don't. Perhaps that is why, in days gone by, it was administered without modern anaesthetic. I was highly traumatised. Fortunately the nurse in charge noticed my swollen, reddened hand, but only after the event, when I was in recovery. I think that is why they believed me when I told them what had happened. The hospital Trust paid for me to go to Marchwood Priory to have a specialised therapy (EMDR) used to treat post-traumatic stress syndrome, in an attempt to lessen the impact of this medical 'mishap'. I did not lodge any sort of complaint. I knew that even the best doctors were fallible and no one had been unkind. They gave me no further ECT treatments at that time. I *did* start to eat and drink again, perhaps more insightful, perhaps wiser that resistance was futile.

This was the general pattern of all of my hospital admissions: at first I would have to remain on the ward continuously, then as I began to improve, the gradual process would start of rehabilitating me back to home. I might be allowed out for an evening or part of the weekend. This would be increased in a stepwise progression and once I was felt to be coping, a whole weekend including an overnight stay would be granted. Then there may be overnights during the week, times at home alone until finally it would be deemed appropriate that I could be discharged. The slow process also allowed time for any community support that was required to be put in place. Being on a Section did not change this system, but it was more gradual and the progression more cautious. Every time I left the ward a form (Section 17 leave) had to be signed authorising the departure. This had to be signed by the consultant in charge of my care and it could not be done retrospectively.

At the end of October, it was considered that I had improved sufficiently to be finally allowed out of hospital, but only on prolonged Section 17

leave. This meant that I could be returned to the ward at any time. I applied for a Mental Health Tribunal review in an attempt to have the Section overturned. I was still extremely resentful about what had happened.

November 1996

It seems that life was improving a little. I was still at home and sleeping better. (I had been particularly bothered by either extreme of being unable to sleep or over-sedated, feeling generally groggy and sleepy during the day.) There was a lot of activity to attend to as the children prepared for Christmas shows and concerts. Andrew Eva my CPN was visiting regularly again, as was the social worker. It must have been a relief to Phil that I was back at home. While I was in hospital he had had to arrange for someone to pick the children up from school and look after them until he got back from work. Every week was a major organisational exercise. However, my application to be released from the Section had been refused. I was having a lot of intrusive thoughts and it was decided that although I was not hearing voices at that time, the thoughts were of a similar nature (termed psychosis). I was started on another antipsychotic drug in an attempt to bring these under control.

CHAPTER 6

Concerns for everyone

So far this account has concentrated on me and how I felt, but in fact this illness affected many people close to me, especially Phil and the children, but also my wider family, as well as our friends.

It is obvious to all that Phil was deeply involved. How he coped I do not know, but somehow he found the inner strength to continue. Much of the time, he lived on 'autopilot'. Life was very hectic as can be evidenced from the family diary. During the week the children had many after-school activities, mainly of the sporting variety for the boys and Stephanie like her sister before her had several different dance classes to attend. At weekends he had at least one return drive to Richmond Park in London, in order that Rebecca could spend the weekend at home. On many occasions Phil's mother did one of the journeys also. Like many children of those ages, they also had social activities, parties, school concerts, etc. . . . If Phil could not do these himself, he was still responsible and therefore had the task of finding willing friends or one or other of our supportive mothers to do this for him. We will always be very grateful for the help we received during that time.

However, Phil's life was much more than activity co-coordinator. My care and treatment was given by a multidisciplinary team of the psychiatrists, the nurses on the ward and the long-term involvement of my psychotherapist. However, Phil was not only my husband but my principal carer. His opinion would be sought whilst I was in hospital but much more so once I had been discharged. Then the Community Plan Approach or CPA was put into action. The community team consisted of the social worker, occupational therapist (OT) and community psychiatric nurse (CPN) and my GP who were involved in my care while I was at home. The social worker would organise any home support I required. They expected updates from Phil and his opinion when I was at home. He was also obliged to monitor my condition and take responsibility for my safety. Phil had lost me, his friend, his confidante and his lover. He was living in his own nightmare.

Despite his apparent stoicism, Phil recalls times of utter despair, leaving our house to arrive at friends totally disconsolate. He says that for most of the latter part of my illness, he was expecting to get a call to say that I was dead. It was like I was terminally ill, but this was not recognised even by those close to him. In fact that was pretty near to the truth. He assumed

that it was just a matter of time, but yet he continued to hope and pray, although by the time six years had gone by, even those aspects were dwindling to an all-time low.

Surprisingly perhaps, the doctors involved did not always provide support for him or even understanding; communication fluctuated from being very good and consistent once I was admitted at the Old Manor to being non-existent when I was seen back at the DOP. However, this changed when Prof Chris Thompson took over my care. Certainly in the later years all the doctors involved were much more communicative with him, perhaps realising how much they relied on his support and his ongoing commitment to care for me.

Phil was also very concerned that if he were to show any weakness, a heavy-handed social worker would decide to interfere with the care of our children. At the back of his mind, he was afraid that the children might be 'taken away', something he never had the opportunity to express to those involved. There was never any overt suggestion of this, but nonetheless the fear remained for much of the time. He thinks this started early on in the illness when a social worker recommended that they should have 'input'. With the best of motivations, I am sure, he suggested placement of the children in a social services based 'after school' programme. In fact this was the last thing our family wanted. The children needed to be with loving friends or family after school, not strangers. Unfortunately this lack of understanding of our needs made Phil reluctant to ask for any sort of help. He was still nervous as a result of the media reporting in the 1980s of the way social services had abused their powers. I am glad he didn't share this thought with me ... it would have added greatly to my distress.

Since my recovery, there have been numerous occasions where I have been asked whether my husband is still with me. When I say that he is, there is often great admiration expressed for Phil. He deserves this in every respect. He was undeniably a man of immense courage and determination. I have been told that later on in my illness, the multidisciplinary team involved had decided that Phil was 'too good to be true'. Prof Thompson put them right. He reminded them that Phil had an active faith and that he loved his wife.

As much as for me, the children gave Phil the fortitude to continue. When it all started at least they were not old enough to comprehend what was happening. They carried on life and living as children do. They were also rewarding in providing their love and affection; there was the delight and enjoyment that watching children grow up brings. They still laughed and joked, were naughty and silly and funny as children are. However, as they got older and passed from the innocence of their childhood into adolescence, their understanding evolved. It came at a price. No one was let off the hook.

White Lodge offered Rebecca some protection in that she was away from

home during the academic year and quite often the periods of my discharge home would be during the school holidays. However, she knew that her mother was seriously ill. It was a hard burden for her to bear away from home. There was an occasion where she was sent home from school unwell and tearful, remaining in this state for two weeks while I was in hospital unable to give her the comfort she needed. Yet she was strong and came through it, doing well in her exams and graduated from the school, having been made head girl.

Simon thought that my job had made me very tired and that was why I went to hospital. As he grew up, he didn't learn much more except that he knew that my illness was embarrassing and certainly not something you talked about. A few of his close friends knew I was in hospital, but that was the extent of his and their knowledge. He accepted the situation – life was as it is. In retrospect he knows that his schooling was affected, but he thinks that was to a large extent to do with the circle of friends he was in. Unfortunately the inevitable teenage experimenting with cannabis became a regular habit and Simon says he enjoyed being 'stoned'; it took away the reality of life. He never talked to anyone about his feelings, but once he was smoking weed on a regular basis, he didn't much care anyway. We did not realise that this was happening to him at the time.

All four of the children lived as though they had a mother who wasn't really there, not part of their lives and in reality it was true. Jonathan and Stephanie were even younger when my illness started. So, like Simon, they had little in the way of questions about why it had happened or what it was about.

Stephanie was noticeably more affected by the time she was a teenager. She became increasingly homesick and regretted her time at White Lodge. She left in the middle of the term during her fourth year, unable to return after her usual weekend at home. She also suffered with a mild depression and needed help from our GP.

Both the girls gave me strong spiritual encouragement as they grew older. They wrote me notes and cards encouraging me to trust God. They took on a responsibility and concern for my welfare – it was the wrong way round, I should have been doing this for them.

Interestingly, when Jonathan entered secondary school, his best friend's mother had died of cancer and so was likewise looked after by a combination of his father and grandmother with helpful friends stepping in. I do not think this was a coincidence. They had a lot in common.

My parents had an incredible struggle with the diagnosis of depression. They found it very difficult to understand, particularly because it had never been experienced by anyone in our family. They were very concerned that a cause had been missed, especially since we had been to Hong Kong and the Philippines less than a year before the onset of my symptoms. Their worry centred on the fact that I had been taking the anti-malarial drug

Larium. It was at this time that an association was found between this drug and developing psychotic symptoms in some predisposed individuals. They were convinced that this had been overlooked. It was hard for them to accept that this was not the reason for the depression.

It was also difficult for them because I was expressing negative thoughts and attitudes towards my childhood experiences, particularly boarding school. I was relating events that occurred which, if they had been heard of before, would have been long since forgotten. They felt wretched that the education which my father had worked so hard to provide for me could possibly have a part in causing my illness. They did not understand our relationship with the church and were worried that this was in fact a malevolent influence on my life, concerned that our non-denominational, non-conformist church could have been responsible for undue pressures.

Everyone was desperate for an answer. Why Cathy Wield? Why wasn't she responding to treatment? How long was this going to continue?

I had a good circle of friends, but some of them could not cope either. I had dropped out of work, I had dropped out of church life and I dropped out of my social life. I became increasingly isolated. We did still see good friends when I was home, but it was a great strain for me, so no doubt it was a great strain for them too. It is never easy to keep visiting sick people when they don't get better, let alone depressed sick people. Somehow visiting in a psychiatric hospital does not have the same appeal. Funnily enough the flowers, presents and cards which seem to be commonplace in other hospitals are not part of the deal. No one knows whether they should visit or not, and if they did, what would they say? The truth is that psychiatric hospitals are frightening environments for the first time visitor. There are 'strange' people around, but is that not the case anywhere you go? Now I was one of them. Many relationships fell by the wayside. Of those that remained, I am so grateful for their support. Dave and Marie were two such friends who were particularly helpful to both of us. They were kind, loving and consistently willing to listen. They visited me throughout the illness and supported Phil as well. They talked to us, prayed with us and gave us spiritual counsel and encouragement. There were others too. It would be difficult to name everyone individually, but thank you for your friendship, even doing small things like giving a lift to one of our children meant so much to us.

The church that we attended was very supportive but, as in all walks of life, understanding of mental illness was sometimes lacking. When I was out of hospital, I would sometimes attend the Sunday meeting (service). Once again, friends who knew me well stuck by me. I wanted to be prayed for because I wanted to get better and I really did not care how. However, I had no means of resisting challenges to my spiritual life. I had to be careful who I allowed to pray for me. The depression spent all day telling me what a bad person I was and how I had failed. Other people adding their views

to this made it even more convincing. However, it was not just church attenders who gave me advice. Anyone who learnt of my plight would have a suggestion for my cure, ranging from cranial massage, acupuncture and alternative therapies to various self-help books. All came with a recommendation; everyone knew of someone who had been helped. Unfortunately this just added to my feelings of failure. I felt that I was letting these kind people down, but nothing seemed to help me.

We still have on our shelves some of those books about depression, given or recommended to us; some of them written by Christian authors but certainly not exclusively. I am sure many people do find the root of their problems revealed during the reading of these books, but I did not. The one thing which I really did believe in, Christian healing prayer, made no difference either. In fact, I never lost my faith in God and I cried out to Him in desperation on a frequent basis. The problem was that any sort of criticism implied or otherwise went straight to my spirit.

I know intentions were good and many people shared a terrible sense of frustration at seeing our struggles, wondering how they could help. I gave up. It amazes me that some of our faithful friends stayed the course. I am so glad they persevered.

CHAPTER 7

Torture made perfect

December 1996

Two years had passed and once again Christmas held no memories despite the photo prompts. The children had a good time that year judging by the look on their excited faces. Oh how remarkable – there's someone who looks just like me. No, it can't be, I wasn't there. What do you mean I was? I'm sure I can't have been ... I don't know whether this was a side effect of the numerous ECT treatments that I had had by this stage or a result of my severe depression. It is academic perhaps, since both reasons are equally valid. I keep looking at the photos with a sense of wonderment. Was I really there? The children look happy and normal, but their life was far from normal. Their acceptance of the situation is very understandable. Nothing had really changed. Mum was at home, but for how long? At least stability was maintained by the wider family, their consistently loving and hard-working father and our faithful friends. After Christmas we went to Center Parcs. I wish I could remember it. I know that it was one of the children's favourite holidays. After their life in Bangkok, they were definitely water babies! Simon had been superb at diving, doing forward flips off the diving board at age four. Rebecca, less adventurous than her younger brother, was also good at diving and swimming. Stephanie was by now swimming with her head above the water as well as underneath. Of course Jonathan had been too young to do anything other than enjoy the water in Thailand, but now Center Parcs suited them all. We returned home in time for New Year and even held a party. It was something we loved to do. Phil would make a Thai curry for as many as turned up and we would organise lively party games. I am sure I put on a very good front. I could do that.

January 1997

The holidays were over. The usual pattern continued. It seems that the psychiatric team had not yet made the connection – improvement prior to school holidays, deterioration as soon as they were over. I stopped one of the medications because of side effects and they were inclined to put my deterioration down to this; however, I restarted it again but continued to

go downhill. I was still aware as they were that they had the power to admit me at any time since I was still on the Section. Fortunately it seems they chose not to use their authority for two reasons, one of which was that there were no beds. But there was also a well-considered rationale. Prof Thompson felt I would not trust them any longer (should they insist I return to hospital) and that they had spent considerable time and effort trying to regain my confidence since the last admission. They were right there. I had become very wary.

I had started to self-harm again. But this time it was different, I would pour boiling water over myself. I remember doing this. It seems such a drastic way to inflict pain, but very effective. I knew it would not scar, at least not in a stigmatising way. I have tried to rationalise it; the physical pain certainly distracted me from my thoughts. It gave me some sort of temporary relief from the exhausting mental anguish which was part of my life. I would wake in the night, unable to sleep and so creep downstairs, boil the kettle and do the deed. I remember my heart beating fast as the kettle was boiling and then the feeling of determination that it had to be done. It was excruciating, but I did not cry out. There was no one who understood the significance of this act. I was being tortured inside my head, day in and day out. Sleep was the only relief and when that was hard to come by, I would torture my body. This physical pain was better than the deep-felt anguish. Why, oh why is there no morphine for the soul? No relief to be had? Somehow it was like a message. To whom I don't know. Maybe to God, maybe to the world. It was certainly not directed at anyone in particular. People talk about 'a cry for help' and 'attention-seeking' behaviour. How little they understand. This was far more profound than that. There was perhaps an element of punishment, certainly an element of escape from my mind.

There is no doubt that when I spoke to people about how I was feeling or shared some of my thoughts, their understanding did bring me some relief. But I felt I had exhausted the sympathy and comfort of everyone I knew. Talking to those who were not paid to listen made the guilt worse. I still felt entirely responsible for my illness. Much of the time, I believed it was self-inflicted and yet I had no way of getting myself out of it.

Within our family, Stephanie was also facing a challenge. Like Rebecca, her love of dancing and obvious talent was evident. She had spent the last three years doing a monthly session with the Royal Ballet School Junior Associates (just as Rebecca had done), before she was invited to audition for White Lodge. Unlike her sister though, Stephanie was not quite so sure that this was what she wanted to do. This predicament would be difficult enough for any 10-year-old, but I know for Stephanie it was much harder having such unsettled home circumstances. She decided not to go ahead. However, the Royal Ballet School Director asked Phil to let her know if Stephanie changed her mind. She did! The competitive entry process was

daunting. The auditions were a round of elimination exercises over a weekend in March. At each point, girls and boys would leave, usually tearful at failing to get a chance to attend this prestigious school. After the final class on Sunday afternoon, those left of the hopeful girls were gathered with their parents in one room. (The boys' audition was held separately.) Each family would be called into the Ballet Director's office in turn to hear the final verdict. We sat with Stephanie on tenterhooks, Rebecca and her friends nearby. I am not sure what I really felt. We had been through this before and had already let one daughter go. But then Rebecca had been so convinced of her calling. Stephanie was also offered a place, a cheer went up from the waiting White Lodgers. I faced the prospect of both my girls spending their weeks away from home. However, Rebecca seemed happy, the education was good, the dancing was excellent. Of course we would need to find more money to supplement the government grant. Ballet shoes, uniform and all the additional extras were very expensive.

Over the next three months, I was repeatedly offered hospital admission, but like me Phil was also keen that I should stay at home. Stephanie had found the last admission very distressing and had cried on many occasions. Jonathan had started crying every time I visited outpatients, fearful that I would disappear again. Thankfully this prevented another compulsory admission as the doctors did not want to go against Phil's wishes.

Letter to GP from Prof Thompson (my explanations in parentheses)
Cathryn is still in a pretty desperate way but hasn't burnt herself for the last 10 days. She still has occasional auditory pseudohallucinations which insist on her burning herself but she controls these with chlorpromazine (an antipsychotic drug).

She is established on L-Tryptophan (a drug for resistant depression) and is coping with this. She has no side effects. She seems to be gaining a bit of weight and appeared calm today, but obviously not well.

Essentially I think we are just holding on by our fingertips and I again offered her admission to hospital which she refused. Given that Phil, her husband, does not want her to come in I do not think that we can section her but I think that everybody realises that she is at risk.

She is on a full regime for resistant depression, together with two different antipsychotics. The only extra manoeuvre might be to switch her to Depixol injections ... this would give her more side effects but may help to control the hallucinations and self-harm urges better ... we will review this.

Apparently, I began drinking heavily, but that was also short-lived. I was amenable to reason and when I realised that this was yet another futile exercise to combat my distress, I stopped. However, I was continuing to burn myself on a regular basis and had internal voices commanding me to do so. Prof Thompson tried increasing the dosages of the antipsychotic drugs he had prescribed, but that did not help. Once more the drug regime was changed in a further attempt to control the situation but to no avail. A stay at Marchwood Priory was offered once again and this time I agreed to the admission.

April 1997

The stay at Marchwood Priory was uneventful, although greatly preferable to the DOP. The scalding with boiling water continued even in hospital. It was a noticeable feature of all the admissions so far that the staff were often too busy to talk or, more importantly, to listen. Strange though it may seem, once admitted to a ward, NHS or private, there seemed little in the way of dialogue. I wished that the nurses would sit down with me on a daily basis; I am sure they did not realise quite how valuable their input was. Being listened to by someone who appears to understand and empathise is the only painkiller I know of for this illness. But like all analgesia, regular doses are required! You know that improvement is occurring when you need it less frequently. The trained nurses were often preoccupied with the processes of admission or discharge, the routine of handing out medication and stepping in when crises occurred. Visits from Andrew, my CPN, and the weekly psychotherapy sessions seemed to be the only times when I was able to convey how I was really feeling. Being in hospital was a very lonely business.

Thankfully this admission only lasted three weeks. Despite being on full treatment for 'resistant' depression, my illness was at best controlled. It was certainly not showing signs of abating. Once again I was discharged, but under constant vigilance.

June 1997

Prof Thompson's senior registrar saw me regularly in outpatients. This is an extract from one of the letters he sent to my GP:

> ... there is an ongoing risk of suicide, but no evidence of harm to the family. I have on many occasions discussed Cathryn with Professor Thompson and we now both feel that Cathryn is best managed by outpatient care with extreme vigilance and regular contact. Her CPN Andrew continues to visit daily. The offer of crisis admission still stands. I will keep you informed of any changes.

One of the awful consequences of having a mental illness is that there is always felt to be a potential risk to any children of the family. There is some justification for this in that a mother may neglect her children as a result of her depression or, worse still, on rare occasions may want to harm them. It is a hard burden to carry for all concerned. I am grateful that this area was always handled sensitively for us.

July–November 1997

As I write this, I have found the photos which I took. My sister Mary was married on 5 July. It was a beautiful wedding by all accounts, taking place in my parent's village in Wiltshire. Stephanie was a bridesmaid. Simon is looking very smart and little Jonathan has a matching waistcoat and bow-tie. Apparently Rebecca was involved in a Royal Ballet performance on that day. I wish I could remember being there. I wish that seeing what I photographed would trigger a memory. I want to pretend that it does. I want those years back. In fact at times I am overwhelmed with a sense of loss. I move on and see the photos of Rebecca taking part in the Scottish dance at White Lodge later on that month. I remember the stamina that was required. Yes, I think I have a vague recollection of the event. Then there was a visit to Legoland. There is obvious enjoyment on the children's faces. There is even a picture of me sitting with my grown-up Rebecca, smiling! Who would guess from that photograph what a chaotic, night-marish world I was living in? There's Phil playing tennis with Simon, Stephanie being face painted and Jonathan man of the match. The spidery writing on the back of the photos with the date and place is just recognis-able as mine. Where have all these memories gone? How much of a mother was I to my lovely children? I certainly was not much of a wife to Phil.

Despite the summer holidays I could not even maintain the 'status quo'. By the end of July I was persuaded to become an inpatient at the DOP and agreed voluntarily. This time it was to a different ward, B ward, to which I would return again and again. Unfortunately I was beginning to lose the protective element that the children had given me, which so far had prevented me from acting on the suicidal thoughts. There was a change in my thinking, so that I was apparently expressing 'disregard for the family'. I was reportedly agitated and I had uncontrolled intrusive thoughts of a disparaging nature. Thoughts would just come into my mind saying such things as 'you are such a terrible person, it's all your fault, you are doing this deliberately because you are so selfish … ' I definitely believed that these thoughts were true, but at the same time wished they would stop. My medication was changed once again with a degree of success in controlling the thoughts.

Surprisingly this admission lasted only two weeks. I was discharged on

Me with the children during the summer of no memories.

15 August and was glad to get back home to appease my conscience of leaving the children in their summer holidays. So life went on, with every day being a struggle over tiredness, lethargy and the relentless misery of my illness. I began to eat less and by the autumn the weight loss was noticeable. I admitted at one of the outpatient appointments that this was deliberate. My desire was *not* to become thin (I was not trying to control my body weight like an individual suffering with anorexia nervosa). Rather it was another self-inflicted punishment, or at least that is what I told them. In fact it was much more sinister than that. It was a 'slow suicide attempt'. I was trying to starve myself to death, but the psychiatric team did not know that – yet. This continued all through the autumn.

On top of all this, I once again had developed very intrusive thoughts, this time of a violent nature, wishing death on those whom I loved. Yet I knew that these were not my thoughts and I did not own them. They came into my mind involuntarily as if planted there. It made me feel so awful, so vile and degraded. I hated myself, hated the fact that this was happening to me and I didn't have the ability to control it. I felt unclean, dirty, evil even. I was repeatedly offered voluntary admission to hospital, but refused until finally in December I was persuaded to go back in.

Phil was due to go on a business trip to the Bahamas in January and I would be able to accompany him. This was the leverage that made me agree to enter hospital – in order that I would improve sufficiently to make this trip with him.

CHAPTER 8

The therapeutic environment

I think I should tell you some more about the wards at the DOP. Each of the wards had the same layout and each was named by a letter, A–D. This alone illustrated the lack of imagination which was so well engendered by the building. Imagine entering an entrance hall which has an old carpet, blue or brown, I can't remember, but worn and stained. The smell was of stale cigarette smoke. The choice to go up to the wards was by lift or stairs. The lifts were often dirty, the inside walls covered in graffiti, even etched onto the metalwork of the doors. If you chose this method to get to the upper floor, you ran the risk of being shut in with 'undesirable' characters. For instance there was a patient on the ward with me whom I will call George. He was a young man, had a 'punk' hairstyle and was heavily tattooed. He wore hobnailed boots and had several body piercings. His general attitude and demeanour was aggressive. He swore often and profusely with the worst language I had ever heard. I had seen him in an outburst of violent rage. His eye had a glint in it and I was really petrified of him. I hated it when he looked at me and so would avoid catching his eye. I am sure at times he must have been high on drugs. I do not know why he was there or what his illness was. I do know that quite frequently a mental illness will coexist with drug or alcohol addiction. I just knew that he was one of the more disturbed patients that frightened me with unpredictable, rude and aggressive behaviour. He was just one example of why I would rather use the stairs. Yet, we were housed together, forced to live within the same premises. Was this a therapeutic environment? (I met George again years later when I was recovered; he was a patient in A&E and I was still scared of him then!)

A ward accommodated 26 people. At the door you had to ring the bell to be let in. Through the square window of the doors you would often see hopefuls standing nearby, vigilant, maybe waiting for meal times, maybe waiting for a chance to flee. The nurses were genuinely under pressure. There were not many trained staff and those who were RMNs (Registered Mental Nurses) were often tucked away in the office, dealing with administrative work. The nursing assistants were a mixed bunch. Some were very kind and helpful, but others had little understanding of the needs of this diverse group of patients. Looking back, I am sure there was a fair amount

of burnout. The staff were weary. A welcoming smile, in fact any sort of joviality, was rarely seen.

So once officially greeted, I would be shown to my bed, usually in one of the two female dormitories. Occasionally I would start off in a single room, but this was only ever for a day or two. Then I would be moved. The dormitory consisted of six beds, each with curtains which could be pulled around the bed at night or for privacy. Even the curtains were awful, brown and flowery. I remember them well as I would be left staring at them for hours, following the monotonous pattern.

My desire was to get a window bed; then at least I could stare out and watch the cars coming and going in the car park below. Also it had a windowsill, which became highly necessary when the hospital management thought they would replace all the lockers with cupboards. This left no surface for drinks, for cards or ornaments. There seemed to be some sort of conspiracy to make sure that you could not even make your bed space your own. On admission, someone would come and log your belongings; one nightdress (blue), one pair of slippers, one dressing gown, one bra, four pairs of knickers, one box of tissues . . . why was this done? It was not only irritating but also humiliating, particularly when comments were made about your private property. Any electrical goods like a hair-drier were taken away for a safety check by the electrical department.

There were two sinks in the dormitory; again, curtains could be pulled around for privacy. At some point all the dormitory lights were replaced with the sort that switches on in response to movement – a bit like those to deter burglars! The problem was that when you were washing behind the curtain, suddenly the light would go out. Then you would be left fumbling, desperately trying to get round the curtain with enough movement to activate the light, but not enough to forego the privacy that they were designed for. I would have found this very amusing if I had been well! Instead I found this just another source of irritation. Of course the converse was true at night. Whenever anyone got up or a nurse walked in, the lights would switch on – clearly not designed for relaxing sleep.

The queue for the bathroom was worse than school. At least there it was timetabled. Here it was pot luck and they were often dirty. I have recollections of occasions when excreta had been left on the walls. It must have been unpleasant for the cleaners, probably so unpleasant that they would rather not deal with it. As a result, it would remain, sometimes for days, despite our protestations. Either that or the perpetrator would repeat the act on a regular basis . . . who knows? (I have seen this confirmed in letters handled by the advocacy service when formal complaints were made.)

Complaining to the nurses about anything was a risky business. It put the already pressurised staff under more pressure and could be counterproductive. You had to choose the moment carefully, choose the staff member

and choose what was worth the effort. It was an effort. It was much easier to keep quiet.

Generally speaking, psychiatric patients do not do well when complaining. All too often, they are not taken seriously. Stigma comes into play here. Even after my recovery, I have been shocked at how many people have questioned my ability to report the situation accurately. 'After all you were ill, not in your right mind.' 'How do you know it really happened?' Although my memory of those years was greatly affected, I had my own written records (including a diary later on). Not only that, I have consulted with other patients, nursing and medical staff as well as the advocacy service that was in operation during the period of my illness. Unfortunately, my conclusion has to be that not only are these events real, but that complaints from mentally ill patients are not taken seriously. I did make a formal complaint, which I will describe in detail in a later chapter.

This hospital had high quality medical staff, psychiatrists who were leaders in their field of expertise. Many of the consultants are also employed by the university as lecturers to do research and teaching. They were and still are providing the most up-to-date in medical treatments. Sadly, the wards do not reflect this; the physical conditions, the staff training and morale lagged behind by at least 20 years. It is well recognised that the psychiatric services have suffered from lack of funding for a very long time. I know there are concerted efforts being made to put this right, which are way overdue and I understand that there are now plans in place to rebuild the hospital.

There was not much of a routine to the day. You were woken for breakfast, which for most patients was taken in the dining room downstairs, so of necessity you had to get dressed. You were encouraged to get up and go to the dayroom rather than stay on your bed which I often preferred. There was a separate room for smokers, which as a non-smoker I cannot tell you about, except that I could see through the open door that the walls were yellow with nicotine staining. A drinks trolley would be brought in mid morning and a few patients would help to wash up the cups afterwards. I remember doing this on many occasions – at least it made you feel useful! Then it was back to the dayroom, socialising, watching TV or not as the case may be, the monotony of the day continued. There would be lunch, a similar mid-afternoon tea trolley and then supper. Before bed the trolley would come out once again, but this time there would be a warm milk option to make Horlicks, as well as biscuits. If you were confined to the ward then the day could certainly be classed as tedious but I had no desire for activity so it suited my depressive inertia.

During one of the earlier admissions I had been sent down to the dining room for my meals, which is the norm for most patients – you queued up to make your choice of food from a service counter as is usual in canteens. However, one of the male patients had discovered, I am not sure how, that

I was a doctor. I was extremely keen to keep this fact to myself. Obviously the nursing staff were aware of it, but I certainly would not have made it known myself. This particular patient decided that he would announce it to the dining room which also fed patients from the other wards. I was mortified. From then on, I would receive a string of comments as people walked by: 'What's up doc?' 'How you doing, doctor?', often accompanied by amused grins. I became a laughing stock and the subject of many unkind jibes. I couldn't stand the bullying and fortunately Karin (a nurse from B ward) stepped in. From now on, I was to have my meals on the ward. This meant that I had to fill in a menu sheet, which would be presented to us each day. The problem was that sometimes it did not happen. Then it became a lottery; you would either get no food or any food! The busy nurses were not amused if they had to go down to the dining room to get something for you. If it was not to your liking that was 'tough'. I became fairly obsessional about making sure the menu was done, particularly if I was out for the weekend when I would need to submit my requests for Monday.

In the dayroom, I began to interact in a limited fashion with some of the other female patients. I heard terribly tragic stories. I realised that my home circumstances were *so* good and it often seemed to be no accident that some of these poor women ended up here. Many had recurrent problems and had been in the hospital numerous times over countless years. For some it was a way of life. Being middle class was the exception, but I met one or two others from not dissimilar backgrounds. We stuck close, supporting one another. There was no one else to talk to. I was lucky as my primary nurse on this ward was Karin. She was a dichotomous character. Some of the patients disliked her purely because of her manner; she could appear hard and at times unfeeling as a result, but she was always good to me. She was very caring and understanding and I looked forward to her being on duty. The sad thing was that even as my primary nurse, she only had time to speak to me once a week. Then we would go to the 'ward round' room and she would ask me how I was and how it was going. I just wanted someone to listen and she did that for me. I just wished she had more time.

Medication was dispensed at regular intervals throughout the day from the 'clinic' room on the female side of the ward. It was up to you to find a place in the queue, particularly important at bed time when all patients would be receiving some sort of medication and so you could be waiting for well over an hour. There were no chairs, so we used to sit on the floor or lean against the wall. Sometimes we would save each other a place in the queue. There was not much communication at these times, more a resolute silence. The major frustration was waiting for the two nursing staff to come and start the process.

Laundry day was always difficult, linen had to be changed. It happened

fairly frequently, which should be no bad thing. The beds were stripped. If you were still sleeping, then never mind, it was time to get up. Regularly there was not enough clean laundry, so once the dirty sheets were removed you could be left with an unmade or semi-made bed! How can a hospital run out of linen? More often the supply of clean towels would run out. It paid to be selfish and I learnt to hide a clean one away for such eventualities.

There was nowhere to hang damp towels; we had no chairs by our beds, which compounded the whole ridiculous situation. Unfortunately I could not hide blankets and being cold was another unnecessary misery which I suffered. I was never personally without sheets, but I witnessed it happening and have seen a letter of complaint handled by the advocates, following my recovery. The hospital executives always promised an improved service. I sincerely hope this is in place now. Such things began to matter a great deal to us. It was these seemingly unimportant details which dominated our lives.

The other major event of the week was the ward round. Various consultants would have patients on the ward. They would arrive with their entourage – junior doctors, medical students, maybe a social worker. They would sit with the nurse in charge in the 'ward round' room. (This was situated near to the day room and contained a number of fairly comfortable chairs, covered in the standard issue NHS orange material.) Their patients would be called in one by one. It was a time of anticipation. In particular, it seemed to be the only time when decisions were made. Throughout the week, nurses would often be heard saying 'just wait until the ward round', 'we will discuss it at the ward round', 'we will ask at the ward round'. No wonder it took on such significance for us patients. Then of course, there were times when the consultant wasn't able to come or had not finished on another ward or, worse still, ran out of time. The patients involved would be devastated. This was the highlight of the week, remember! It was also the only time when you would get to see your consultant.

It was not surprising, I suppose. Once clerked in, on admission by the most junior member of the team, that was that. New treatments would be instigated on the instruction of the consultant and there was no need for further senior doctor involvement. Rapid improvement in the context of psychiatry means over days! If something new arose like a side effect or a physical complaint, then the ward SHO would deal with it. After all the diagnosis had been made and treatment within the 'therapeutic' and safe environment was taking place, so weekly review should be sufficient. I think what was most sad in all of this was the general sense of abandonment which many of us felt. The environment was not conducive to recovery. The fact that patients did get better was probably despite the ward not because of it.

Patients may have been in and out of the hospital for years without

making much, if any, progress. That is not to say that the staff didn't help. Most certainly tried, but their best efforts were hampered by lack of qualified nursing staff, lack of time to spend with patients for those who were there and lack of training for their assistants. I also observed that some of the nurses were demoralised and as a result cynical. Some of the staff came across as unfeeling and therefore uncaring. But some patients were rude, some violent, many had access to drugs or alcohol. Unlike me, some patients were allowed to come and go as they pleased. Undoubtedly illicit drugs were brought onto the hospital premises. The nurses had more to do than just care for patients. They became the ward police and the ward security.

Another gloomy fact was that a number of patients knew how to 'run the system'. They knew precisely how to get the attention they required. The nurses had no time to be proactive and I know from my own experience that if you wanted a 'chat', undoubtedly the answer would be 'not now, later'. As a result, some had learnt other ways of gaining attention.

I got to know a lovely lady, Jean, older than myself. She was also depressed and had been employed in a worthwhile and stable job before her illness. She explained to me how she had been asking time and time again to speak to someone, but no nurses were available, so in the end she systematically began to turn over the tables and chairs. Suddenly all the staff were upon her, shouting at her, demanding that she should stop. Someone angrily asked her why she was doing this. 'I wanted to talk to someone,' she explained. An offer of medication was made and an indelicate promise for dialogue when they were less busy.

This behaviour would have been totally out of character for Jean. How could this have happened? Yet it was not unusual. Suddenly this group of adults was behaving in a way more akin to kindergarten children. I started to sit and watch.

I did a lot of watching, a lot of observing. As I became more used to the ward and its inhabitants, I felt more part of it. I appreciated some of the other patients and we became friends. We kept each other going, protected one another when harsh words were said, shared our likes and dislikes of the staff who were there to care for us. However, this was prison not hospital, or at least that is how it felt.

CHAPTER 9

Attempt at a slow death

December 1997

Three years had passed. I had been back in hospital for a week. This nightmare was reaching new heights of intensity. I realised that I had made a very big mistake in accepting admission. I wanted to get out, but unfortunately it was not just to get home. My brain was telling me that I needed to die. My life was not worth living. I was a useless wife, a useless mother, a burden on all our family and on society. The fact that I was not getting better was clearly my fault. I was probably not really depressed, just a complete failure as a person.

My attempts to get discharged were fruitless, as they guessed my intention. That was the problem: now I was here, I could not leave. I had been admitted suicidal and when I was asked directly, I could not deny suicidal thoughts. (I have always been very bad at lying – my face always gives me away.) When I packed my bags ready to go, a nurse applied a Section 5(4), which they can do to prevent someone from leaving until they have been examined by a doctor. The doors were locked. I was trapped. The doctors agreed that I needed to stay in hospital and I was placed on a six-month Section 3. Once again I was an involuntary patient. Involuntary and resentful.

Unbeknown to me, they were carefully examining the fact that I would hardly eat anything. They were looking for additional diagnoses. It's interesting just how confused everyone was. The notes from the ward rounds during that period describe the different members of staff putting forward their theories. They considered anorexia nervosa, personality disorder, even straightforward manipulation during those few weeks. They even consulted a behavioural psychologist who suggested that my not eating was a protest, in part due to the fact that I had been robbed of my freedom, i.e. sectioned. Well, I am sure that could have been true, but it was certainly not the whole story.

It seems that it took some time before they realised exactly what was going on. Although I admit, I was probably not terribly forthcoming. Looking at it with hindsight, it seems so obvious. They all missed something which was far more fundamental to my depressive illness; despite the

complex analytical process that was being applied to my behaviour. I was trying to starve myself to death. I had been doing so since the autumn. Why would that have changed? I had admitted that it was deliberate in outpatients but I guess that had probably been forgotten. It seems amazing to me that the medical staff devoted quite so much time in their analysis, as documented in my notes. However, Prof Thompson told me recently that they found it extremely difficult to know exactly what I was thinking. I was manipulative in some ways because I would often tell them only what I thought they wanted to hear. They were well aware of this and to some extent they felt that they could not trust me to tell them the truth, especially now I was on a Section. They were mindful that although my thinking was slow and illogical, I had not lost my intelligence.

Starving oneself in the presence of food is not an easy thing to do, but my weight was gradually falling to dangerously low levels. The problem was that my food intake was being watched like a hawk. The nursing notes are full of entries of the exact quantities I consumed. 'Lunch: two lettuce leaves and half a slice of ham. Dinner half a cheese sandwich'! Sometimes a friend would come to visit and I had discovered that I could go with them to the League of Friends shop where they served snacks and drinks. This also earned a comment. 'Cathy was seen at the Friends shop accompanied by her visitor. It is not certain whether she ate anything or not.' How ridiculous it seems now.

I was in a terrible quandary. In fact I can remember something of the dilemma, which I was plagued with throughout the whole illness. I also remember how very difficult I found it when trying to work through this. I cogitated on this problem for years. It would go round and round in my head endlessly. Sometimes I would come to a conclusion. In this case it was to starve to death. The quandary went something like this.

When at home, I was with the children, thereby freed from the guilt of 'abandoning' them, which I absolutely believed I was doing whilst in hospital. However, I found that I was exhausted and under considerable strain trying to put on a front at home, to cover up my serious unhappiness. I felt very unwell and I wanted to stay in bed all day. I had no energy for even small household tasks, plus I wanted to die. Yet I was afraid to do this, not of the actual event or action leading to my death, but of the consequences it would have for my children. My maternal instinct had always been strong and my desire for their welfare was extremely powerful. It gave me protection, but at a terrible cost in terms of enduring the pain of my illness.

In hospital, once I had recovered from my anger at the Section, I admitted to myself that I felt safer. I was protected from myself and the consistent, ongoing suicidal thoughts. I was also absolved from household tasks and to some extent the responsibilities. The downside was that I hated the burden I felt that I was placing on Phil and the children, and the

extreme guilt which came with it. On top of this, I felt that the medical and nursing staff were not in fact doing anything for me that was making any difference. I was not making any real or lasting progress. I was afraid of sharing my thoughts with them, fearful that I might not be believed and fearful that if they did believe me, more restriction would be placed on me. I was afraid that I might not even be allowed to visit home in the evenings or at weekends as had become the routine once I started to show some improvement.

By January, my predicament focused on the business trip Phil was due to make to the Bahamas. I did not want to let him down, but I knew I would not cope with the trip. In fact the decision was taken away from me by my inability to persuade Prof Thomson that I was well enough for him to lift the Section. I recognise now how much I did need to have my life decisions taken out of my hands during that period of time. My memories are not good ones, but whilst I do not bear resentment over the decisions to section me, my experiences at these times could have been made more bearable by some of the staff involved. Having said that, as always, there were some very caring nurses working on the ward. I do not underestimate the extreme pressures under which they had to work.

Through all this, starvation seemed an answer. It was punitive and my mind told me constantly that I deserved punishment. I believed that to die in this way would be a good outcome, without a 'suicide' tag. However, the longing to be understood and listened to eventually forced me to confess. I think that once I had disclosed my intentions, it did at least help the staff to have some understanding and the alternative diagnoses were abandoned. However, it did not bode well for the future. I would have been mortified to discover that they thought my behaviour was manipulative; I am even now, in retrospect. However, they had not known me prior to this illness, so it was hard for them to make a judgement.

This may be a salutary lesson to anyone working with those whose mental health is disturbed. To understand is not easy, but to the sufferer, being understood is often the only comfort possible. However, as I have said before, it is a bit like taking a painkiller – it wears off!

The management of my illness was changing. Initially there was hope of 'cure' or at least remission. Now the hope was that the severity would decrease. There was acceptance that I was suffering from a chronic resistant form of depression, so the drug treatment was under continuous review.

There are various treatment regimes for resistant depression using different classes of drugs. All of these require time to build up to the maximal dosage and then time to allow a response to occur, often amounting to weeks. In the meantime I was kept in hospital because it was felt that the suicide risk was too great for me to be at home. ECT was still the only form of treatment that I had shown any response to so it was

becoming the mainstay of therapy. As time progressed, a gradual process of return to the community was attempted, although this was particularly slow because of the renewed suicide risk. There was recognition that for me as a mother, being able to spend time at home was essential. Not surprisingly, the children found visiting me on the ward very distressing and it was not a suitable place for them to be. The medical team fully understood that both for my sake and the children's, regular contact was a necessity. They were careful to ensure that as soon as I was considered well enough, a timetable of home leave would start.

One year earlier a request had been made to change the sort of psychotherapy I had been having to Cognitive Behaviour Therapy or CBT. It is seriously in vogue at the moment, having been the only 'talking' therapy to have stood the test of the medical gold standard, randomised controlled trials and been shown to make a lasting difference in mild to moderate depression. Unfortunately, there was an insurmountable problem. My depression was so severe that I was unable to concentrate for long enough or to remember the contents of the sessions, which is vital for the treatment to be successful. So despite a prolonged assessment, it was decided that this was not a suitable treatment for me at this time. My original psychotherapist Ian left. I was passed on to a lovely lady named Lee, who was going to attempt a more supportive type of psychotherapy.

Lee truly was a godsend. After a while I felt able to talk to her, although it was not easy to begin with. She persisted with me and I began to trust her. Once again we explored every avenue of my life. My childhood was analysed in great detail, as was every aspect of my later life, as had happened with Ian. I am not certain this was of any great value except that it gave me an opportunity to talk. Lee was kind and she listened. She was challenging and sometimes I found this upsetting, but I wanted to keep going. I found it very difficult when she went away on holiday.

She was convinced that there was a 'psychological' root cause for my depression. I detected her antagonism to physical treatments, including ECT, but no one could deny that it seemed to be the only way of pulling me up from the lowest depths. Looking back, I can see great value in the time I had with her, but I also wonder whether the continuous probing prompted additional negative thoughts. Who knows? We were all looking for an answer. I certainly was. It was inconceivable that this illness could happen for no reason. I was just as convinced as she was that there must have been something in my background that could be responsible.

I cannot accurately describe to you what went on during the three years of therapy with Lee. I could not do justice to that with so little memory and also no notes to fall back on. However, I do remember some of what we talked about. We looked at my early childhood – separation from the nanny when I left India aged one, my memories of nursery school and school in Nairobi. I told Lee about the turning point in my life when I first

realised there was right and wrong, just after the episode when I had lied to the police describing to them the criminal that I had not actually seen, the episode that had left me with so much guilt. We discussed in detail the experiences of boarding school – the bullying that I witnessed during my first year, the death of one of my friends but, in particular, the unhappiness I felt towards the end of the holidays in anticipation of the return to school. I described the traumatic departures at the airport and how I cried so much on the flight back to the UK. We discussed the fact that I had started to enjoy Badminton School when I began to achieve academically, only to be moved to the second school, St George's, and my subsequent loneliness there.

I told Lee about my experiences of illness, how the matron had not believed me when I had broken my arm and, when I was finally taken to hospital, how I had it manipulated without an anaesthetic. (This would never happen to a child nowadays!) I told her how I felt about being in hospital with Sydenham's chorea (a form of rheumatic fever) during my 'O' level year at school, while my parents were themselves worrying so far away in Thailand. I remembered how the doctor had asked me how I liked school and then subsequently told me to pull myself together when I could not stop the involuntary shaking which was the prime symptom of the condition from which I was suffering.

We talked over the stressful experiences at medical school when I was pregnant and then being a new mother trying to cope with a new baby and exams all at the same time. I relived the early years of our married life and the financial pressures we had faced. I remembered the panic and distress I felt when we were asked to return a gift of money we had been given which had long since been spent. I remembered the pain we felt when we had to remove the children from the church's independent fee-paying school where they were so happily settled, having had our application for a bursary refused.

By now I was quite adept at retrieving from my memory any and every situation that had some negative aspect to it and I found it difficult to see the positive side even when today it seems glaringly obvious! I think Lee was more interested in the relationships I had had throughout my life and how I had felt towards the people involved, how I had coped with disappointment and rejection and whether I was directing my negative feelings back onto myself, but that is probably an oversimplification.

Dave and Marie were very helpful, though, because through the recollections of the past I could easily have apportioned blame or held resentment towards people who may have unwittingly been a part of the experience I had recalled. They encouraged me at every step of the way to release my memories to God in prayer and to forgive anyone that I felt badly towards. I am so glad that they helped me to do this. I am only too well aware now that I was suppressing memories – the good ones!

I now know that some of the multidisciplinary team of doctors, nurses and psychotherapists were wondering whether some form of abuse had occurred during my childhood. This was not the case at all. It had also been tempting for them to blame my depression on the fact that to some extent my childhood unhappiness had not been recognised. (There was definitely a 'stiff upper lip', 'grin and bear it' culture during my childhood.) However, the depression did not get any better despite 'working through' these experiences with Lee. Concerns had also been expressed about my church life. Perhaps I had been 'brainwashed' in some way, maybe the church I was part of was extremist and my lifelong commitment was indicative that I was involved in some bizarre sect. None of these things were true and as time went on, it became evident that there were no specific answers, although the childhood experiences were labelled as 'vulnerability factors'.

This spilled over to my parents. They were also extremely worried. I had now been ill for over three years. They wrote on a number of occasions to Prof Thompson with their own suggestions. Phil and I knew of some of their concerns, particularly over the church. We found that hard, particularly as our most supportive friends were Christians. Family tensions mounted as the sense of frustration grew. We recognised though how difficult it was for them when my childhood was 'placed under the microscope'. It must have been nerve racking wondering where this would end up. However despite it all, my parents remained supportive throughout the illness.

In fact Phil and the children continued to be given a lot of help from many different sources: parents of our children's friends, our close friends, as well as our respective families. We are indebted to the love and care they all gave us. Our Christian friends continued to pray faithfully, not giving up, even though the situation showed no signs of improving.

January–June 1998

The hospital admission went on and on and on. It must have been interminable for Phil as well as for me. I was well and truly institutionalised. My life was focused on the small events that took place on the ward. The position of my bed was incredibly important to me. I needed to be beside the window. I spent a lot of time looking out, either at the sky or watching the car park. It was not exactly entertainment, but it was all I had.

As I improved a little, I would be allowed out for increasing lengths of time with Phil, and this began to involve weekend leave. When I returned on Sunday evening and found that my bed had been moved, my belongings shoved into a hospital property plastic bag, it upset me greatly. The same reason was always given. A new patient had been admitted and required my bed. I lost my window position and had to continuously request to be

moved back, waiting for the next change around. What was most harsh was the unsympathetic response that greeted my despair. The nurses clearly did not understand what I was making such a fuss about. I would get a shrug and a curt explanation. No provision was made to satisfy my request. I knew I was a nuisance. To them it was trivial. To me, my little world was further disturbed. The lack of compassion or understanding felt very cruel indeed. I began to realise that I had very little control over any area of my life. I used to pack my own things up each weekend, so that at least my few belongings left in hospital would not be disrespectfully and randomly thrown into a bag, a clock with shampoo, the box of tissues squashed under a pair of shoes ...

Some of the nursing staff really did not recognise how their behaviour and attitudes impacted on us patients. If only they realised that little acts of kindness were precious rays of light in the darkness of the dungeon. Through their own pressures and stresses, I think too often they forgot the reason for which they were employed – to care for patients. Care seemed to be the forgotten word, the forgotten sentiment. The ward was run to avoid trouble, to administer medication, to keep paperwork in order. We were often treated as naughty children and so not surprisingly that's how we felt. Respect and self-esteem were at an all-time low. We were a major inconvenience to the smooth running of the ward.

In the family diary, Phil had made a column through the week which indicated where the boys were going after school or who was coming in to look after them until he got home. A tick beside the name was confirmation that they would be meeting Jonathan after school. Stephanie was now away at White Lodge during the week so there were fewer after-school activities to organise. Nonetheless, there are many names down as well as the faithful grandparents. Phil would have come home from work, picked me up from hospital if I was allowed out on leave and had to prepare the evening meal. Fortunately Thelma (Phil's mother) came down to South-ampton with meals for us, often two or three times a week which helped enormously. I did try and help with the clearing up when I came home. But I cannot remember how much nagging would have happened over the homework, probably not enough! The boys would be encouraged to bed. I would have to be dropped back down to the DOP. No doubt Phil would be needing to phone the helpful friends to organise the next few days and I suppose somewhere in this he would find time to deal with washing, bills and other mundane tasks. I know the grandparents helped with cleaning and shopping, particularly Thelma. In the midst of this, his wife was terribly ill and I was no joy to be with.

The awful thing is that this admission lasted six months. My formal discharge was on 2 June 1998. This episode is a blur, the memories which will stay forever of the significant events on the ward could have occurred at any time during the illness. Once again there had been a Christmas.

There had also been two sets of school holidays and two half terms. This time there are no photos. Oh well, no lost memories to cry over. Then suddenly I think of all the birthdays I have missed, all the growing up that must have happened. Simon had been at secondary school for two years and I haven't even mentioned it. It must have been a real landmark in his life. I know now how difficult the adjustment was for him to go from a friendly junior school into an all boys comprehensive.

CHAPTER 10

Last resort

July 1998

I was now at home and the Section 3 had been allowed to expire. I could no longer be called back to hospital against my will. What a relief! I still had to attend the ward for review.

Letter to GP written by his Registrar
Professor Thompson reviewed Cathryn as an outpatient on B Ward on 21 July 1998. Cathryn has made some improvement in that her weight has gained and she is managing to do some housework with the help of her support worker. Her children have started their summer holidays and she is motivated to give them as much help and support as she can.

She has an extensive community package including day attendance at B Ward three times a week and community support input twice a week. She is seen regularly by Andrew Eva her CPN. She also receives occupational therapy and is seen by her social worker. She continues to see Lee for her psychotherapy.

At the review it was clear that Cathryn wanted to use some of her time to pursue activities at home. Prof Thompson was keen to support this as long as she does not retire to bed and reduce her activity. It was agreed that she attend the ward once a week on a Tuesday. The ward will phone her at approximately 09.30 on Mondays and Thursdays to remind her to get up.

The next few weeks will be a turning point in that, hopefully she will continue to improve and we can provide less hospital input and more community support. However, there is a risk that she will withdraw to bed and we will have to monitor the situation closely.

We went to Spain that summer, during the last two weeks of August. I remember the drive. It was extremely long and hot. We had no air-conditioning in the car and had erected a series of sunshades to try and lessen the effect of the sun's hot rays. We stayed at a Eurocamp site on the Costa

Brava and the photos show some lovely beach scenes. We visited Barcelona and the boys were very excited, purchasing football kits when we visited the stadium. Once again I have no real memories apart from the hot drive. How sad that it is the negative memory that has stuck. It looks as though the whole family enjoyed the break and you certainly wouldn't know that I was suffering from severe depression looking at the one photo with me in! However, as I have said, I was good at rising to the occasion, as long as it didn't happen too often.

Letters to the GP over that autumn period are uninteresting. Basically the team were making valiant attempts to keep me at home; increasing the dosage of medication, putting additional community support in place, then arranging extra visits to the ward. I am described as becoming increasingly withdrawn and spending more time in bed. I was having progressively more suicidal thoughts and there was a new phenomenon; I was becoming distressed by thoughts that something catastrophic was going to happen to Phil and the children.

November 1998

On 4 November the unavoidable happened, I was recalled back to hospital. By this stage my suicide plans were well made and included a violent death. However, the medical staff were pleased that I agreed to be admitted and the initial plan was for a period of respite care. Unfortunately this planned *short* admission lasted for nine months!

Once again I received ECT, another 14 treatments. I was self-harming on a regular basis by pouring boiling water over my arms and abdomen. Yes, surprising though it may seem, even in hospital this was possible. The kitchen was not locked and there was a constant supply of boiling water from the machine on the wall. The nursing staff knew I was doing this but I can only suppose that since it neither threatened life nor limb, they were not too bothered by it.

Phil was back in the old routine. I guess I was too. I have little recall specifically relating to that period and no writing to help me out. It all became a 'blur', this hospital life. The ECT lifted my mood slightly and so I was soon allowed out to spend some evenings and weekends at home. The medical team decided that I needed to see an endocrinologist in case they were missing anything 'physical'. He had little to add except to start me on treatment for osteoporosis (thinning of the bones) which had occurred. My hormonal cycle had shut down in response to the severe depression and weight loss. My thyroid gland had ceased to function earlier on during the illness, so I was already taking thyroxine regularly. This can happen some-times as a side effect of lithium treatment, which was one of the drugs that I was taking. But it never recovered even after the lithium had been stopped for some time so it is unlikely that this was related to the drug.

Another Christmas went by. I was on home leave for the festivities. We even had a New Year's Eve party, just like old times. No doubt I would be leaving those who did not know me well with the impression that there was nothing much wrong. If only that were the case.

January–July 1999

I was still far from well and remained an informal patient on B ward. However, early in February, I wanted to discharge myself from the hospital. I told the staff not only of my desire to leave but also that I intended to do so. I had been scalding myself repeatedly and they felt the risk of letting me go was too great. Once again, an emergency Section was applied and by the following day it had been converted to the six-month Section 3. Once again I was held against my will and all home leave was stopped.

I cannot remember any noteworthy events during this period. The medical records are rather monotonous. The admission seemed to run a fluctuating course; increasing my leave so that I could spend more time at home, then restricting it again because the suicide risk was felt to be too great. Medication was altered, ECT was given but the reality was that the illness was unremitting. There was no respite from my agonising misery. There was no reprieve for Phil and the children with their own distress. There was not only physical separation between me and the children, but also an emotional vacuum. I was not aware of how my absence was really affecting my family. I think if I had been, then it would have made the situation even worse, if that were possible.

March was particularly difficult, not just for me, but for the whole family. Simon was not very communicative about his feelings. This may not be particularly unusual for a 14-year-old boy, but he became upset and told me that he was fed up with me being ill and that he thought I would never get better. He did not know that his thoughts were shared by many people including the medical staff. The reassurance he received lacked conviction.

I was upset that Andrew Eva had moved away and so I was allocated another CPN. Even though most of my time had been spent in hospital, I still found his understanding nature and willingness to listen a great help. Fortunately his successor, Ruth Paley, turned out to be a lovely lady and, like Andrew had been, very supportive. She also seemed to understand me very well which helped a great deal. I met her while I was still on the ward and then she visited me when I was at home on leave. When I saw her about writing this book, Ruth told me how she soon came to realise, like the other members of the team, that I was not going to get better. In fact more than that, the consensus was that I was going to die. A successful and intentional suicide was thought to be the most likely outcome. She said she found it extremely difficult to accept, but she had not come across

anyone so tormented. She said that she had to be careful not to become too emotionally involved with me. As she came to know me better, she found herself searching for a glimmer of light in the darkness, but there seemed to be none. She did not give up, but at the same time, she acknowledged that there really did not seem to be much to hope for.

Towards the end of March, Rebecca had been sent home from school unwell. This compounded my feelings of guilt and I really wanted to be with her. I requested discharge, feeling that the strain on the family was becoming too much. She was 16 and in her GCSE year. She had done very well at White Lodge and had been made head girl, but unfortunately the additional pressure upon her of her imminent assessment for the upper school was also getting the better of her. I wanted to be a support to her so much and this time I was given extended home leave, where I just sat with her as she lay on the sofa, exhausted and tearful. Fortunately the Easter holidays gave her sufficient time to recover and she returned for the summer term in full health.

Every time I went on leave for an overnight stay, I was given a supply of my medication. By some oversight I was given more than I required and this had meant that I was able to accumulate some of the highly toxic tricyclic antidepressant that I was prescribed. I was biding my time to have enough to be sure that death would be certain. But someone became suspicious (probably Ruth!) and the plot was discovered early in June. I was extremely angry. There seemed to be no hope at all. Every aspect of my treatment was failing. I was in fact highly compliant with medication. I was so petrified of becoming worse that I always took the correct doses. But by July the drug regime was changed again since no improvement had occurred with Clomipramine, the most recent drug I had tried.

None of the antidepressant drugs are addictive but it is not unusual to require a slow decrease in dose to minimise the unpleasant effects of withdrawal. Chlomipramine was no exception and at the same time I was started on another two different drugs. Fortunately I started to feel better and this coincided with the summer holidays. I was also offered more sessions of psychotherapy with Lee, but I felt that I was wasting her time. I had no idea how I could carry on with life at home, but I had no choice. The community care package was reinstated and I was allowed more time at home. The Section 3 was not rescinded but the plan was to allow it to elapse in August. However, I was not to be discharged from hospital. I was on 'extended leave'.

August 1999

When I reported to the ward in early August, things were clearly changing. I said I felt 'high' and full of energy. I was looking forward to going on holiday and in the notes it is even recorded that I was smiling. This note-

worthy event was sufficiently unusual to be commented on! However, the team was careful in their evaluation and rang Phil. He was surprised at how much I was doing at home, but said that by the evening I was low and very tired. He said I was getting angry on occasions which he saw as a good indication that normality was beginning to be restored, but he was also well aware that if I was going to show an improvement, the summer holidays seemed to be the time.

We went away to a cottage in Devon. One of Rebecca's good White Lodge friends and her mother joined us. I do have a few memories of that holiday, but not as many as Phil and the children have. I had a lot of thinking to do. Rebecca was moving on to the English National Ballet School. We had been supporting both girls with their education. The Royal Ballet School fees are one of the highest of all the fee-paying schools in Britain. Like all UK citizens, we had been able to take advantage of a government-run scheme for aided places and had received a substantial grant for both of them. Nevertheless, Phil's salary alone was insufficient for all our needs. Rebecca had won a scholarship to the English National Ballet School for her last two years of training, but we still had her living expenses to pay for; she would be living in the centre of London and both the girls had the expenses of the inevitable extras such as their pointe shoes which need frequent replacement. We had used up our savings and we had to remortgage the house. I had been registered for receipt of Disability Living Allowance so that also helped, along with the generosity of our parents which enabled us to go on holiday. However, I was acutely aware of the struggle that life had become on this practical level.

We were applying for council tax relief. This is the letter written by my GP to answer some of the local council's questions.

> ... you were seeking clarification as to whether CW is severely mentally impaired and whether her condition was covered by the definition laid out by the department of health.
>
> I have read the document you have sent me from the Department of Health and certainly CW does have severe impairment of her social functions and at this stage it appears to be permanent. I have spoken to her psychiatrist who gives fairly gloomy prospects of her prognosis and at this current time we have to presume that her function will remain significantly impaired.

I remember being at home in the sitting room. I do not know the date. I was having a conversation with myself. It went something like this:

'Well, Cathy, there are only two ways out of this. Either you die, which would not be good for the children would it? Of course they may get some life insurance money, but can that be guaranteed? Or you pull yourself together and get back to work. I know it's hard, but you have done hard

things before. After all, you are not really ill. Tell them that you are much better and get back to that flexible training job (part-time medical post), God will help you.'

I wrote this at some point over this period of time, but I am not sure when exactly.

First and foremost I am utterly selfish and very, very stupid. The things I've done while I've been ill here are just disgusting. I am a loser and I ruin everything. I want someone to tell me it's not true but the evidence speaks for itself. I want to walk away – distance myself, stop seeing anyone, stop the drugs and psychotherapy. The trouble comes when I'm alone, as long as I distract myself that's OK but I am always finding myself phoning Ruth (my CPN), planning my days around the contact I'm going to have. I'm addicted to it. I am so ashamed and I feel so guilty but especially ashamed.

So where to from here? Where indeed? Shall I just try and pick up where I left off as though nothing has happened. I don't know, will it work? I know I could pretend everything's OK, and it will be in the short-term, but I'm seriously worried. Also worried: what if Phil finds out? Also worried what Prof Thomson will think. I am so embarrassed.

Maybe I could explain the work situation to Prof Thompson – if I planned to go back in February, it wouldn't be so bad after all – six sessions as an elective. Maybe I can pull round from this, snap out of it – I could if I tried. My one concern is my alone times. I don't know whether activity then is best or not. I'm still dreaming about taking the tablets, just leaving it in God's hands – that's having taken them – but if I survived the children would hate me. There are lots of nos and yet one YES and it'll be all over, finished.

I phoned up Rodger Sleet, the consultant from A&E, who had by then retired, and arranged to meet. He seemed extremely pleased to hear from me and suggested that I speak to one of the new consultants (Lynn Williams had left by this stage) and arrange to become an observer back at Southampton General A&E, in order to prepare for a return to work. I also had to contact the Deanery to get my funding sorted out. This was a difficult step, but I was determined to carry it out. I had been away from work for almost five years. However, it was not as long as the gap between qualifying and first starting work, so it did not seem impossible.

Here are some extracts from the letters written to my GP from outpatients by Prof Thompson.

25th August 1999

Cathryn came back from holiday on Friday and the care program has gradually been put in place again. She has seen her psychotherapist and will recommence twice a week now the summer is over. Ruth, her CPN, gave her a Clopixol injection yesterday. She remains on the discharge medication and I suggest this continues until she settles back in at home. She of course has a crisis point coming up in two weeks when the children go back to school.

When I saw her she was reporting a high level of negative feelings . . .

Two weeks later:

Cathryn is under a lot of strain at the moment and is really not feeling as well as before. Happily, she is able to talk about her feelings and engage in sensible conversation about her predicament. The children go back to school soon. Her sleep has become poor and she has begun having severely obsessional thoughts about killing herself. Obviously she is at significant risk but I think probably no more than she has been at many times in the past.

She asked me if she could have ECT as an outpatient. This is a possibility, but I want to discuss it with her psychotherapist as the memory disturbance may interfere with the psychological treatment. She realises this and seems committed to the psychotherapy. My inclination is not to interfere with that.

A couple of positive things have happened, but characteristically these have been converted by her depressive thinking into negative events. Firstly she has arranged lunch with Dr Sleet A&E consultant to discuss her return to medicine. She is aware that she must make no plans at the present time, but it is rather nice that they are to have lunch. Second there was an accident outside her house and she assisted capably at the scene. Afterwards, however, she felt she had been 'hopeless'.

I have made sure that she has crisis numbers to phone if she feels acutely suicidal. The medication is to continue.

This day, 9 September 1999, was memorable for one particular reason – this was not actually written in the letter to the GP, but is recorded in the handwritten medical notes, simply as '*discussed leucotomy*'. This was the first mention of brain surgery. I felt like I'd been struck by lightning, such was my surprise. For a start I had never heard of an operation for depression. It had never occurred to me that it could be a possibility. The only

concept I had of this sort of thing was what was portrayed in *One Flew Over the Cuckoo's Nest*!

This sort of operation, formally termed psychosurgery, is now known as neurosurgery for mental disorder or NMD. For once I prefer the new name; it has fewer historical associations and reflects more accurately the fact that this is indeed a new operation which uses very precise techniques.

During this initial conversation Prof Thompson described it to me as a relatively simple procedure, this stereotactic surgery. With the advent of new techniques the exact area of the brain can be located so that a discrete lesion can be placed in order to interrupt the abnormal neural pathway thought to be responsible for this type of depression. I would be left with two scars on my scalp, I couldn't remember where, there was a very small risk of fits and that it might not work, but that was all. I was left to think about it. My mind was spinning. I felt out of control. What was this coming to? Here I was talking about work and here my doctor was talking about brain surgery. In principle I had no reason to object. Nothing else had made any difference.

I was scared at the suggestion, scared that I might not have any choice and scared of the consequences of either accepting or refusing. I felt that I had little to lose. My most significant concern was whether it would affect my personality, but was assured that the risks of that with this modern operation were extremely low. I was also worried that it could be done against my will. But since it is never done without the patient's full consent, I could at least rest assured on that point as well. I was still bothered by the idea of refusing this treatment. I felt that if I did turn it down then it opened up the possibility that I was unwilling to get better. I think initially it was my own internal standard of how to be a good patient which was driving me to accept any treatment that was being offered. However, I was at no time pressurised into considering this option by anyone other than myself.

In the end, though, I could see that there was no harm in exploring this alternative. I was referred to the nearest unit which carried out this surgery, the Maudsley Hospital in London, but not until December 1999.

I used the crisis number that Prof Thompson had left with me on 14 September and was admitted to B ward. However this was the shortest admission of the whole illness. I realised my mistake after one night. My reasons as recorded in the medical notes were that 'the toilet was blocked, the shower didn't work, there was loud music, the food was horrible and I wanted a life!' I had also learnt that Jonathan, now aged 10, had cried all night. I promised that I would not carry out any suicidal plans. I was described as having psychomotor retardation, little eye contact, softly spoken and expressing suicidal thoughts. But despite the fact that I was still obviously severely depressed, they decided that it was time to move 'out of the realm of Sections' and put some trust in my judgement and

requests. I was allowed to go home with review on the ward in a few days' time.

It seems that the medical team was not at all sure about what was going on. They were hoping that I really was beginning to recover. Clearly, they were not immune to wishful thinking or misplaced optimism either! I now had the opposite problem to the previous one of weight loss. One of the drugs had given me a voracious appetite. I was rapidly putting on weight. Of course this was not causing the medical team much concern, but I had to come to terms with my changing appearance and expanding waistline.

CHAPTER 11

Winter of discontent

October 1999

I think it was the mention of brain surgery that fuelled the fire of my determination. I was not going to let this beat me. I was going to make myself better. So I did not stick to the agreement with Prof Thompson not to pursue the return to work. Instead I made plans, which were accepted, to become an observer in Southampton A&E department. I was to attend for two half days a week. On the first day that I arrived, I was introduced and shown around. I felt very uncomfortable, like a fish out of water, and no one else was aware of the courage it had taken for me to do this. I was told to go to the medical staffing department to sign my honorary contract and to obtain a name badge. Again this was another huge step for me. To my horror, I was told by the medical staffing officer that I could not sign any contract or go near a clinical area until I had clearance from the Occupational Health department. With my heart pounding, I went over to Occupational Health. I knew that disaster awaited me, and my worst fears were realised. They needed a letter from the consultant psychiatrist to say that I was well enough to be present as an observer. I could not even bring myself to go over to A&E and tell them what had happened. I left the hospital grounds, weeping, despondent and utterly miserable. I had failed. It was a terrible setback.

After a few days, I wrote a note to Prof Thompson telling him what had happened and their request and I was very surprised that he agreed to write to the Occupational Health department, but the damage had been done. He was suggesting to me that in the meantime I do something a little less stressful. He suggested that I offer to work in a charity shop for instance, but of course that made me feel even worse. The little self-esteem that I had somehow clung on to was shattered and so was my grand plan. Clearly I could no longer just return to work, it was going to be a far more complex process.

I had also noticed the advance in technology that was happening, although I was still not very interested in anything that did not affect me directly. Phil had a PC at home and I thought that perhaps I should learn to use it. I enrolled on a word processing course for the autumn

term. It was only for one morning a week and it was free of charge. I hated going to it though. I felt so slow; I could not type and I found it hard to concentrate. I found that the most difficult thing was retaining information for the next session. However, I was still quite resolute that I was going to pull myself out of this illness one way or another. My mother was coming over once a week and Phil's mother came twice a week. Each time they would bring meals or cook them for us. The boy's were both playing in different football leagues and Stephanie was going to be in *The Nutcracker* at the Royal Opera House in December. Life was very full.

November 1999

With continuing community support, I had managed to stay out of hospital. However, Prof Thompson obviously realised that my plans to return to work were completely inappropriate.

I wrote him a letter using my newly acquired word processing skills.

> Dear Prof Thompson
> Reluctantly I have taken your advice and written to the Associate Dean for flexible training to postpone my starting work date. However on reflection I think you are mistaken in thinking that 'starting work' is the reason I've been feeling down as it wasn't my intention to do anything but assume that the funding wasn't available until next August. I think the thought of eventually going back to work has been the supreme motivator, allowing me to read magazines etc to fill my time. I have been very diligent in filling up the week by seeing friends, exercising and trying to stay on top. I don't feel able to do that now, especially while I'm so tired, but I don't see why I should be blamed by you for having brought it on myself.
> As for hearing that I abuse your trust by saying 'I want to die', well, it's real to me, but I will keep quiet in future. I realise that I am not a good little patient who does the decent thing and gets better without a struggle. I have tried and will probably try again, but for now I'm too tired. I am grateful for the time you have given me and for the graciousness with which you saw me when I entered your private office. Thank you.
> I can't come into hospital; it would just be to difficult for the family.
> Hand signed Cathy with PS I don't want further communications sent to my GP; it's just too embarrassed.

I was clearly not too hot on my grammar and very upset and angry with my extraordinarily dedicated doctor. Apparently I had sought Prof Thompson out without an appointment.

I was going downhill. I had started scalding myself with boiling water again and four days after this letter was written, I was once again persuaded to accept hospital admission. I also phoned up Guy's Poisons Unit to try and find out the fatal dose of one of the drugs I was on. After I had done this, I imagined that they had realised that it was not a genuine call. I was petrified of the consequences, worrying that I would be tracked down and punished.

This admission was back to C ward, since there were no beds on the usual B ward. Unbeknown to me, Prof Thompson was preparing to take up another post. He introduced me to Dr David Baldwin, a Senior Lecturer in Psychiatry and also a specialist in the treatment of depression. He was doing research into the clinical psychopharmacology of anxiety and depressive disorders and also the prevention of suicide and non-fatal self-harm. I was to see Dr Baldwin with increasing frequency as the responsibility for my care was to be transferred to him when Prof Thompson took on his new role as dean of the Southampton Medical School. They decided to stop the present drugs and start a special class called MAOIs. This particular class of drugs requires you to be on a special diet as certain foods are able to react with them, producing a serious side effect, namely a catastrophic rise in blood pressure.

I had a miserable time on this ward, to the extent that Phil even phoned up requesting that I be transferred; this did not happen, but fortunately I soon progressed to home leave. Interestingly, events that happened led me to make a formal complaint. Now when I think back to what had happened so far, I find it somewhat surprising. I had been given ECT paralysed but not anaesthetised, but had not made any sort of formal protest; now I was prepared to try out the system.

What precipitated this was in fact an occasion on 17 December, which was a Friday; I was being picked up to go home for weekend leave by Jo, my new carer from social services. I was always very anxious that I would get my medication to go home. The staff had taken some time to go and fetch it and when this particular nurse came back, she was addressing Jo about my drugs and not me. I was asking the questions, but she insisted on giving Jo the answers. It was as though I did not exist or even worse that I did not have the capability to understand. In fact the reverse was true. Jo had no medical training and when we eventually left, she told me that she had no idea what they were 'going on about'. I felt so humiliated. It was the last straw. In addition various other situations had arisen over the past week.

This is what I wrote on 17 December 1999. The names I have entered are fictitious:

Dear (Complaints Manager)

I am writing to you because of a number of incidents which took place while I was on C Ward at the DOP. I am loathe to complain because I realise that it may affect the way I am treated, should I have the misfortune to be in hospital again. I have been admitted to B ward on many occasions and although not perfect, I did not feel I had cause for complaint as I do now.

This morning I was due to go on home leave. Two days ago I asked the staff if there were TTOs (medication to be taken home) for me as I knew my doctor (Dr Boyd) was away. I was told that there were some in the cupboard and a further request slip that hadn't been sent to pharmacy yet. Today I was ready to go and Holly went to get my TTOs. After *some* time in the office, where my carer and I could see her chatting to staff, eventually she emerged and informed me that I would have to wait as the TTOs were for seven days not three. She told this not in fact to me but to my carer Jo, who remarked to me afterwards that she had no idea what Holly was talking about. I protested and after some unsympathetic exchanges, Holly went and asked another staff member, David. Again she kept addressing Jo and not me, even though I was holding the conversation. I felt she had been unnecessarily rude with a very unhelpful attitude. David has been courteous and helpful and said that it was alright for me to take the seven day supply home.

The previous week: 5/12/99

The patient in the next bed had developed a bad back and was put on bed rest. The staff had agreed to her smoking there. No one asked me if I minded. I did but kept quiet. The following day she returned to bed in the evening and with her friend decided she would like to smoke again (she had been in the smoking room earlier), again she asked the staff and her request was granted. At the same time her friend was present and they talked together loudly – the f-word and other swear words were used liberally. That evening I had had enough. I asked the staff if I could be moved but was told that I would have to wait until morning. The morning staff told me to wait for the afternoon staff. Finally Alison, my primary nurse, informed me that no more smoking would occur but I was sufficiently upset by this time that I wanted to see the doctor to get discharged home. During all this time I was told by Holly to have a sympathetic attitude towards other patients, when at no time had I expressed a lack of sympathy and had requested that *I* was the one who should be moved.

My upset had been added to because that lunchtime I had gone into the dining room and asked for my lunch. The N/A Judith was

there and told me that I was not on the list. I explained that I had been out for the weekend so may have been missed off. She became very forceful and said, 'you are not on the list, you have to eat downstairs.' She told me to come with her and we went into the office where she repeated her statement. In front of everyone I explained again how I had been bullied by a patient downstairs in the dining room for being a doctor. B ward had always let me eat upstairs and Karin (my primary nurse on B ward) told the staff about the situation when I was originally admitted to C ward. Judith went back to the dining room, (I had been given permission to stay upstairs) and I sat down. After a while I asked if I was going to have any lunch. She replied that I could if I asked and without any graciousness fetched me something. This is an aside but I was repeatedly having to explain why I had to eat upstairs – apparently no one thought it appropriate even though I was hardly eating and the doctors had asked the staff to encourage me to do so.

I am a doctor but I am mentally ill, I know I feel fragile. Why is it that I feel positively discriminated against because of being a doctor? There are some good staff (mentioned by name), but my experience has turned me away from a potential safe haven and I never want to go to C ward again.

Yours sincerely

I did not undertake this lightly. I was afraid of the consequences and afraid that I would be badly treated by some of the staff if I complained. That is why I was careful to refer to the 'good staff', although I admit that I was not exactly liberal with praise for anyone. I remember feeling quite paranoid that my confidential complaint would become public knowledge. How right I was. I was absolutely stunned to find not only a copy of my complaint and the reply given, but also entries in the medical notes that it had been discussed in the ward round and that the reply was sent to Prof Thompson for approval before being sent to me. It had nothing to do with the medical staff at all and I now know that what happened went completely against the NHS complaints procedure. This should never have been filed in the medical record and it has now been removed! However it's a bit late now. The damage occurred in 1999 and no apology from a hospital administrator will erase the torment I felt at that time.

It took two months for me to receive a reply.

In the meantime Prof Thompson had decided that they really had come to the end of the usual treatment options. This is the referral letter that he wrote to the Maudsley on 15 December 1999:

I would be most grateful if you could assess this doctor with regard to Neurosurgery for Mental Disorder. As you might guess this is

not something I do every day, but in this case the depression has been going on for such a long time with such ferocious intensity that I would very much appreciate an assessment. I have discussed this with her and she is prepared to come and see you for assessment without prejudice to the outcome.

I enclose an annotated summary of her history from the onset of the illness in 1994 to the present time. The key points are as follows.

(Quite a bit about early childhood experiences including boarding school) ... When Cathryn gets depressed her weight plummets and it is very difficult to get her to eat anything at all. In addition to the very strong depressive symptoms there is a history of deliberate self-harm. She has poured boiling water on herself, both to her arms and stomach in order to raise blisters. While these remain painful, she discontinues further self-harm, but as they improve she starts again. The behaviour does seem to be related to her depression as it gets worse in parallel with the mood. However recent psychotherapy seems to be dissociating these two features of her illness. She has also made decided efforts to commit suicide and at the present time has internal obsessional thoughts about this. She keeps medication stocks in order to carry this out and has run out into the road on occasions in attempts to be run over.

You will see from the four page annotated history that we have tried most things that we can think of.

Currently the situation is more settled than it has been when she has been admitted on Section 3. At the moment, she is using the hospital as a place of asylum and we have a much better quality therapeutic relationship with her. She is having dynamic psychotherapy twice a week which she is finding extremely difficult. Cognitive Behaviour Therapy was ineffective. She is also on quite a cocktail of medications. This includes Clopixol injections, mirtazapine and reboxetine, lithium and zopiclone. When she can't sleep she also takes thioridazine.

We have been struggling with this lady's care now for five years, almost continuously. She has been through phases where the only way to keep her out of hospital was to provide her with daily contact with the community team. She remains at high risk of suicide with pronounced obsessive symptoms as well as other symptoms of depression such as profound fatigue and insomnia. She has had a partial response to ECT in the past. I have been reluctant to restart ECT for several reasons.

This is a chronic condition and I am holding the possibility of ECT for acute deteriorations.

She appears to have a pseudo-cholinesterase deficiency causing anaesthetic problems on a number of occasions. On one occasion we had to do some post-traumatic stress counselling after she was paralysed while still awake. Although she is prepared to have ECT again she understands the need for caution.

At this stage we would very much appreciate another opinion and be particularly interested on your views on the appropriateness of neurosurgery.

I was upset by the events on C ward for some considerable time. The Trust's reply to my complaint was far from satisfactory. It said that I had become angry and shouted at the care assistant. This was exactly the sort of treatment that I had suspected of being meted out to mentally ill complainants. Basically counter-accusation. It made me feel very afraid and I am sure this is part of the reason that patients dare not protest. It would end up as my word against hers and I knew that I would lose. Even so, I was shocked by this and extremely distressed and eventually sought out the services of Advocacy Matters. They were very sympathetic and were willing to help me through the next tier of the complaints procedure. But I did not have the energy to continue to pursue the justice which I badly wanted.

What I was totally unaware of was the fact that Prof Thompson was having correspondence with the chief executive of the Trust, not only on the subject of my complaint, but also because he was asking them to fund the referral he was making to the Maudsley Hospital for me to be assessed for suitability for neurosurgery. I had no idea of the bureaucracy involved to obtain the finance for an ECR (extra-contractual referral).

The new millennium

Fortunately after the regrettable month which I had spent on C ward, I was allowed out on leave over Christmas 1999 and for the millennium celebrations. Stephanie was in *The Nutcracker* at the Royal Opera House, so we did not see much of her over the Christmas holidays. We went and watched a performance and I was so proud to see my little girl on stage. I had spent the Christmas weekend at home, but apart from the performance mentioned, I do not have any memories of it.

Phil had been hard at work managing the debugging of his company's software in preparation for 2000. He was on call all over this period. However, we actually spent New Year's Eve at Central Hall, the building where our church is based. I remember that occasion. Stephanie was at home for New Year. She and her friend decided to try out the mulled wine at the party. Unbeknown to us, they carefully went around our various friends asking if they could just 'try a little'. Once we discovered their little game it was too late. On the way home, we had to pick up Simon who was also a little worse for wear. Stephanie was put to bed but calling out from her room, 'I love you Mum, I love you Dad ... could you video the room because it's so funny the way it keeps going round and round!' At least we felt like a normal family having to deal with the usual problems teenage children bring!

January 2000

The festive lift of my spirits did not last for long. I admitted after Christmas that I felt I had to 'cover up all the time' when I was at home. I was reported to be lethargic, depressed with no interest, not wanting to do any enjoyable activity, no appetite, subdued and retarded.

I still remained on home leave but Ruth, my CPN, was very concerned. She faxed the department having seen me at home:

> FAO: Prof Thompson
> I want you to have this prior to seeing Cathy as planned on Monday
> 1 She continues to burn her arms badly and regularly (at least every other day).

2   Her mood is very low even though she is telling people that she is getting better (otherwise 'they will get fed up with her').

3   She has a plan to kill herself on Tuesday with very clear images associated with this.

I was admitted to A ward, but transferred to B ward a few days later. The scalding had continued and I had several burns on my arms, all at different stages of healing.

I was very low indeed and continuously asking to leave the ward during the week of 23 January. I was still a voluntary patient, but it was made clear to me that if I attempted to leave, I would be placed on a Section again. However, I had my psychotherapy session with Lee on Wednesday afternoon, the 26 January. I was escorted to the waiting area and left by the nurse. It was my golden opportunity. I escaped. I had no coat on, but I had some loose change. I ran out of the building and through the grounds of the hospital. I couldn't keep it up. I had so little energy. I was free now, but had to take action. I did not know the area well at all, but I spotted a chemist and went in. I knew buying paracetamol was no good – there was an antidote – so I bought aspirin and also Phenergan in order that I might at least feel sleepy. I found another shop which sold drinks and then I sat on a wall at the far end of a rather empty car park. I took all the tablets with the intention of dying as a result of the overdose. It was harder to do than I had imagined. I felt very lonely all of a sudden and I felt worthless. I remember how cold it was; a grey, overcast January day. No one saw me and I disposed of the empty packages in a bin. I still had a little bit of money left over, enough for a coffee. I decided that a café would be warm and I knew I needed somewhere to go while the tablets took effect. I wandered near to the town centre. I must have looked a little strange when I bought a drink in the John Lewis coffee shop which was not far away. I sat at a table alone and forlorn. This wasn't the way it was meant to be. I wanted to curl up somewhere warm and die. Then my mobile phone rang. I had forgotten about that. I panicked and switched it off. However, it got me thinking about Phil and the children. I had no paper so I couldn't even write to them. Where was I going to go now anyway? I was in such a dilemma. The coffee shop staff seemed to be watching me. I had finished my drink and was sitting there doing nothing. No shopping bag, no coat. I felt terribly conspicuous. I turned the phone back on and predictably Phil called again. I could hear the anxiety in his voice. I told him where I was. I still could not formulate a plan and when he came to get me, I was crying 'I'm sorry, I'm so sorry … ' I moaned it over and over again. He was reassuring, but had no idea what had happened. He took me to the car and he was saying, 'It's alright, I've found you now. You're safe … ' All I could think of was what was going to happen. I was beginning to feel drowsy. 'I'm sorry, tell the children I'm sorry … ' Just as

we were arriving back at the DOP, the penny dropped for him. He suddenly realised that my apologies were far more serious than running away from the hospital. He drove straight to Southampton General A&E.

Apparently I did fight with Phil, but I don't remember it. However, I didn't resist for long. I had no energy to resist. They asked me what I had taken and I told them. The Phenergan at least sent me to sleep. However, I hadn't taken enough. I was admitted to the medical ward and by the following morning apart from ringing in my ears, I was fine.

Well, physically I was fine, but mentally the torment was terrible. I had messed up. I was a doctor and I couldn't even get this right. I felt sure I was being laughed at and then I heard them talking about me. There were two or three people discussing me. I was so upset at what they were saying, although I had to agree with them – I was completely useless, a terrible person and I deserved to die. They were better off without me and I was so stupid that I couldn't even do it properly. Of course I was an attention-seeking, selfish woman who had no right to be here ... I couldn't bear it any more, I wanted to tell them to shut up, but when I pulled back the curtain, there was no one there and the voices carried on and on. I so wished I had been successful, I wished I was dead, but I would rather be at the DOP than continue here in my vulnerability on the medical ward. I wondered what the A&E staff thought of me. I hoped I hadn't been recognised. I wondered whether anyone would have any sympathy, but I doubted it. Was I sympathetic five years ago when I worked in that same department? The honest answer was no. It wasn't cool to be kind to 'time wasters', like those who took trivial overdoses. Now the tables were turned. I could never return to work now. I was a low life with no prospects. I was locked into my ill-fated and pitiful world. There was no turning back and I could not undo the past. I was relieved to be taken back to B ward.

February 2000

I had started to see more of Dr Baldwin as Prof Thompson was soon to be leaving. I found it unsettling and was reluctant to trust yet another person, but Dr Baldwin was also very kind and he soon gained my confidence. I had also got to know their staff grade doctor, Dr Harriet Boyd, very well and appreciated the consistency, particularly with the long hospital admissions. I saw Harriet two or three times a week, which I found very helpful.

I do not have any memory of most of what I am relating for this period of time. I have used the medical notes, our diary at home and my snippets of writing to put this account together. I remember some of the feelings and some of the experiences, but I have little memory of detail. Sometimes what I have read in the notes has been very difficult to take in or relate to, but I do recognise myself in it. Dr Boyd in particular wrote copious and detailed notes when I saw her either alone or during the ward rounds. She

often wrote in quotes exactly what I had said and she noted what had been going on in my life, including the events at home. I have not included every detail, sometimes because it is tedious or recurrent and sometimes because it is too personal for such an account. Likewise I have not given detail of the drug treatments, purely because it is hard enough for me to understand without a psychiatry training, let alone a non-medical reader.

When I returned to B ward, I was no better. My failed suicide attempt only served to make things worse; my relationship with the nursing staff was not perfect and now I had to endure their disapproval. There was some cause for optimism though. I had an appointment for my assessment at the Maudsley. I was beginning to think that brain surgery was a good idea. Really it was my only glimmer of hope in this ghastly mess I had got myself into. Either that or I would have to find another opportunity to kill myself. I had a good look at the ceiling system, wondering where a noose could be attached and so now even my dressing gown belt had been removed. I was on 15-minute observations. I was still hearing voices and wanted to leave the hospital. This is what Dr Baldwin wrote:

> Ms Wield is suffering from severe, resistant depression with mood congruent psychotic phenomena including delusions of guilt, delusions of persecution, second and third person object space auditory hallucinations and fleeting visual hallucinations. She had made a serious suicide attempt, has persisting suicidal thoughts and intent, and has a long history of deliberate self-harm. She had made frequent attempts to leave the ward two days ago with the express interest of wishing to kill herself by taking a second overdose of medication.
>
> She is at present detained under Section 5(2) and in view of her severe psychotic depression, suicide intent and reluctance to continue with informal treatment, she is being assessed for detention under the provisions of Section 3 of the Mental Health Act.

The Section 3 was applied. I was detained in hospital for another six months of involuntary treatment. A decision was made to start ECT again, only I was also suffering with postural hypotension, a side effect of the new drugs and I fell and sustained a head injury, leaving me with a nerve palsy and double vision. Life was not good.

I was called to the Maudsley Hospital for an assessment with a view to having NMD. The conclusion was that I had a severe refractory depression with a strong biological component to the illness so would be put on the waiting list for an inpatient in-depth assessment for suitability for surgery. We were told that the waiting list was at least four months.

The lithium was stopped since I had been on it for five years with no response; the MAOI was stopped since it was not effective even at

maximum dose. I continued on a combination of other drugs including antipsychotics in order to control the voices. The ECT was restarted (once I recovered from the head injury) as a holding measure and the psychotherapy ran on twice a week.

I remember little, apart from the long days filled with ongoing misery and my inherent dislike of the hospital. I have no idea how my faith was. I wrote this at some point.

Psychotherapy
Sometimes it's helpful just to talk but more often I find myself being criticised. When I'm on the ward, a nurse might say, 'you're thinking that because you're feeling low' (yes, I need the obvious pointing out), but Lee tries to correct me and often resorts to the phrase of 'there you go again'. I keep explaining that I'm not trying to be bad, but I feel as if I can't do anything right. I'm so scared that if I don't keep going, her prophesy that 'it will happen again' will come true so I feel trapped into swallowing this very bitter medicine.

I do not know what I was talking about. I think I was excessively sensitive and I could never get past the feeling that I was constantly being criticised. I do not know whether I was or not, but I do know that the nursing staff were finding me hard work.

I tried to smuggle some drugs on to the ward, but they were discovered in the search. This is what I wrote:

A long night up courtesy of two zopiclone (sleeping tablets)
This has been a long week and I really made a fool of myself this time, but I thought it might help if I tried to explain myself, if nothing else I might feel better for it. I am not playing games. I'm not functioning all that logically though, I admit that. When I brought those drugs in, I really truly wanted them to be there should I have the impulse to kill myself. I'm not like anyone else on the ward; as I am regularly reminded, 'you're a doctor'. This means I can't afford to make another mistake, get found too soon, take diazepam or paracetamol ... I've got to get it right. If I was to have an 'accident' and it wasn't fatal, then they would all be saying 'attention seeker'.

One of the reasons I haven't gone through with it is that Stephanie's best friend at school – her mother – is dying, in fact not expected to last the weekend. She stayed with us recently and I

can't even mention her mum without tears welling up. It's a stark reminder of what I might do to my children.

So why am I writing this? I think I am still terribly misunderstood and though my good times have been good, my bad times are so awful and frightening and then I can't think that I will ever get out of this or recover totally. I think if I do well, then it's just waiting round the corner to get me again. But the brave face comes out at home; maybe the hospital is just a relief from that.

At the same time, I remember how I used to be envious of people having cancer. I wanted to die from something which I saw as legitimate. How sad and how awful that I was wishing a terminal illness on myself. But unhappily it was true, although it was not something that I would have readily admitted at the time. The illness had made me become incredibly self-centred and even when I did try to think outside of myself I could not do so without feeling the burden of guilt associated with my perceived sense of failure.

By the end of February, I was allowed out on weekend leave. I had had a better week, was smiling more and moving more quickly. However, I did not want more ECT, I was finding it 'scary'. I felt also that I was ruining the children's lives and I was extremely worried about the thought of brain surgery. My driving licence had been taken away, which I also found very upsetting and was to repeatedly ask over the coming months that the team write to the DVLC to say that I was well enough to drive once I got home. They repeatedly said 'no, not yet'.

March 2000

My memory problems were becoming more evident. I was often confused about times and dates even though the ECT had been suspended during that time. My mental state seemed to be improving and the team were thinking of rescinding the Section (although I was not aware of this). I was to be allowed out on one week's leave to see how it would go. Unfortunately I was back within two days with suicidal thoughts and intent. I was described as having delusions of guilt and nihilistic delusions – meaning that I was convinced that I was totally worthless as a person and could not be persuaded otherwise. I agreed to have more ECT and once again the medication was altered.

April 2000

They continued to allow me to visit home at the weekends and weekday evenings and I felt a bit better when I was at home with the children. I

was very worried that the assessment at the Maudsley would coincide with Simon's GCSEs. (I don't know why, since I did little to support him anyway!) That was not to be a problem; unfortunately the waiting list was going down extremely slowly.

Easter was coming up. I knew I ought to be at home and felt that I was 'letting the children down badly'. However, I was also scared. I found it difficult to maintain enough energy and to keep up a front. I felt a terrible failure. I was hearing voices again and had lots of intrusive thoughts about harming myself. When on the ward, it was noted that I was not interacting with the other patients and seemed preoccupied. I burned myself over Easter, but seemed to think that the ECT was helping. My joints were painful and I needed painkillers to help me sleep. X-rays showed osteoporosis.

By the end of April, I was allowed home for a full four days and I was once again telling everyone that I felt much better. My 'much better' was clearly not that much of an improvement. I was reported to have pronounced psychomotor retardation, to be pessimistic with feelings of hopelessness.

The psychotic element of the depression was very evident. I had terrible feelings of impending doom, was quite paranoid and needed to do things when at home to distract me from the voices. I was convinced that everyone thought I was weird, which fed my low self esteem.

I was obviously happier at home and my CPN, Ruth, was convinced that I should spend more time there and try to do other activities, not just housework! I had no energy for anything else and found what I did do a tremendous effort. Pushed by guilt at leaving tasks to other people, mainly Phil and his mother, gave me some motivation to do some household chores.

The next few weeks were a seesaw of a little improvement to being suicidal and obsessed with thoughts of self-harm. I was ever more preoccupied with the latter and needed all my strength to control the urges to act on them.

There was still no word from the Maudsley and I was finding the concept of surgery increasingly difficult. I was frightened at the thought of it and frightened at what would happen if I chose not to go ahead. The whole world had taken on a sense of unreality and déjà vu. Apparently this was another psychotic phenomenon. I do remember this feeling quite well. It is very strange, like having a high fever and not at all pleasant. I wished this world of mine wasn't real and even now, I still wish it hadn't been. There seemed no end to it all.

CHAPTER 13

Summer, pain and shame

June 2000

By the end of May, my home leave was being increased again. I wanted the Section to be removed. I had had 18 ECT treatments in the last two months. I was still very unwell, weepy and 'down', with a tremendous sense of guilt and dogged by unremitting thoughts of suicide. I was angry at life and although I didn't know how I was going to cope, I knew that I had to test my capabilities. 'I just want to go home and be okay.' The medical team agreed.

However, I was to come back to hospital once a week for 'maintenance' ECT on a Wednesday so as not to interfere with extended leave. The other stipulation was that I was not to be left alone at home. I have no idea how that was supposed to have been adhered to since it was difficult enough arranging for care for the children, let alone for me!

Around this time the pattern of my self-harm changed. I started to cut myself, having smashed up a quantity of disposable razors and removed all the blades. They were very small and easy to keep hidden away. I cut my abdomen, requiring stitches from one of the SHOs on the ward. It was decided that the leave needed review, which led to more time in hospital. Another ward round discussion ensued. Basically Dr Baldwin and the team felt I should take responsibility for my actions. Meanwhile I was caught in my familiar dilemma. Anyway, I denied any suicidal plans and was very worried about how the family were coping at home. My misplaced anxiety included concern about the hamster and I would phone home to check whether he had been fed!

We had a holiday in France booked for the end of July and I would be allowed to go since I would be under Phil's constant supervision. We thought this would be our last family holiday because of our increasingly difficult financial circumstances and the fact that Rebecca would only have one more year at school. Phil and I both independently thought this would be our last holiday together, because I would not be alive for another one.

Dr Boyd noted that I had gained considerable weight, almost two stone over a very short period. I didn't like being overweight but being fatter made the cutting less dangerous! The nurses had started to search me

whenever I entered the ward (e.g. after an evening at home) and had found a blade. However, for a short time they decided that searching me just made things worse, by 'reinforcing the challenging behaviour' that my deliberate self-harm was felt to be. This lack of understanding displayed by some of the nurses strengthened my desire not just to go home on leave, but to be fully discharged. I started telling everyone that I was actually much better and inexplicably I even started talking about returning to work in September after the summer holiday.

On 14 July, I told Dr Baldwin that I was 'really quite good'. His notes did not bear this out, 'downcast, subdued, little spontaneity of speech'. The decision was made that they would allow the Section to expire while I was on holiday, but that I was not to be discharged. I was to be 'on leave' as an informal patient, but return to the ward for review on my return from France.

August 2000

Once again, I look at the photos with amazement. My memories are scarce, but I do remember one day which we all enjoyed. We went wild water rafting and we stopped for lunch by the side of this mountain river. We had a barbecue over a fire made with brush wood accompanied by French wine. We had met up with our friends, Phil and Sheelagh Clarke, on this holiday and we all had a good time, sneaking up and pushing each other into the freezing water! It awakened something of my former self – what a shame it did not last. I found the laughter and normal frivolity of a family on holiday difficult to cope with and often retired to bed in the mobile home. I was trying to read but found that I was easily distracted and concentration was very difficult. Normally I would have read avidly, often a book a day, now it was an achievement to get through a single chapter.

Mindful of Dr Baldwin's plan, I was afraid that I would be readmitted on my return from holiday, but I was allowed to stay at home still on 'extended leave'. Since it was time for yet another alteration to the medication, I was asked to attend the ward each week for review by one of the medical team. I was making a lot of mistakes when I spoke, like asking for a cup of gin, when I meant tea! The children found this very amusing, but I did not. I was reassured that this was part of being depressed and not a side effect of the ECT, which is what I feared. I was reporting that Phil and I were having a lot of rows, but when Dr Boyd spoke to him on the phone, he assured her that in fact they were more like minor disagreements, primarily because I bottled things up. He also felt that I had shown no real improvement during the holiday. (Phil has since told me that however difficult it might have been, he avoided conflict at all costs.) Despite the fact that I was expressing a lot of frustration at not being allowed to drive and therefore ferry the children around, Phil felt I was pretty uncoordinated

and physically clumsy. He agreed with the team that it would be unsafe for me to drive. I thought Prof Thompson was being mean because he would not agree to me driving.

I made a second large cut on my abdomen. It was decided that the maintenance ECT should in fact continue. I felt that Phil was 'slogging his guts out for me' and I was being of little help. My plan to return to work to ease the situation was being weighed up against the possibility of obtaining life insurance money if I died.

Neither of these things happened. Instead we got a lodger! I remained at home through September and the plan was for a care worker to be found once again. I told the medical team that I had lost faith in the medication which I had so consistently been compliant with, but they told me that I would go on a 'drug holiday', i.e. have them withdrawn when I was assessed at the Maudsley.

It seems that every entry with a positive note contained within it would be followed by a decline on the next occasion I was seen. The cuts continued to be repeated with increasing frequency. It seems that I used the cutting to control the tension caused either by the situation or by the intensity of the thoughts. There were times where I wanted to be back in hospital, but the team were convinced that it was not a solution and that I would do even less, in terms of activity, than I was doing at home. However, they made sure that I could be admitted in an emergency and also that I was not formally discharged. The Maudsley was still not able to come up with a date for the assessment. I made plans for another suicide attempt, but made a partial disclosure to Ruth, my CPN. However, when I was seen by Prof Thompson, I kept the plans quiet and expressed ambivalence about coming back to hospital. He decided to let me stay home if accompanied, but to have a bed ready for an emergency admission.

Simon had started this academic year at sixth form college to do AS levels; Jonathan was also making a new start at secondary school. I am not sure I was of much help to either of them.

November 2000

Two days after I had seen Prof Thompson, Ruth came to see me and she felt that this time there was no question, I required readmission. I was confused with a sense of impending doom and once again feelings of unreality. At least there were no voices at this time. Once back on B ward, I was still encouraged to go home for the evening and weekends to see the children, but with the proviso that I should not be left alone. That was fine by me; I was frightened when I was alone, scared that I would be unable to resist the urges to kill myself. Somewhere in the recesses of my mind there must have been some self-preservation instinct, although my concern for the wellbeing of the family was probably the most powerful protection I

had – part of the reason why the medical team were keen for me to maintain as much contact with my children as possible. The delay in admission to the Maudsley was not helping the situation. I had suddenly lost patience. I decided that it was no longer worth waiting for and I wanted to leave the ward. Rather a familiar pattern for the staff, but not for me. I had no active memory of the last few years. Apparently I was tearful, distressed, no eye contact, no rapport and it took an hour to persuade me to wait until the morning. I waited, but over the next 48 hours nothing changed. Dr Baldwin was asked to review the situation. This is what he wrote:

Nursing staff have requested a review of Cathy who is wishing to leave the ward, but has caused some concerns about risk of self-harm.

At interview
Cathy has thoughts of wishing to leave the ward, with a view to going into the town centre to buy tablets to take in overdose (probably aspirin). These thoughts have worsened over the last two days coupled with a sense of not wanting to be on the ward or at home. A nurse found Cathy preparing to take an overdose, took her supply of medicine and also found her to be concealing a razor blade in her underwear. At the same time, Cathy has images of her family around her grave in her 'mind's eye'. She is ambivalent about whether she wishes to live or die.

Cathy's depressive symptoms are otherwise unchanged; amongst these she describes some recent reduction in appetite and increase in tension. She also feels reluctant to accept visits.

Mental state examination reveals evidence of non-reactive low mood, psychomotor retardation, suicidal thoughts and images and partially completed plans. There are no signs of psychosis, no cognitive impairment and her insight appears full.

These are grounds to recommend her detention under Section 3 of the Mental Health Act. Cathy cannot assure me that she will remain in hospital and I am therefore recommending that she be detained.

At the same time things were going wrong for Stephanie. She was travelling back to White Lodge as usual after her weekend at home, but she broke down in tears halfway up the M3, saying she did not want to go back. Phil brought her home again. Despite a few more days at home, Stephanie's feelings did not change. She wanted to leave White Lodge. Phil made arrangements for her to join Jonathan at the local comprehensive school. It was a very traumatic time for Stephanie but she was resolute

that she did not want to go back to boarding school. This made the situation even worse as far as I was concerned. I felt desperately guilty that I had once again got myself in this position of being in hospital. I was allowed to go home and see her, but it did not stop me from cutting again. I knew the nursing staff were far from pleased with me when I got back to the ward and I felt that I was wasting their time. I sat in front of the TV, watching but not taking anything in, miserable and bombarded by intrusive thoughts telling me to 'do something really nasty'.

I started to notice a change in the children when I went home. They seemed independent and even Stephanie didn't really need me. Back in hospital, I became less communicative and when asked questions would reply, 'I don't know, I don't know what to say, my mind has gone blank'. I had frequent images of dying and graveyards. I was cutting myself frequently and needed antibiotics for a wound infection. I felt that the doctors did not really mind about the self-harm. I knew the nursing staff did and I found it puzzling that they did not understand that if I did not cut or burn, I would do something else. Karin became angry with me. My response was that she has 'every right to get cross as it's a waste of everyone's time'. I felt better for the pain. I now felt that the children would not be upset for long if I was to die and that they would get on with their lives. There was no part of me that wanted to stay alive. Everything was in conflict. I felt numb and could no longer cry. I cut very deeply. This time, though, the ward SHO felt it was too extensive for her to repair. I was taken to A&E. Well at least I had made my debut a few months earlier. They knew already that I was a no good loser, but I still felt ashamed and embarrassed.

11 December 2000

The medical team received a phone call from the Maudsley. They were no longer going to be offering a service for NMD. The only place that could do this in the UK was Professor Keith Matthews in Dundee. Fortunately for me, Dr Baldwin wasted no time and phoned him immediately asking for an urgent assessment. A letter was to be sent ASAP.

By the time Dr Baldwin saw me on the ward round, he was able to tell me the good news that I would be assessed in Dundee, so that the shock of hearing about the Maudsley was greatly lessened.

CHAPTER 14

Dear Diary

January 2001

The notes in early January say that I had a good Christmas, was able to put on a front and enjoy it, but the good feeling did not last.

My parents were by now offering to pay for me to have private treatment, such was their desperation, but news from Dundee was good; there was no waiting list.

The psychotherapy had continued all this time. Lee was a little concerned about the deliberate self-harm and was keen that I disclose my intentions. I told the team that I was planning on bleeding to death, but I guess there was not a lot they could do about it. I was being searched on a regular basis and it was clearly felt to be my responsibility. I had another idea as well which was to give myself peritonitis; that way I felt I could die without the suicide label. My thinking was clearly irrational. Why would I assume I would die from it in this day and age of advanced treatment and antibiotics? They offered me the option of taking out my feelings in the seclusion room. This was a small room with no furniture. There was no carpet on the flooring and it had padded walls. It was usually used when a patient was violent, in order to give them time and space to calm down. The offer was that I could go in there and punch a pillow. I can't think why I turned it down! Instead I cut myself and there followed another trip to A&E.

The voices were back again by the middle of January as were compelling intrusive thoughts. This is what Dr Boyd wrote in the notes; I was obviously being asked to describe the experience.

> It's like voices, but not through the ears, like her own voice, different from ordinary thoughts. She is not sure if it is her own voice – a voice. She needs to block it out, get anger out, but it does not work. When she decides to do what the voices say (cut), she gets peace. The voice crescendos towards the end. She tries to block it out and has tried her walkman but it does not alleviate her symptoms.

The team increased one of the antipsychotic medications.

I started to do a consistent diary on 29 January 2001. I was finding it very hard to remember anything from day to day, in particular the contents of the twice-weekly psychotherapy sessions. I think this may be why I decided to start writing things down in a notebook. I am sure that I then subsequently forgot that was the reason why I started it, since I did not look back very often. As a result, it is quite repetitive, but I also notice how the pattern of my thinking changed over a relatively short period of time with no reference to what I was thinking previously. When I had completed a notebook, I would leave it hidden away at home. Once I recovered it took me a good six months to be able to bring myself to read what I had written. I was very tempted to burn it all!

I have tried not to alter what I originally wrote, but sometimes have had to in order for it to be comprehensible. I have deliberately left out names of fellow patients and have changed names of the nursing staff to ensure their confidentiality. The exceptions to this are Ruth Paley my CPN, Lee the psychotherapist, Karin who was my primary nurse, the doctors and a few others who were also exceptionally kind, understanding and helpful.

The contents are fairly simple; childlike often, but each entry took considerable effort. This is evident by the form of my writing, which was sometimes spidery and clearly shaky, sometimes virtually illegible. If the entry was long, the writing would often become progressively worse towards the end. There are gaps indicating that I did not necessarily write the whole entry for a day at the same time. I remember ongoing themes, but not many of the specific events, unless of course they were of the sort that one could never forget. I cannot put faces to names of people who I met on only a few occasions. I cannot even remember all of the nurses or all of the patients with whom I had prolonged contact.

I have added comments in parentheses as explanations where necessary. The children all have their nicknames – Bec, Simon remains Simon, Steph and Jona.

---

29 January 2001 Monday
Phil's birthday today.

Very cold in the side room – put in it after my bed was taken at the weekend. I was at least more prepared for this than before and had packed my things away. I'm still terrified I'll be moved back into a non-window bed.

Had psychotherapy this a.m. – talked a lot about self-harm. Lee says I'm converting emotional pain to physical pain and that I need to learn to tolerate the emotional pain. She also says that I am torturing myself and hurting our family including Phil. Phil took two days off work last week and that surprised and frightened

me. Will I ruin his work too? Lee says that I shouldn't be surprised that it affects our family.

Yesterday I talked to Steph and apologised for not being around after school. She said 'it's alright Mum, we know you can't help it' and also pointed out that other parents are at work or separated.

The experience
It was on Wednesday (17 January) – I'd had psychotherapy and spent about an hour on the phone to Mary (my sister) and promised her I would not kill myself that day. I had tried running away but had been caught. Anyway I decided to give in to the thoughts and cut myself. I wanted to cut right through to do myself some 'real' harm. I was taken to Southampton General by Vera (one of the nurses) and went straight to the stretcher side. They did my obs (temperature, pulse, blood pressure etc.) which must have been OK and I was told I would see a senior doctor straight away. An SHO came, looked at the wound and said 'oh, we'll just stitch you up'. But then a surgeon arrived and took my pulse and announced that I had a tachycardia (raised heart rate). He explored the wound without any local anaesthetic and it hurt like hell – I was screaming and pushing him off, but then I felt terrible, sick and faint. I was really breathless. They tipped the trolley up and gave me oxygen. They put two venflons (intravenous lines) in and gave me fluid and took me straight to theatre. The anaesthetist was really nice and stroked my hair. I had to sign the consent and wanted to refuse. I asked if they could just let me die and he said 'no', so I signed.

The next thing I know, I woke up in recovery. I was taken to the ward. The nurses were surprisingly nice. I was expecting them to be punitive, but they were fine. The first night I catnapped only because they kept doing my blood pressure. I had to stay in until the drain was out and I had to have a blood transfusion.

I was seen on B ward by Dr Boyd once I was transferred back to the DOP a few days later. I had obviously found the experience pretty traumatic and repeatedly said that I would not do it again; I did not like the feelings associated with the blood loss and did not want to die in that way. At that time it was thought that this might become a deterrent for the cutting behaviour.

The centre at Dundee had been on the phone as Prof Keith Matthews had decided that I needed to be transferred up there for a full assessment, since I was a 'complex' case. Dr Baldwin agreed. There were, however, problems over the paperwork since I was on a Section 3. The Scottish

Mental Health Act is different and they needed to ensure that this difficulty could be sorted out in order to cross the border. Arrangements were being made.

---

30 January 2001 Tuesday
I feel like I don't know how I feel; inside there's a voice inside saying I'm a liar, I could snap out of it if I wanted to. Sometimes I just don't know what's the truth. I want to be well, really well, no pretending, no pushing it back in so this happens to me again. Do I feel low or am I just trying it on? Am I just feeling sorry for myself? I can't cry – I think it would be good for me, in a way. I feel numb. I don't want to go home as I feel more secure here even though it's such a horrid place. I want to talk to Karin but she'll probably be too busy. I'm so scared that going to Dundee will all go wrong – I'm so afraid that they'll say no. I know I've got to trust God about this. It's easy to say though, but not easy to do.

Yesterday I had ward round with Dr Baldwin and he says I can go to Scotland in mid-February. I'm really scared it will go wrong. I feel guilty because I think I try to make out I'm worse than I am. I do want to cut myself again but the memory is still there – the stitches are due out tomorrow.

It was Phil's birthday yesterday and we had some wine so Marie (our friend) brought me back. She wants me to meet this woman who's had depression, self-harm etc. and come through it. I don't want to go but feel obliged to otherwise they'll think I'm not trying. At least I'll get to talk to Marie on the way.

1 February 2001 Thursday
I was strip-searched today and all my things were gone through but they didn't find the blade. I panicked and had a chat with Miranda (nurse) – the thoughts are quite prominent now. I've had the stitches out and I do want to do it again. I'm not sure about wanting to die today. All I know is I want to be self-destructive and it's a matter of when, not if, though I am trying to hold out. I just don't know what to do. I want to go off the ward and decide but probably I can't.

Lee says I will be a different person after the operation if I go ahead. I feel like piggy in the middle and to crown it all Prof Thompson's on holiday, Dr Baldwin's on study leave and Harriet (Dr Boyd) is on holiday, so who can I talk to? That's why I called Ruth (CPN) and it was she who alerted the staff to the blades, because when she asked whether I had some, the look on my face gave it away.

2 February 2001 Friday
I cut myself this a.m. as soon as I was awake – unfortunately the blade was lousy, though in retrospect at least I didn't have to go to A&E. Now I feel down, but the tension has lifted and the soreness helps. I've packed everything up for the weekend in case I get moved again. I hate the thought so much and I would feel a lot easier if I knew I would be coming back to the same bed. It's not so bad if they move the things nicely like Sue (a really helpful nurse) did at the beginning of the week, but usually everything's just thrown into a bag which is why I've packed up myself. God please look after me. Karin is too busy to see me.

4 February 2001 Sunday
Back at the DOP and all of the worry over beds is for nothing. I feel guilty at leaving the hamster and not cleaning the bathroom and stairs. I did want to do them but just lack energy. At least I've been to Sainsbury's today and cleared up the dinner as well as doing washing yesterday.

On Saturday went with Marie to see this woman, she is a 'Theo-therapist' or TT for short ... It was an interesting time and I think she knows what she's doing, but once again it's back to childhood forgiving myself and loving myself because God does. OK on the intellect scale. Of course she's very suspicious of the operation – the thing is I don't want the depression back. I don't mind tackling the weaknesses in my character/personality BUT I do NOT want to get ill ever again and I think the op might help that.

6 February 2001 Tuesday
I'm finding S (a patient) really annoying, she's obviously very distressed but some of her 'confusion' doesn't seem genuine to me. Mind you I find J (another patient) annoying with her constant shaking. When I get attention it doesn't make *me* feel any better. The other thing is S had a razor – it makes me feel really guilty as she's obviously copying me.

I told Dr Boyd about choking all the time, but she says I've had odd symptoms and they've cleared up on their own! I must admit I do keep thinking there's something wrong with me but then I'm aware that when you're depressed you do think hypochondriac thoughts. I might be called up to Scotland any day now – I hope, I wish, I pray it's soon.

The session with Lee was OK except she blames my lack of memory on the drugs whereas Harriet (Dr Boyd) says its short attention span – I find it hard to remember the contents of the session.

Mary (my sister) is ringing virtually every day and sent me some beautiful flowers, it's a bit of a pressure though.

Serena (a nurse) says I should see the op or not having the op as in God's hands and not rely on being suitable for the op. Easier said than done, but I'm trying. I recognise that I can't stay here forever and she suggests I think about what could be different if I go back home i.e. not staying in bed all day.

7 February 2001 Wednesday

Been feeling low – got a bollocking from Lee re operation – she totally denied saying that it would change my personality. Anyway we discussed it and the possibility of me not being suitable. I think there are two options – suicide or pull myself together with TT (haven't told Lee about the TT bit). I still feel numb most of the time though I cried with Lee and also keep thinking I'm making this up and could just be fine if I wanted to, so I also feel guilty. What's real?

The lights

All the pull-cord lights have been replaced by movement-sensitive lights. However, in our room one is on permanently and the other when you walk past switches on, but when I was cleaning my teeth it went off twice. This happened before on the toilet and I was waving my arms frantically and the stupid thing wouldn't go on, but did eventually.

8 February 2001 Thursday

Just feel like staying in bed today but got up at teatime, still feel low and doing a lot of thinking about suicide and cutting. I'm afraid of what will happen if they refuse the op and also next week. How am I going to cope? It's an addiction; I mustn't do anything which would jeopardise my trip to Dundee. But when? The staff say my leave form is being changed so I can go out at the weekend but I'm worried. If Bec wasn't coming home then I wouldn't mind.

The other thing that's worrying me is my weight is going up. I'm so hungry except first thing in the morning. Mary says go with what your body tells you and worry about it later – I hope she's right.

9 February 2001 Friday

What I dread about going home for the weekend is a) all the things that need doing especially shopping and b) having to put on a front, but I just have to bite the bullet as they say. Once again I'm worried about losing the bed and will pack everything away.

My stitches are due out today but I'm not sure if I'm going to say anything or not.

S is annoying me with her groaning and 'confusion', only because I think she doesn't try to help herself – not taking her tablets.

Yesterday Phil brought his friend to see me to talk about his wife. He said he wouldn't have thought I was depressed and I tried to explain why I don't 'act' depressed because of learning to cover up feelings as a child. Is this true or am I making it all up?

This was something I found difficult throughout my illness – comments along the lines of 'you look alright to me'. I was doing my best to behave 'normally' towards other people and suffered tremendously from guilt. These comments always hurt me and made me feel worse about myself. I wished so often to have had what would be considered a legitimate illness instead. If I had been suffering from a serious physical condition, then maybe the comments would be 'isn't it great the way she tries so hard to be cheerful' or 'she's so uncomplaining'. It was quite common for there to be little or no acknowledgement of my suffering.

11 February 2001 Sunday

Weekend not bad, very tiring, trying to keep up with all the chores. Still dead scared about the bed and Phil wants me to come to church – some guy with a healing ministry. Love seeing the children, lots of hugs and cuddles with Bec.

I got prayed for at church. What I remember is to be set free from the spirit of self-rejection and the spirit of death. I prayed loads when I was outside the DOP – I want this to be real, Lord help me to accept your healing. Audrey also prayed not to look back in self-condemnation. Tony prayed against the chemical imbalance.

12 February 2001 Monday

I've just heard I'm going to Scotland on Wednesday!! Just been to see Lee, it went OK although I make out I agree with her, when either I don't understand or I don't really agree.

13 February 2001 Tuesday

I've just remembered more. Tony prayed against the chemical imbalance and the German guy for lifting the depression. I'm feeling surprisingly peaceful about tomorrow, I just hope Phil can get all the transport sorted out. I've just tried art therapy – I'm not much good at it but had a go anyway.

CHAPTER 15

North of the border

18 February 2001 Sunday (Liff Hospital, Dundee)
I haven't been writing, a combination of I can't be bothered and forgetting. So much has happened – psychological tests mainly. I had a long interview with Prof Matthews – he's very nice, sweet bloke. I still feel a fraud. Yesterday I came back at 4.30 even though we had booked out till 8 p.m. (allowed out with Phil). I just feel so tired. They let me lie in both yesterday and today thank goodness, mostly we get woken and have to dress for breakfast at 8 a.m.

I am still having horrible symptoms and wonder whether it's anything sinister (cancer), but then I don't care if it is.

I've told Prof Matthews that I'm terrified of being turned down for surgery – where's my faith in getting healed? I'm also terrified of this interview with the cognitive behaviour therapist. I was turned down in Southampton and I'm worried this guy will say it's the answer when I've already been turned down.

My literary capabilities were obviously severely limited as illustrated by my description of Prof Matthews. I failed to mention that he has the typical build of a rugby player, mid-late 30s, bald, shaved head with a beard and a Scot. He did not look in the least bit like a psychiatrist to me! He was most offended when I told him of my description of him as a 'sweet bloke'! However, he was very kind. I do not remember the interview that I had with him but it would have been very thorough. He assesses a good many patients, most of which he finds are not suitable for surgery because they have not been tried on all the different treatment options. He must have told me this and I guess this was why I became so nervous of seeing the cognitive behaviour therapist.

I cannot remember Liff Hospital except I have a vague recollection of large rooms in an old building with wooden panels on the walls. It had snowed quite heavily when we arrived apparently.

I remember that the Scottish nurses wore white uniforms whereas in England psychiatric nurses wear their own clothes. At least you knew who

was who! I don't remember the journey up to Dundee. Phil accompanied me and we flew from Southampton to Edinburgh and hired a car. He had to stay in a local hotel.

---

19 February 2001 Monday
Had a shower and breakfast and went back to bed. Still feeling numb. Don't think anything is happening today except the hairdresser is coming about 12 p.m. for a trim! I really need it and my face is awful at present.

Tomorrow is the CBT session, I'm dreading that he'll say I need it. I am prejudiced but as Phil suggested, I just haven't got the energy to go through a full course. I want the surgery, risks and all, I can't keep going and waiting.

I am trying to go to sleep but suddenly remember two embarrassing moments – this happens repeatedly – must tell Lee.
My scars are sore and itchy. I've been thinking about cutting myself virtually all day.

20 February 2001 Tuesday
I've just been told I'll see Dr Durham CBT at 1 p.m., just 10 mins away. I am so nervous of the outcome.

It was 'short and sweet'; he said that a course might have helped but my present therapy is forming contact with the past but in a less structured way. He also reckoned I was too depressed.

I'm feeling lots of self-harm thoughts and I've just talked to staff. They're going to see if they can get some chlorpromazine.

21 February 2001 Wednesday
I saw Prof Matthews with Phil, this a.m. and it looks promising about me going ahead for surgery, but the earliest will be May and I need to be here for 3–4 weeks. We need permission from the Mental Welfare Commission and funding from the trust in Southampton. He asked Phil about the weekend and he admitted I stayed in bed most of the day. I hate doing the shopping and can't do it alone, sometimes I can do washing.

We now have to wait for some paperwork to allow me to leave Scotland so it's just going to be boring.

Side effects: a bleed and therefore a stroke, epilepsy, operation takes 6–9 months to take effect.

I feel really bad, self-harm and suicidal and eventually asked for help. The suitcase with the blade hidden in has been taken to the office and I've been moved to the six-bedder so a closer watch can be taken. They have all been very kind and I've been very upset.

At last I have good news that I can have the operation . . . all the anticipation and upset, yet barely any comment. I could not even feel relieved let alone any ability to feel pleased. Instead the awful self-harm thoughts had taken me captive. I remember those feelings of desperation, a senseless, gnawing sensation almost like a craving longing to be satisfied. They were overpowering and literally devoured me. I could not switch them off until finally I was compelled to act on them.

---

22 February 2001 Thursday
I've been put on 'Obs' so basically one to one in England. I am feeling terrible – still want to cut, use the emergency blade and I really thought about hanging myself but there's nowhere and I have had the dressing gown belt taken away. I just feel so low and want to hurt myself so much. I hear we might be able to travel tomorrow so it is imperative that I stay safe, that much I know. They can't find the blade in the suitcase so I don't know why it's been locked away. I mustn't forget to get the belt back.

23 February 2001 Friday
I am awaiting a phone call saying whether I can go back this afternoon – it's murder, must be even worse for Phil. I've had a shower and am trying to keep upright till my hair is dry. I've been trying crosswords but not been much success. I so want to get back now, even though it means being in the DOP this weekend, at least the children can visit.

Phil has told them I have a blade and after extreme pressure and distress I gave in, but I have a spare, however I have no intention of giving that away.

I feel so awful in myself. I don't want to carry on living; I've thought about hanging. I don't want to see the children and their smiley faces and I've just found out its Liz's wedding tomorrow.

24 February 2001 Saturday (Back in Southampton DOP)
No one cares about how I feel only about if I cut myself so they don't look bad 'not keeping me safe'. I was searched – nothing was found but I know it's going to happen soon. I can't go on like this. The thoughts won't go away. I just can't keep it up. I was distracted today when Phil took me to Liz's wedding and it was lovely and I cried. But I've just wanted to come back here so much because I feel I can't face the real world and when I do it's a cover-up. I'm *so* tired. I feel like I'm a sham, a fraud, a nuisance. I just don't understand.

25 February 2001 Sunday
Feeling very low and tired. Went home for the day and did some washing. Phil's so good to me. I talked to Karin when I got back, tried to explain how I'm feeling. I'm going to cut after I've seen Lee unless she can change anything and before ward round because I can't stand them all 'congratulating' me on how well I've done. It just makes it worse. In fact the long gap in between cutting feels like failure not success – must ask Lee why.

26 February 2001 Monday
Saw Lee and discussed cutting at length – she says I need to keep thinking about my feelings. Also something about 'triumphing' over people. I don't know but I did it anyway. I saw Dr Boyd and Dr Baldwin. Uneventful. Still waiting to go to A&E even though it happened 1½ hours ago. I could be dead by now!

I spoke to Mary yesterday and she was going on and on about the surgery 'on the brain'. 'No one knows what they're doing; how come they're not doing it anywhere else?' It's awful and I just said I needed support not scepticism. Phil says it's my decision and they should MYOB! I also spoke to Thelma (Phil's mother) and she was sweet and has got me photocopies of the latest literature from the Oxford Book of Psychiatry.

The cut was 2 hours ago now.

My parents and Mary my sister found the concept of Neurosurgery for Mental Disorder very difficult. They had looked on the MIND website and so they read with horror the MIND views on psychosurgery. (Even though MIND have now updated their site and include an accurate description of the modern surgery, they are still fundamentally opposed to this as a form of treatment.) Fortunately, Thelma, who was herself a retired doctor, was able to do her own independent literature search – it went much further than a psychiatry textbook! She found a paper specifically written about neurosurgery for intractable psychiatric conditions. She was at least able to ease some of my family's fears. This was further helped by the information received from the centre in Dundee. I was not that interested in the research or ethics surrounding the operation. I was in a desperate way and this was offering me an alternative treatment with the possibility of recovery. If it did not work, then at least I would have tried. Whatever the risks, I was living in torment and the only other option was death. I wanted this operation. I was not aware of how important it was that I should be freely consenting, I had had my doubts about the surgery initially, but now I was sure that I wanted to go ahead. Unfortunately for me, Karin was retiring so I lost a staunch ally and advocate for my life on the ward.

28 February 2001 Wednesday
Karin's last day; I'm really sad she's going. Continuing the saga from Monday, I eventually got to A&E, eventually seen and referred to surgeons. I ended up having a GA and staying overnight. Of course they had used my bed in the meantime. Now I'm back in a non-window bed and the only positive thing I can think is that if they move me at the weekend I needn't worry.

I'm feeling knackered today and low but now I'm at home its easier to look okay to the children anyway.

1 March 2001 Thursday
This evening I've been terrible and I even tried the chair on the bed to see if I could get a belt up there on the ceiling. I keep having these images of me hanging. Anyway I prayed that I could speak to someone and was able to see Janet. I'm also very tired and hope it won't be long before I get my drugs – Janet is going to ask if I can have them early. No word from Mary, I expect she's given up on me.

4 March 2001 Sunday
I was searched and they discovered a blade. I feel so annoyed at being found out especially since they checked the socks I was wearing and not the ones in the bag and I had swapped them around. My mother on Friday said that the staff has the responsibility to keep me safe and I know it's true. Still I have my emergency one and no one is going to find that. I still feel very down away from the children and Phil. I still make an effort for him but I can't for others like Marie, even though she's so kind – I just don't want to see anyone right now. I've got this awful curtain bed, no table either. I feel really let down by God and then I think it's all my own fault.

5 March 2001 Monday
Saw Lee this a.m. and told her about the embarrassing moments, but I can't for the life of me remember what she said. Then I was supposed to see Prof T, but he didn't turn up; there's a surprise. Feeling a bit better this afternoon, had a sleep. Now I'm waiting for Phil.

I'm thinking about the weekends, they are such a strain, but I know I have to put up with it for the children's sake. I don't know how I am going to face my parents visiting tomorrow. I also want the bed by the window. PLEASE GOD

Having visitors was much appreciated. However, I did not find social inter-action easy and as always made the effort to put on a front. It must have been so painful for my parents as they witnessed the continuing deteriora-tion and heard about the inexplicable acts of self-harm that I was commit-ting. Phil lived with this day after day, but made every effort to make sure I came home when allowed or he would visit me himself. I cannot imagine how he must have been feeling. However, I was one of the lucky ones, there were quite a few patients who had no family able to visit them. Yet this link to the outside, 'normal' world was so vital.

6 March 2001 Tuesday
None of the nurses can see me today – I am really fed up with them. Serena asked Janet if she would talk to me but she didn't, even though I said I was low.
Mary phoned – she is going to the Far East with her girls for six weeks. She is so lucky!

7 March 2001 Wednesday
I had my session with Lee and we talked about 'them' i.e. docs wanting to stop the psychotherapy, but she said they would have to make a very good case for it. I talked about the hanging thoughts and OD (overdose) and she says once again that I can't tolerate mental pain or the fact that I think others don't care, so I act destructively. It's true.
   I talked to Janet in the afternoon and cried quite a bit; still feel v low generally and she suggested that I tell them at home but I didn't get the chance what with Phil going out to take Steph etc.
I want them (the staff) to know I'm serious about killing myself but Lee says they know already. Its just people don't seem to show it.

8 March 2001 Thursday
Feel terrible, want to die and voices saying 'fraud' and 'liar' again. Tried to escape but got caught, deliberately tried to get up on the chair (to hang myself). I was found. So no escape because other-wise I would have carried it through. Still wanting to cut also but thinking of how much I don't want to go to A&E.

9 March 2001 Friday
Went to A&E last night – only a small cut and I'm back feeling like I want to REALLY hurt myself. I tried to run away today to get some aspirin but got caught in the hall. I don't know why I'm so unsettled. Obviously the weekend's looming and I think I'll need some help and somehow I need to convey to the children that I

don't feel good. I wish I knew what makes me feel so unsettled. I'm really cross with M (fellow patient), she has my window bed and never opens the curtains but won't swap. God please sort it out for me. I mean all of it.

11 March 2001 Sunday
I am SO pleased, I've got the window bed back! Long may it last – I do feel guilty as M is in the single room and wants to come back but they are always juggling beds. I must try not to feel guilty.
Steph ran away today after Phil told her off – he was quite reasonable; we eventually found her at Chloe's.
I had a really bad night last night with restless legs. I was awake past 2 a.m. I feel tired now but I think it will hit tomorrow. I have felt low and lacking in energy and Phil's been very helpful, but I FEEL GUILTY leaving all the work to Thelma.
I know Phil's keeping all our tablets, paracetamol etc., locked up, but we haven't talked about it.

12 March 2001 Monday
Lee thinks embarrassing thoughts are surfacing because of being searched, especially strip searched. She also pointed out that Steph is the only female in the house most of the time and is therefore under domestic strain.
Just had ward round and lots of suggestions drug-wise. They say that Steph running away is quite normal for her age and me being irritable is a sign that mood is improving.
I feel awful that I've been in here so long – I need somehow to pull myself together and get out. I am worried though that they'll think I don't need the op and I do, so that I never suffer from this again. HELP.
I've just got back from home, I can't turn it on and off. Right now I'd like to cut myself really, really deeply, even stab myself or use a Stanley knife or jump off the cupboard or hang myself using a sheet.

14 March 2001 Wednesday
With Lee talked about operation – not being the 'miracle cure' – but I said psychotherapy was obviously not the miracle cure either, nor the drugs. Phone call from Sarah (my sister) – she's engaged.

Lee was not in favour of the surgery. She had grave reservations and was still searching for a breakthrough with the psychotherapy. A new issue

arose when we learnt that Cognitive Behaviour Therapy (CBT) was suggested to help patients recover after the operation. Since Lee was using an analytical approach, I would need to see a different psychotherapist. This filled me with anxiety. I did not want to lose contact with Lee, who I had been seeing twice a week for over two years now. This situation was further compounded when some of the ward nurses started telling me that I should be receiving CBT now and that the therapy sessions with Lee were making me worse. Of course CBT may well be the right approach for some patients but I had been assessed by two competent consultant psychotherapists who had decided that I was too depressed and did not have enough working memory or concentration to be able to take part in CBT let alone benefit from it. Of course I had no means of challenging the nurses. I believe they drove me towards greater dependence on Lee. She was at least a sympathetic listening ear.

CHAPTER 16

The padded cell

15 March 2001 Thursday
Had quite a good day, visit from Suzie (one of my friends) went OK and being chatting with S. Need some space now. Have found I'll have to sleep back here on weekend days because of the blood pressure after high dose venlafaxine.

16 March 2001 Friday
I'm courageous today. I escaped but needed the loo so went to the friend's shop and got caught coming out. I really want to get out on my own and OD. Don't know why, just do.

I don't feel part of my family. I feel alone and they would be better off without me.

J is back in and she makes me feel so angry as she refuses to take tablets – am I angry because it reminds me of my own bad behaviour, like cutting? I just don't know. She refuses therapy as well.

17 March 2001 Saturday
Went home. Phil had done some washing and I carried on with it and we went to Sainsbury's. It was lovely to see Bec. She has injured her hip and so can't dance at the moment. When I hug her, I think maybe this is going to be the last time.

Feeling v tired now, was searched on the way in, just want to go to sleep.

Sometimes especially after reading the bible, I think I'm just pretending – I don't know for sure but I feel so GUILTY that I should just pull myself together.

19 March 2001 Monday
Saw Lee and can't remember what she said. Had WR (ward round) with Dr Baldwin – Prof Thompson is becoming head of the medical school. Apparently Lee has sent an 11-page letter to Prof Matthews.

Escaped and bought 72 aspirin and phenergan. I know it's all a

game of life. I did pray. I bought some writing paper and envelopes.
I think I'll write some suicide notes to get them off my chest.
I have an idea – Friday evening my parents are coming down. Phil
won't need time off work – the ideal time– still frightening though.
However, I do need to do something or lots of cutting – it's driving
me crazy.

What was I thinking of? I somehow thought that I could go and commit
suicide at a weekend and that Phil would not need any time off work! I
obviously had no idea of what he was going through, no idea of what he
felt for me. My world had become so black and white, so limited. I was definitely devoid of reality. Although this seems shocking to me now, I am also
glad in some ways that I didn't know what Phil and the children were
going through. I think if I had done, it may well have spurred me on even
more, if that were possible, to ensure that I did end it all one way or
another.

20 March 2001 Tuesday
Saw Lee and talked about the above. However, I had Steph cry on
me because she won't see me for two days and Jona cry when I
talked about children blaming themselves. The other thing is that I
can't stay out for the weekend because of the blood pressure stuff.

21 March 2001 Wednesday: first day of spring
It's been a dreadful evening thinking about cutting. I'm in the
seclusion room trying to avoid it. I want to run away and buy a
Stanley knife and have a really good go at it. I can't take in all the
advice. I've got the pills as well.

22 March 2001 Thursday
Last night was spent in the seclusion room. I felt so terrible,
feelings kept overwhelming me in a great tidal wave – it did lessen
when I was away from everything. I need to hide the pills better
though in case they go in for a search.
 I managed to run away but I got caught at St Mary's car park. I
so want to go and get the knife.

Being put in the seclusion room meant at least that I could be observed in a
'safe' environment, but actually it did nothing for me. I was given a pillow
to punch, but it was not something that I would do or had done at any
time in my life! There was no furniture, so that meant lying or sitting on

the floor. There was no mattress, so it was a very uncomfortable place to be. In retrospect it seems totally inappropriate to me, especially when I was left in there all night.

'Running away' was a major achievement. I had to get out of the ward – the doors were constantly locked. I would probably have sneaked past when they were opened to let another patient in or out. I could not move fast and I had very little energy. It's no wonder the staff caught up with me once they realised I was missing. These escapes were opportunistic so I would undoubtedly be without a coat. I carried a small purse with me with only small amounts of money and I usually had my mobile phone. Even before I was ill, I did not know the area surrounding the hospital well. I was disoriented once I got outside. My thinking was extremely slowed and I would find it difficult to know what to do next. This is probably just as well and I am sure it preserved my life. For instance I would have had great difficulty in working out where to go and buy a knife!

---

23 March 2001 Friday
I've had not a bad day, went home with my parents. Steph confided in me that her friend may be pregnant and we arranged for Steph to take her specimen to her doc. Then one of Steph's other friends phoned in great distress and we went and got her before Phil dropped me back here.

I had quite a good chat with J & S but when I went back to the bed, the urge to cut was really strong. I'm in the seclusion room and it's still terrible. Serena has told me to write it down. I WANT TO HURT MYSELF. I DON'T KNOW WHY BUT I CAN'T JUST SAY NO, BUT I'M TRYING TO.

24 March 2001 Saturday
I have TOTALLY and absolutely messed up by cutting myself. I would have had pizza with the children and Jona has hurt his arm. I am so STUPID. God help me, please help me. Oh I hate this so much. Everyone's telling me off. Well it's all done now isn't it? I've made the mess. It's all my fault. I have to live with it. Oh I hate myself and I hate this situation.

Tell Lee on Monday: I've been feeling bad all week but I resisted until Sunday.

I think the staff honestly believed that if you were given any sympathy it would increase the chances of you self-harming again. How little they realised that this behaviour is so often linked with people who have very low self-esteem for whatever reason. It means that when they are treated

badly or come across punitive responses to their self-harm, it just feeds into the vicious cycle and in fact it will make it even more likely that the self-harm will be repeated. I came across this sort of negative attitude being expressed when I worked in A&E this weekend. One of the trained nurses gave his opinion that stomach washouts should be brought back as they are so unpleasant for the patient. He said 'that should stop them from doing it again. It would stop me.' I tried to explain to him that not only was it shown to be no deterrent, it was cruel and in fact often made the situation worse by washing tablets further down the gastrointestinal tract. He shrugged and persisted with his opinion that such patients deserve no sympathy. 'They should all be "rodded"' (A term used for the forcible placing of a stomach washout tube.) I did not have the courage to admit that I have been one of these patients he so despises. How can these discriminatory attitudes be changed? I know that not all staff are like this, there are many who are more enlightened and very kind to all their patients whatever the circumstances that have led to their admission to A&E. So as I write this, I reprimand myself for my spinelessness yesterday. I should have challenged him directly. Have you ever felt like this? Have you ever known such desperation that you would hurt your body or take pills to poison yourself or kill yourself? How dare you even think of punishing people who are in so much pain, who come to hospital to receive your help. Do you actually think they enjoy the experience? Do you actually think that the attention you give them is so worthwhile that they would repeatedly harm themselves just to get more of it? You have a very high opinion of yourself if you do. Think about it! If they are doing it again and again and visiting this A&E department is the motivation for doing so, then what are their lives like, that this could possibly be an experience worth harming themselves for? I want to shout it from the rooftops. Can't you see their pain? What if it was your wife or your daughter, your brother or your son or your best friend or your lover? Would you still want to 'rod them'?

---

26 March 2001 Monday
I didn't arrive back from A&E until 9 a.m. in the morning on Sunday. I felt so absolutely terrible and so worried about the bed. I had 18 stitches and they offered me to have it under GA but because of the bed, going out with the children etc, I chose LA (local anaesthetic). I didn't get any sleep all night.

At 10 am Phil came and we went and called on his Mum as a surprise – it was Mother's day. It was quite a good time with them, then we went and had a drink on the way home, but although it was good to be able to talk, secretly I was worried about leaving the children on their own.

They gave me the most super cards and the one from Bec said

'God will make you well, trust in Him!' Chocolates and flowers. They are such lovely children.

27 March 2001 Tuesday
Had a text from Steph saying she was so unhappy and so it was good to see her and give her lots of hugs this evening. Spoke to Bec on the phone and she's having an MRI on her hip soon as its been painful for several weeks now. Jona is happier and going back to school tomorrow. Simon was working.

28 March 2001 Wednesday
I saw Lee today and talked about cutting again. Then she mentioned the talk she'd had with Dr Boyd – apparently the letter she had written to Prof Matthews was all about me and not as I had thought – anti-operation! Now I would rather not change to another therapist for the CBT before the operation and I feel everything is confused. I need three pillows because of the reflux (indigestion) which is really bad tonight.

29 March 2001 Thursday
I have been tired all day, otherwise it has not been a bad day. I'm thinking of Steph and hoping it all goes okay when Phil takes her to see Barry (GP).

30 March 2001 Friday
Sleepy again. Not sure if I can go for the whole weekend, but Sue (nurse) says if someone's put in my bed, she'll move me back. She's lovely. I've been daydreaming about taking an OD and it leaves me feeling peaceful.

1 April 2001 Sunday
When I got back, I found my bed gone. They didn't tell me. But because I was so upset they asked J to swap with me so I'm back in my old bed. I feel all the staff are being horrid to me and don't like me. J's a sweetie.

2 April 2001 Monday
I apologised to Bridget (senior nurse) yesterday and she said she doesn't bear grudges, but I don't believe her. I told Lee all about it, this a.m. I feel with all the staff that I've made such a fuss which I have. I'm v tired. I slept v badly, awake from 3–6 a.m., so I've slept all afternoon. Maybe I wanted the excuse to OD, but panicked at the same time. I feel very low.

I remember Bridget only too well. She definitely did not like me. I apologised to her for 'causing a fuss' by wanting to move beds. She was a bully and unfortunately I was one of her victims. Now Karin had left, I no longer had an advocate. I am sure this contributed to the worsening of my relationship with some of the B ward staff. I wonder what made Bridget become hardened. Was it the nature of her work, the pressure, the poor environment? I presume that she went into psychiatric nursing as a caring individual; I wonder when her attitude changed.

---

3 April 2001 Tuesday
Dreading ward round – feel low but don't think anyone knows about it; they just think I'm a selfish troublemaker, which I am. Was thinking last night about OD again and wonder if I should do the letters now.

5 April 2001 Thursday at Southampton General
I took an OD yesterday – I've managed to survive. Apparently Phil was with me in A&E but I don't remember. I know I was very confused during the night. Phil's such a sweetie, he doesn't appear angry and is very loving. Yesterday I went to Lee's session and ran away afterwards. She did try and persuade me out of going out, but she didn't know I had the tablets.

6 April 2001 Friday
I'm still here at the General. I'm waiting for transport back to the DOP.
    Yesterday Bec came over with Phil and we both cried – she says to have faith in God.
    Back at the DOP – all the nurses seemed so unfriendly except Steve. I kept crying. Sheelagh (friend) came down and I cried on her too.
    Now I have a non-window bed adjacent to the phone, but I'll just have to make the best of it, won't I.

Thank you Steve. I do remember you and it is so good that there are nurses like you who are willing to show kindness and look beyond the behaviour. I suspect they don't get enough encouragement and unfortunately the patients who appreciate these little acts of care are the least capable of expressing this. It was in fact a serious overdose, I was unconscious and I had a fit. My intention would have been to kill myself and I am fortunate that my memory was so poor that I was incapable of working out the lethal dose. I remember thinking that I had! Once again I felt the disgrace of not achieving this despite my medical qualifications. I felt terrible.

7 April 2001 Saturday
Phil and Jona came last night and I was OK with them.

Today we went to London to see Steph dance at the ENB Easter school It was lovely to see her, but very tiring. I came straight back here to the DOP and have been trying to be on my own, which has been difficult because S keeps wanting me to socialise.

8 April 2001 Sunday
Went home and saw all the children – plenty to do housework-wise. This woman got knocked down in the road, well tried to – she said she wanted to die so I left her in the capable hands of the ambulance crew to take her to A&E. Wouldn't it be weird if she ended up here?!

Talked with Miranda about need for isolation and people being cross with me, but she says it's just they have to put the responsibility back on me, but why can't they say comforting words? Like 'it's OK, we understand' or 'it's going to be alright'.

9 April 2001 Monday
Saw the team this a.m. after Lee – can't remember much of what was said, something about turning my frustrations of other people not caring onto myself. Apparently I had a fit in A&E after I had taken the OD. They're going to fiddle around with the drugs and renew the Section – don't care right now – just want to be left alone.

11 April 2001 Wednesday
If Lee hadn't said they would stop psychotherapy if I absconded again, I would have. To be perfectly honest, even more aspirin seemed a good idea. I feel rotten and have done all day.

Had a care plan session with Serena, which was awful – can't bear these 'goals' etc.; as Lee says, it's condescending. Hopefully over the weekend, I'll manage to write down how I feel, so I can present it to her. Can't be bothered right now. Haven't gone home tonight. I just want to go to bed. I haven't listened to tapes or read magazines or done anything since the OD.

12 April 2001 Thursday
I don't feel like going home at all. Still feeling low and lying down doing nothing for long periods of time.

13 April 2001 Friday
I'm so angry with the ward staff and the way they've treated me. I hate Serena. I hate Vera. I wish I could humiliate them. Oh, I know. Pray for them.

> I told the children (about the OD otherwise I thought they would find out). Steph was very, very upset. Jona was upset but seemed to recover. Simon didn't say anything, but Phil has talked to him today.
>
> **14 April 2001 Saturday**
> Quite an active day, trying not to eat too much, but went to TGI Friday and bowling in the evening. I lost. Feel very tired, but the children all seem quite happy.
>
> **16 April 2001 Monday**
> Yesterday went OK, fairly tense lunch but what else do you expect. The LETTER I would like to send to Bridget.
> Who do you think you are, claiming to be caring, but all you want is not to lose face? When I came in after the OD you said 'this is just ridiculous'. No sympathy, no questions to see whether I'd be OK and two days later when I come back to the ward again, no expression of sympathy, no 'how was it?' no welcome back. Oh yes, you say people care by spending time with me, well that's your job. It's like a doctor's bedside manner and as far as I can see you score zero in the equivalent.

The nursing staff were not good at acknowledging my distress. I would be told off when I disclosed thoughts of self-harm and they were often angry with me if I had actually cut myself. I had hoped that this would have changed. But when I went back to work I met Vera, the very same nurse who had consistently been unpleasant to me on B ward. She still worked there and on this particular occasion was accompanying a young girl who was a patient on the ward. This poor girl had tried to hang herself and came into the resuscitation room unconscious. I was the receiving doctor. Suddenly the tables were turned and I was asking Vera exactly what happened to the patient. Vera's reply was dismissive, she said: 'you know, she's always doing things like this, I've seen her with things round her neck before, so I didn't take much notice.' She rolled her eyes as she tutted. I was aghast. So here was a patient whose life was in danger being seen as a nuisance. I was very angry. I still am. More so that this kind of attitude continues to prevail in the very place where patients are taken to be cared for and treated, often against their will. I realised then that nothing much had changed and there are countless, vulnerable people who have no voice, living with this attitude which amounts to little less than abuse. I am a voice. It needs to change. It must change. This is totally unacceptable in a civilised society.

CHAPTER 17

Impatient and in disgrace

17 April 2001 Tuesday

When Janet did my blood pressure she basically said the staff are very frustrated with me 'overdosing and cutting' and that Dr Baldwin wanted me home as much as possible because being in hospital didn't help me. I made her repeat it in front of Phil and of course she watered it down and made it sound nicer.

Oh I hate this place, I feel like just going home and have done with it. I just can't think of a situation where I can get out of here as Lee says that if I escape, when I am seeing her, they'll stop the psychotherapy.

I've just had a situation where S had tablets, she told me and I reported her and I've spent some time comforting her. IRONIC or what, but why don't the nurses do any comforting?

18 April 2001 Wednesday

This a.m. had meeting with the hospital managers and saw Dr Baldwin. He said Harriet (Dr Boyd) will come up and see me, but of course she hasn't! I am just assuming they will continue the Section 3. Forgot to ask if I can complain about the nurses!

S's driving me a bit nuts as she's so possessive.

I haven't written how I feel, for a while. I quite often feel like taking a fatal amount of aspirin but won't because of the children and I'd love to cut myself. I don't feel as low as last week but the tension's building up and I'm wondering about (cutting) tomorrow at home or wait until I get moved to a grotty bed!

20 April 2001 Friday

Yesterday I cut myself in the evening. I had tried to speak to Colin – Vera was my nurse and he suggested her, but NO WAY. I asked for chlorpromazine and at home I tried to ring the ward but Steph was on the phone. I'm hurting now but the thoughts are gone. I'm staying in tonight as Phil's gone out with a friend, but I'm going to spend the day at home tomorrow. Ruth didn't come which I found disappointing; I wish she hadn't said she would.

21 April 2001 Saturday
Went home today and had a busy time. I'm just thinking such morbid thoughts like Phil and Steph being killed tomorrow and what I should do. Horrible.

22 April 2001 Sunday
Just heard from Steph, they have ½ hr left of their journey (Steph had been for an audition for a summer school in Birmingham) and want to know if I want to come out. I've said no 'cos I think Phil should have an evening in and I really don't mind staying in. I just hope its OK for the children's sake.

I wrote this 'Care Plan' for the nurses
Voice 1 Take a fatal dose of Aspirin and die
Voice 2 No don't
Voice 3 Cut yourself really badly
Voice 4 No cut yourself shallow
Voice 5 Ask for help
I haven't had any response from them yet.

I keep thinking really morbid thoughts like Phil's going to die and what will happen to me and the children and maybe I would kill myself and leave them to the Clarkes.

Seen Serena, cried and tried to explain. Having some chlorpromazine to see if it helps. I feel a bit calmed down so I think it helps.

24 April 2001 Tuesday
Lee – went OK, can't remember anything much.

WR (ward round) – also went OK.

Another patient said today I didn't look depressed, it hurt because then I think, am I? I've had it confirmed that the Section 3 has been extended.

Phil was quite moody but I got him to talk about it. I think it helped.

I can't write down what I think or feel except I'm dreading meeting Bridget, but I have prayed that it will be in God's hands.

25 April 2001 Wednesday
Last night I saw Bridget – she totally denied that she tried to make me phone Phil and I felt I hadn't a leg to stand on. She also said 'I don't know what you want me to say' after I told her how no one helped me that day. I was too scared to say, an apology. Anyway it's ended. I just pray that God will prick her conscience.

J got put in seclusion after trying to break a window with a cot side. I don't quite know how to relate to her.

Lee says have low expectations of the staff so I won't be disappointed. I'll try.

26 April 2001 Thursday
Rotten day. Feel bad, feel worse after yet another search. This occurred after J and I planned to get out. I know it was stupid. Anyway it backfired and everyone got cross. Fed up, fed up, fed up, not talking to S or anyone. Enjoy listening to Scarlet Feather.

27 April 2001 Friday
Steph's birthday and I forgot to sign her card. Phil says it's OK. I'm very fed up with this lifestyle.

29 April 2001 Sunday
What a weekend – lots of chores, Phil broke down on Sat night and cried and cried and said 'please don't die'. I felt I couldn't say anything like, 'no I won't'. Then on Sunday when Steph came back from visiting White Lodge, she started crying and couldn't say why. We took her to the Clarkes while I came back here. Almost had a run-in with Bridget, but explained I was upset. Still don't want to talk to S or anyone for that matter.

30 April 2001 Monday
Session with Lee – talked about the weekend and also the swallowing problem. She says I can't live without blame – judgemental, which is true.

Session with Dr Baldwin – OK, no change. Told him about Steph and Phil. Being referred for the swallowing/choking problem.

Got the razor in my purse found. Said to Janet I feel like cutting.

1 May 2001 Tuesday
I've been really upset, frustrated, low and I want to cut myself but can't because of seeing Steph tonight. Maybe I will at home, changed into maroon trousers so blood won't show.

Later: I've been in the seclusion room but I CAN'T punch pillows, it just isn't me and anyway it smelt of urine and there was cigarette ash on the floor.

2 May 2001 Wednesday
I did it last night and got back from A&E at 1 a.m.; at least I got to sleep in until 11.40. When they sew the wound up using local anaesthetic, often it still hurts because they don't numb it enough, but I don't say anything, because it's my fault anyway.

I mustn't forget Lee today. I do feel less tense and frustrated but guilty of being so much trouble.

They took my nail clippers away last time I was searched so I'm hoping to keep them this time since the night staff are coming on. It's so pathetic. What could you do with nail clippers apart from clipping nails? I'm so tired and just want to go to sleep.

3 May 2001 Thursday

Ok a.m. slept quite a bit. I keep having horrible thought about things which make me feel nervous and afraid like Phil falling off the ladder being stung by wasps.

4 May 2001 Friday

S has just told me she's taken some tablets, so I got the staff, 16 Anadin, I don't know what she's playing at.

I'm very tired but have been listening to a book tape which helps. Low as usual, dreading being picked up and having to talk to my mother, don't like talking to anyone, especially when they say positive things or hopeful things when there's nothing positive or hopeful.

I found it so hard to talk to people at this point in the illness. It was difficult to make light conversation and I had little that I could talk about. My mother was, as always, trying to be positive and optimistic. Unfortunately I could not relate to this at all. She must have found it very difficult too. My ability to 'put on a front' was not as good as it had been so I found it difficult to be with anyone, even close friends like Marie and yet I felt abandoned if I had no visitors, so I did appreciate their visits. I say little about how I spent my day apart from the general ward routine. My concentration was poor but I started to try and listen to book tapes as well as music on my walkman. I was never particularly good at crosswords but would attempt to do the more straightforward ones in magazines. Cryptic crosswords were way out of my league! Magazines were useful for my short attention span, but I had never been one to read many prior to my illness. I spent much of my time in hospital doing very little, that is why I was so keen on having a window bed. Looking out of the window was my major source of entertainment!

7 May 2001 Monday (Bank Holiday)

Funny sort of weekend. Lots of housework and Sunday in particular, I felt ill and spent a lot of time in bed. Went for a walk with

Phil, Simon and Steph this afternoon. Spoke to Bec yesterday, must keep in touch more often.

S did a minor OD and spent 5 hours in A&E. I have no trace of compassion – aren't I mean. I just can't cope with other people's problems.

8 May 2001 Tuesday

No news, no change in ward round. Feeling desperate again about cutting myself with the kitchen scissors; I'm sure it puts my heart rate up.

Went home and Marie popped in. I couldn't even look at her, let alone talk. I tried to explain to Phil afterwards. The thoughts are terrible.

Bec is to be a principal in her end of year performance at ENB (English National Ballet School) – she's really pleased and so am I!

9 May 2001 Wednesday

Waiting for psychotherapy, tired morning. Scared that A in bed opposite is leaving and that nasty W will be brought back into the dormitory.

Main thing on my mind is WAITING. Please God may there be some dates soon. WAITING WAITING WAITING trying to be patient but very frustrated.

Later: Lee explained the (cutting) thoughts as anger and frustration at the waiting turned in on myself. Chris spoke to me and I explained (about the thoughts) without saying about the scissors. He said they would monitor me and see about tomorrow.

Felt calmed down this afternoon with the book tape and a sleep.

10 May 2001 Thursday

Woke up quite early and watched TV a bit with J. Now I'm back at my bed the thoughts are there. I wish Ruth (CPN) would come. N is back (schizophrenic), she had a big upset in the night and I got the staff.

Someone has pooed on the floor and the disabled loo is disgusting as well; it's blocked. This place.

I'm waiting to speak to Jane and have my stitches removed, neither of which I think will happen. The thoughts are on my mind all the time, but I can't tell them exactly what; otherwise Phil will be told or I won't be allowed home. Bed by the window is my security.

Was about to cut myself after a shower. But I didn't, too tired and I want to do it properly.

11 May 2001 Friday
Ruth came and I told her about the thoughts. She's told me to tell Phil that I mustn't be left alone. I still feel dreadful and thought about asking someone to take me home so I could do it. I tried to go out this a.m., to 'sign out' at the desk – they didn't fall for it.

Bec's been asked to do class with the Birmingham Royal Ballet Company after someone came and visited them yesterday!

Guilt thoughts: you could get better if you wanted, you could be healed if you wanted, you're not really ill. I want this op to make me completely better and never have it again.

12 May 2001 Saturday
None of my clothes fit, I'm really fed up. At least I got my carrots! (trying to diet) Bec arrived as a surprise! She looks well. I feel SO tired and I've thought loads about cutting, but I'm seeing the gastroenterology doctor, Dr Fisher, about the choking on Wednesday.

13 May 2001 Sunday
Cooler today. I just saw Mark & Penny's baby Nathan before we left – almost made me cry. I was very quiet with Phil, hope he understands. Thoughts – leave for Thursday.

15 May 2001 Tuesday
Taken 80mg Phenergan – hope I'll sleep, if not another 80. I don't want to get caught, just to sleep. The thoughts were at me all last night when I was trying to sleep.

Phil seemed in quite a bad mood yesterday; I think it's because he's got so much to do. Taken another 80. V disappointed. I feel a bit shaky but not sleeping. Tell Lee . . . (illegible presumably due to phenergan!) . . . feel quite calm, but want to eat. I am trying to lose weight but it's so difficult.

Talked to Deborah the hospital manager and said that I don't often get an 'easy time' after cutting/OD. Wish I'd said about Bridget but decided to leave it be. Still not sleepy but drowsy. Fewer bad thoughts.

16 May 2001 Wednesday
This a.m. talked to S, trying to drum some sense into her, and then beckoned Serena to come and speak to her – as if I haven't enough problems of my own.

Visit to Dr Fisher: probably a primary motility disorder – will need investigation in the next 2–3 weeks.

17 May 2001 Thursday
I'm planning on doing it today – Steph is going out and I could do it before Phil goes out. The only snag is that Janet might warn him.

I may die, but I need to get these thoughts appeased. Please God help me. I pray that He will protect me and that He'll stop me if that's what he wants.

If I die and you're reading this then that wasn't the purpose. I love you Phil, I love you Bec, I love you Simon, I love you Steph, I love you Jonathan. It's not your fault and it's not because I didn't love you. Its just the thoughts won't leave me alone and I have to do what they say.

18 May 2001 Friday (at Southampton General)
It all went horribly wrong – I got thro' the peritoneum with my knife, but I didn't cut deep enough with my scissors so I have just been stitched under local with a drain in. I am being observed on the surgical ward. I just want to go back to the DOP. My mother is due to take me at 4 p.m. and I just need to be discharged by a doc. Please God. I am trying to relax. If I've lost my bed by the window then it's all my fault.

Phil has had to go and get Bec as she's hurt her back and needs to be taken to physio – apparently she can hardly walk.

19 May 2001 Saturday
I can't describe how awful I feel, worse to find I had been moved beds again. Of course I couldn't tell them about that, but I think it was the straw that broke the camel's back. I did a lot of this in front of my mother and ended up not being allowed home. So I cut all my stitches out and refused to be sewn up, but got persuaded to. I'm now being on one to one, so I feel dirty and generally awful, but I will try and wash later. I hate having to go to the loo in front of people. I still wish when I cut the stitches out, the stupid blade could have cut right through the peritoneum like I envisaged. Its by no means over – the thoughts remain, although I feel calmer. I'm worried though about how Phil will cope this weekend. It's all MY fault and I'm in a bed next to M who doesn't even open her curtains. GOD PLEASE HELP ME TO ENDURE THIS.

At this point, the duty psychiatrist did not know what to do because I was refusing treatment. He involved the hospital managers and the consultant. Between them they decided that they owed me 'a duty of care'. When I was taken back to Southampton General to be stitched up, it is recorded in

the notes that the surgeon on call was not impressed. He asked me whether this was because 'I did not like their handiwork'. I can imagine how frustrated they were all feeling with me. Yet they had no insight into the continuous torment that ravaged through my mind. I can remember something of my feelings then. I felt oh so humiliated. It was terrible having to return to A&E, knowing that the likelihood was that attitudes would not be sympathetic. I felt so weak and vulnerable. I was overwhelmed with misery and then I met just what I dreaded, an unsympathetic surgeon. I remember many occasions when I was not given enough local anaesthetic, but I would not complain. I think this was one of them. I wonder what he was hoping to achieve. To make me feel guilty perhaps – he succeeded. To make me feel bad about my behaviour – I already did and now I felt worse. It was after times like these that I would wish I was dead. It was at times like these that B ward was some sort of sanctuary if only because I could hide on my bed and do nothing. I hated myself and had no reason not to, after all the rest of the world were in agreement with me. I was foolish, childish, a waste of time, attention-seeker, crazy, loony, sad, mad and bad. That's exactly how I saw myself.

20 May 2001 Sunday
Still one to one but don't know why. Had a bath while being watched. Eating a bit today. Phil and the girls came up this a.m. then they were going to Sal's (Phil's sister) for lunch – grandma's birthday but Phil had to take Jona to his cup final. I didn't confide in them. I do feel calmer but the thoughts are still there and the accusations too. I hope they will let me go to psychotherapy tomorrow. I still feel tired despite a good afternoon sleep.

Saw Phil and told him what had happened – he didn't react. I'll have to speak again. I SO want to be by a window.

21 May 2001 Monday
Saw Dr Baldwin this a.m. and he cancelled all my leave and I'm to have ECT. I still feel a little afraid. I'm still on one to one and find having a period and being constipated difficult to deal with as the nurses watch me go to the loo. I just feel totally dull, not thinking much, but just black. Lee wasn't there this a.m. S has left and given me an HMV token!

22 May 2001 Tuesday
Saw Dr Baldwin again this a.m. and now am reduced to 5 min obs thank goodness – went to the loo and had a bath in peace. What I'm really worried about is that Dr Baldwin said he was trying to get the health authority to agree (to fund the operation) and he's

been passed on to someone else. He also said 'depression has a natural remission you know', so I think he's worried about getting funding. I KNOW I MUST TRUST GOD. Also I want a bed by the window and I know they just put it off, even though there is one empty. I MUST TRUST GOD. I haven't asked for any painkillers today and it hurts but it pales into insignificance compared to the other problems. Vera shouting is getting on my nerves. Poor Phil I put the burden onto him. I hope God looks after him.

I suppose Mary's lawyer who said you could sue them for failure of duty of care could be used against the health authority, but I need this operation so much.

Went down for psychotherapy and waited and waited. Wrong day!

Ruth came today and was lovely as ever. I cried. THEY'VE MOVED ME BACK TO THE WINDOW BED THANK YOU LORD! It now feels a bit of an anticlimax.

Thoughts of suffocation using a carrier bag or throwing boiling water on myself. I've done my best to contaminate the wound but knowing my luck nothing will happen.

Phone and watch in knicker draw.

Ruth continued to visit me on the ward even though as my community psychiatric nurse, she needn't have done. She gave me the opportunity to express myself and tell her what was going on between me and the ward nurses. Thank you Ruth for being a lifeline, you were such a sympathetic listener, which is why your visits were so important to me. You accepted me without condemnation, which helped numb the awful pain and torment I was feeling. I will never forget your dedication and I am very grateful to you.

CHAPTER 18

Interminable battle

23 May 2001 Wednesday
Seen Lee. Had ECT. Thelma coming. Feel nothing. Went to psychotherapy and Lee was really strong about me hurting other people by my actions.

Thelma brought me hair clips which were lovely. J's back after a paracetamol OD. M and D are both annoying me in their different ways.

ASK BRIDGET FOR KARIN'S ADDRESS.

24 May 2001 Thursday
I feel so fed up. I woke stiff all over but since having a bath I don't feel so bad. I'm still on 5 min obs – it's almost as bad as continuous obs except at least you can have a bath with them just knocking on the door. I've tried to contaminate the wound without success. The image of the knife and scissors isn't so strong but the image of my head in a bag with Sellotape all round my neck is. I guess I'll get some chlorpromazine.

25 May 2001 Saturday
I couldn't be bothered to write yesterday. I had ECT after all and then spent most of my waking hours with J. Today my one plea to God is that he'll protect my stuff from D. She steals. I really want her moved.

I'm still taking chlorpromazine but haven't talked to a member of staff for ages. I wanted to get the wound infected but it's fine. I'm allowed home for a couple of hours today – it'll be good to see the children. I don't know what I feel, pretty numb I think.

28 May 2001 Monday
Home for most of the WE and good to catch up with the kids. Saw Dave and Marie today – they are so lovely but I'm still not OK with them. Phil IS really wonderful, he does so much for all of us. Still feeling numb, thinking cutting thoughts but trying with the

help of chlorpromazine to not become obsessed again. It was Suzie's birthday but I've forgotten a card!

29 May 2001 Tuesday
I got up around 9.30 and had a bath. I've done nothing except look out of the dayroom window at planes and trains. Thinking horrible thoughts. Forgot till now it's ECT tomorrow and then Lee. I feel bad I'm not at home with the children.

30 May 2001 Wednesday
Prior to ECT: went to Lloyds yesterday pm. Bec goes today, I'll miss her. She missed the ENB audition and she was told she would have got in so she would have. She's very disappointed but pretty well accepting Essen (she had been offered a contract in a Ballet Company in Essen, Germany).

Jona's had his hair cut off. Grade 2. Phil's lost 9lb with the Vitality plan diet and walking while I continue to grow out of my clothes.

Slept well, to see Lee, docs today, quite nervous about the latter. I'm fed up to the back teeth of waiting for everything – Dundee. Just had psychotherapy and cried about the summer – Bec going to Essen, waiting for the op, generally unable to trust myself as far as the self-harm goes. Phil's ill so I can't go home tonight.

31 May 2001 Thursday
Just had a chat with Serena – don't feel she really understands at all. Going on about having an hour to myself at home. Yeah, yeah, as if. The worst thing is waiting for Dundee – please Lord, please. I can't keep going and trusting.

Need to wash my hair after ECT.

Need to get a new notebook.

I'm feeling like nothing, don't want to do anything except eat, drink and sleep. Mind on cutting a bit, trying to look to the future without doing it. Stitches are due to come out.

1 June 2001 Friday
Watch etc. in dressing gown pocket.

Had ECT this a.m., parents came p.m. with nice new skirt. They have offered to pay for mental health commissioner's flights. I'm feeling fine. Could go home if I was allowed, but I'm not.

2 June 2001 Saturday
Stayed in till about 2 p.m. and then went home and did various things – washing etc. Phil did pizza and I knocked over a glass of

red wine onto my jeans so I'll have to put them in the wash tomorrow. Steph came home from staying with Bec and doing Senior Associates (a class at Royal Ballet School). Simon has been working! How do I feel? In some ways I feel quite elated though it's not going to last for long I don't think. I am very tired and I've brought back some phenergan. I don't know when I'll use it but at least I've smuggled it in! I'll tell Lee. The girl in the next door bed is being v loud on her mobile. I wish she'd shut up.

4 June 2001 Monday
ECT. Watch in d'gown pocket. No psychotherapy or ward round. Did see Dr Baldwin and said about my parents' offer – he said he thought we wouldn't need it. Let's hope he's right. Hurry up. Feel like doing nothing today – haven't listened to tapes, don't want to. Stitches are out so once again thinking about cutting. Try not to though. KS is here, but not in the mood for her either at the moment.

Mavis (nurse) is around being nauseatingly positive – she really annoys me. I wish Ruth would come up.

Got either rotten hayfever or a cold. I'm not going home tonight as Phil has a meeting at Cantell (Jonathan's school).

5 June 2001 Tuesday
I cut late last night. eight stitches at A&E but not too bad a wait. Woke up late this a.m. when they were making beds. I've put my PJs and dressing gown for a wash as they had blood on.

Last night D called me a bitch and said I had thrown her socks out the window! Hope we don't get a repeat today. Still got bad hayfever and feel quite low. ECT tomorrow. J reminded me I've got phenergan but I can't remember where I've put it, but it could be very useful.

D was a lady with schizophrenia. She was a volatile individual and in fact there were times when I felt pretty scared of her, but I had no choice but to share the same dormitory as her. It was good to have some sort of relationship with those patients who were in hospital for some days if not weeks with you. As time went by, she became more settled and we were even able to talk a little. However, I never lost my wariness of her. Stealing was another issue. There was nowhere to lock things up and it was upsetting when such things as sweets or toiletries were stolen, even worse when you knew who the perpetrator was!

6 June 2001 Wednesday
Had ECT today followed by psychotherapy after lunch. I was in a complete muddle and needed this to remind me of days gone by. I don't know why I had ECT on Monday nor did Lee. We talked about CBT after the surgery and I asked whether I could come back to her if I didn't get on and she said I could. The limiting factor is the doctors – oh well, we'll see. Lee is still very anti the surgery and ECT, but she is good for getting things off my chest.

D is being nice again or at least friendly. I wonder how long that will last. I'm going home this pm although Steph is working late at the beauticians. I need to try and get Simon a good luck card for his exams.

10 June 2001 Sunday
WE at home. Phil and I had quite a bad time yesterday because he lost his temper over the cutlery drawer and spilt pasta all over the floor and I just couldn't cope. He doesn't want me to say except to Lee as he's afraid that they'll say he's unsuitable for the children. Today we spent most of it in the garden getting rid of the built-in barbecue. We went out for a walk but I fell down, cutting both hands and generally bruising them and my hip so we went home. It was 'Power in the Park' (a small pop festival) and the children spent most of the day there. I missed them. They are so busy with friends. Marie came over and prayed for me. I know I need it but I can't cope. Bridget searched me and found a blade. The other one remained hidden but I've forgotten what's happened to the third. I must get some fruit. Tomorrow is ECT I think and at 5 p.m. is the video swallow test – I'm dreading it. My mouth is sore.

I need to get in touch with Ruth about the tribunal.

Phil rarely became angry, but like most people, he has lost his temper occasionally through his life. It should have been no great surprise that he did need to express his feelings from time to time, but of course I did not have the emotional reserve to deal with this. I was very distressed and worried by his outburst, more so because of his own anxieties already mentioned – 'the possibility of a heavy-handed social worker'. I wish he could have talked to Ruth or one of the medical team himself as I know they would have reassured him.

I am sure Bridget finding the blade must have added to her negative attitude towards me. I discovered later on that she suspected me of giving them to other patients, which I never did. What a complete disaster life on the ward had become!

I was due to attend a Mental Health Review Tribunal as I had been on a Section 3 for six months. This would have been an appeal to prevent the extension of the Section. I am not sure who initiated this, whether it was the hospital managers or me. I cannot remember attending but I know that the panel are independent. Ruth had agreed to accompany me.

---

11 June 2001 Monday
ECT cancelled so saw Lee. Told her about the WE and how Phil lost his temper. She talked about anger and how I connect my angry feelings with aggressive actions. Then I had ward round – the Scottish people are due to come mid-July. Why do I have to wait so long? The hayfever is terrible and they won't let me have a Piriton as well but are starting something else. What?

After lunch Ruth came and we chatted about Friday's tribunal. I also talked about Phil and she said that he shouldn't worry, it's normal to get cross occasionally. Then I had a sleep.

The video swallow wasn't as bad as I anticipated – it was barium and showed up some neuromuscular dysfunction.

Feel so lonely. J is out. No one to talk to. At least I'll go home tomorrow evening. I'm thinking about escaping and buying some high dose phenergan but worried about it being taken away.

12 June 2001 Tuesday
Awful day – awake in the night again – hayfever and feeling sick. No HF tablets so in the end I took my remaining Phenergan. I had several confrontations about it. Janet said I couldn't blame pharmacy whereas I said if they had provided the tablets, I wouldn't have taken the Phenergan. Serena came and was equally hard. I just ended up crying and crying. Liz Gibson phoned and I couldn't help crying to her so she came down to see me. Oh yes, I saw this social worker about Friday and she asked what I was planning to say – nothing. I just feel I want to die – I'm fed up with being told I'm childish just because I don't live up to their expectations. I'm obviously a nuisance and they think I should make myself better. I want to cut myself with scissors or take a huge OD. I don't want to talk to anyone anymore (ward staff I mean). I've tried to escape twice today but been caught.

Once again I was confronted by angry and unsympathetic staff. Why should I not blame pharmacy? They did not provide the antihistamines. The rationale for taking the Phenergan was benign and not unreasonable –

to help me to sleep because I had severe hayfever and the hospital staff were not treating my symptoms. No, I should not have done that, but if I were at home I could have driven to Tescos and picked them off the shelf! This episode did not stop me.

---

13 June 2001 Wednesday

When I arrived home yesterday I had to cheer up for Steph. She was doing a talk at her cell group on joy and so we talked about 'the joy of the Lord is your strength' and she talked about forgiving people. I know all she said was relevant to me. However, when I got back here, they went and got a metal detector and I refused to let them search my back as I had some Phenergan I had found at home, but Serena was totally convinced it was a razor.

I've just had ECT and I'm very confused about what day it is and I don't remember writing the above. I want to escape after psychotherapy but I remember that they would stop it altogether if I do, so I'd better not. I've had awful reflux so it was impossible to lie down after dinner. I can't remember where the phenergan is – oh yes, I've stuck it to the roof of a drawer.

I've seen Lee and I can't remember exactly what she was saying but she says that all the things I do will hurt me. I want to escape so badly. I have just asked if I can have my stitches out and if I can have my dressing gown belt back – Janet says when Phil gets here. I was told to wait on my bed for Laura to come and remove the stitches, but she never came or even sent a message. I sit and look out the window in the day room at boats, trains and planes and on my bed at people coming in and out of car parks.

14 June 2001 Thursday

Talk with Laura this a.m. while getting the stitches out. She went on and on. Goal not to cut for 2 days – well I won't anyway because of tribunal followed by weekend. Have every intention of serious cut with scissors. Laura also went on about CBT, saying I have got worse with psychotherapy. Why are they all so anti? Hoped I might escape but gave up. Taken some Phenergan – hope it takes effect soon.

I slept quite a lot this afternoon – missed all the tea breaks.

I've had a brief talk with Serena as I think she's being particularly vindictive over cutting and self-harm etc. she said she would see me later.

D has had a chat with me, telling me all about the hard times she's having with son and daughter and friend. She has been having a go at the nurses – just so long as it's not at me.

It's been raining so hopefully the pollen count will drop. Dr Boyd won't allow an increase in chlorpromazine or Piriton.

I saw Serena and she went on about goals and how I'd get nowhere unless I had them. Apparently she and Janet are going to have a meeting about it with me. I admitted to having taken the Phenergan and handed in the last eight tablets. The doctor who came was not at all worried, which supported what I was telling Serena: 'they're harmless they just make you sleepy'.

I have just had a row with Bridget – she wouldn't give me any medication even though she hadn't asked the doc. I had asked to speak to the doc myself but Bridget won't let me. I've taken the plastic off the pillow and I'm going to use it – I told Bridget but she didn't seem to care. So if you read this post mortem, sue the staff for negligence and failure in their duty of care.

15 June 2001 Friday
I did try it but I was found on the floor. I was very breathless and vomited several times and they got me back to bed. Eventually around 2.30 a.m. I got to sleep.

Now its 7.30 and just waiting to hand the sick bowl in. Asked Janet for medication and she says she's got to ask doctors – don't know the result.

Briefly saw Dr Baldwin and tried to explain last night but cried a lot. He says he'll see me at the tribunal. A certain Dr Edwards is coming to see me to do with it.

All happened. Had the tribunal and obviously not allowed off the Section. I had the medication I asked for from Martin. I feel Janet is being deliberately awkward. I can't wait to go home this weekend.

17 June 2001 Sunday
I've made it in with the scissors just need to decide when. Been quite a good weekend – affection from the children, cuddles with Jona, sitting next to Simon, kissed Steph when she went to bed. Phil goes away to Guernsey (for work) Wednesday to Friday. Jenny is coming to stay. Steph is trying to persuade the boys to come to 'the big story' whatever that is (a church youth meeting). Sue Beare is back and came round for a chat. She says she will pop round when Phil is away. Phil's on a diet and is being quite successful.

ECT tomorrow so I'll miss Lee. I must tell her how Serena and Janet say I've got worse with her, which I really find unhelpful.

Just spoken to Bec about Essen and her sore feet! She's been resting today. She's doing a solo and pas de deux at the end of

year performance. I DO hope I'll see her. She's such a lovely daughter. I'm afraid I'll miss her so much but hope we'll be able to go and see her.

It was Father's Day today: Bec is sending hers, Simon gave Dad a mug, and Steph and Jona unknowingly got him identical cards and presents! Phil's making superb bread.

Mustn't forget tomorrow: toothpaste.

18 June 2001 Monday
Had ECT. I've written a note to Lee trying to say about Serena without mentioning names. I do hope she gets it. I desperately want to cut but am scared I'll lose the bed by the window. Also Phil's going to Guernsey and I don't want to worry him. I'm very tired and feeling sick – I couldn't eat all my lunch. I should go on a diet.

I've cut myself and am going to ask Phil to take me to A&E. I don't want the nurses to know. Janet said she'll see me at 4 p.m. – its now 4.04.

Mustn't forget toothpaste.

Seen Janet, admitted to cutting and had to hand in razor. She confirmed what they think about my sessions with Lee, i.e. that they're not helping. I hate it so much. Got to see the duty doc.

I am so perplexed that the nurses persisted in their judgemental attitudes, particularly in telling me that the sessions with Lee were unhelpful. I wonder just what they were hoping to achieve. Clearly it was not improving my relationship with them. If anything it was making things worse since I became more convinced that they were not trying to help me.

CHAPTER 19

The Health Commissioners' visit

19 June 2001 Tuesday
Got stitched up in A&E and had to come straight back here. Apologised to Phil.

I must take home washing, as the machine here is playing up, also toothpaste.

D's being friendly – help, long may it last. I just don't want to upset her.

Janet said yesterday that cutting is worse than burning and that I've got worse under Lee. I tried to say how helpful Lee is, but it didn't get through.

Had my time with Lee and we are considering what to do – I told her about Serena and Janet. I do find her really helpful at the moment. I told her that having the bed by the window stopped me doing anything really drastic.

I think I really MUST go on a diet. I didn't even like my lunch. My tummy is in rolls and straining the zip of my trousers.

Tonight: pen, all bran, fruit, washing

I saw Jona at home and had a hug. Simon went off to work, Steph has gone with Jenny to see a show. Jenny's staying from tonight. I managed to do my washing, empty the dishwasher, wash up and watch Eastenders.

20 June 2001 Wednesday
Had ECT and stayed in bed a lot.

21 June 2001 Thursday
The longest day today! I've had so much reflux from lunch and been sick despite two lots of Gaviscon. I'm getting on well with SJ in my dormitory and quite well with D. At psychotherapy yesterday Lee re-emphasised the need for a meeting with the Drs and S R (CBT person).

I feel quite numb, but pleased to have a date for the mental welfare people, 5 July. Now I'm just so nervous I won't be found right but I need to trust God.

My parents are coming at 3.30; hope that goes OK.

Went OK, they had a good time in Russia. Apparently Sarah (my sister) is selling her flat to buy a house with Charlie.

I was sick after lunch so I need to be careful after supper.

22 June 2001 Friday
Simon's birthday!

Had ECT and thought I'd lost my watch, but it was in my dressing-gown pocket. Been quite confused today but helpful reading the diary. I don't know what time Phil will be back – not late I hope.

24 June 2001 Sunday
Home yesterday a.m. and Bec came home too which was nice. The children have such complex social lives. Steph got Simon along to Sublime (youth meeting at church). He stayed overnight at the Lloyds.

It's been really hot and I have horrendous hayfever – like a running cold with itchy eyes. We had a barbecue in the garden. Bec found out that her flat in London has been broken into – hope it's OK. She's trying to learn German now and is quite excited about Essen. I just MUST see her perform because she's the main part.

Back here. S is back with a horrendous black eye. Apparently she tried to escape and fell over in the attempt. I didn't spend much time with her because she's too uncommunicative. It's too much effort.

I don't want ECT tomorrow a) hayfever b) Lee c) Dr Baldwin.

25 June 2001 Monday
Where are my nail clippers? Try and get them back, I thought I had but I can't find them. I've had my obs done for ECT so I guess I'll have to have it.

I've received a letter from a mental health commissioner in preparation for the visit on 5 July. It says I should have received an information sheet about the operation – I haven't so Serena has phoned to ask for one.

Dr Boyd says we will not have ECT on Mondays so I can have psychotherapy and also after surgery have CBT AND see Lee – that is good. I can't wait to tell Lee. I've sent her a note.

S is back in, she tried to escape and in the process of being

stopped got pushed by one of the nurses – now she has a horrendous black eye.

26 June 2001 Tuesday
Alastair's birthday (my brother) I did remember the card thank goodness.

I slept through most of the morning after making up the bed myself with clean sheets. This afternoon most of the time I sat with S, then came to bed after some chlorpromazine. I was worrying about when the stitches are due out – it'll be 10 days on Thursday, but I already want to cut myself again. I'm trying to persuade myself not to because the Scottish people are coming. Also I would like to lose weight. I told Phil I was getting nerves over the op. When I arrived back Miranda searched my bag and found a razor I had lost. RATS. At least I've found my nail clippers in my dressing-gown pocket.

I do not know why the nail clippers became such a source of concern! I wonder what they represented for me. Maybe they were a symbol of my autonomy. I certainly had so little of that.

27 June 2001 Wednesday
Just signed consent for 10 more ECT but not sure I'm happy about it.

Had ECT, lunch, washed hair – want to go home. I found my pyjamas by the sink – I don't know why. I suspect someone took them from my bed. It makes me want to go even more. Apparently the woman in the next bed was very confused ... she's gone to SGH (Southampton General).

Had long chat with Miranda where she put the blame squarely on me – if I didn't cut, if I didn't overdose, made me feel even more miserable.

I had a few words with Steph as she was upset but didn't seem to be helping any. I've just had a message saying not to blame myself about it, but I'm not sure who it's from.

I've been looking out the window and I've taken the dressing off. Stitches need to come out tomorrow. I WANT TO CUT.

28 June 2001 Thursday
I woke late this a.m. and had my tablets brought to me. I took a bath and CUT the stitches out – quite a mess. Now I'm waiting to let Miranda know and expecting a bollocking. I'll suggest steristrips.

I got taken to A&E and waited 2 hrs before even going through and then longer until stitched. 15 stitches. Got told I might do myself serious injury (I can't think of anything better). Had some talk from Laura mostly about how selfish I am and how I've got worse seeing Lee. I hate it. When I got back there was no food left for me, had my own snacks.

Phil is going to come down this evening as Steph and Jona have been off school, Jona – sick. Steph – unhappy and we'll go for a drink at Ocean Village.

D is going tonight; some relief as she asked me why I was crying and was not sympathetic when I told her.

29 June 2001 Friday
Got up with medication, had breakfast and then a bath and then back to bed.

Poor S didn't get any lunch as she's supposed to eat downstairs (in patient's dining room). I managed to get her a pudding.

Laura hasn't passed it on that the wound needs inspection today. Just make sure that I feel bad, that's the only priority.

Mary phoned about Sarah's wedding. She wants Phil's email code – what ever that is.

Bridget cleaned the wound and has given me stuff to do it at home. I lay on the floor and Kim came and had a chat about how guilty I feel. I also put my head in a bag but Mary's phone call interrupted that.

1 July 2001 Sunday
We went for a brief walk in the New Forest before picking up Jona. I arrived back here, was thoroughly searched which included a metal detector, and had my wound redressed after inspection by the SHO. There's a numb patch which is hard and another bit that looks pretty grotty.

I want my nail clippers back. I've got the information sheet on the operation. I feel pretty low altogether and at home feel the constant need to do housework even though it's a strain, but I really find it hard to relax. I feel terribly sorry/guilty on what it's doing to Phil. Whenever I write or think something like this, I have another thought saying 'you're making it up – you aren't really low, you don't need to cut yourself'. In fact I don't know why I do it – the thoughts, but so what? The whole situation is very strange but I CAN'T snap out of it even when I feel everyone else thinks I should.

Phil's on a low fat diet. I weighed myself; I'm over 11 stone so I'm joining him. Day 1 and its hard. I desperately want chocolate.

I've asked for my nail clippers and I hope if and when I get them I won't have them taken into custody again.

2 July 2001 Monday
Woke at 5 a.m., asked for chlorpromazine at 7.30, got it and got back to sleep again. Didn't wake up till 9.30 and had to ask for medication and breakfast – no one seemed concerned that I'd missed it all.

I tried escaping without success but got given chlorpromazine by Miranda – it hasn't knocked me out. Tomorrow I must ask about:
Is the op definite?
Wound – is it OK?
Lee – continue with her
Swallowing – follow-up appointment
Feeling faint

I listened to 'sixth sense' even though I wasn't concentrating and I couldn't remember the beginning which I listened to some time ago.

I went home as usual and after tea we went for a walk around the common. I found it really tough. I'm dreading repeating it but Phil is very keen.

There are two new people in the room, I hope they are nice and don't snore!

When I got back I was searched as usual and didn't appreciate the comments but I guess I'll have to put up with it.

3 July 2001 Tuesday
I woke early again and got knocked out with chlorpromazine.

Saw Dr Baldwin, they've decided I must not have ANY home leave because of the cutting. I can go out for 4 hrs a day as long as it's not home. I couldn't cry, but I did later. They say it's not a punishment, just that the cuts are serious.

How on earth are they going to manage – plants, hamster, beds etc. I feel such a failure, worst of all I still want to cut and I've hidden the one blade I have. I have a feeling they're going to do a search.

Phil came with Jona and we went and sat outside – he wasn't cross but we couldn't talk properly as Jona was there. I told him to look after Juicy (the hamster)

4 July 2001 Wednesday
ECT today. Pretty bad night.

Later: I'm just thinking of tomorrow and the mental welfare commission coming. Normally I'm very sleepy after ECT but

because of my nerves I'm wide awake. Just considering what I'll do if they say no. Thinking about dying, I know it'll be devastating for Phil and the children but I really can't stand this anymore. Hopefully God will look after them and provide Phil with a new wife. It's pointless me trying to guess who. I've also thought about trying again to make myself better by sheer determination. It's so hard being in this period of waiting. Please, please God will you bring about what's best.

Apparently I'm not allowed home, just 4 hrs with Phil, so it'll have to be the razor if I can remember where it is – I hope I have one.

Oh yes, I remember now, it's under the bed. I'll tell Lee about how I feel but not that I have a razor as she might tell. The other thing I could do is run away after Lee next Monday – I must remember to take some money with me.

Just had a session with Lee – apparently I am to have CBT after the surgery – IF I HAVE IT. Dr Boyd and two nurses said I didn't want it in case it worked. The absolute cheek. I'm going to have to tackle it, how can they say such an awful thing. It makes me really mad.

I just released S from a neck tie thing – she was trying to strangle herself. She is really a lovely girl. She's been razoring her arms. I wish I had razors like that. I've asked her for some and she says I can steal one. Laura came to talk to her. I am so glad to hear that Laura is leaving soon.

I've re-read through the operation notes and have decided that if they say 'no' then that's OK – that's the first time I've felt like that but the notes aren't exactly optimistic, so now I commit this into God's hands.

Helps half: 1/3 do well; 1/3 small improvement; 1/3 no benefit

Risks: 1:100 stroke, 1:1000 death, 1:50 fits, 1:10 one fit in 10 years

Side effects: facial swelling, weight gain, bladder problems, confusion

5 July 2001 Thursday
Today is the day and its 10.25 a.m. I actually went back to sleep after breakfast and now I feel nervous.

Seen the commissioners and answered lots of questions. Phil saw them too. Dr Baldwin came up and explained that I'm to be transferred to Mayflower (Psychiatric Intensive Care Unit), so I'm all packed up. They have said yes to the surgery.

The three mental health commissioners came down from Scotland to make sure that I was freely consenting to have the operation. They had formal interviews with Phil, Ruth my CPN, Serena as a member of the ward nursing staff, Dr Baldwin and the consultant psychotherapist who was briefed by Lee to act on her behalf. Their report consisted of a four-page document. This is their conclusion.

> Dr Wield has a severe treatment resistant depressive illness with endogenous and sometimes psychotic features. No physical treatments have produced any sustained improvement and she has not to date been considered suitable for cognitive behaviour therapy. In her present state there is a high risk that she will die either from straightforward suicide or through self-harming behaviour that leads on to death. In my medical view she should be offered neurosurgery for mental disorder and there is no other reasonable treatment approach available at present. All three of us decided without difficulty that she is able to consent to the procedure and is so freely consenting.

Dr Baldwin had decided that if the commissioners agreed to the surgery I would be immediately transferred to Mayflower Ward – the psychiatric intensive care unit. That would at least give me the best chance of arriving in Dundee alive! Just five days earlier the ward had received a phone call from one of the consultants at Southampton General A&E expressing the opinion that the damage that I had done to my abdominal wall was such that my life was at risk. I had areas of necrosis and he was concerned about the possibility of serious infection.

Being moved to Mayflower and being put on 1:1 observation was a shock to me. I did not know of the existence of this ward. To enter it, a bell was rung at the entrance and a staff member would come and let you in through an airlock, i.e. two sets of locked doors. There would definitely be no means of escape now! Each patient had a separate room with just enough space for a chest of drawers and a chair. It was a great improvement on the dormitory. There were far more staff and it was a very controlled environment. A member of staff was present in every area of the ward. It was to my recollection in much better condition generally compared to B ward, it looked cleaner and more recently redecorated. It was situated on the ground floor and there was a small garden area which was grassed and surrounded by a high, solid-looking wooden fence.

> Arrival on Mayflower, room 6, this is absolutely awful. I'm being sat with. They've been all through my things but haven't found anything. I've had lots of things confiscated including my

walkman, all tapes, tape cases, nail clippers, coat hangers, a bottle. They are quite friendly staff but I still hate it. I saw Dr Baldwin and asked about seeing Bec next week and the gastro doc. I will 'have to be good'.

Practically everyone smokes and in the 'non-smoking' TV room. Phil is going to bring a TV for me.

They are going to take the pen away after I've done this 'in case I self-harm' with it. It all seems ridiculous. I hate having to go to the loo with someone in the room. All in all I feel beastly and don't know how I'll survive until tomorrow especially having to give this pen in. God help.

CHAPTER 20

Mayflower or high security prisoner

6 July 2001 Friday
Woke early. Around 9.30 the news was that someone called Joseph (pseudonym) had committed suicide overnight. There are police and all sorts of people down the corridor. The body is obviously about to be moved as this irritating woman who is 'sitting with me' today has been told to come in here and shut the door.

How awful that even in this environment someone was able to take their own life. However, I was to learn that there were different levels of observation. You could 'earn' time on your own as a privilege for good behaviour. I didn't know this at the time. For most of my stay, I was on the highest level of observation. The rooms were very small so, having a nurse in the room with me all day was very intrusive. But I saw this tragic suicide advantageously – I remember thinking that at least, even here it could be possible for me to kill myself. I wanted to know how he had managed it!

My parents came and my mother offered to come to Scotland with me for the operation. We talked quite extensively about St George's (the second boarding school) and the illness in the fifth year.

The chaplain Alastair has just said 'hello'. I have decided to read one chapter of Acts at a time.

Phil came with TV and aerial – it needs to be approved by the hospital. Bec phoned and said she'd had a bad dress rehearsal. She doesn't mind me missing the graduation ceremony, the day after the performance as she says it's just handing out bits of paper.

I met Dr Brown today – he's in charge of the unit. He's keen that I do go to the performance.

I've got a John Grisham book to read but I've read some of it

and can't remember a thing. I don't know whether to go back to the beginning or carry on hoping it comes back to me.

I was surprisingly disciplined during this stage of my illness and I remember trying to make myself read a chapter of a book a day. I found it hard to concentrate for even that amount of time and, as you will see, I found it difficult to remember what I had read before. This is difficult for me to understand now in retrospect as usually I have no difficulty in reading a novel in less than a day and it seems so awful that I was unable to do this when I had so much time on my hands! I used to listen to 'book tapes' as well, which Thelma used to get for me from the library. However, I know the same thing happened – I would have difficulty following a storyline because I could not remember what I had previously heard particularly when I listened over several days.

7 July 2001 Saturday
I washed and dressed in front of a female nurse. Also been so embarrassing going to the loo in front of one too. I don't see the point.

I had a chat with a male nurse about cutting, the past and what led up to me becoming ill and trying to fathom out how the self-harm started (without success). I do know I mustn't do anything in case they stop me going to see Bec.

R (another patient) is really annoying. He gave me a whole bunch of rubbishy magazines, but he plays his music really loud. The most annoying thing is he comes into my room to talk to whoever is sitting with me and I can't understand a word he says.

Must ask Phil a) what about the gastro appointment b) phone Mary with email code.

8 July 2001 Sunday
The nurse has been very nicely chatty, showed her my photos including Bec in Swan Lake – just remembered Dr Baldwin asked to see them too.

I feel guilty that I'm giving the one to one nurses sitting with me a really boring time. Sometimes I don't want to talk.

After lunch I couldn't get hurting out of my head, I tried to suffocate myself by putting my head inside a plastic bag but got caught, tried holding my breath but couldn't, tried head banging but got told to stop. I wish I could die. I wish I had cancer. I wish Phil and the children wouldn't care if I died but I know they

would, so yes, it is selfish. I must get better otherwise it will be the suicide option. I can't keep going like this.
It's definitely harder a) not going out b) not having friends.
Phil and Jona came to see me this evening. I am to remember to leave around 4 p.m. on Thursday.
I felt like head banging again, but persuaded not to by Kim – she says I'm brave and that I must tell them when I feel like harming myself.
Remember Monday psychotherapy
Stitches out
Gastro appointment
London Thursday

Thank you Kim for being so understanding. Generally speaking, the Mayflower nurses seemed much more sympathetic and constructive in their approach to my self-harm. I am sure observing a patient on a 1:1 must have been almost as difficult for them as it was for me.

9 July 2001 Monday
Woke quite early. In the night someone who sat with me made me have both hands above the cover and woke me up when I didn't.
Lee: talked about the move to Mayflower and the shock it caused and she said it was just people expressing concern, but why all of a sudden is what I want to know. It's crazy. Talked about lack of privacy and how humiliating it is going to the loo with someone watching – the embarrassment – but just have to put up with it.
Saw Dr Baldwin and he said 'NO' to the Dr Fisher appointment – too high a risk. I can only go to Bec's performance if my 'mental state is going in the right direction'. I got him to increase the chlorpromazine. I'll have to sleep and pretend to be OK.
I had some more chlorpromazine and then had a sleep. When I was asked if I was alright, I said 'yes'. Apparently the man who died here died of suffocation – bag over his head – no wonder they're concerned about me I suppose.

10 July 2001 Tuesday
I've just woken up and had breakfast. I'm waiting to bath. Apparently Marion (a friend) is coming this afternoon – must get her phone no.
Fine hot bath and hair wash.
Written a note to Lee, mustn't forget to give it to her. Had a sleep before lunch.

Phone message 44********* Marion

Luckily she phoned the ward as I have tried to text back and rubbed it out. I can't do this texting.

Lunch – pilchard salad – I'm sure I didn't chose it. Pretty sleepy but I don't mind.

Saw OT then Marion arrived. Apparently the 44 on the no. is equivalent to a '0'. Marion brought me some pretty garden flowers and miniature heroes.

Phil came with Jona and was told children aren't allowed on the ward. Fortunately they let him in.

I had a horrible supper. I'm sure I didn't order it. Anyway I've done tomorrow's menu.

Don't forget ECT tomorrow

Children visiting

Bec's performance – Thursday

Dr Fisher – reflux

TV

Shave legs

Lee 1 p.m.

11 July 2001 Wednesday

I had ECT. I was extremely disorientated afterwards – forgotten I was on Mayflower, which room I was in, where I kept my stuff. I had a sleep then dinner. I saw Lee and discussed at length whether or not they'll allow me to go to London tomorrow to see Bec. If they say 'no' I'll go absolutely mad!

It's very windy today and quite showery. I'll have to get a Ladyshave as they won't allow me to use a razor.

I'm having awful reflux and not allowed to see Dr Fisher.

I've received a sick note request and benefits will be stopped if they don't receive one by 21 July 2001 sent to the hospital address. Officialdom is crazy.

I had ward round with Dr Brown; he is a funny fellow but anyway confirmed the OK for tomorrow but was concerned that I couldn't get anything to self-harm. (Quite the reverse of this was obviously what I meant to write!) He said the children can be seen in a room outside the ward. Apparently Harriet (Dr Boyd) is sorting out Dr Fisher.

I saw the OT – she's brought three 250-piece jigsaws and I've started one with the help of Lucy, a student nurse. I've eaten all the chocolates Marion brought yesterday – greedy pig!

12/7/10 Thursday

I'm so worried – they haven't done a Section 17 leave form. They

say this guy Steve Brown is coming down – a consultant. Please God may he come. I've been tidying up, getting organised – bin emptying, blanket put away. I'm feeling very, very tired but can't sleep until this is done.

Went to London and saw Bec, went for a meal afterwards and then took her home. My biro must be in the car.

Sadly I have absolutely no memory of the performance. It was Rebecca's graduation where she was the lead role in *Les Sylphides*. I wish I had written something more about the day so that at least I could have the possibility of it triggering a memory. However, I have looked at the photos. No, there is nothing there. Another landmark event that I would have wished to have cherished. I am still glad that I went though – maybe one day something will come back to me! My diary was becoming more a factual record of events. I often wrote down exactly what the meal was. I have left that out as it is rather tedious.

13 July 2001 Friday
Bec was really superb. Phil has gone up to her graduation. I had ECT and a long sleep. Salad for lunch then I did my jigsaw. This pen has come from my property. After ECT and during lunch I was looked after by a nurse called Steven. He wasn't very nice.

14 July 2001 Saturday
Woke up to R's awful loud music. The nurse looking after me talked about me being a doctor and I had to explain that I was trying to keep it quiet.

Nursed by Neil and heard lots about his life. I started to bang my head – it was stopped of course but I can't explain why I want to do it except I want to cut but why that? I'm sure I've gone over this in psychotherapy.

15/7/10 Sunday
Up, breakfast, bath, all being watched which is uncomfortable. Cup of coffee and discussion re TV. Phil is going to Guernsey for work Tuesday and back Wednesday 6 p.m.

16 July 2001 Monday
Lee at 10. I've got the TV in my room now and watched Silent Witness all night (well, till 10.55). If Dr Baldwin comes
a Dr Fisher reflux and choking
b Clonazepam
c Dr Boyd saying I don't want CBT in case I get better

I need my nail clippers.

Lee: discussed the anger, self-destruct pattern. It might be helpful to write down what makes me angry. She thinks that the amount of time I have without self-harming may decrease the desire – not so far.

- My mother's positive attitude when I express negative thoughts – 'look on the bright side'.
- Not being believed as a child.
- People denying the existence of God.
- Being music captain at school and having to make people play hymns in assembly when they didn't want to.
- Being here and having things confiscated

I thought our house no. was 210 but somehow I knew it was wrong. It took me ages to remember what it is.

I got Phil to buy me a blue biro since I lost my last one and they insist that I have to give it in after use. I cannot understand why. I'm not allowed chlorpromazine till after 10 o'clock either.

Phil came with Bec and Jona. He's brought the *Observer* article which compliments Bec's performance – it's really lovely. Jona might be going to do Latin – he was really tired.

I still feel like banging my head and having thoughts of being flogged and then secondary thoughts 'you've made it up'.

17 July 2001 Tuesday

I started a period last night and I don't know how I'm going to cope with it. I wish I knew what it was they're scared of me doing with a pen.

I managed to get a shower and cope with tampons etc. then went for breakfast and felt faint.

Had a phone call from Ma to say they are visiting at 3.30. Feeling very subdued but still.

Still feeling ill. My pen goes to whoever's looking after me but I'm having to ask for it back.

Tomorrow at ward round

Pen

Clonazepam

Dr Fisher

Walkman

I'm worried about home. I know Grandma helps.

My parents came and brought maltesers. I can't remember what we talked about but I showed them the article about Bec. They are going to ask friends what Sunday papers they have so they might find another write-up. I don't know how Phil found out about the Observer.

I managed to win a concession over the pen. Apparently someone has stated that I self-harm with one – I haven't the faintest idea how to self-harm with it. So now I have the pen but have to hand it to the next nurse who gives it straight back to me. I drew a very bad picture of me being flogged.

18 July 2001 Wednesday
Ready for ECT. Period pain to deal with.

Post psychotherapy – no lunch first so I wasn't really with it, should have been woken earlier.

Seen Harriet – she says walkman not allowed because of the wire, but I will ask Dr Brown. She doesn't have any idea when the surgery will take place.

Been annoyed about R's music but having been in the garden it's a bit better.

Seen Dr Brown – discussion re observation – whether I'm safe or not. I confessed that I had the urge to cut so he's going to discuss it with my key nurse. Forgot about Dr Fisher. Talked about the pen and he thinks I can have the walkman back. Said I'm worried about home in general terms.

Had quite a cry afterwards and talked with Rachel, my key nurse. Basically I felt I should have lied, then I would have been allowed off obs, but they are telling me it wouldn't have helped. Phil was very supportive during his visit and he had a chat with Rachel before going home.

19 July 2001 Thursday
Slept really late this morning and had a shower. Not worth having breakfast. Had some time with Clare (OT) – she filled in a referral for art therapy and got me some cards and another jigsaw. I've also got the magazines to read and do crosswords. I need to
  a shave legs
  b nails
  c washing
  d walkman
  e ask Phil for: bacon crisps, toffee crisps, bananas, oranges, biscuits, Olay daily renewal face wash, cola

20 July 2001 Friday
No ECT as no anaesthetist and I woke really thirsty in the night – not allowed a drink! Phil didn't come yesterday as had to go to Steph's parents evening. I did 'glass painting' in OT this a.m. with the help of Clare.

At lunch Dr Boyd showed me a letter from Dr Fisher – apparently nifedipine might help.

> S came to visit me (from B ward) and she told me about her being diagnosed as borderline personality disorder as well as depression. She's gone to buy me a chocolate shortbread.
>
> I'm going to write down what time I had meds so that I don't ask for them before they're due. 7 p.m.
>
> I know it's silly but I think I'm too well to need 24hr obs. I'm tired now but it's such a bore to get a female to take me to the loo.

Suddenly it came to me as I was writing this out that I remembered patient 'S'. I encountered her again in A&E when I was back at work. She had taken a non-lethal overdose. When I saw her as a patient, she kept saying, 'don't you remember me?' and I was racking my brains trying to think who she was. I remember now, she was a young girl who had come to Southampton as a student before being admitted to the DOP. She had no family near by, in fact they had all disowned her, so on the notes under 'next of kin' there was written 'none'. It was S who then came into A&E after an attempted hanging. She survived but subsequently was placed in a secure unit herself. Oh how sad that I had not remembered her. She had been so kind to me. I wish I could have remembered her in time to at least have been able to thank her. I hope I did not hurt her too much by not recognising her.

CHAPTER 21

A date at last

21 July 2001 Saturday
*10.10
* 4.05
   Talked a bit about how I feel with Andy, self-harm thoughts and suicidal thoughts. Needed Gaviscon after lunch. Bec and Phil may be home by 5 p.m. – they've been sorting out Bec's flat. I don't know if they'll come and see me.
*8.30 p.m.
   Saw Phil and Steph for 20 mins. She asked why I had to have someone with me all the time and I replied to stop me hurting myself. I don't know how she took it. I hope she talks to Phil.

22 July 2001 Sunday
* 9.27
   I just feel upset this morning. I phoned Bec as she was getting on Eurostar. I love them all so much. I'm listening to music but thinking about suicide. I have a bag. I don't really want to die for the family's sake, but for me I do.
   I got caught, inevitable I suppose, even though I pretended to go to sleep and snuggled down under the covers. Kim asked about more – no, knives – no, scissors – no, razor blades – I refused to answer. I'm terrified they'll do a search. I need it here so much. If it got found I just couldn't bear it. They've told Dr Brown. HELP.
*2.30 p.m.

23 July 2001 Monday
Went up for psychotherapy at 10 a.m. Talked about destructive thoughts and feelings and the fact that I'm not looking forward to the op. Also expressed my concern about going home and trying to be a normal mum, how will the children be able to take me seriously, I wonder? I'm especially worried about Steph since I told her I hurt myself. What does she think of me? Lee says they will

just think I was ill but I don't think it'll be quite that simple. Apparently I'm due to have an interview with someone, Joyce, I think, about CBT.

*11 a.m.

I was going to have a sleep but they came and got me for OT. Then I've got to do the care plan.

Had interview with George, art therapist. I've got to tell Lee and apparently it's a good complement to CBT.

I sat out in the garden for a while, watching the flying ants and just about tolerating Julia's company (care assistant). I quite deliberately answer her as little as possible. She was on when Phil came and she sat just outside the door ... some privacy. When Suzie (one of my friends) came, the nurse with me disappeared totally. Why can't she do that?

Oh Phil said they are all going to my parents' anniversary do next Saturday, so I'll ask. I'll try not to forget with the ECT. Had chlorpromazine and Gaviscon around 5 p.m. – told to try liquid to see if it works quicker.

24 July 2001 Tuesday

*6.30

Woke at 5.30 a.m. and found my carer person was asleep so I got it into my head to cut myself now. I did, but unfortunately someone else got suspicious as she saw me trying to stick the razor to the back of my bed. So I was found out and my whole room searched and blood cleaned up with special cleaning fluid which smells of bleach and has wet my newly made bed.

*1.30 p.m.

I was stitched by the SHO on call. I had a bath even though he said 'no' but I just did it anyway. Then I slept. I'm not talking to anyone unless it's just basic needs, like I want the loo.

My parents phoned and asked if they could see me. I phoned back asking for some Bic razors, but I doubt if my mother will get them for me.

I head banged really hard and Julian (nurse) comforted me to the extent that I stopped. I want to do it more and more. I'm listening to Sleeping Beauty (Tchaikovsky). It makes me think of Bec and I'm so sad she's going. I haven't felt this sad about it before.

My parents came and brought cherries and Immac, not razors. They did not understand when I tried to explain how I felt and how I can put on a front if necessary, like when we went to see Bec. My father said I seemed 'perfectly alright'.

I do hope Sue (our friend) will be able to help for the holidays as

I'm worried about Jona. I've had a chat with Val and had chlor-promazine 9 p.m. I feel so much trouble to them all.

25 July 2001 Wednesday
Slept in my clothes so that I just had to wash face and go to the loo before ECT.

Just seen Lee: told her about the cutting and how I wasn't given enough local and how the doctor doing it didn't care. Also it was on the bed of that man who committed suicide. I also discussed Jona and how he was monosyllabic and when asked said his friends and their mothers didn't know I was in here, so I told him to tell them so they would understand why he doesn't invite them over.

She seems nothing but amused by art therapy. I tried to get her to explain to me what it was about but she said no more than they interpret pictures.

Ward round with Dr Brown, only change is escorted off the ward leave with two nurses. *No* to parents' anniversary do on Saturday. Phil has just left – he came straight from work – loving as usual. Dr Brown popped in and says I can ask to see him any time.

26 July 2001 Thursday
Been talking to Rachel re care plan. It is to do with what to do when I feel like harming myself. Met briefly Joyce who I will see a week today – I think she is the CBT person – seems surprisingly nice, but I can't bear these plans e.g. hands on ice.

I've put coffee on the bleached patch on the carpet. Phil isn't coming down tonight – must give him a shopping list:
Bananas
Bacon crisps
Oranges
Toffee crisps
Alastair (my brother) phoned on the mobile but I didn't get it and couldn't get back through.

27 July 2001 Friday
Had ECT this am – uneventful, then salad for lunch.

Had reminder for sick note but don't know who does it.

Phoned home and spoke to Steph; they all seem alright – busy. Had my dressing changed.

I spent most of the day doing jigsaws – Steven joined in and we finished one and he got a 1000-piece one and it is so hard!! I mean it. I really need help.

28 July 2001 Saturday
Golden wedding for my parents today and keep thinking that Phil and the children will be killed on the way. Horrible. Feel if I deny it, it's more likely to happen. Also having weird sensations. Taken chlorpromazine.

I got really worried when Steph phoned earlier asking where Dad was, his phone and wallet at home. After several phone calls I discovered he'd been for a jog.

Been doing the 1000-piece jigsaw with Steven and other staff members – it's really hard. I would rather stick to the 500s. I've done them with help.

I've not been allowed more chlorpromazine this time. I feel worried about Phil and the children. I feel annoyed by the staff around trying to help me.

29 July 2001 Sunday
Steph has been invited to be locum nanny by Mary and be paid so apparently she's very keen.

Everyone keeps asking about visitors and I have no idea. Anyway I feel yuk, v tired, funny sensations again.

30 July 2001 Monday
Dr Baldwin and Harriet came in which was really good. Apparently the surgery MIGHT be at the end of August. I also told them about the voices and sensations and asked if we could increase the chlorpromazine again – it's under review.

After lunch and more jigsaw, taken for walk around the hospital and came back to the fan in my room. Phil came and we talked about the timing of the op and Bec going to Germany. She's been away and comes back home on Sunday. Phil's going to Guernsey tomorrow – I'm still afraid. I had a nice card from Thelma (Phil's mother) today.

I'm afraid people don't really think I'm ill. I don't know how to behave. Apparently it's unusual not to get angry! I don't get angry. I have a fan in my room because last night apparently I was really restless, so they thought I might be hot.

I had my first session with George – art therapy. We didn't do any art as he was finding out about me and my life so I don't quite know what it'll be like but he seems a nice enough bloke.

1 August 2001 Wednesday
Had ECT and felt perfectly fine, ready to go home and it's been painful having reality dawn. The reality of Mayflower ward and

harming myself has come with a bit of a shock, but as I remember the bad feelings have come back.

Then I had ward round with Dr Brown – it was OK I suppose, though I can't have home leave, but he wants to stop the 1:1 gradually. At least it will mean I won't have to put up with that.

3 August 2001 Friday

Yesterday was our wedding anniversary – a huge bouquet from Phil and some sparkling white wine that we had got permission for, from Tim. We left some for him but he didn't get it. I wanted the bottle to break and cut! Still, that's my secret.

I had a 'care plan' session with Rachel and ended up with toilet privacy and later 5 min obs!

I went for a walk with Stephen and Anne. He was trying to find out what was wrong, but I wouldn't say. Basically I feel miserable because I want scissors to cut me and Phil might bring them tonight but I doubt it – that's why I feel miserable and I can't tell anyone

List: notebook

Oranges

Bananas

Toffee crisps

Bacon crisps

Diet coke

Toothpaste

Soap

4 August 2001 Saturday

4 a.m. I'm wide awake. I've been banging my head and my hand and last evening got quite a bruise.

I got chlorpromazine and my walkman and I eventually fell asleep. Breakfast was in the OT room and I did one of those glass colours and went for a walk round the grounds. They had lost the bathroom key and started a room to room search including mine but fortunately found it *before* they had completed the search.

5 August 2001 Sunday

4 a.m.: went to bed early, had meds at 8.30 p.m. as I was wall banging. Now wide awake, had chlorpromazine. Not sure what to do as I want to bang but I'm being watched. Want so much to knock myself out.

Later: Now every time I go to the loo, I hit myself. I do so at other times but get stopped and have suggestions made of what I should do, which I don't like. My head hurts, my right hand hurts

and knuckle on left hand is swollen. The duty doc saw me and wants an x-ray of my wrist. I spent most of the afternoon in front of the dreaded jigsaw with Steven; he kept coming and getting me.

6 August 2001 Monday
Lee's leave: 15 Aug – 3 Sept
I managed to sleep through my alarm and so had a rush to the session. I think they are pointless now. I'd rather have ECT – all we talk about is my destructive behaviour. I'm being chaperoned by Julia again – I find her intensely irritating.

I saw the new SHO and she agreed my wrist is not broken but x-ray just to be on the safe side.

George's leave 10–17 September had art therapy – just history taking.

No x-ray today – good – more chance to do something drastic. I really want to hurt myself and I hit it every time I go to the loo. I want to go onto 5 min obs so I'll try and talk to Tracy about that.

7 August 2001 Tuesday
Been awake since 5 a.m., listening to Sleeping Beauty and imagining Bec. They're not removing obs because they say the level of self-harm is serious i.e. requiring x-ray. However, there's going to be a meeting with me and I can negotiate.

Had some chlorpromazine and walking past TV room heard them talking about me being a doctor. I suppose I'll never be free of that now, thanks to G's big mouth.

I had a bath at 10.15 and got so annoyed with Julia, for a start she wouldn't believe I was allowed in by myself and then she kept shouting 'are you OK?' and not hearing my reply.

I asked to go out and was allowed so just ran for it, but must have tripped up, grazing my hands and toes and landing on my chest.

8 August 2001 Wednesday
Very confused from ECT but just read this and it explains. Phoned Phil and apparently his mother bought me two pairs of trousers, so feel better now I know where they came from.

Taken to psychotherapy and left so I escaped, almost got run over but managed to get to Hill Lane and get a taxi back home. Cut myself and then went to the sitting room and found Jona fast asleep. When he woke up we both had a long cry about me being away. Phil phoned and was very nice to me despite the trouble I've caused. He took me to A&E and then I got joined by Tony from Mayflower. I had to have an x-ray and wait 4hrs. I'm back now

and searched but nothing found. The whole thing was awful and we got soaked and I can't have a bath until tomorrow. Everyone is sort of kind but you can tell they are not exactly pleased.

9 August 2001 Thursday
Last night wasn't brilliant because I was cold and they kept saying they wanted my hands out and visible. At least the self-harm thoughts are satisfied. My hands are really bruised.

11 August 2001 Saturday
Woke, had a bath and had breakfast. When I got back to my room, did some jigsaw and not much later Steven came and we did some till lunch. I've had all my 1:1 people helping and then got dragged to the OT room by Steven to do one of the new ones there – a boring train, difficult too. Now I'm fed up with jigsaws.

I'm trying to read some of *The Street Lawyer* – I'm up to chapter 23 – trying to do one a day. The Bible is there untouched. I watched 'You've Been Framed' then I was going to watch Poirot but couldn't concentrate on it so I've just got ready for bed and hope I get my drugs soon. Vera (nurse from B ward) is down here in charge – it seems rather odd.

12 August 2001 Sunday
I've just had drugs and got only one clonazepam, instead of usual dose of two and Tracy is going to try and find another. Having a cup of coffee meantime and had to put up with this nurse ?name telling me that he'd heard coffee can stop sleep – he asked if I had heard that!! Got the clonazepam at 10.25.

Gone to bed, all ready, then asked for my hands to show and feel like saying 'f**k off' but managed not to.

13 August 2001 Monday
At psychotherapy, Lee was on about how I must be angry that's she's going on leave. Afterwards I went out and no one was there to take me to the ward. I didn't do a bunk – sorely tempted. When I got back, I found out that not only have I been given 2hrs leave but that it includes home with family – I'm so pleased.

I went for a walk round the block with Steven and then did jigsaw – lunch – jigsaw – art therapy.

14 August 2001 Tuesday
Woke at 6 a.m. but managed to fall back to sleep till 10.15. Had a bath, breakfast and went straight to Steven and the jigsaw.

Had quite a good talk with the chaplain about life in general,

the kids, wanting to die etc. then I went into the garden. Suzie visited and met the other patients and staff. Even had interaction with G (he's the one who knows I'm a doctor). My bruised hands are hurting – serves me right I suppose.

I went out with Phil, Bec, Steph and Jona – we had a drink at Ocean Village. I went to the loo ALONE – it's so much easier to 'go'.

15 August 2001 Wednesday

Woke 4 a.m.–7 a.m. Tried crossword, book, had a drink of Horlicks and eventually fell asleep till 9.30.

I'm about to see Dr Brown. I don't know when I'll get to see Dr Baldwin and get a date for the Op. I REALLY want one. At lunch I knocked my coffee onto myself by accident and burnt my thigh.

Saw Dr Brown and discussed leave, bathroom privacy and cutting. They don't seem to mind me banging my hands. We have to negotiate, but it seems I'll be allowed 3 hrs leave once a week. The bathroom privacy is up for discussion. I talked at length to Kim about it, but I find I just can't talk about it. (Self-harm) I find the whole subject hard to understand myself let alone explain it to others. I'm not going to be getting more ECT.

I went out with the family to the Lloyds and we had Chinese takeaway. Marion brought me back and I got searched with the metal detector. We gave the staff a bag of prawn crisps – I think they appreciated it.

I'm going home tomorrow at 10.30 but I'm still awake 12.30 a.m. due to the noise so I hope I'll be up in time.

16 August 2001 Thursday

Eventually slept around 1 a.m. – woke near to 10 a.m. – done all my jobs, washing, changing flower's water, emptied bin.

Saw Joyce (CBT person) – was OK – talked about self-harm and the issues surrounding it. Phil phoned me. The operation is 20 September and I have to go to Dundee on 10 Sept!

I've shrunk my navy cardigan so must ask Phil's mum if she can make me another.

Found another navy cardigan at home. Had a 3 hr session at home doing odd jobs and went to Cowherds for a meal.

There is only a brief mention of the fact that I now had a date for my surgery. I had been anxious and impatient about this for months. Now it's here and I barely comment even though I must have at least felt relieved if nothing else!

Likewise, Rebecca was leaving for Germany to start her first job as a professional ballet dancer the following day. I do not even mention this and yet it was such a momentous occasion. The meal at the Cowherds was the family goodbye to her! Knowing how I feel now when any of the children go away, I would imagine I was actually very upset, but this is not alluded to at all. Phil had decided to take Rebecca by car so that she could take all her belongings for her new life. Stephanie went with them and Phil had arranged for our good friends, Phil and Sheelagh, who lived a few doors down, to check up on the boys. Simon was very keen to be left on his own, by now aged 17. Unfortunately his plans to have a few friends around for a small party went horribly wrong . . .

Allowed out for a family meal before Rebecca goes to Germany.

CHAPTER 22

Never a dull moment

17 August 2001 Friday
Dr Baldwin visited me today. He's really pleased with the news. He needs to get me transferred to the Scottish Mental Health Act. Afterwards I did a jigsaw with Steven and Tony and we finished it after lunch with Andy. Then I went for an hour's walk with Steven including West Quay (the new Southampton shopping centre) which I had forgotten all about.

Just now I invited N into my room because she was upset and managed to calm her down. We read Psalm 91 and I lent her some tapes.

Phil phoned to say they arrived safely and Bec has a tiny room. I phoned the boys – they are both having friends over. I've told them to phone if there are any problems.

18 August 2001 Saturday
Woke up 10.35, had a bath during which M threw a guitar through the smoking room window so the corridor is now covered in glass. It took the best part of an hour to clear it up so I didn't get breakfast till 11.45. After lunch went and tried Steven's 1000-piece puzzle with no success so came back to my room.

My parents came about 4.30 with photos of Russia and fruit for me, which was kind. Sue Beare arrived with Jona and stayed for quite a while – till supper time. I had salad and orange, but since then I've eaten all the cherries and a toffee crisp. I've had my stitches out and transferred a blade to my dressing gown pocket. I feel awful and I've had chlorpromazine.

I've cut myself, pretending to read a book, but I don't want to tell anyone – I think I'll wait till morning.

They found out when I went to the loo.

Even on this close level of observation I managed to elude them. Unfortunately this did not help my case when I became so upset at having to have my hands visible above the sheets when sleeping. It was an awful

thing to be woken from sleep to show my hands, but in fairness to the staff, I had managed to harm myself quite adequately by hiding what I was doing. I had been moved back to continuous 1:1 observation after the escape.

---

19 August 2001 Sunday
It took ages in A&E, arrived home after 5 a.m. – by ambulance there and back. I'm exhausted but it's 11.30 and I've dressed, had breakfast, put my washing in, changed my sheets. Had to have pain killers as I've got pain in my shoulder tip.

Phoned Simon – no reply, phoned home spoke to Jona and then Simon. He had to call the police and clear everyone out, dope was being smoked. His phone was stolen. The carpet was burnt. Later Jona phoned in tears as our neighbour bent down to pick up some glass, cut her hand, slipped and broke her arm. I phoned Sheelagh. She and Sue then went down and helped the boys. Sheelagh phoned later – apparently it's much better now.

20 August 2001 Monday
I did four pieces of Steven's difficult puzzle – very proud of myself. No one's talked to me about the cut – it's really weird. Went up to art therapy and did a sort of picture of me with a knife, a bag, a bottle of pills and a blade. The talk we had was really good – he didn't try to analyse the doing of it, more accepting and said we would travel down that path week by week.

When I got back to the ward, I was introduced to some people doing a survey on mental health facilities, so I told them about the extreme lack of privacy in going to the loo and having a bath.

Sue Beare dropped in, she's staying with the boys tonight.

I'm feeling really low.

21 August 2001 Tuesday
Session with Joyce. We talked about cutting and emotions surrounding it and the fact I don't cry. I told her about the anger at the lack of toilet privacy. This morning I went to the loo and had to get Julia to turn the tap on. When I went back to bed, my hip ached and I kept rubbing it and she kept telling me to keep hands above the sheets. I got very cross and in the end had to get some pain killers. I did fall back asleep.

1.30 Thursday Joyce next week.

I am waiting for this doctor to hopefully confirm my leave for this afternoon.

I got leave after Thelma got a lecture about how she was

responsible. I did a bit of cleaning at home and saw the boys, which was lovely. Thelma was very nice too.

22 August 2001 Wednesday
Went to the bathroom and I was so uncoordinated.

Just found out that Jona has been chosen as mascot for the first premier league Saints match on Saturday. He had been entered into a competition by the Lloyds.

Chlorpromazine *5.30, – 3/10 – this is the new way of assessing whether it works for the SHO.

*6.52 5/10

23 August 2001 Thursday
*1.27 1/10 feeling v low * 3.01 – 3/10 rolled off my bed earlier in attempt to hurt myself. We went to the Lloyds and had a drink of wine and some fruit and coffee. Now I'm back I feel terrible. *10.30 so so tired. Marion has given me some lovely flowers from her garden.

25 August 2001 Saturday
Woke reasonably early but had to wait for a bath as no females were available to take me. Went to the football at 2 p.m. – saw Jona as the mascot, then he was brought up to us. Afterwards I got worried about being late back and Phil said I should've said something. I just feel totally useless and down. I've had some chlorpromazine. I admitted that I feel like hurting myself. Now I just feel terrible

26 August 2001 Sunday
My parents came and we had a difficult time as I was so low and didn't feel like talking and couldn't answer some of their questions. Forgot to wish them a good time when they left – they're going to Virginia, USA on a house swap and will be away during the op.

27 August 2001 Monday
Bank holiday. Woken by Julia's loud talking. Last night woken by Bill because my hands were not visible. I slept all morning and then had lunch. Most of this afternoon doing jigsaw with Steven. Kim also 1:1 and was very sweet. I managed to knock the finished jigsaw onto the floor. I told them about being woken up in the middle of the night because my hands were under the covers and they have passed it on to the night staff that it's not on. My ankles have been very swollen again.

Phil phoned – he watched Steph dance at the Birmingham Royal Ballet summer school and then took her to Mary's.

28 August 2001 Tuesday

Up early-ish, then Steven and jigsaw. That continued till lunch. Wasn't very hungry so gave away my chocolate pudding. They have locked the cutlery draw and lost the key. They wouldn't even let me have a plastic knife for my oranges. After lunch I went for a walk with Steven to buy some fruit and then sat in the garden but had to come in 'cos M was so annoying.

I asked W for a blade but she wouldn't let me have one. I head banged and wrist banged and tried to suffocate myself but Tony stopped me and called Rowena. She lectured me on why I should distract myself and what's worrying me – the op, no visitors in Scotland, our debt. I felt she didn't understand at all. Just said all the 'right' things. I feel I want to die or at the very least cut.

29 August 2001 Wednesday

Steven took me out to take the bad oranges back that I got yesterday and got a refund. I still feel really bad. Tracy has lent me a John Grisham book for Scotland.

I've had a bad afternoon but at least Andy has been helpful by just being understanding. I can't sleep even though I try and no one cares when I head bang. M has been a complete pain – swearing and shouting. N has also been a pain wailing and then asking me questions when I've just been crying in the ward round. That was pretty terrible, dominated by Rowena – they want to speak to Phil before deciding on more leave. I asked about hands out of the covers and they agreed while I'm asleep it should be allowed. The reason is because of the last cutting but I dare not admit that I wasn't trying to be asleep as I want to cut again and it's so hard to think of how.

I saw Phil with Rowena and they decided I can go out but not home. I cried. I told Phil how I felt about Scotland and cried again. I told him I'd make it up to him one day. He spoke to Dr Baldwin today and I'm going up on Sunday 9 – I wish he'd come and see me.

30 August 2001 Thursday

Woken by Kim and Rowena chattering – at least they brought me coffee. I'm making lists of what to take to Scotland. I then slept till lunch.

I got it into my head that Joyce was at 3.30 even though I wrote down 1.30 so she phoned down for me. Didn't like the session. Getting photocopy of 'what we agreed'.

Cut myself while Val was reading a book and I was 'doing' a cross-word. Didn't get to A&E till around 7 p.m. though, as M was in seclusion and all sorts was going on. Val took me and we got back at 10 p.m. to find all the windows except a few behind the fence were all smashed! (By M)

31 August 2001 Friday
Woke up, had breakfast, went to bed and then remembered that I needed a blood test. I'm anaemic and need 'haematinics' before going on iron. No wonder I'm so tired. I had a little go at a jigsaw and met AJ from B ward – she has stitches on her forehead and two black eyes from some incident with staff. What a place!

Sheelagh came to visit; apparently there are lots of people praying about the op.

I've watched the news and I am waiting for Phil to visit – he's gone to Sainsbury's and is waiting for Steph who is coming back from Mary's. Mary phoned to say how much she enjoyed having her and Sophie (Steph's cousin). Written to Bec.

I went to a pub with Phil and Steph at 8 p.m. Steph was talking all about her visit to Mary's. We got back here about 9 p.m. and I watched some TV. Bill was my 1:1 and we didn't exchange a word.

1/9/01 Saturday
Went out to the forest with Phil and Simon for lunch – they still won't let me home, we went for a walk dodging the animal dung. Simon has a really bad cough.

I did a jigsaw in the afternoon and then went and watched the football for the sake of boredom. AJ was there and she had a tearful chat afterwards – apparently she had tried to hang herself so the black eyes etc. may be from when she was cut down. Now waiting for meds and bed – I get furious when they go on about having my hands outside the covers.

2/9/01 Sunday
Gave Phil a copy of the list I made for what I need from home and Sainsbury's. I talked to them about the arrangements or rather lack of them. Phil knows much more than the ward – they don't even know I'm going a week today! I've carried on with the jigsaw but it's really hard and I'm a bit fed up with it. Tea was OK, talked to AJ and suggested her husband talked to Phil since we're both in the same boat. Being 1:1 by a new nurse, who has been telling me about her constipation, even showed me her belly! Honestly, how stupid!
]

3/9/01 Monday
Woke up early and I wasn't going to have a bath but Anne said my hair wasn't OK so I did. N's lost one of my tapes – I hope she finds it. Had a session with Lee and got upset. She says I harm myself because I'm angry with people. She says I can request to see her after the op as I'm worried I won't get on with Joyce.

Saw Dr Baldwin briefly and he said I'm coming back to A ward and he'd got the travel arrangements wrong but that's been sorted out now. Val and John are taking me. Anyway I feel very upset and angry about the A ward thing. Yet another ward and new people. I've told everyone and I've cried on and off all afternoon. Mary phoned and we talked about everything.

In art therapy I did traffic lights, autumn and summer with the amber and the squiggles between as the op, only I feel like I'm going from green to red. HELP! I want to cut my stomach open with the kitchen scissors. I'm so tired too. I saw Ruth (CPN) and cried loads with her, but I can't get any help from her as she's on holiday from today.

My mobile went completely empty battery – it's never happened before – it made a funny noise. I had some salad and two cheese-cakes for tea.

4/9/01 Tuesday
There's been an outbreak of D&V and we all have to have our own named mugs.

Been to psychotherapy and left Lee in tears. I still want to cut myself and I know I'll run away from A ward.

N's going back to Milton Keynes and she's very upset – I do understand and try to encourage her but I feel so low for me and head/hand banging.

Sue Beare came to see me as she's going back to Zimbabwe soon. Apparently she helped us dismantle the BBQ and take the concrete and bricks to the tip – I really can't remember doing it.

Rowena has supported the straight to A ward business but suggests a preliminary visit, which I've agreed to. I cried a lot again and said about running away and scissors.

Phil's coming on his way home just for a visit as I said I was not having a good day.

I forgot to say, more bacon crispies and bananas and about AJ's husband.

5/9/01 Wednesday
Last night I fell asleep about 6 p.m. and nobody woke me until 11.30 to give me meds.

Dr Baldwin came – I had to do this questionnaire about mental things. I also said about my fear of A ward but I don't think I've changed his mind. I still think I'll just run away.

I've just been black all afternoon, started to take out the stitches but Charles wouldn't let me – started head banging. Rowena came and said I could take them out and gave me some chlorpromazine and a chat.

Had my other wound looked at by the SHO and managed to persuade her that I didn't need antibiotics.

Phil said he'd pop in since I'm feeling low. I want to go out.

6/9/01 Thursday
Last night I was woken up by something and then turned round to go back to sleep – Julia came over and told me to put my hands out; I can't remember what I said to her but I know I was angry.

I went with Julian to buy some bananas and I fell in the street and hurt my hand; it hurt to write this. I just remembered I forgot to wash my face.

Sue and Hannah came and prayed for me and all the family. It was very good and relaxed – I didn't feel under pressure. Sue said how they lowered the paralytic man to Jesus and all the man had to do was let them. She said that God's love and our friends' prayers would be with me wherever I go.

I wasn't really appreciative of any spiritual input at this stage. I didn't want to be prayed for as it made me feel as though friends were expecting the operation to be successful. I wasn't at all optimistic at this point. I felt under pressure and repeatedly told Phil that I didn't want prayer. It felt as if no prayers had been answered in the past seven years and I certainly was not full of faith.

7/9/01 Friday
My hand is very painful but I don't think it's broken. I need pain-killers though. Saw Dave and Marie for 15 mins and they prayed. Dave prayed over my hand.

I had my hand x-rayed – it's OK. I've started sorting things out. I can only just fit into my maroon jeans. Went out with Phil, Simon and Steph to the Crown – Steph had some lovely photos of her stay with Mary – it was lovely seeing them all.

Harriet came to wish me luck and even hugged me! Dr Baldwin phoned and said Phil could phone during the week and said arrangements were all in place and wished me luck.

8 September 2001 Saturday
Last night was horrendous as dreaded Vera from B ward was on and this care assistant. They decided to bug me because of my hands not showing. He stood over me and basically kept moving around so I turned to face the wall. I pretended to be asleep but was furious so didn't fall asleep until after the day staff arrived.

After lunch I finished the last chapter of *The Street Lawyer*.

I went home to get some things with Phil and saw Simon, Steph and Jona. I managed to secretly get a blade and hide it in my coat lining, but cut my thumb.

I hope I sleep better tonight.

9 September 2001 Sunday
Woke early and couldn't go back to sleep, although I had a good night this time – no Vera. Had breakfast with the staff. Finally the taxi came at 12.30. I hadn't been hungry for lunch. We got to the airport and had a drink. Val and John were very nice, but Val was scared during the take off and landing!

Now I'm at Ninewells Hospital, it's a lovely unit, all new.

CHAPTER 23

The end of the road

I remember the Carseview Centre very well – the unit which houses the psychiatry wards at Ninewells Hospital, Dundee. My two accompanying nurses were no doubt very relieved to have delivered me there safely. They had stuck closely to my side, which was just as well. I remember while we were waiting for the train at Edinburgh thinking about the possibility of running for it and jumping in front of the train. I thought better of it though, thankfully.

This unit was entirely different from what I had experienced of the NHS up until now. It was newly built under the public–private enterprise scheme, having only been open for a few months. The ward I was taken to was a mixed ward but every patient had a single room with en suite bathroom. I said goodbye to Val and John and was taken to my room. I was very impressed, especially when they left me on my own. Things were looking up. I know Val had felt under pressure on the journey, unable to enter the cubicles in the various ladies toilets that I had to visit. At last I was going to experience privacy. Unfortunately, Val and John must have put the Dundee nursing staff right as regards my 'observation status'. Before I had time to fully unpack, I was escorted out of my lovely single room and taken to a larger 2-bedded room. Apparently the Carseview Centre intensive care ward was only for male patients. Females requiring this kind of care were unusual and so kept on the general ward but in this room, together! I was bitterly disappointed, not only was I to share a room, but I still had the same level of observation and the nurse would enter the tiny en suite shower room with me, even when I just needed to use the toilet. In fact I was not allowed to use the shower but was accompanied to the bathroom so that I could be directly observed in a bath! I did not get much chance to see any of the rest of the ward at this point, but I noticed that there was a courtyard area and a small TV lounge (for non-smokers) and a dining area. The floor was carpeted and being new, there were no horrible smells or stains!

Apparently the centre had had a certain amount of difficulty with the heating system. The nurses' office was incredibly hot and they had a fan going, but there was a huge differential. The further the distance was from this hot area, the cooler it became – as I was to discover! It was in fact

quite cold in some of the rooms. I was glad that I had brought some winter clothing with me.

The nurses wore uniforms, unlike psychiatric nurses in England, so at least I knew who was who. Quite naturally, most of them spoke with Scottish accents, some of which were quite broad, and I didn't always understand what was being said. I felt very stupid having to ask them to repeat themselves. I also felt as though I stood out like a sore thumb with my English accent. It was all very strange. Other things were confusing too, for instance 'supper' was the pre-bedtime drink and substantial snack rather than our English evening meal.

The diary continues:

---

10 September 2001 Monday
Had a good night's sleep though I didn't get my meds until 11 p.m. I don't get bathroom privacy which is a pain and I hate going to the loo with nurses there.

I've met one member of the tribunal, been interviewed by my named nurse Gill and examined. A final-year medical student took blood under supervision of an SHO. Phil phoned – the mobile has no signal, so he has to phone the ward no.

I've asked if I can watch TV – 'no'. I'm confined to this room with L. She just threw a wobbly – I don't blame her – everyone came running in as one of them (nurses) pressed their alarm.

I've been trying to read and trying to listen to a book tape but my concentration is awful. At least they've got me a cup of coffee that's actually hot.

At 8 p.m. more coffee and a sandwich. It was horrible but I ate it since I didn't eat their tea.

I've just remembered John probably went off with my return air ticket. I must tell Phil next time he rings.

11 September 2001 Tuesday
The start of another miserable day. I had a bath which was nice as the nurse just kept popping her head round the door instead of being in there constantly. I woke twice in the night, vivid dreams again. I've reorganised the top of my chest of drawers so that I can see the photo of all of us taken by the Lloyds before Bec went.

I found the lovely photo and bible verses Steph had done for me and I started crying. I feel low and fed up with this obs business. The worst thing is being confined to this room – no TV, no exercise.

I can vaguely hear titbits of a news report that two planes have crashed into the World Trade Center. I'm trying to do crosswords

---

and look at magazines and had four sweets as a treat. The nurse came to have a chat when I was upset. She says I have tests tomorrow.

I had a sleep then it was tea. We are to have another woman in the room so the beds have been moved. There is a radio in here. I was shown and heard all about the awful terrorist attacks in the USA – four planes and a car bomb, thousands killed and injured. I assume my parents are alright.

A new girl has come into our room and our beds have been moved to fit in another one as a result. I hope it's not for long.

I vaguely remember that day that the rest of the world will never forget. I remember overhearing the nurses talking about it, but until we had the radio on in our room, we did not really know what happened. Even then we did not see the event on television as most other people would have done. I had no idea of the significance of the event – that aspect totally passed me by. The world I was in was very insular and it was quite a shock later on to find out exactly what had happened.

12 September 2001 Wednesday
Kept waking up with vivid dreams and felt so tired when woken for breakfast. Had to get ready as its start of tests.

Went by ambulance to the back of Ninewells and it was so complicated to get to various places – Prof Matthews did a video and then some questionnaire-type questions and I have a whole load to do as 'homework'. I asked to come off obs but its 'no' but hopefully a bit more freedom, like TV and phone Phil.

Lunch was kept: mince, overcooked sprouts and potatoes. Not for me. At tea I managed to get some sandwiches and pudding but I'm not hungry, had an orange.

Just spoke to Phil and Steph on the phone. He's coming on Monday now as Sunday flight is fully booked. I'll have to manage a WHOLE weekend.

Had an attempt at head banging since I was so frustrated, but it was stopped rapidly and I was given chlorpromazine. I'm listening to tapes while wishing time would fly. Someone remarked we are like goldfish in a bowl as everyone can see us in this room, the door is open. Especially as everyone comes for their drugs in the treatment room next door and you can see them peering in.

13 September 2001 Thursday
Woken for drugs, no sugar puffs, but they managed to find coffee –

that had run out too. I've had my bath and the dressing changed. The wound is all dried up but looks nasty. I hope the doctor gets the message to take the stitches out. I also want some Gaviscon.

I went to do the computer tests and then x-ray. They refused to do it as there wasn't the right information on the card.

Phil has sent some beautiful flowers – a lovely surprise!

L has been moved out, so I'm just in with G, she's getting a lot of freedom which also means more for me as the 1:1 person can come with me. We watched the news on TV.

14 September 2001 Friday

Just been visited by two more doctors from mental welfare commission to check that I'm freely consenting. They weren't here for long. Last night I got really uptight about wanting to cut myself and had very close 1:1 and they wouldn't let me bite myself or hit my head. Got given this elastic band to flick on my wrist, actually it does hurt.

Had a lovely card from Bec, I need to write back to her. Can you believe it, they've run out of coffee, milk and sugar puffs?

I slept this afternoon and they saved me some tea but I didn't like the look of it so had some sandwiches. I watched Eastenders and some other TV tonight which has helped the day pass. I've hardly done anything else. It's cold in here today.

15 September 2001 Saturday

Still very tired and yawning all the time. Tried to sleep after breakfast but couldn't. Just like Southampton the fire alarm keeps going off for trivial reasons and the fire crew were here – one just wonders what would happen if there was a real fire, as no one takes it too seriously.

Another fire alarm after lunch – I got offered a salad for the first time since being here! They've got some coffee from the other ward thank goodness. I feel 'blue' and tired. Don't want to get out of bed; been trying to read magazines, but got bored.

Apparently I go to ward 23 (a neurosurgery ward in the main hospital) on Wednesday and back here Friday or Saturday, so in a week it'll all be over. I want to cut an artery but then the op won't go ahead. I don't know what to do with these thoughts.

I've been thinking of how I'll run the house if/when I get home. I do hope it happens, being 1:1 isn't much fun. I have just discovered that L, who was in my room is a doctor and has children too! Had a good long chat with L about our families and illnesses. I'll never tell anyone just to 'hope', though, as SO many people have told me to. It makes it even worse.

16 September 2001 Sunday
Woke a bit later than usual as apparently they don't have breakfast until 10 a.m. on a Sunday. I didn't get mine till 10.30. I was
feeling very impatient. Oh well, now I'm showered, clean sheets on
the bed, Gaviscon, water for the flowers. I'm fed up with Greg – a
N/A. He keeps on laughing and joking.

I watched some TV then went back to lie down. I felt down and
felt an impulse to die. I tried the plastic bag over the head, got
caught and given chlorpromazine and lorazepam – it hasn't
touched me. Hoping that Joy will leave her coke can in the bin so
maybe I can cut myself with it.

Got taken out for a walk round the block by Joy – lovely view. L
came in crying because another patient upset her so we had
another chat and showed each other photos of our families.

I phoned home and spoke to Steph, Jona and Phil and asked
them to tell Simon that I'm missing him – he was at work.

17 September 2001 Monday
Feeling awful and been given chlorpromazine – next problem
reflux, can't bring myself to ask for Gaviscon. Had a card from
Marion, Thelma and Suzie. The nurses insisted on sticking the
banner Suzie sent on the wall.

I've watched the domestics clean the bathroom. If a bug was
going around everyone would get it. The same bucket carries cloth
for loo, cloth for basin and loo brush. She wears the same gloves
and washes the floor around the loo and then the shower floor –
no rinsing between.

18 September 2001 Tuesday
I was taken to the main hospital to have an ECG. We went by taxi,
two escort nurses and a student nurse. I suggested we walk back,
it's not exactly far, but NO, we had to go by taxi. When I got here
I found Phil had arrived (he was coming from Southampton to be
with me for the surgery) and gone off again so I cried. It wasn't
long before he returned but I was well upset. Helen (one of the
nurses) told me the operation was under local anaesthetic. I
flipped, but Phil said to ask a doctor because he was sure it was
wrong. It was and Helen apologised.

Went out for a meal with Phil – I'm going over to ward
23 tomorrow, both Phil and I will see Prof Matthews. It was
nice food but I could only manage one course. I spoke to Mary
but could barely hear what she said except 'we all love you' at the
end.

I need a good night's sleep. Phil prayed. Apparently Graham

Cooke (a church leader) gave an important prophesy about restoring families.

19 September 2001 Wednesday Ward 23
Woken up for breakfast and then had to wait around for an ambulance. Fortunately Phil came in at 10 a.m. so I had company. I'm fed up with being told that everything's going to be OK.

The anaesthetist arrived and asked if necessary could they put the frame on my head under local anaesthetic but I said I wasn't happy so I pray it won't be necessary. I've met the surgeon Mr Eljamel and he gave a brief explanation of the surgery.

Flowers have been sent from Alastair, Mary and Sarah, also Tony and Hannah. The room is nice, with a comfortable state of the art bed with push button controls. There's also a TV. Phil arrived and then Prof Matthews – he stayed and talked for some time.

The surgery is at 8.30 am. I'm trying not to think about it.

I was moved to the neurosurgery ward (ward 23) in time for the operation on the following day, the 20 September 2001. I was to have a Bilateral Anterior Cingulotomy. Mr Eljamel was the consultant neurosurgeon. This is a stereotactic procedure which means that there is a very accurate implantation of two electrodes into this anatomically specific area of the brain – an electric current applied then heats the tips, causing a lesion at that area. In order for this to be carried out successfully, the patient's head is kept still in a frame and scanned with it on. It is from this that the surgeon is able to accurately determine exactly where to place the electrodes. I was told to have a shower and wash my hair first thing in the morning. I had to put on the tight-fitting white stockings known as TED stockings, which help prevent venous thrombosis or blood clots from forming. I was greatly relieved to find that the whole operation would be carried out under general anaesthetic. I had been completely petrified at the thought of being awake for any of it and when there was mention of the frame being put on my head under local, I panicked and almost pulled out. My rather factual diary did not convey this, but I remember thinking that I would refuse. I was really very frightened.

I remember waking up back in the room with a 'turban' on my head. I had the worst headache I had ever experienced and I was given morphine for the pain. Two physios came to get me out of bed, but I was very sick when anyone tried to move me, so they left me alone. I remember Phil visiting briefly. Other than that, I cannot recall any other events of that day.

21 September 2001 Friday
Yesterday was just a blur of headache, sickness and sleep. I'm back at Carseview – much more awake. I've been sick again but I'm very thirsty. I look such a sight, my hair is all stuck down – I can wash it tomorrow.

22 September 2001 Saturday
Feel even worse today but trying to survive on painkillers. I don't feel nauseous anymore but not hungry either. I've had such a terrible headache, neck ache, back ache and swollen left eye. Earlier I had an 'assisted' wash, very grateful as I think the water from the shower would be very painful. I've been sleepy most of the day so Prof Matthews has stopped some of the drugs. Phil came to see me three times today.

I'm worried about my thoughts which are still self-harm but I'm too much in pain at the moment.

Apparently the eye swelling is a CSF leak (the fluid that surrounds the brain and spinal cord) but I have a fever and low blood pressure. The headache is much worse especially when I move. I'm drinking loads. The SHO has gone to phone the neuro-surgeon.

23 September 2001 Sunday
Phil called in to say goodbye – he has to go back home. Afterwards I cried. I've generally felt better today – less headache, more steady on my feet. At last someone has turned the fan off. I felt so cold.

I've been given clonazepam as my legs are agitated.

Still no idea why the temp.

24 September 2001 Monday
I'm feeling much better today but still tired. I've had a bath and hairwash from one of the nurses. My temp is down, but I still have a headache.

My temp is up again. I looked for the razor, couldn't find it and got very upset. It makes me more determined to escape from the DOP when I get back. If only I could get out of here. At least they'll think I'm safe soon.

25 September 2001 Tuesday
Rebecca's birthday – I wish I could ring her. Its only 5 days since the op but it seems like 3 weeks.

I've just had a cry again about the self-harm. Talking to Greg, he says we're all responsible for our actions. I can't cope with the

un-understanding of it. I spoke to Prof Matthews this a.m. and we mostly talked about the last 5 days.

26 September 2001 Wednesday
Everyone keeps saying how much better I look but they can't see what's really going on. I want to buy a Stanley knife. I can't find the blade still. Yesterday I gave up hope and had another crying session. Given lorazepam.

27 September 2001 Thursday 11.45 p.m.
Waiting for lorazepam to work. I've had a busy day. I attacked myself with the ring pull from the can and now being more closely observed. Had a go at the jigsaw – I can't do it. Got a headache. Don't know why I can't sleep apart from the noise.

CHAPTER 24

Light at the end of the tunnel

It was now eight days after the operation. My physical recovery from the surgery was going well. The facial swelling had gone down. I no longer had a fever or headache. However, I had lost my appetite and felt nauseous. Psychologically I felt terrible. I remember making a decision that as soon as I was transferred back to Southampton I would definitely find a way to escape from hospital to go and kill myself. I knew that I could not break out from this ward and even if I did, I would not know where to go. At this time I very much regretted that I had agreed to have the surgery, I thought that I had made a big mistake – although why I thought this I do not know, as I still firmly held the belief that I had now 'tried everything'. I no longer felt any obligation to wait for the possibility of improvement. My impatience to get back home was growing.

> **28 September 2001 Friday**
> I'm not hungry. Saw Prof Matthews this a.m. and he said I'm going to have to continue 'the prison' (my words not his!) when I go back home whether that'll be 'obs' on A ward or back to Mayflower.
> Had the jigsaw out but got fed up. Had a walk round the block in the rain and watched TV. Found it hard to get to sleep again.

This was the day it happened and yet I made no mention of it in the diary! I know why. I could not believe it myself.

I was sitting in the TV room with the nurse beside me quite late in the evening. L, the patient who had shared the room with me before the operation, came in. She had returned from home leave and was clearly fed up. She slumped into a chair, saying, 'All I want is to be at home with my husband and children.' I was thinking 'I wish she would just be quiet' when all of a sudden a light switched on in my head! It was as if a power cable had been connected and the generator had gone on; this tremendous sensation of light blazing through my innermost being happened in an instant. I was amazed, startled, almost bewildered. I started to cry, realising that the darkness had gone, the depression was over! Now I echoed her, all

I wanted was to be at home with my husband and children. I felt completely different and asked to leave the TV room so that I could be alone to assimilate what had happened. (Of course, I could not be truly alone since I was still on 1:1 observation.)

As I left the room, I experienced a very clear internal voice. It did not seem to have come from me at all. 'What about the self harm?' I answered it defiantly. 'I do not want it anymore. I want to be at home with my family'. It left me alone. This happened on several occasions and each time I answered it the same way. After three days it left, never to return again.

At first I was not totally confident that this was a permanent state of mind. I also realised that there was no one I could relate this to. After all, it was a Friday night and the nurse had not seemed surprised at my tears (of relief!) – I could hardly expect her to believe what had happened to me. I was pretty confused myself. I went back to my room and to bed slightly shocked and very puzzled. I remember lying there trying to work it out. I realised that I faced a considerable challenge as the other big revelation to me was that I became aware of where I was. Not just the physical surroundings, but the reality of my situation dawned on me. Here I was in a psychiatric hospital, on a Section in Scotland, 500 miles from home. I had a nurse with me wherever I went including the bathroom and toilet. I became quite anxious. How was I going to get out of this? No wonder I had difficulty getting to sleep that night!

From this day onwards, my memory improved in leaps and bounds. When I returned over a year later for post-operative assessment, I remembered the area, including the way from the Carseview Centre to the University Department of Psychiatry in Ninewells Hospital – no mean feat! But more so I remembered the beautiful rolling hills that surround the town, the view of the Tay river with the sunlight glistening on the water and the small airstrip running just beside it, envious of the light aircraft which could take off at any moment. I continued to write the diary, but only for the next 10 days; now it is only a helpful reminder.

Phil was arriving on Sunday and Rebecca had decided to come and visit me from Germany. The hope was that I would soon be transferred back to Southampton. But Prof Matthews still had the post-operative tests to run, as all his patients were being evaluated both before and after surgery as part of the NMD research programme which he was running in conjunction with Mr Eljamel. I needed to do the videoed interview, the computer-based neuropsychological testing, the re-evaluation by the clinical psychologist and the depression scores. It was hard doing the testing, I was asked about my symptoms in the previous two weeks, but there had been such a change. I wanted to be completely honest and I wanted to qualify my answers, but psychological tests do not give you that liberty. I would also need permission to travel by way of a warrant issued by the Mental

Welfare Commission to return to the jurisdiction of the English Mental Health Act.

Saturday was a real trial. I was *so* bored and impatient waiting for Rebecca and Phil to arrive. I was still reluctant to describe to the staff exactly what had happened to me. It sounded so way out and implausible, but I think they noticed a lightness in my mood. I kept crying with relief and the emotion of it all but I knew that it could be sending out the wrong signals! I told them that I was feeling better but I was not confident enough to say any more than that, mindful that the timescale for recovery was expected to be around 3–6 months. I was still confined to my room for most of the day and had little to occupy myself with. I had a jigsaw with me, but I was not really interested. I was desperate to get out. The room was of a higher calibre compared to the DOP, freshly painted magnolia, but nonetheless easily identifiable as NHS hospital. I was fascinated by the design of the bathroom. There was a small strip on the floor separating the shower area and a plastic curtain. When the shower was used, the water naturally spread as far as it could go, well over the strip, so for the rest of the day, there would be a puddle of water on the bathroom floor. I wondered who was responsible for this great design but at the same time mindful of the tremendous luxury of having an en suite in an NHS mental hospital.

Later I was taken out for my usual walk around the block accompanied by two nurses, I started laughing with them as we watched the decorating of a car taking place for one of the nurses who was leaving. Later I wanted to know how he had reacted to the jam they had placed beneath his car door handles! I would not have been the least bit interested in 24 hours earlier. Now I enjoyed the joke, but more than that I was noticing the weather and enjoying the fantastic views of the river which could be seen from our vantage point on the hillside. I became more and more keen to be taken out for a walk – not easy for the nursing staff on that busy ward to spare the time to go with me.

However, despite feeling so much better, I hated the imposition that the continuous observation caused.

I felt more of a prisoner during those two days after the 'light switched on' than at any time in the illness. Over the months I had really grown quite used to being on 1:1 observation, but now I was shy and I sneaked into the loo without my escort. The first time, the nurse did not seem to notice, but thereafter it became a battle. I started resisting but then thought better of it. After all, I would have to be co-operative and compliant in order that I would be believed when I finally could tell Prof Matthews what had happened – it was a bank holiday weekend so I knew I would have to wait until Tuesday to see him. Later on Saturday evening, I phoned Phil, but I did not know what to say. I was worried that I would just cry with the sense of relief I felt and that I would not be able to explain

myself properly, so I just said 'something has happened'. He was having a meal with our friends the Lloyds at the time and he said that the minute he heard my voice, he knew that there had been a change. I sounded different.

---

29 September 2001 Saturday
I can't wait for Phil and Bec to arrive tomorrow. I have decided that I am not going to harm myself any more. I just want to go home. Thank you, L! I suddenly feel this change. I just want to go home. Thank God and please may I go home next Sunday.

I did the jigsaw all morning and then went for a walk round the block before lunch. The nurses are all playing games and had done up Dave's car; two of them were putting jam under the handles!

I ate lunch in the dining room but I am still feeling sick. My tummy is not right at all. I am just trying to patiently let it settle. I don't think having Bran Flakes for breakfast was a good idea. Never mind! Phil and the kids are going to the Lloyds for a BBQ tonight. I wish I was there and Bec.

I watched quite a lot of TV and then spoke to Phil on the phone and said how I feel. I was able to be quite unemotional about it thankfully. He's coming 5–6 p.m. and I need to get hold of Prof Matthews to confirm that I can go out with him. I'm so looking forward to it. I'm so tired. I've been chatting with L. It's been lovely weather here this evening.

30 September 2001 Sunday
I'm waiting for Phil and Bec – they could arrive any time now! I'm allowed 2 hours out to have tea! I hope they won't be late. The weather's not too bad and I've had a few walks. My tummy is a bit more settled today.

I'm just trying to fill my time. I got up late today, have done jigsaw, crosswords, read book and a rubbish newspaper! I still feel the same but no tears today. I've thrown the can away. (I had kept this as a potential instrument for self harm!)

I went out with Phil and Bec to Nosey Parker (a pub/restaurant) – it was great and lovely to see them. I just keep talking to various nurses about how much better I feel. I can't wait to tell Prof Matthews. I told Mary on the phone, she sounded really sceptical about it. But I just want them to see how different I am. Thank God! I really mean that!

1 October 2001 Monday
Had a great day with Phil and Bec. We went to St Andrews and trotted around, had a sandwich. We then returned to Dundee and

had a little rest at the Guest House where they are staying before going out for supper.

I spoke to my mother and Alastair on the phone. He's engaged to Natasha!

Phil and Bec are going to a film tonight and they're coming over in the morning. I need permission from Prof to take Bec to the airport tomorrow. I also want permission to go to the bathroom alone.

I have asked the nurses to be quiet outside my room tonight – we will see! Often they have been talking which has kept me awake!

3 October 2001 Wednesday
Yesterday: I went for the interview with Prof and managed to tell him how much better I feel. I have been taken off obs, moved to a single room and allowed to go out afterwards. We went to Edinburgh, visited the shops and then took Bec to the airport. It all went without a hitch but I was upset at seeing her go. Afterwards we went and met some friends of Tony's who live in Edinburgh.

On the way home, I spoke to Steph – the travel warrant had arrived at home! Phil had to get her to take it to her singing teacher to fax it to the Guest House. We found another place to have supper and I returned for 8.30 p.m. My room is not warm so I go to bed well wrapped! I met up with L and we had a long chat.

Today: I got up having woken myself at 8.00, showered etc. Last night I slept better except I woke cold in the early hours. I'm a bit fed up with the way the nurses keep on asking how I am, but at least I'm no longer being watched in the bathroom etc.

We went to visit the Discovery and then went back to the Guest House ...

I was so relieved that Prof Matthews did not doubt me. He has told me that he was pleasantly surprised but that he could tell from my face that my experience was genuine – he saw the real me for the very first time! The level of observation was stepped down on that day – my liberation had commenced! I was still very worried about how I was to cope with the continuing expectation of me as a patient. Suddenly being in hospital was all wrong. I was so aware of the situation, so aware of the way I was spoken to and how I was expected to behave. Having to queue for medication seemed belittling, especially now when I was wondering why I even had to take the drugs. I wanted to stay out with Phil in his hotel, but Prof Matthews was not prepared to go quite that far. I was also still on a Section and kept thinking forward to how I was going to cope on my

return to Southampton and the DOP. I was excited and happy at having my life back but very apprehensive of the approaching need to persuade Dr Baldwin that I really was well. The enormity of the situation was sinking in. I still had to go back to the Carseview Centre each evening as a patient when for most of the rest of the day I was living and behaving as a normal person on holiday in Scotland! The very act of walking into the ward and being signed in was increasingly painful. I wondered how any well person would feel if they were in my situation, held against their will in hospital on a Section. Yet I knew that I had to bide my time, be patient, not make a fuss and 'play the game'. I think that's what kept me from being totally ecstatic, as I was gaining confidence in the fact that I really was no longer depressed.

Phil now felt that I was secure enough for him to let me know what had been happening back home without my knowledge. He said that he had been reluctant to tell me since I had been so opposed to the idea of anyone praying for me prior to the surgery. (I had told him that it put me under pressure to 'respond'.) A group of Christians had started meeting together specifically to pray for me. These were not people that I had known; in fact I had never even met them. They did not all come from Southampton or our church even, but had heard about my desperate state and felt called by God to pray for me. They started meeting with Phil at David and Marie's house a short time before my surgery. I was deeply moved by their dedication, that people who did not even know me could do this for me. I felt humbled by their kindness.

---

4 October 2001 Thursday
I've been out with Phil all day. Feeling so much better physically as well as mentally. We went to Glamis Castle, home of the Queen Mother; it was very interesting.

Spoke to Steph and she's out tonight so Jona will be on his own. I've just phoned him and he's OK having his tea. I can't wait until I'm discharged and I admit now that I am worried about sorting out the leave etc. BUT God did not give us a spirit of fear, but of love, peace and of self-discipline 2 Tim 1:7. The Lord has done so much for us, I really must learn to trust Him again, even though it seems such a big thing to me. I want to sleep better tonight, not be so cold. The wind has dropped so hopefully that will be possible.

5 October 2001 Friday
Just two more days to go – I can't wait! I know it'll be back to the DOP but at least it's near home. I can start packing tomorrow. I want to NOW! My hair looks like a Mohican when it's wet with

the hair loss from the glue by the scars! I did sleep better but I heaved on those ghastly tablets again this a.m.

Phil and I saw Prof Matthews: he was telling us all the possibilities and I know he had to but I had to keep saying (not out loud) NOT ME – deteriorating at 3 months when the oedema (swelling) has gone, needing further surgery etc. etc. my overwhelming thought is stick to 2 Tim! He thought that it would be OK for Phil and I to just go home for a little while after we arrive back – but we won't tell anyone, as we should go straight to the DOP! Good. We can see the children and I can unpack.

Apparently Dr Baldwin is in Japan, back next week! Prof Matthews maintains my hopes by suggesting that he (Dr Baldwin) might assess my need for detention and observation from a fresh perspective.

We went to Perth, to Scone Palace. We went out for a nice meal, but I could not eat much. However, I had some wine.

I've been chatting to L most of the evening. Bec phoned and she sounded very cheerful.

I have noticed how discoloured my teeth are and my gums are bleeding – I do hope I haven't neglected them too much. I am also so fat! I don't know how I could have let myself get like this.

6 October 2001 Saturday
My birthday – 42 today. Oh heck! Last complete day here.

Phil took me to St Andrew's and we had a walk, lunch in the pub and read the paper. We were invited to L's house and met her husband and children! She had prepared tea, snacks and a cake for my birthday!

Phil and I at St Andrew's. My smile is back!

CHAPTER 25

What on earth is email?

> 7 October 2001 Sunday
> We had some time before getting to the airport. Phil and I had a
> heated discussion about children's literature!
> The flight was delayed for half an hour, but we got back to find
> Steph had cooked a lovely meal. I couldn't believe that she could
> do this. I guess she's grown up so much. So has Jona!
> I returned to A ward and found that they had given me a single
> room! It was so hard going in, but that pleased me.

I remember the meal, it was lamb cooked with fresh rosemary and in red
wine. It seemed so amazing that my children had grown up so much to be
able to do this. I was so elated until once again the reality dawned that I
still had to go back to the DOP – being back home was only a little detour.

> 8 October 2001 Monday
> Saw Dr Baldwin – he couldn't believe the difference – 'flabber-
> gasted' was his word! Still he didn't let me off the Section, just
> gave me 8 hours accompanied leave at home. I was very disap-
> pointed.
> On the way back to the ward this evening, I became very angry
> and cried. Phil calmed me down.

I remember meeting Dr Baldwin and Dr Harriet Boyd that day; it was
wonderful to see their reaction. I enjoyed being asked about depressive
symptoms, suicidal thoughts and thoughts of self-harm because now I
could say 'no, not me, not now, no longer'. I could be completely honest
and deny any symptoms. I revelled in their surprise and amazement. They
had never seen me well and I was quite determined that I was completely
fine. I understood their reluctance to trust me, after all I had been quite
explicit that my intention was to return to Southampton and end my life.
However, I could not disguise my disappointment at not being discharged

from the Section and hospital at that first meeting. My parents picked me up later that first day and we went and had a meal out at Ocean Village overlooking the yachting harbour before going home. Watching the tranquil water and the swans swimming about with no cares in the world was lovely, but knowing that I had to return to the DOP that evening put a damper on my desire to celebrate. However, my parents were delighted at my progress; my mother's eyes filled with tears repeatedly, so very pleased was she to see me back to my normal self.

After our evening meal, Phil had to take me back to hospital. When we arrived at the DOP, I could not face going back in. I sat with Phil in the car in the car park, crying my eyes out. The hospital seemed a totally alien place. I no longer belonged. I felt completely well but had to return to the environment I hated so much. The previous evening when I had been 'readmitted', a nursing assistant had logged my belongings. She had made comments about what I had brought in with me – 'a box of tissues, we're expecting a cold are we?' I had found it very difficult to keep my feelings hidden. The DOP had been a sanctuary at times during the last few years, which had made life bearable, but now I had no need of that. Phil reminded me that if I entered 'in a state', I would find it much more difficult to convince the staff that I really had recovered. He helpfully suggested that it would only be a few weeks longer. At this I erupted again: 'Weeks! I can't last weeks in there ... ' He hastily tried to retrieve the situation. Eventually I calmed down enough to go back in, drying my eyes, hoping that the recent tears would not show. I found that my belongings had been moved to a bed in a dormitory. My patience was stretched to the limit.

This is the last entry of my diary.

---

9 October 2001 Tuesday
I feel less frustrated, openly, but keep praying that Dr Baldwin will let me go! I just hate it here but am trying to accept that I'll have to be here for a while.

Dr Baldwin let me go! I left hospital with Thelma (Phil's mother). I was so thrilled and I started to become jubilant. I was ecstatic and kept shouting at the world 'yes, yes'. I was like a footballer who had just scored the winning goal. I was over the moon, I had spent my last night ever in the DOP and I practically danced to the car. Despite the fact that I was not 'discharged', either from hospital or from the Section, and had to comply with strict instructions, I was free. I had been released from the captivity of my illness and from the imprisonment it had led me into. Nothing was going to wipe the smile off my face now. I still had to report to the ward daily initially and then the reviews went to twice a week. My CPN Ruth

Stephanie and me. I am so thrilled to be at Sarah's wedding.

started to visit at home. I was instructed that I must still take the prescribed medication for at least one year. I have to say that I had no intention of complying with that!

The following week was my sister Sarah's wedding and I had not even met her fiancé; it felt strange to realise how much of life I had missed. It was wonderful to be able to enjoy getting ready. I was rather perturbed that I had grown out of all my clothes and reluctant to buy new since the aim was to lose some weight, but I had to get myself a new skirt. The wedding was beautiful, Sarah looked stunning and her new husband was charming. I was amazed to meet my sister Mary's two little girls and to be at Mary's manor house for the first time.

When I reported to the ward the following day, Dr Boyd tried to encourage me to slow down. She reminded me that I had been through major surgery. But I could not 'slow down'; I had been sitting doing nothing for the last seven years. Now I was determined to live life to the full.

I was still on a Section, still officially 'on leave' from hospital, but I knew from now on my struggle was downhill. I remained delighted with the freedom and I made several decisions about my day to day life.

1   I would exercise every day to build up my stamina, even if it was just a walk to the shops and back.

2   I would go on a diet – eat three meals a day and only healthy snacks e.g. fruit in between. I was allowed one 'treat' a day.
3   I would stop all medication possible, but comply with what was insisted upon by Dr Baldwin – must lessen his anxieties!
4   I would take over running the house, including cleaning and washing, although I agreed that Phil should continue cooking for the time being.

The biggest challenge of all though was getting to know my husband and children again. The children had grown up so much.

It was very exciting! There was good reason for leaving Phil to do the cooking though. I had not done it for most of the seven years – I couldn't even remember how to use the microwave. I did start to cook after about two weeks, but it was not an easy task after so long. However, there were all sorts of nice surprises in store. I discovered that peeling potatoes for instance was really not a strenuous task. My memory of it, obviously from when I was ill, was that it was a time-consuming, difficult thing to do. I was so proud of myself a few weeks later when I successfully cooked my first shepherd's pie!

Walking down to the local shops was equally a treat. I must have been beaming because not only was I aware of the smiles and greetings of complete strangers but one older man said 'I don't know what you've got to be so happy about!' I accompanied Phil to the club where he had obtained membership to use the swimming pool and soon I was borrowing his bike. Otherwise I had to use the buses to get around as I was not allowed to drive for six months after brain surgery – I realised that cycling was a more efficient and less frustrating way of travel. I was once again finding my way around Southampton, relearning the map, familiarising myself with road names which once I had taken for granted. Cycling was hard work though. I pushed myself, making sure that I did a little bit more on each occasion. I can't say I enjoyed the aching legs and the breathlessness associated with the physical exertion, but I did enjoy the thrill of being able to exercise.

Another challenge was technology, as I realised that advances had passed me by. Even though I had started the word processing course in autumn 2000, I remembered nothing of it. I was like a complete beginner. One day when Phil came home from work and I asked him, 'What on earth is email?' He burst out laughing. I kept hearing people talk about it but had no idea what it was. Phil was very patient as he taught me how to do basic tasks on the computer and before too long he had set up my email account. Once again I was delighted. Similarly I had no idea what the internet was and it took a while to get to grips with the basics. It seemed unbelievable what changes had happened during my 'time away'. That's what it felt like – as though I had been held hostage and now I was

released from my captivity. I wanted to take up where I had left off, but I knew that I had a lot of catching up to do.

Our house had been kept clean by Thelma, but it is a big old Victorian house and she had only been able to do the superficial tasks. I think she was amazing to have done what she did. She had come down to Southampton at least twice a week, armed with meals, homemade biscuits and cakes. She had also tried to keep the garden in check, which was an enormous task. She still came down to visit us and she used to take me supermarket shopping since I could not drive. She was also worried that I was doing too much, but knew me well enough to do no more than express her anxiety!

I started on the serious business of 'spring cleaning'. I enjoyed this as well, but sensibly only took on one room per week. We realised that redecoration was also required throughout most of the house but that our limited budget could not stretch to that at the present time. However, I was back as the 'home maker' and relishing my new role.

One thing I found very puzzling was seeing myself in the mirror. My abdomen was covered in scars, my arms also, but to a lesser extent. It looked such a mess. How could I have done this to myself? It felt unreal. I could not relate to it at all. I would stare at myself in amazement. Me? Why? I didn't want to remember the thoughts and feelings that led up to the assault upon my body – I buried the diary notebooks at the back of a drawer. I was only interested in how I felt at the present time and I was not going to betray myself by delving into what I now saw as the past. I started to try to remove any reminders. Fortunately, I was losing weight, which gave me the excuse to buy new clothes, but I systematically started to get rid of anything that triggered the bad memories of the last few years. This purge of the past extended not only to everyday wear such as my dressing gown and coat but also to many of my possessions. We also decided to take on the task of redecorating the house from top to bottom – this was the sign of my fresh start.

Through all this activity, I was not as sensitive as I could have been to Phil's reaction to this sudden change. He was exhausted and I was impatient. I had been doing next to nothing for years and now was full of energy. Quite often I would tactlessly ask him why he was not celebrating as I was. I did not fully appreciate the trauma that he had been through himself. I had recovered in an instant and I could not understand why those around me were not 'bouncing back' with the same rapidity! We had a turbulent time. We had not talked properly for years. I had been meek and mild and suddenly I was back to my old self, which meant forthright and opinionated. We struggled to relate to each other again. Many people asked both Phil and me, was I the same Cathy, had my personality altered? The answer was 'no', but inevitably our life circumstances had changed us both to some extent. We fought each other and argued frequently, but

fortunately we were able to resolve our differences. It came down to the basics; did we love each other still? We were both able to reassure each other that yes, we did! We had been through so much; we were not going to give up on one another now. Prof Matthews had warned us that this might happen. We have great admiration for his wisdom.

I don't know to what extent the children were aware of our conflict. They weren't really children any more. Rebecca was living in Germany, still working as a professional ballet dancer. Simon was in his last year at Sixth Form College. Stephanie was doing her GCSEs at a local comprehensive. Jonathan was a few years below her.

I did not see much of Simon and when I did he was not very communicative. He had seemed really pleased with my return home but was very involved with his group of friends and his work at the local shop. We had not guessed that he was using cannabis on a daily basis. I was concerned that he did not seem bothered by his A levels approaching and that he did not seem to have any motivation to study. He listened to my worries and acknowledged them, but he made little response and seemed uninterested in what he would be doing after his exams were over. He was a friendly boy and seemed very laid back. He clearly had an active social life and he did not seem unhappy. I told myself not to worry. I had missed his teenage years so it was not surprising that he was having some problems sorting out his future. I was naïve and ignorant about what was really going on.

Stephanie on the other hand was very conscientious with her studying for GCSEs. It was not easy for her as she had joined the school mid-way through courses, which were different to what she had been studying at White Lodge. She and Rebecca seemed to show the most overt delight at my recovery out of all our family. We spent hours talking together and she told me all about her friends and social life; she described to me why she had the change of heart in regard to dancing and that she had several non-dance career aspirations. She admitted to me how hard she had found her last few years and how much she had missed me. I realised that we have similar personalities and occasionally we had our clashes. However, I felt that was healthy, a sign of return to normality.

Jonathan had changed a great deal. He had just had his thirteenth birthday and was so independent. He also seemed quite resentful when I started using my motherly powers to tell him what to do! I remember demanding that he go to bed 'right now'. He glared at me as he stomped up the stairs. A couple of days later, he rang the doorbell when he got home from school. I answered it but to my surprise he would not come in. As he stood there on the doormat, he asked me 'are you ever going back to *that* hospital?' I shook my head and answered him: 'No, never.' He took a huge breath, breathed a sigh of relief and came in. From that moment on, his attitude changed towards me and I was able to become a mother to him once again.

I went back to church and beamed at everyone who asked me how I was. It was really strange going back. I looked around at the large congregation and realised that there were a lot of new faces. I was introduced to people who asked me whether I was new to the church. Once again, a reminder of just how much of life I had missed. There were children now grown up, new babies born to young people who I didn't even know had married. After three weeks I asked permission to stand up in front of the congregation and tell them what had happened to me. There were about 600 people seated in the main auditorium of Central Hall. They all clapped loudly at the end and I appreciated the opportunity to say thank you to those who had prayed for me and although they were not there at the time, I was also able to publicly thank the doctors and nurses who had helped me through the illness. Without them, I would not be here to write this book. I had surgery to my brain, but it seemed as though an incredible acceleration in the recovery process had occurred. I believed that God had stepped in and his healing touch had been upon me. No one could give me any medical explanation for what had happened, but whatever anyone believes, there is no doubt that something truly remarkable had put me back into life without the need for any of the extensive rehabilitation programme which had been planned.

CHAPTER 26

Future considerations

I was encouraged by Dr Baldwin to keep the appointment with Joyce for CBT (Cognitive Behaviour Therapy). I was refusing most of their suggestions and felt a certain obligation to 'co-operate'. I had turned down input from an occupational therapist as I felt I didn't need one, neither did I want any assistance from social services. I was also reluctant to continue taking the antidepressants. I discussed going to CBT with my GP and he advised me to go to see her, if only to tell her what had happened. I certainly had not felt that I had clicked with this lady in the couple of sessions before the operation and so it was with some reluctance that I attended the first appointment. I entered her office and sat down with my – by now normal – smiling face. Joyce was to me the archetypal psychotherapist. She was late middle-aged, wore long skirts, had her long hair in a bun and had dangly earrings. She asked me how I was and I replied 'very well, thank you!' She looked puzzled if not a little perturbed. She then went through the routine of trying to tease out any residual depressive symptoms but I denied any of these. She looked very thoughtful and finally admitted that she had never seen anyone after neurosurgery and wasn't quite sure of what she should be doing with me. In addition she was not sure that there was any therapy for someone with no symptoms. I found this answer simply delightful! She asked me for more detail of what exactly had happened, but it did not give her any further clues. I could tell that I was presenting her with a dilemma. Finally she decided to talk about how I dealt with normal, everyday experiences which had a negative aspect to them. She decided that she would like me to think about this and do a diary for the next meeting in two weeks. I was to write down any negative experience and how I dealt with it. I agreed to do this but felt very uneasy. Joyce was quite a dominating lady and I felt a little intimidated by her.

When I left, I changed my mind as I knew that I could not go through with this. I had no desire to concentrate on any negative aspects to life! I had done that for the last seven years, now was a time to move on. I also felt that this was not a normal thing to do and since I was determined to live as normal a life as possible, I decided that I could not do what she had asked.

I returned for the next appointment two weeks later. She had now 'got her act together', had lost her initial hesitation and was completely in

control. But I had not done my homework and Joyce was not amused. There followed a rather heated discussion. I told her that I was not prepared to spend my life analysing my responses to various situations. I thought that she did not in fact believe that I was really well and symptom-free. Her response was 'you have fallen off your horse once; you will do so again.' I knew from that moment that I could not see this lady again. I would not make another appointment with her and a few days later phoned up her secretary and asked to be fully discharged from the psychotherapy service. I was angered by her attitude, particularly as I felt that she was trying to put the blame on me for my depression and also I could not cope with her pessimistic outlook. Joyce did not seem delighted at my recovery and that was something I failed to understand. Even if my assessment of the situation was not entirely reasonable, it was clear that she had little respect for either my autonomy or my wishes.

I tried to contact Lee. This was not because I wanted help but because I wanted to 'show myself off' to her. In the end I had to make an appointment. When I met with her, she seemed overwhelmed. She listened to my account and looked at me with an air of disbelief. As I rose to go, she was in tears and she shook her head. 'I'm sorry I couldn't help you' is what she said. It was my turn to be flabbergasted. She had helped me so much. She was wonderful in just being there for me, listening week after week. She had been incredibly patient and very kind. I am very grateful to this lady. I just wished that the psychological therapies service would at least acknowledge that their treatments and physical treatments were and are not mutually exclusive. I had sensed antagonism before I was well and my recent experience confirmed that this had still not been resolved. In fact I heard that both the psychotherapists were of the opinion that my recovery was purely a 'placebo' response to the operation. How wrong they were!

Unfortunately the psychotherapists were not the only people to doubt my recovery. I found it very trying whenever I met or heard from people who with the best of intentions would ask 'are you *still* well?' Part of it was that as the weeks passed, I wanted to shut off the experience I had been through, to close the door on that period in my life. I wanted to move on. But I also hated the expectation that I could possibly relapse. I remember one particular occasion shortly after one of Stephanie's friends had been tragically killed. We sat together in church both weeping as we could not put it out of our minds. Some time later, a lady said to me 'I'm so sorry to see that you are unwell again.' Since it is such a large congregation, I did not know this lady well. She was referring to this occasion when she saw me weeping! The fact that later on in the meeting, I had asked the leaders if I could lead the congregation in prayer for this girl's family had passed her by. I was hurt by her assumption and rather too brusquely informed her that I had a right to mourn a tragic death as much as anyone else.

However, the experience has made me wary of expressing emotion openly. I hate this sort of misunderstanding.

We had a final CPA meeting at my home.(We had been having these regularly through my illness, during the periods of time that I was discharged.) I did a depression rating scale with Dr Baldwin and jokes were made about how the staff were more depressed than I was! I found it uncomfortable when they got to the bit in the form where they had to identify signs of relapse. I was convinced that this would never happen to me again. In fact I could not tolerate even the thought of becoming depressed ever again. When I was asked what I would do, I could not understand the routine nature of the question. I felt like a prisoner who had just been released from Belsen. Would you ask one of them what they would do if they knew they were about to return? I told them straight out. I would find a very high building and jump off. I did not do myself any favours. It probably made Dr Baldwin more nervous, but thankfully he said that he understood. I was grateful for that and they pressed me no further. Later on I realised that committing suicide did remain an 'escape plan' which I kept to myself. I then had to do business in my prayer life and I agreed to surrender my future to God. I agreed with him that if I thought that this dreadful illness was returning I would get on my knees and pray. He had seen me through this; I could trust him for the future also. There are times when I have had to remind myself of this.

I continued to see Ruth at home and Dr Baldwin in the outpatient clinic. I left them in no doubt that I was completely symptom-free. I liked seeing Ruth as she was so delighted at the transformation, but before long I felt that I was wasting her time. With some reluctance I asked her to discharge me! Likewise, seeing Dr Baldwin was not difficult. It gave me such pleasure to be able to answer negatively to all the symptoms that could occur in depression. However, I was finding it increasingly hard to comply with taking the medication. Once I had been so scared to miss a single dose, now I hated the very act of swallowing the tablets. I admit I maximised the side effects and felt wholly justified when I told him that I had stopped one of the antidepressants which was making me a little drowsy in the daytime. I was now left on one antidepressant and did agree that for the purposes of the research trial for NMD of which I was part, I would take it for one year. But even with this I decreased the dose and had weaned myself off it by nine months. I hated taking medication!

Phil and I were asked if we would attend a case presentation at the DOP so that the medical staff could ask us questions about our experience. I was delighted to be able to do so.

Since the autumn of 1994 I had suffered with severe depression:

- I had been admitted to five different hospitals, under the care of seven consultant psychiatrists.

- I had been on 13 different classes of drugs.
- I had ECT more than 100 times.
- I had psychotherapy at least once a week for seven years.
- I had involvement from occupational therapists, social workers and carers in the community.
- I had nursing involvement from three CPNs.
- I had spent a total of $4\frac{1}{2}$ years in hospital, $2\frac{1}{2}$ years of which was on a Section 3.
- I was first referred for NMD in December 1999.
- Eighteen months later I had the operation.
- Eight days after the operation, a sudden change took place.
- Seven years later, at last, I was well!

My diet was going well and I was losing weight, I was exercising every day. The house was becoming more like home as I tidied, sorted and spring-cleaned. I had made a start on the decorating. I was getting to know Simon, Stephanie and Jonathan again. Phil and I invited friends over and we were having dinner parties every week. We made new friends as well as catching up with old friendships. Christmas 2001 was really special and Rebecca was able to fly over from Germany to join us.

I was thinking about my future career. Phil was very settled in his job and he earned a good salary. However, we were in debt from the financial strain of the past few years. We did not feel that it was right for me to continue to receive Disability Living Allowance, since I was no longer disabled! I wrote a letter to the DSS informing them of my recovery. They replied with a form. Well, it was more than a form, it was a booklet used for assessing the client's need, to determine whether or not they needed support. I left it blank and wrote to them again. 'I do not need DLA as I am now completely well.' Shortly afterwards a letter arrived at our home. I opened it.

'We regret to hear of the death of Dr Cathryn Wield ... '

I phoned them up, laughing, and informed them that I was very much alive!

I enrolled on a theology and bible study course at the church which took one day of my week, but I also decided that I should start preparing to return to medicine. I was warned by medical and nursing friends that a lot had changed in the seven and a half years that I had been away. I was left wondering whether I should retrain in a completely different field of medicine. I thought that I had only one area of experience over those years – psychiatry. I bought relevant textbooks and read them. I started to read general medical journals as well and had to agree that enormous advances had been made, not just in technology and drugs, but even in the training

of junior doctors. It did seem daunting. I knew that I would prefer to work part-time because I still needed to be at home for the children. I was certainly not going to compromise our family life after the last seven years.

In February 2002, I applied for a post in psychiatry of the elderly and was shortlisted. This was very encouraging since I had submitted my CV which of course included my $7\frac{1}{2}$-year gap (career break is the politically correct term!). I had explained my absence from medicine, thinking that it was wiser to be open and honest about my illness rather than leave people guessing. After all I had fully recovered. But I did not know that when the job advertisement stated that 'part-time applicants are welcome to apply', it was just political talk. I was very disappointed when the interview committee called me in to say that they wanted a full-time doctor. However, they were very encouraging and told me that I had interviewed well.

Shortly after this I was able to start driving again. It was wonderful to start up the old mini and I was exhilarated as I drove around. I used any excuse to drive the car, so the children had no trouble getting lifts from me. I have to say that did not last too long, but since Simon was 17, I decided to teach him to drive, with the added benefit that I was much cheaper than an official driving instructor!

As a result of this job application I had asked Lynn Williams, my consultant back in 1994, for a reference. A letter arrived from her – she had been surprised to hear from me after so long, even more so that I was applying for a psychiatry post. We had a telephone conversation during which she assured me that it would be perfectly possible to return to A&E and positively encouraged me to do so. She arranged for me to meet a colleague who lived locally since she had herself moved away by this time. Her colleague seemed a little less certain of the wisdom of my return, but nonetheless he arranged for me to become a clinical observer at Southampton General A&E.

I think I had good reason to be apprehensive: after all, I had failed at my last attempt and since then I had been taken there as a patient on how many occasions? Of that I was not sure. By the time this was arranged it was April 2002. I tried to work it out: the last time I would have been a patient was now over six months ago. Nobody would remember me surely. Anyway, I had lost weight, had my hair cut and I was told that my whole demeanour was different. Junior doctors change their posts every six months, so ... I persuaded myself that I could do this.

Just a few days before I was due to start I remembered Anna. Anna was a lovely doctor who had worked in A&E for very many years as a staff grade. I used to be good friends with her and so I thought now was the ideal time to renew our acquaintance. I gave her a ring but she was not in so left a message with her husband. I phoned again later that day and Anna came to the phone. She was clearly shocked. She told me how she

had thought I was dead. She had heard about the awful self-harm and had been in the department on occasions when I had been brought in. When my visits stopped, she just assumed that I had died ... I told her of my plans to return as an observer. She questioned my judgement of the situation. 'Surely they won't remember me, will they?' I asked innocently. She put me right. I had been notorious, a 'regular', everyone knew who I was.

This was sobering. How was I going to cope with my return now, I wondered? I had already made the arrangements. I decided that I would just have to be brave and go for it. After all, I had been ill. It was not my fault, was it? No, they needed to know that 'normal' people can become ill and do these awful, weird things to themselves, but then recover. I was going to make a stand. I needed to do this not just for myself, but for the sake of others who are mentally ill. It was then that I knew I must start to fight against the stigma which surrounds mental illness. I decided that I would be open about it; I would not try and cover up my dark years. I remembered the previous experience with Occupational Health so I decided to pre-empt it this time. I asked Dr Baldwin to write to them and confirm that I was recovered and I managed to get the paperwork sorted out before I started.

I walked to Southampton General Hospital for my first day as a clinical observer. I was incredibly nervous, mentally rehearsing how I would cope if I was recognised. I wondered whether it would evoke memories of my visits, which until that point were few and far between. As I walked up the hill to the hospital, I kept saying to myself over and over again: 'It's OK, you were ill. You're well now. Lift your head up high, there's nothing to be ashamed of. Look at what God had done for you. You have every right to be here ... ' When I walked in, I felt like Daniel in the lion's den. It seemed as though all eyes were turned on me. Momentarily I wanted to run. The reality was that most of the staff did not know me – what a relief – but then I caught the eye of one of the nurses whom I had known all those years ago even before I was ill. She stared at me with a look of disbelief on her face and then walked away. I kept repeating to myself: 'Hold your head up high; you have every right to be here.' I was shown around the department and then left with one of the SHOs.

The department had changed radically since I had last worked there almost eight years before. It had been renovated, something I had been oblivious to as a patient. As well as the refurbishment, there were clearly far more staff and it seemed an awful lot more busy. When I left there were only two consultants, now there were four. I had only met one of the current consultants and I was glad that he was unaware of the connections I had with the department. Suddenly I had to start being a doctor again. I had thought my role as an observer would be just that, an 'observer', but the SHO I was with was having none of it. She suggested that I go and see a patient and present my findings to her ... I was thrown in at the deep

end. I had no choice but to sink or swim and I was determined that I would swim. I was not being paid since I was there purely for educational purposes which at least meant I could dictate my hours. I made it through until lunchtime and then excused myself. It had been a very nerve-racking morning but I had done it – I had survived my first step back into medicine! When I got back home I frantically got out my books on emergency medicine; they seemed woefully inadequate and out of date but nonetheless my programme of study began. Over the next few weeks I began to settle in. There were several nurses that I had known and I started to be able to talk to them. After two or three days, one of the sisters came up to me and said, 'Welcome back. It's good to see that you're the same old Cathy!' That was music to my ears.

Phil was called away on a business trip to the Bahamas. Once again I had the opportunity to accompany him. It was very tempting but this time I had other commitments.

CHAPTER 27

A taste of the past

Being an observer in A&E was just what I needed to feed my enthusiasm to get back to work. On my second day there, it was characteristically very busy. One of the SHOs was looking very hassled and my instinct was always to 'help out' even if it meant mundane tasks such as filling out x-ray request forms. She had another idea. There was a paramedic who was in the department to acquire skills in putting up intravenous lines. Claire asked me to help him. Before I had time to say that I had not actually done so myself for quite a while, she was gone. I decided that I could at least watch him. It turned out that he was extremely nervous and was visibly trembling. Not surprisingly, the attempt was a failure and he asked me to take over. I did so and without any problem sited the line. He looked at me with admiration, the patient looked at me with gratefulness. This was so good for my confidence and self-esteem. I was not just about to admit that it was my first time in over seven years!

I started to see patients but had to report to one of the doctors to check my work. It was a bit like being a medical student again, but that did not last long. After six weeks, I was asked to do a locum and at the beginning of August 2002, I started work as a flexible trainee SHO (flexible training in medicine means part-time). It had only taken seven and a half years to get there!

This was timely. I had once again entertained the sensible option of finishing off my GP training as I had only six months to go, but I had received a letter back from the JCPTGP (the central body which regulates GP training) which curtly stated that if I wished to become a GP, I would have to repeat all of my previous training. I was shocked and dismayed. Fortunately, the faculty of A&E medicine were more lenient and encouraged me to return to the speciality and continue where I had left off. I was very grateful for this, particularly as it enabled me to go ahead and sit my postgraduate A&E examinations within a year of my return to medicine. I also received encouragement and support, both from the nursing staff and from the consultants in the department, in particular from Diana Hulbert, who had faith in me even when all the odds seemed stacked against me! I am very grateful to all of them.

As I settled into the work at Southampton General Emergency Department, my confidence increased and I found myself once again enjoying my

work. However, there were many different sorts of surprises in store for me. One day I was treating an elderly gentleman who had crashed his car. He was not seriously injured but admitted to me that he knew his health had not been good and he had had several episodes which could be fits. He had not reported these to his GP in the knowledge that he might be prohibited from driving. Just then his son arrived and entered the curtained off bay that we were in. We immediately recognised one another. He was one of the nurses from B ward – one of the really good ones. He asked me to reprimand his father and forbid his driving. He had been trying to persuade him to stop for several weeks. It would be easy now since the car was a write-off. It felt unreal, this sudden role reversal, and I left the hospital at the end of my shift elated!

There were several occasions when I met patients from the DOP who came to A&E for treatment. Some I remembered and tried to avoid, like George, but some I did not, like poor 'S', whose suffering continued. I also met them in the street or when shopping. I found it very difficult, particularly because without exception none of these acquaintances would readily believe that I was well. An especially memorable occasion occurred recently when I was accosted in West Quay shopping centre. A woman came up to me and said loudly 'You were in the DOP with me, weren't you?' I looked around hoping that no one I knew was nearby. I had no memory of her but politely told her that although that might have been the case, I did not remember and I was completely well now. 'You can't be' she said. 'No one ever gets well. No one gets better.' I assured her that I had and hurriedly excused myself, feeling very uncomfortable and yet a little ashamed that I did not want to associate with her.

Sometimes working in A&E brought me face to face with my past, particularly when I had to deal with patients in similar circumstances to those I had been in. I remember seeing an elderly gentleman who had taken a near-fatal overdose. He was upset that he had been found and was still acutely suicidal. I did my best to reassure him that he would be cared for with respect and that his dignity would be preserved. I was trying to explain depression to him and in particular how his illness was treatable. He would feel differently in a few weeks time is what I told him. However, he persisted in his wish to die and I knew that he would be sectioned once he had recovered from the physical effects of his overdose. I am glad that he did not know just how much I empathised with him.

The other major difficulty I faced in A&E was negative attitudes expressed towards patients attending after an act of self-harm. The problem which all of us face is that a number of patients who come to A&E either after an overdose or after a physical act such as cutting are not depressed. People do these things for a variety of reasons and often it is not easy to unravel what lies behind this act. There is a subgroup of patients who will do so on a regular basis and they become quite well known to the depart-

ment. I was of course one of them. However, unlike me, some of them have done this for most of their lives in one way or another. They are quite well in between episodes and for some it has become part of their life style or life habit. This latter group is particularly difficult for A&E staff to deal with.

An example of this came home to me one day.

A lady came into our department claiming that she had taken a massive overdose of paracetamol. Even though it was the middle of the day, she was still in her nightdress. She was curled up on the trolley, crying profusely. Her boyfriend was with her. She was very reluctant to talk but gave me good indication that she was depressed and that she had not sought out any help for her symptoms. She said that she had never done anything like this before and that if she could, she would go off and repeat the overdose. I was very worried about her. I spent almost an hour trying to get her to agree to have blood taken to confirm her massive overdose and then to start her on the antidote. She eventually agreed. When I had taken the blood sample, she then ran out of the department just dressed in her pink nightie! Our security porters were unable to stop her and so we had to give her description to the police and hope that she could be brought back safely for treatment. In the meantime her paracetamol levels came back – they were not raised which confirmed that she had not taken a dangerous overdose after all. It turned out that she was using another name as she was recognised by one of the mental health team nurses who happened to see her flee. The police brought her back. She had a glint in her eye. She seemed to be enjoying this. It was almost as if it was a game. It turned out that her boyfriend had no idea that she had done this before. In fact she had done this many, many times before. Sadly, despite counselling and various other treatments this was a habitual behaviour that she indulged in. Initially I was furious. I understood the comments my colleagues were making and I joined in – 'time waster', 'manipulative', 'scheming' ... I could not believe that I had been so naïve and spent so much time with her. I felt betrayed and angry. Here I was trying to promote a culture of respect and tolerance to people who self-harm, and then one patient could destroy even my moral high ground.

It challenged my thinking, it challenged my beliefs. I knew that I must not let this lady ruin the care that I gave to any patient who presented in this way. I also knew that I needed to at least try and understand what drove her to this extraordinary behaviour. It made me look at myself again and think back to the way I had been treated. It made me wonder why I had repeatedly harmed myself. It was not easy to think about and I wondered what on earth people thought about me when I had attended A&E. I did not want to know.

Fortunately my angry feelings soon dissipated. Once again I took on the role of patient's advocate only this time I had to deal with attitude expressed by an orthopaedic registrar. One Sunday afternoon a young man

called Peter came into our department. He had dislocated his patella (kneecap) earlier that day and been seen at another hospital, who had placed his leg in a plaster cast. He came to us with severe pain. As part of my assessment of all patients, I ask them as a matter of course whether they have any medical problems and what medication they take. He suffered with mild depression and was on antidepressants. I recorded this in the notes as I would any answers to these questions. What a mistake that was – well, from the patient's point of view anyway. It turned out that despite the plaster, Peter's patella was still out of place. His knee was grossly swollen and I needed to give him morphine to relieve his pain. He was a large man and neither myself nor the consultant could get his patella back into position. I had to refer him to the orthopaedic registrar on call. He came down and before seeing the patient, read the notes. The note about depression clearly struck a chord with him. 'I don't know why we can't call them loonies, that's what they are. Mad, completely mad. Nutcases! He's not in pain, he's just a nutter!' I was appalled and was glad that we were out of earshot of the patient. Fortunately the x-rays convinced him that the patient needed orthopaedic assistance, but it made little difference to the prejudicial attitude that had been displayed. If this is the way 'educated' professionals behave, then what hope is there for the rest of society? But in fact I suspect that a large majority of the general public would have been dismayed if they had witnessed this shenanigan. For me, I knew that I had work to do. I have to speak out about my own experience. Stigma and discrimination against people who through no fault of their own are unwell must stop!

There is also some satisfaction to be gained when I have been able to talk to patients who are suffering from depression, knowing that I can honestly say to them that with the right treatment, they will get better. I tell my patients that the brain is a very complicated organ and unfortunately it can go wrong just like other parts of the body. There are many different treatments and I was one of the unfortunate few who did not respond, most people do. I am sympathetic but optimistic in my approach.

I was quite distressed to come across gross ignorance this time from a church attender. He asked me how I was getting on being back at work. I replied positively as usual, but he had his own agenda. 'It must be difficult dealing with you know the, hmm ... ' – he hesitated – 'mentally ill and all their violence.' I felt like he had just struck me across the face! I was stunned. 'It's not the mentally ill who are violent,' I exclaimed, 'you can blame alcohol if you want something to attribute it to.' I was so irritated by this and part of me was left wondering – he knew I had been ill myself, so why did he say that ... ? Then I thought of the media coverage and even some of my favourite detective programmes like Frost or Morse. Every series will have at least one episode where the murderer is depicted as a psychiatric patient. This leaves people with the impression that violence is

commonly committed by mentally ill patients when in fact the reverse is true, it's rare. Most murders are committed within the home and most violence is related to alcohol. Yes, there is a great need for education!

CHAPTER 28

Postscript

Wouldn't it be wonderful if every story had a happy ending! However, life can seem a never-ending struggle for some people. Our time since my recovery has not been easy, but we have also had the privilege of seeing the children enter new walks of life. Rebecca met Ben in Germany and is now married to him. She has developed insulin-dependent diabetes and so continues to live the uncertain life of a professional dancer, now back in England.

Simon became a Christian, he gave up cannabis and his life changed as he gained a new perspective. After a year spent as a volunteer doing youth work, he has gone on to university and is hoping to train as a teacher.

Stephanie had given up on ballet but after her first year at sixth form college realised that she just had to dance. She was able to identify that her aspirations were not purely for classical ballet and chose to audition for the school of her choice, Central School of Ballet. This is giving her the broad base that she requires, which opens up more opportunity, with a diversity not available from the Royal Ballet School.

Jonathan also decided to become a Christian, is enjoying all sorts of sporting activities and is just about to take his GCSEs. However, all of us have had different struggles to get where we are today. We have had to learn to be a family again. We have had to cope with our memories as I have been writing this and it has not been easy.

For me, many good things have happened. Work has gone well for me. Despite the rather harrowing events that I have described, I have enjoyed being back in my job. I like the variety of patients who come for many different reasons, varying from sprained ankles to heart attacks. It's good to work in the A&E multidisciplinary team and, although the shifts can be tiring, for me there has been a real satisfaction in returning to the career that I had to leave behind so many years ago.

I have managed to pass my postgraduate examinations and with support and encouragement, applied for and was appointed as a specialist registrar in A&E in November 2004. However, Phil and I knew that writing this book was going to be a challenge. When I started writing this, I had not imagined what an impact revisiting the past would have. Seeing my notes was very difficult, as was reading the diary. There have been many occa-

sions where I wanted to give up, but I knew that once this process had started, I needed to complete it.

I have met and spoken to key people involved in my care – Andrew Eva, Ruth Paley, Prof Chris Thompson, Dr David Baldwin and Prof Keith Matthews. I have heard them tell me of the gloomy prognosis before surgery and how surprised and delighted they have been by my rapid recovery. But I also learnt how treating me was very difficult for them as people. I was not an easy patient and they found it hard to see not only my suffering but that of Phil and the children. I had no idea that I had caused sleepless nights and despair for some of them. I had not given enough credit to just how much care and attention I had received from the medical services. Reading the notes was especially painful.

After a few weeks of sleeping particularly badly, I began to realise that perhaps I was experiencing some depressive symptoms. I looked back at the past three and a half years and realised just how wonderful it had been to live life totally free of this. I hated admitting that there could possibly be a relapse, but was grateful that I was able to have the reassurance and support of both Prof Matthews and Dr Baldwin. This minor episode was short in length and as soon as sleep returned, I felt better. It has made me realise that I am not invincible! I still possess vulnerability for this condition.

However, I am grateful that help is available and more so that there are men and women who have made it their life's work to tackle this potentially fatal disease, despite inadequate resources, despite lack of understanding, despite stigma. I am especially grateful to Prof Matthews, Mr Eljamel, the neurosurgeon who performed the operation and the team in Dundee who continue their research into NMD. They gave me my life back! Thank you. I am grateful to all the psychiatrists who treated me, but especially Prof Chris Thompson and Dr David Baldwin, who did everything they could to treat the illness before referring me for surgery. I know they sectioned me and gave me treatment against my will but it was right to do so. I am alive and well today as a result.

I am grateful to the nursing staff at the four psychiatric hospitals that I was treated at, please don't lose heart and remember just how much your kind words mean to patients in your care. I am grateful to Southampton General Emergency Department for patching me up so many times and then for having me back and supporting me in pursuit of my present career.

I hope that everyone who reads this will understand just a little bit more about just how easy it can be to put labels on people when we do not understand the circumstances around their life and being. I want stigma to stop. Please join me by talking about it! I want people to put their hands up and say: 'Yes, I've seen it, I've experienced mental illness, but I'm a normal person!' In this way, perhaps, understanding and tolerance may

increase. The medical services will get the resources they need and the hidden suffering will decrease. For those who continue to suffer, their friends, relatives and carers – don't give up. You may never know from when or where the breakthrough will come.

Life after darkness – a family photo at Rebecca's wedding, August 2004.

In sickness and in health

Phil Wield

It has been an interesting, sometimes difficult, task to relive these memories. After three years, it already seems to me like a different, distant world but it has been important to come to terms with the past and to empathise with those who suffer the same experience.

Like Cathy, I think our children were our salvation. The desire to care for them, and the realisation that this situation was more frightening for them than for me, gave my life a structure and purpose to keep going.

During this time I only attempted to keep regular contact with a small number of close friends; I was fortunate to have their support. I know that some people find it difficult to talk to someone who is going through a dreadful experience because they don't know what to say. I realise now that when I am in the opposite situation, I don't need to have the right thing to say. I don't pretend to know what they are going through, all I can do is show friendship, and not cut them off by being embarrassed or feeling guilty about their predicament.

I was also very fortunate to have understanding managers at work. I knew that when a crisis phone call came, I could just disappear and explain later. This meant that I could function normally at work, which also helped me to cope with life as a whole.

When talking to people after Cathy got better, especially those who cared for her, we have been struck by how many are surprised that our marriage survived the illness. As well as the factors I have mentioned, it was important that we had medical people who recognised that we were a family under threat, not just a patient.

It is also important to say that the recovery period has also been a stressful time for different reasons. Like two people separated by war, we were two individuals who had to learn to live and relate together again. Although people admired the fact that I had not left Cathy, I had not been a perfect husband and I emerged from the seven years mentally exhausted and dazed.

We have spent the ensuing three years forging a new relationship which I think will be stronger because of what we have been through. We have had to forgive each other for things in the past and agree to move on and make a new life together. I believe that is the challenge of suffering: to be

beaten by it or to use it to make life a richer, deeper experience. For me that is the truth of Christian faith: not a crutch against a painful world, but a weapon to take charge of it.

June 2005

A doctor's view

David Baldwin

A resolute approach to treating depression

Recovery from depression can take a long time. Although the vast majority of patients (around 80%) recover from an episode of depression within two years, longitudinal studies suggest that approximately 10% of patients remain troubled by depressive symptoms, even after 15 years. Research indicates that patients with chronic depression (i.e. symptoms that have lasted more than two years) have the highest rates of social and occupational impairment, greater psychiatric co-morbidity (for example, higher rates of coexisting anxiety disorders or alcohol abuse) and an increased risk of suicide and non-fatal self-harm.

One of the factors known to be predictive of chronicity in depression is 'inadequate' treatment. Despite public education and professional training campaigns, many depressed patients still do not receive treatment, even when it is clear that they are likely to benefit from it. Sometimes depressed patients are 'treated', but with approaches that are not evidence-based. In others, effective treatment is recommended, but either prescribed or taken at doses that are insufficient, or for periods that are too short. But when a patient has received a succession of evidence-based treatments (pharmacological and psychological) at an adequate dosage and for a reasonable time, and still remains troubled by significant depressive symptoms, all sorts of additional problems can ensue.

One problem is that people start to question the diagnosis. Health professionals start referring to 'personality issues', and patients can acquire the diagnosis of personality disorder, even when it is clear that there were no such 'issues' prior to the onset of depression. Theories develop as to why the patient might wish to remain depressed. Some patients and their relatives find themselves wondering whether some underlying physical illness has been overlooked; others become convinced that prescribed antidepressant treatment is in fact worsening the depression, rather than attempting to relieve it. Worse still, staff members can begin to fall out, with strongly held but widely differing views as to whether depression is indeed present, how it might have arisen, and how it should be most effectively treated. Focus is lost, the team is split, and the patient suffers further.

I believe that much success can be achieved in caring for patients with chronic depression, providing the focus remains fixed on achieving recovery, staff members work together in an atmosphere of mutual respect of their individual differing expertise, and the patient is involved as an active participant in treatment decisions. Of course, the latter is not always possible, when depressive symptoms are as severe as to compromise insight. Sometimes decisions have to be made against the expressed will of the patient, but this is unusual.

When I first assumed partial responsibility for the treatment of Cathy, my first goal was to review all the treatments she had received: to see whether she showed any signs of improvement, and if so how she had tolerated the associated side effects. During this review, it was clear to me that she had not received treatment with an antidepressant from the class known as monoamine oxidase inhibitors (MAOIs). When given at the right dose, these antidepressants can prove highly effective, but they are not easy for patients to take, partly due to the need to follow a fairly stringent dietary regime. My decision to institute MAOI treatment was welcomed by Cathy, but sadly the results were disappointing, and I feared that she might lose confidence in my continuing care of her after this early failure.

Surprisingly, this did not happen, even when it was necessary for me to recommend Cathy's detention in hospital under Section 3 of the 1983 Mental Health Act, not once but twice. At a Mental Health Tribunal, I had to argue against Cathy's appeal that her involuntary detention in hospital should be ended. Thankfully this Tribunal avoided some of the unfortunate adversarial atmosphere that can sometimes occur, although Cathy's disappointment was clear, and I had some nagging doubts as to what more could be offered to Cathy, other than hoping she would remain alive long enough for natural remission to occur.

The decision to refer her to the specialist unit in Dundee was made swiftly, having received the disappointing news that the Maudsley Hospital was no longer able to offer a service for neurosurgery for mental disorder. I was appalled that Cathy had waited for one year for the initial assessment, only for the possibility of this alternative approach to her treatment to be removed. By contrast, I was most impressed by the immediate response from Dundee to my initial email and phone call, and was therefore able to tell Cathy that alternative arrangements had been made, when giving the news about the Maudsley.

Dundee is a long way from Southampton – so far, indeed, that some aspects of Mental Health Law are markedly different. Provisions that apply in England do not in Scotland, and vice versa, and there was an almost comic feeling when discussing the mechanisms to arrange her safe receipt at the Scottish border. In addition, the Trust here had expressed some concern about the financial costs of arranging her transfer for an assessment in Dundee, and similar reservations were expressed about the possibi-

lity of a further admission there to undergo the neurosurgical procedure. People seemed more bothered about who would pay for the procedure, rather than offering Cathy an additional possibility of recovery. A management colleague stated: 'But what if the operation works? Won't everyone want one?'

I was delighted to read that Professor Matthews and his team in Dundee considered that Cathy might benefit from neurosurgery. However, approval for this operation has to be sought from, and approval granted by, three Scottish Mental Welfare commissioners, and the five-month wait for their assessment of Cathy in Southampton seemed interminable. Once they had granted their approval, I made arrangements for her transfer to the Psychiatric Intensive Care Unit, with the intention that Cathy remain there until the time of her operation. Cathy was often subject to one-to-one constant nursing supervision, which greatly upset her, but everyone was concerned to ensure that Cathy would arrive safely in Dundee, preferably in one piece.

I was indeed 'flabbergasted' at the change in Cathy, when I saw her back in Southampton, three weeks after the operation. Of course her dramatic improvement brought new challenges – for example, she was still subject to detention under the Mental Health Act. It seemed churlish to detain a symptomless patient but I was concerned to ensure her continuing recovery was carefully monitored, over increasing periods of leave. I also wished to convey to Cathy how important it was that she stay in contact with her community psychiatric nurse and to continue attending the mood disorders service outpatient clinic. Perhaps I brought her back to too many outpatient appointments. I remember that when Professor Matthews described Cathy's response to neurosurgery at a scientific conference, he stated: 'She eventually managed to discharge Dr Baldwin.'

It is unclear what the future holds for Cathy. Relatively little is known about the outcome of neurosurgical intervention over the long term, although Professor Matthews and his team are helping to reduce that uncertainty, by the systematic and detailed follow-up of all patients seen in their Unit. It was a privilege to participate in the care of this extraordinarily courageous woman, and I have greatly enjoyed the opportunity of seeing her again in recent months, whilst she wrote this account of her journey.

David Baldwin MB BS DM FRCPsych
Senior Lecturer in Psychiatry
Clinical Neuroscience Division
University of Southampton

Honorary Consultant Psychiatrist
Hampshire Partnership NHS Trust

Appendix A: Glossary

A Doctors' training

Once qualified, every doctor must obtain full registration with the GMC by doing PRHO pre-registration house officer posts. Once registered, the next grade is SHO (senior house officer). This progresses to specialist registrar (SpR) and then consultant, or GP registrar to GP. The time spent in all grades varies according to the speciality. Even though the posts are termed 'training grades', this refers to ongoing acquisition of skills and experience which parallels the doctor's work. The training structures are about to change, although the grades will remain.

Flexible training is the term used for doctors who wish to train part-time.

Staff grade doctors are also known as non-consultant career grade doctors and are permanent posts held at a particular hospital.

Anaesthetic

Having an anaesthetic involves being put to sleep – sedated – with relief of pain – analgesia – and relaxation of muscles – muscle relaxant or paralytic. The drugs involved vary for each individual anaesthetic but on each occasion the anaesthesia must be induced with an 'induction agent' before a paralytic agent is given.

Antipsychotics

Drugs which are used in the treatment of psychosis to relieve the symptoms such as delusions and hallucinations. Can also be used to boost the response to an antidepressant.

Antidepressants

Drugs which are given to relieve the symptoms of depression (and some anxiety disorders), to speed up the natural remission or to decrease the risk of relapse.

Auditory pseudohallucination

An abnormal voice heard and recognised as such, being within the mind. It is not subject to conscious control or manipulation.

Borderline personality disorder

A personality disorder which is particularly characterised by intense, unstable relationships, recurrent, impulsive acts of self-harm and uncertain self-image. There is a proneness to brief episodes of psychosis.

ASW

An approved psychiatric social worker. They recommend the Section, although theoretically the nearest relative could also do so. The Section is enforced by the hospital management.

CBT (cognitive behaviour therapy)
A system of psychotherapy which uses a structured approach to identify differing thought patterns and use 'correct' or 'normal' thinking to influence the way the individual behaves in a given situation.

CPA (care programme approach)
Introduced in 1991, a system for the organisation and delivery of specialist psychiatric services to patients when discharged into the community. It involves assessment of the social and health problems and needs of the patient and whether there are risks posed by the patient to him/herself or others. Services which can be provided are identified, as is the key worker to take responsibility for delivery of the care plan. The patient and carers are involved in the creation and review of the plan, which should be flexible so that it can respond appropriately to changes in the patient's needs should they deteriorate. Signs of relapse are documented, as are the actions to manage any risk which might occur as a result of relapse or default by the patient. The care programme is signed by the parties involved and a date is made for its review.

CPN
Community psychiatric nurse.

CSF
Cerebrospinal fluid, which is produced in the brain and surrounds the brain and spinal cord.

Delusion
This is a falsely held belief, which is not in keeping with the patient's social and cultural norms or values. The patient cannot be persuaded out of it and firmly holds the belief to be true, e.g. delusion of guilt – the patient believes that they are responsible and culpable for the event/situation/ occurrence even when this is manifestly incorrect.
Common delusions: guilt, persecution, nihilistic.

Depot injection
An injection of a drug in a form which enables it to last for up to six weeks before a further injection is given.

Depression scores
There are various scales for assessing depressive symptoms, all used in an attempt to assess severity and judge the response to treatment, e.g. Hamilton score: < 15 unremarkable, 15–20 mild, > 20 moderate/severe, > 30 severe.

ECR (extracontractual referral)
This means that the hospital trust or primary care trust has to pay the receiving trust for the patient's treatment!

ECT (electroconvulsive therapy)
This is given as a course of treatment under full general anaesthesia. A muscle relaxant is given so that the convulsion is not able to cause the muscles to contract. The only evidence of the convulsion will be flickering

of the eyelids, and an EEG tracing. It is given as a course of treatment, usually 2–3 times a week, until significant improvement in the patient's condition is seen. This will vary from individual to individual.

It is only given to patients who have a severe depressive episode and is particularly helpful to provide a rapid improvement when the situation is life-threatening either as a result of suicidal ideation or food and fluid refusal.

The electric current could be applied to one side of the head (unilateral) – the non-dominant side – or to both sides (bilateral). The latter will often result in more memory impairment but its effects are more rapidly produced.

EMDR (eye movement desensitising reprocessing therapy)
A psychological technique used to combat post-traumatic stress syndrome.

Hallucination
This is a sensory perception which is not created by an external stimulus, e.g. 'voices' which are actually heard even though no sound has created the voice.

Hamilton scale
A rating scale used by psychiatrists to assess the severity of the depression.

JCPTGP
Joint Committee for Postgraduate Training in General Practice.

Major depression
Is defined by strict criteria which are beyond the scope of this book. It is estimated that 20% will have an illness lasting for more than two years, 5% for more than five years – these long-lived episodes are often termed 'treatment-resistant' depression.

Mood disorder
This is the general descriptor for types of depression, including bipolar disorder.

Nihilistic delusion
Falsely held belief of death or worthlessness. Can be applied to a body part so that the patient does not believe that part exists.

Neurosurgery for mental disorder
Anatomically accurate areas of the brain are targeted under CT or MRI guidance and discrete lesions are made. This sort of operation is only offered for intractable depression or intractable obsessional compulsive disorder where all other treatment options have been tried and failed and where the patient's quality of life is very poor due to the mental illness in question.

Postural hypotension
This is a fall in blood pressure when a patient rises from the sitting or lying position to standing and may result in dizziness, faintness or collapse.

Pseudocholinesterase deficiency
A genetic defect which slows down the metabolism of the muscle relaxant suxamethonium, which is often given during the induction of anaesthesia.

Psychoanalytical psychotherapy
A system of psychotherapy which analyses the relationships formed in early life and attempts to explain current relational life events in the light of these and therefore change life situations when more healthy attitudes are adopted.

Psychosis
This occurs in severe mental illness and, broadly speaking, refers to the state where the patient is unable to distinguish between subjective experience and reality. The patient lacks insight and many aspects of personality and behaviour may be distorted by the illness. It is often characterised by delusions and hallucinations.

RMO (responsible medical officer)
Usually the consultant psychiatrist in charge of the patient's care. He/she will have to be approved under the Mental Health Act to be able to take this position.

RCT (randomised controlled trial)
This is one of the gold standards for testing a medical treatment. Briefly it involves taking a set of patients with similar characteristics with the same condition. They are then randomised to receive the test treatment or a placebo; in all other respects their care must be the same. The patient and the researcher ideally are blinded as to what they are receiving in order to eliminate bias. All patients are followed up and the results analysed.

Sections
These are orders under the Mental Health Act 1983 for England (new Scottish Mental Health Act 2003) for the detention of a patient with a mental disorder for assessment or treatment in a place designated by the Act. The different sections of the Act have varying requirements as to who can recommend the section. All of the sections which detain a patient for a significant length of time have to be ratified by at least two doctors, one of whom must be approved as having special experience and expertise for this purpose. An approved social worker is the individual who usually recommends that the patient is detained, although it can be done by the nearest relative. It is the hospital manager's responsibility to apply the Section. There is a system of appeal in place for each Section.

- **Section 2** is an assessment order lasting for a period of 28 days.
- **Section 3** is a treatment order lasting for a period of six months and can be extended for a further six-month period.
- **Section 5(4)** may be applied by a registered mental nurse to a patient in a psychiatric unit to prevent them from leaving for up to six hours. Its purpose is to allow time for the patient to be examined by a doctor when the nurse feels that the patient leaving the ward is a danger to themselves or others.
- **Section 17** authorises the patient to go on leave from the hospital. It

states the duration of the leave and any other conditions which may apply. It must be signed by the RMO.

Drugs

These are broad categories, please note that in other patients they may have other or different uses, e.g. amitryptiline may be used for pain control in certain situations.

- **amitryptiline:** a tricyclic antidepressant
- **clomipramine:** a tricyclic antidepressant
- **chlorpromazine:** an antipsychotic with sedating properties
- **clonazepam:** a sedative
- **Clopixol:** an antipsychotic given as a depot injection
- **Depixol:** an antipsychotic given as a depot injection
- **dothiepin:** a tricyclic antidepressant (old name for dosulepin)
- **lithium:** a mood-stabilising drug. It requires strict monitoring in order to reach and then maintain therapeutic levels
- **lorazepam:** a sedative
- **L-Tryptophan:** a drug used as an adjuvant to antidepressants in chronic, resistant depression
- **MAOI:** monoamine oxidase inhibitors – a class of antidepressants
- **mirtazapine:** a presynaptic α_2-antagonist – an antidepressant
- **nifedipine:** a calcium channel blocker, often used in the treatment of hypertension or angina
- **Phenergan:** a sedative antihistamine which can be purchased over the counter
- **reboxetine:** a selective inhibitor of noradrenaline – an antidepressant
- **thioridazine:** an antipsychotic
- **venlafaxine:** a SNRI (serotonin and noradrenaline reuptake inhibitor)
- **zopiclone:** a hypnotic or 'sleeping tablet'

Appendix B: Neurosurgery information sheet

Patient Information Sheet

Neurosurgery for Depressive Disorder
Anterior Cingulotomy

This information is designed to help patients understand one of the modern neuro-surgical treatments for depressive disorder. Some patients want more detail of what is involved in the operation. We can include a section at the end of the guide with diagrams if you wish.

We know that understanding and remembering information can be difficult when you are depressed. Our advice to you is:

take your time

only read small sections of the guide at any one time

ask other people to help you read it

highlight any areas of concern so that we can discuss these with you.

"Why operate?"

For some patients suffering from depression, treatment with antidepressant drugs, electroconvulsive therapy (ECT) and psychological treatments (Cognitive Behavioural Therapy) fails to relieve symptoms. They continue to suffer from depressed mood, a loss of interest in previously enjoyed activities and they can feel quite hopeless. Usually, they have negative and pessimistic views of themselves, others, the world around them and their future. They may have difficulties with sleeping, eating and concentrating. These persistent feelings and symptoms may lead to thoughts of suicide. When depression does not respond to standard treatments, patients endure great suffering, have a very poor quality of life and may be at risk of suicide. The consequences for the family and friends of the patient can also be severe.

There are many different treatments for depression, but some sufferers do not respond to any of them. After all clinically proven treatments have been tried, patients may be considered for a neurosurgical operation. This brain surgery is also known as **neurosurgery for mental disorder**. Dundee is the only centre performing this type of surgery in Scotland. Currently, about three people per year have operations in Dundee.

"What are the operations called?"

Although there are several different operations performed around the world, the one that is used currently in Dundee is called an **Anterior Cingu-lotomy**. The other main procedure performed is called an **Anterior Capsu-lotomy**. Sometimes, after a **Capsulotomy** has been unsuccessful, or only partly successful, a patient will have an **Anterior Cingulotomy** in an attempt to improve symptoms. The following information refers to the **Cingulotomy** operation. Please note that figures describing outcome and risks of other procedures may be different

"Is this a lobotomy?"

Brain operations to relieve the symptoms of mental disorders have been carried out for many years. In the past they were called Psychosurgery. When surgery was used to treat schizophrenia in the 1940s and 50s, the operation was crude, destroying large areas of brain tissue. The extensive damage to those parts of the brain called the **frontal lobes** led to problems with apathy, personality changes and a blunting of emotional responses and feelings. *The operations conducted today are very different.*

"How are they different?"

First, surgery is only offered to patients suffering from prolonged **depression**, or from a condition called **obsessive-compulsive disorder**, where other treatments have been unhelpful. Second, the surgery involves the insertion of thin surgical probes into the brain causing a minimum of damage. The probes are guided into position very accurately using special machines that produce detailed images of the brain; Computerised Tomography (CT) or Magnetic Resonance Image (MRI) scanners. When placed in position by the neurosurgeon, the ends of the probes are heated to damage the tissue immediately around the tip. This heat-damaged tissue stops functioning. This effect is permanent.

There are two areas, one on either side and close to the middle and front of the brain, called the cingulate. Within the small areas that are affected by a **Cingulotomy** operation there are thought to be a range of different functions. These functions include some aspects of the regulation of

emotion and of automatic bodily responses to events in the world around us. The cingulate is also involved in some aspects of learning, particularly learning which events in the outside world are pleasant and which are unpleasant.

"What will I feel?"

The operation is carried out under a general anaesthetic so patients are asleep during surgery. While the patient is unconscious the frame for the surgery is attached firmly to the patient's skull. Unlike skin, bone and other parts of the body, the brain has no sensory nerve supply and cannot 'feel' pain. However, the scalp and skull do have such nerves and it is normal to feel a headache where the frame has been attached and the probes have been passed through the top of the skull for a few days after surgery. Normally, simple painkillers, such as paracetamol, relieve this.

"How effective is this kind of operation?"

Research over many years in different countries suggests that this kind of operation helps around a half of all patients who have it. Around **one third** of patients seem to do well, with a significant improvement in symptoms. Another **one third** experience a small improvement in symptoms. The remaining **third** experience no benefit. **However, the effectiveness of a cingulotomy that is performed *after a capsulotomy has already failed* is much less well established. A beneficial response may be less likely in these circumstances.**

Most, but not all, patients notice some improvement in their symptoms almost immediately. However, this improvement in the days following surgery may not last. For many patients, it may take 6–12 months before a sustained improvement is obvious.

"Is it a cure?"

Even if the operation is very successful and most symptoms are relieved, there will be continuing difficulties. When someone has been depressed for a very long time, there are usually many problems and difficulties in their lives. These take time to try to resolve. The year following surgery can be a difficult one. It can be very frustrating to have to wait to see if the operation is going to help. If the operation brings rapid relief, it can be difficult to adjust to feeling well after such a long period of illness. Full support from family, friends and the local mental health services is very important. The patient's local mental health services are asked to design a care plan with the patient for this period after the operation. Most patients who have the operation remain in contact with psychiatric services for a lengthy period

afterwards. Continuing treatment with antidepressant drugs and psychological treatments is almost always necessary.

Sometimes, other treatments such as ECT are still required. Please note that some patients find treatments (*such as antidepressant drugs or ECT*) that were previously unhelpful may become helpful after surgery.

"What are the risks of the operation?"

With all surgical operations and general anaesthetics, there are risks. When carrying out operations on the brain, the two main risks are of introducing infection and of bleeding into the brain. The risk of infection or bleeding is low but these rare events can lead to serious problems, rather like having a stroke. This happens approximately **one time in a hundred** procedures. Recent reviews of the outcome of a large number of brain operations reveal that the risk of death is about **one** in a **1000**.

However, there are more common complications that patients and relatives need to be aware of. Around **1** in **50** patients develop **epileptic seizures** in the period after the operation, although this is usually controlled quite easily with drug treatment. Because of this risk of seizures, patients are not permitted to drive motor vehicles for a period of six months after surgery, **(see address for DVLA at end of this document)**. Over a period of 10 years post-surgery, this risk of epilepsy persists. This may lead to **1** in **10** patients experiencing **at least one seizure**. However, when seizures do occur, they are usually controlled quite easily with medication.

Other, more common, short term side effects of the procedure may include **swelling of the face, tiredness, weight gain** and problems with **holding urine in the bladder**, particularly while sleeping. The **bladder problems** tend to occur alongside periods of **confusion**, with impairments of memory and attention, during the immediate post-operative period. For example, the patient may become confused about which day it is. This does not usually persist for more than a few days or, at worst, weeks for most patients. There is **no convincing evidence** that the operation affects the personality of the patient in any negative way.

"If I have the operation, what is involved?"

To determine suitability for surgery, **Professor Matthews** (University of Dundee, Department of Psychiatry) and his specialist team assess all patients either at their own hospital base or in Dundee. This involves an extensive interview with the patient and usually also with their relatives. The doctors and nurses and other health professionals involved in their care are also involved in the assessment. The medical case records, including all aspects of psychiatric treatment, are examined in detail. If surgery appears to be an appropriate treatment for the patient, Professor

Matthews will ask representatives from the **Mental Welfare Commission for Scotland** to visit the patient. The purpose of this visit is to provide a second opinion about the suitability of surgery and to assess how well the patient and their family understand the potential risks and benefits of surgery.

Sometimes, Professor Matthews will recommend other treatment options to be tried before surgery, or he may ask other psychiatrists or psychologists for their opinions regarding additional psychological treatments.

The decision whether or not to proceed with surgery is made jointly with the patient.

Surgery is <u>never</u> carried out unless the patient wishes to proceed. The patient is able to withdraw from surgery at any time. Test results and details of the procedure can be discussed with **Prof. Matthews** and with the neurosurgeon, **Mr M.S. Eljamel.**

"Where do I stay?"

Once a definite decision has been made regarding suitability for surgery, arrangements are made for admission to the **Carseview Centre**, the psychiatric unit on the **Ninewells Hospital** site. Over a period of a week or so, a number of assessments and tests are conducted. These include clinical interviews, the completion of different questionnaires and rating scales, some computer-based psychological tests, tests of learning and memory, and a videotaped interview to record how the patient feels, speaks and behaves before surgery.

On the day before surgery, the patient is transferred to the neurosurgical unit at **Ninewells Hospital** (**Ward 23b**). The patients will meet the neurosurgical team. At this point, the technique and the risks of the surgery will be discussed again, and a final consent will be obtained. The patient will also be seen by the neurosurgeon, the neuroanaesthetist and often by the neurotheatre nurse on the day of the operation.

"What is involved in the operation?"

The operation takes about 3 hours, although much of this time is taken up by brain scans to locate the correct position for the probes. The surgery itself takes about one hour. The two incisions are usually placed on either side of the top of the patient's head, behind the hairline to hide the scars although this is not always possible. The scalp around the incisions is shaved. The scar will eventually fade to a pale line within three to six months and the hair will usually grow back normally where it has been shaved. The skin is closed by a variety of different methods, but currently staples or skin glue is used. Staples are normally removed in about 3–5 days depending on how well the wound has healed. After surgery, patients

remain in the Neurosurgical Unit for 24–48 hours, depending on how quickly they recover from the anaesthetic.

"What will I feel after surgery?"

Although many patients feel their symptoms improve immediately, it is important to be aware that there may be **NO EFFECT** at this stage. This does not mean that the operation will not be successful over a longer time.

On waking up from the anaesthetic, patients usually have a headache. This tends to be around the areas where the frame has been attached to the patient's head and the incisions where the probes have been inserted through the skull. Simple painkillers are given to make the patient more comfortable. This does not usually last longer than a couple of days.

The patient may experience some confusion and problems with their memory, for example – remembering which day it is. This usually settles quickly.

Also, there can be problems controlling the bladder, although normal ability to hold urine will return. There can be some bruising and swelling of the face around the eyes. This is short-lasting and requires no specific treatment.

Most patients are able to return to the psychiatric ward the day after surgery. The length of stay after surgery depends on the patient's progress. Most are ready for transfer back to their base hospital or home within two to three weeks. Before leaving Dundee, all patients have some of their tests repeated. The patient has a repeat MRI scan (see separate leaflet) and a repeat of some of the interviews. All patients are brought back to Dundee for repeated testing (*for example, after 12 months*) to follow progress and to advise on further treatments as necessary.

"What happens after I leave Dundee?"

Patients return to the care of their local mental health services. Professor Matthews will discuss drug treatments with the patient's own psychiatrist and will usually recommend as few changes as possible. The post-operative plan for the patient is then put into action. It is very important that the local mental health services provide a programme of assistance that will maximise the chances of sustained improvement. This may involve psychological treatments. Professor Matthews will review progress after surgery at 12 and 24 months. The first follow-up appointment may be at the patient's base hospital. The others will probably be in Dundee so that some of the specialised tests can be repeated.

"What if the operation doesn't work?"

As explained above, around 1 in 3 patients may not feel any benefit in the **two years** after surgery. If a previous surgical procedure, either a **Capsulotomy** or a **Cingulotomy**, has failed to help, the chances of not improving may be higher. If this happens, **Professor Matthews** will review the situation and he may arrange to repeat brain scans to look at the effects of surgery. Depending on these scan results, patients may be offered an additional procedure. In the case of patients who have had a **Capsulotomy**, to have the different procedure – a **Cingulotomy**. In the case of patients who have had little effect from a **Cingulotomy** they may be offered a further procedure to extend the **Cingulotomy**. This means that the lesions from the previous operation are increased in size. If this is not considered likely to help, Professor Matthews and his team will review and discuss other non-surgical treatment options with the local mental health services.

Glossary

anterior	towards the front, front
capsulotomy	to divide, cut or place a lesion in the internal capsule of the brain
cingulate	part of the brain known as the cingulate gyrus
cingulotomy	to divide, cut or place a lesion in the cingulate gyrus of the brain
confusion	a mental state characterised by a lack of clear and orderly thought and behaviour (in this case temporary)
gyrus	a convoluted elevation or ridge
mental welfare commission	an independent body who have the legal power to protect the welfare and rights of people with mental disorders

Driver and Vehicle Licensing Agency
Swansea SA6 7JL
Web: www.dvla.gov.uk/at_a_glance/content.htm (last updated April 2005)

Professor K. Matthews,
Mr M.S. Eljamel,
R. MacVicar, Clinical Nurse Specialist
June 2005

Appendix C: Directory of organisations

Bristol Crisis Service for Women
Website: www.users.zetnet.co.uk/BCSW
Helpline: 0117 925 1119 run by trained volunteers
Opening hours: Friday and Saturday 9 p.m.–12.30 a.m., Sunday 6–9 p.m.
Office for information: 0117 927 9600

British Association for Behavioural Cognitive Psychotherapies
BABCP General Office
Globe Centre
Box 9
Accrington
BB5 0XB
Tel: 01254 875277
Website: www.babcp.com
Lists practitioners of cognitive behaviour therapies by region.

Doctors Support Line
Website: www.doctorssupport.org
Helpline: 0870 765 0001
A totally confidential helpline run by doctors for doctors.

Doctors Support Network
38 Harwood Road
Fulham
London
SW6 4PH
Website: www.dsn.org.uk
Tel: 0870 321 0642

Manic Depression Fellowship
Castle Works
21 St George's Road
London
SE1 6ES
Website: www.mdf.org.uk
Tel: 0207 793 2600

MIND
Granta House
15–19 Broadway
London
E15 4BQ
Website: www.mind.org.uk
Tel: 0208 793 2600

National Counselling Service for Sick Doctors
Tel: 0207 935 5982 9.30 a.m.–4.30 p.m.

Royal College of Psychiatrists
17 Belgrave Square
London
SW1X 8PG
Website: www.rcpsych.ac.uk
Tel: 0207 235 2351

Samaritans
The Upper Mill
Kingston Road
Ewell
Surrey
KT17 2AF
Website: www.samaritans.org
An emotional support organisation for people in distress and despair as well
as those who are suicidal.
Tel: 08457 909090 or email jo@samaritans.org

SANE
Cityside House
40 Adler Street
London
E1 1EE
Website: www.sane.org.uk
Tel: 0207 375 1002
Saneline: 0845 767 8000

Survivors of Bereavement by Suicide
Centre 88
Saner St
Anlaby Road
Hull
HU3 2TR
Website: www.uk-sobs.org.uk
Tel: 0870 2413 337 (Helpline)

HEALTH LEARNING CENTER
Northwestern Memorial Hospital
Galter 3-304
Chicago, IL